CHATTERIS THUNDERBOLT

The Eric Boon Story

Bob Lonkhurst

Published by
BL Associates

Published by
BL Associates 2012

Copyright Bob Lonkhurst 2012

Printed and bound by
The Berforts Group Ltd
www.berforts.com

A catalogue record for this book is
available from the British Library

Hardback version ISBN 978 09540271-4-8
Paperback version ISBN 978-0-9540271-5-5

DEDICATION

FOR
DAVE 'BOY' GREEN
MBE

A great fighter and special friend
whose contribution to charity and
the sport of boxing over many years
has been immense.

Also by Bob Lonkhurst

MAN OF COURAGE: *The Life and Career of Tommy Farr*

GENTLEMAN OF THE RING: *The Life and Career of Jack Petersen*

EAST END IDOL: *The Amazing Story of Terry Spinks MBE*

FEN TIGER: *The Success of Dave 'Boy' Green*

LIFE IS JUST A SCHEME: *The autobiography of Danny Clark (in aid of charity)*

CONTENTS

As a young lad I knew all about Eric Boon because everyone in Chatteris used to talk about him. Being the first boxer from the town to win a British professional championship he was a real folk hero.

I was thirteen-years-old when I joined Chatteris Boxing Club and my first trainer was Arthur Binder who had also trained Boon when Eric was a lad. Arthur always had stories to tell about Eric and I quickly realised he was a bit special. He was a great puncher and there was no doubt in my mind that he was very unlucky that the war set in when it did because it deprived him of winning a European title and getting a world championship fight.

I first met Eric when I was about fifteen or sixteen and he came to our club shows and presented the prizes. When I turned professional, he was a guest at Cambridge Guildhall for a couple of my early fights which were promoted by my manager, Andy Smith. After I beat Derek Simpson, Boon came into my dressing room and congratulated me on a fine performance. That meant the world to me because of who he was and what he had achieved.

From that day I set out to emulate him. He was my inspiration and when he started coming to Andy Smith's gym at St Ives to train a young lad named Duncan Presst, he always stayed and watched me spar. Although he never attempted to intrude he often gave me encouragement and was complimentary about how I was progressing. "You train so much harder than I ever did," he told me one day.

Eric supported me throughout my career, but never once made comparisons between us. He was an absolute gentleman and despite what he had achieved never once said that he could have beaten me. I always got on well with him and regarded it as an absolute privilege to know him and have his support.

When I fought Joey Singleton for the British light-welterweight title, Eric was ringside at the Royal Albert Hall. He got a massive reception when introduced from the ring and quite rightly so because he was a legend in our part of the country. After the fight he came to my dressing room and, clutching my hand, said: "You were great, simply great." I never forgot that moment.

During the later years of his life Eric travelled all over the country raising money for charity by putting on film shows of old fights. I went to a couple at Chatteris Working Men's Club and the place was packed out each time. Throughout the film of his incredible fight with Arthur Danahar, everyone cheered wildly. It was as though they were watching it for real.

During the late 1970's when Eric was down on his luck, Andy Smith and I were on the committee formed to organise a testimonial dinner for him at the Grosvenor Hotel. In order to attend meetings we drove to London in all weathers sometimes taking several hours to reach our destination. Yet as far as I was concerned it was important to be there because it was a case of me helping somebody who had helped me.

A book about Eric Boon is long overdue because his success in the boxing ring put our town on the map. People adored him and still talk about him today. He had an eventful life and should never be forgotten.

I have known the author for many years. He has a good understanding of boxing and has conducted intense research into Boon's life in and out of the ring. Even the low points have been emphasised with great compassion so as not to degrade the old champion who was a dignified man.

The story is told with warmth and humanity and it is therefore a privilege for me to be given the opportunity to write this foreword. Eric gave me tremendous inspiration and without doubt helped me to reach my own level of success. Most importantly he is very much part of the history of Chatteris and Cambridgeshire.

Dave 'Boy' Green
Chatteris - 2011

ACKNOWLEDGEMENTS

I owe thanks to many people for making this book possible. Without their help and support the finished article would never have materialised.

First and foremost I have received great support from my good friend, Dave 'Boy' Green, a former British and double European champion. Like Boon he was born and brought up at Chatteris and began his boxing career at the local club. It was Dave who first suggested that I take on this task and throughout my research he has pointed me in all the right directions locally. It was therefore appropriate that he wrote the foreword for which I am grateful.

Adam Lazzari, Sports Editor of the *Cambridgeshire Times,* kindly advised his readers of my project in its infancy, which prompted a good local response. A number of people loaned scrapbooks or provided cuttings, illustrations and photographs. I mention in particular Anne and John Stokes, Eric's niece, Shirley Lathwell, Jenny Furlong, Bill Cooke and the volunteers at Chatteris Museum, Bob French of the *Peterborough Evening Telegraph,* Trish Dixon, Editor of *Boxing* News, Chris Jakes of Cambridgeshire Central Library, Rob Strover for his skill in preparing the pages of photographs, Erik Roper, Larry Braysher, Ray Lee, Phil Sharkey, Geoff Williams and Jim Kirkwood. Helpful information was also provided by Dennis Clark, Des Pritchard, Tony Allen, Judith Bradshaw, Vicki Lewarne, Gill Birt, Miles Templeton, Harold Varnham, Harold Alderman and Bert Jackson.

Local stalwarts Rita Goodyear and John Salisbury were of particular help. Rita, a retired schoolteacher and local councillor, knew Boon when he was champion. John was a boy at the time and with his mates often went for rides in the boxer's sports car and got to know him well.

Robert Smith, General Secretary of the British Boxing Board of Control, afforded me access to relevant records, and Maureen Woodard of the Royal Air Force Museum at Hendon patiently deciphered unreadable abbreviations on Eric's service record. The staff of the National Newspaper Library at Colindale provided me with a succession of publications essential to my research over a two-year period. Their service was of the usual high standard for which I thank them.

My good friends Richard Barber and Clare Benfield, a talented writer in her own right, gave valuable support by providing material which would not otherwise been available due to my inability to master modern technology. I am particularly indebted to my long-term friend, Maureen Cox, for her patience and skill regarding the design and typesetting of this book. She has my sincere thanks.

I am particularly grateful for help given to me by Melanie Knight and Fergus McKenna at Mirrorpix in giving me authority to reproduce a number of extracts from articles written in Boon's name in the *Sunday People* more than fifty years ago. This material was essential in adding substance to what is a fascinating story.

Finally, I acknowledge the works of Isidore Green, Maurice Woolf and Jeff Barr, three young but exceptionally talented journalists. They all got to know Eric when he was learning his trade at the Devonshire Club. Close friendships were formed and consequently they frequently got stories, often unconnected with boxing, before their counterparts from the nationals. Although their publications have long since ceased, their reports have been vital in enabling me to present a deeper and hopefully more accurate picture of Boon.

INTRODUCTION

A biography of Eric Boon should have been written years ago not least because his was one of life's incredible rollercoaster rides. The suggestion that I should write it was first put to me back in 2004 by Dave 'Boy' Green shortly after I had published his biography, *Fen Tiger*. As a former British and European light-welterweight champion, European welterweight title holder and two-time challenger for the WBC welterweight crown, Dave had huge respect for Boon. He has always maintained that the old champion inspired him to reach his own high levels.

Although I wanted a break from writing, Dave insisted that Eric was a bit special and a book about him was essential to the history of Chatteris. It didn't take me long to realise that he was right because after some initial research I quickly established that Boon stood out as a very special person both in and out of the ring. Packed with excitement, sadness and intrigue, his story is absorbing and thoroughly entertaining.

A charismatic and flamboyant character Boon was one of Britain's most colourful boxing champions. A natural crowd-pleaser he was arguably one of the country's finest lightweights and certainly, pound-for-pound, one of the hardest punchers to have graced the rings of these shores. Outside boxing he appeared on stage in a series of successful vaudeville productions, had parts in a number of films, was a renowned playboy and had minor brushes with the law.

As a fighter Boon was unique because whenever he was in the ring something dramatic always seemed to happen. From the small halls to the big arenas he generated sheer excitement and, occasionally, controversy. For those reasons alone I have deliberately made reference to virtually all of his fights. Not to have done so would have deprived the reader of vital substance on which to judge him as a man and a very special fighter.

Throughout the history of boxing in Britain the majority of combatants have come from large towns, dockland or industrial areas. Boon, however, was brought up in the small market town of Chatteris situated amid the vast agricultural region of the Cambridgeshire Fens. By the age of eleven he was a brash, angry and aggressive youngster frequently involved in playground and street fights. Even at that tender age he looked to be on a collision course with the authorities, but due largely to the patience, skill and understanding of three respected local men he was coaxed into the town boxing club. There, after a year of intense coaching, he was developed into a compact and controlled fighting machine. The only time his aggression was unleashed was in the ring.

If ever a boy was meant to fight it was Eric Boon and a few months after his twelfth birthday he climbed into the ring on a small local promotion at nearby St Ives for his first fight of a career which would span 20 years and take in more than 160 contests. Although he lost that one his development was incredible and by his mid-teens his two-fisted, whirlwind style of fighting thrilled the crowds in the small halls. It was the same when he graduated to the big London arenas.

The son of a local blacksmith, Boon was indeed special and would become the youngest man to win both a British professional championship and a coveted Lonsdale belt outright. In doing so he put Chatteris firmly on the map. Although ardent fight fans knew all about his development and progress, few knew much about the town or where it was situated. All that changed, however, once he became headline news. His popularity was immense and special trains had to be laid on to take thousands of Fenland fans to London for his major contests. In his home town photographs of him were displayed on the walls of most local pubs and schools.

Boon's rise to fame was achieved through sheer hard work and careful guidance during the early stages of his career. His apprenticeship was one of which champions were made. After 25 schoolboy contests, of which he lost only two, he was stripped of his amateur status at the age of fourteen after being paid ten shillings (50p) for boxing three rounds on a fairground booth. Ignoring British Boxing Board of Control rules which prohibited paid boxing before a contestant reached the age of sixteen, he immediately turned professional and issued challenges at local shows.

Although he boxed at many small hall venues in the Eastern Counties, Eric learned his trade at the toughest school of all, the intimidating Devonshire Club at Hackney in London's east end. There he was taken under the wing of the proprietor, Jack Solomons, a local fishmonger with a burning ambition to become a successful player in the world of professional boxing. He carefully guided Boon along a steady path only pushing him to a higher level when he was satisfied he was ready. Jack also controlled the youngster's finances ensuring that he didn't squander his hard earned purse money. Years later he described Boon as the biggest attraction in the history of the Devonshire Club. When Jack was eventually established as the country's top promoter he admitted that Boon's success set him on his way.

An enthusiastic pupil, Boon built up a tremendous record with most of his victories coming inside the distance. He was only eighteen when Solomons persuaded Sydney Hulls, the country's top promoter at the time, to match him with reigning British lightweight champion, Jimmy Walsh, in a non-title fight over 10 rounds at Chatteris football ground. Although incessant rain persisted throughout the day, the skies cleared by evening and Boon duly delivered with a hard earned points victory.

More successes followed and seven months later Eric became the youngest man to win a British championship when he knocked out Dave Crowley in 13 absorbing rounds. Successful defences against Arthur Danahar and Crowley gave him the Lonsdale belt outright.

The contest with Danahar, described in many circles as 'The Fight of the Century', was one of the most punishing and exhausting ever seen between lightweights in Britain. Seasoned critics agreed that no other at that weight had contained so much scientific boxing, dogged courage, hard punching and thrills. More than 40 years later veteran boxing correspondent, Frank Butler, wrote: "Even all these years later I don't recall reporting a more exciting championship."

No fight had been more desired because it was a natural in every sense, and none which preceded it had so gripped and fired public imagination. It had absolutely everything and the patrons at Harringay Arena that night witnessed one of the finest battles ever seen in a British ring. Even the most hardened fight fans were keyed up to such a pitch of excitement that they would remember it for the rest of their lives.

Whilst Boon's big punching successes had thrilled the crowds, hand injuries became an inevitable consequence. Forced to remain inactive for several months following the Danahar fight, he occupied much of his time touring the country with a successful vaudeville act. Although a world title contest was high on his promoter's agenda, this was scuppered by the outbreak of the Second World War. It was a massive disappointment for Eric because up until this point he had been riding on the crest of a wave. Suddenly, however, his life became one of ups and downs.

A lot happened to Boon after his glamorous, exciting pre-war days when he was the toast of the town and beautiful girls hounded him day and night. Although hundreds cheered outside a Golders Green church in April 1940 when he married nineteen-years-old actress, Wendy Elliott, his lifestyle meant it wouldn't last. The following month he joined the RAF, but was discharged on medical grounds three years later. Serious head injuries sustained in a motorcycle accident were believed to be the cause of him having blackouts.

Ignoring medical advice he continued to box, but was a shadow of the great fighter of a few years earlier. Against mediocre opposition he had only limited success, and after losing his British title to Ronnie James in 1944 and being stopped by five-fight novice, Henry Hall, the following year, he announced his retirement.

Whilst it was a sensible, albeit belated decision, Boon's life was in turmoil mainly because his playboy lifestyle had drained his financial resources. He had opened two nightclubs in Soho, but the Police closed both within weeks because he ignored the Licensing Act. Without a trade to turn to he had no alternative but to return to the ring. In a spirited comeback early in 1946 he scored six quick victories in just three months, but when he faced Arthur Danahar in a British welterweight title eliminator he was stopped in five rounds, albeit very controversially.

Desperate to turn his life around Eric accepted offers for fights in South Africa where he became a massive attraction. He earned good money in winning six of seven contests over a 14 month period. Intending to make The Rand his home, he became involved in a country club business and also secured the leading role in the popular Broadway musical, Golden Boy. In September 1947, however, things went horribly wrong. Not only did his winning run in South African rings come to an abrupt halt, Golden Boy ended when the theatre was condemned. To make matters worse the country club business suffered serious financial difficulties. It was all too much for Boon and he returned to Britain almost broke.

Despite his fall from grace, Eric was one of the few British boxers who would always sell tickets, a situation which Jack Solomons was quick to exploit. In what were described as two of his greatest fights, the Chatteris man was outpointed by Ernie Roderick in a challenge for the British title in December 1947 and knocked out by European champion, Robert Villemain, four months later with just five seconds of the final round remaining.

The financial problems remained and there were even allegations that he was involved in fight fixing. It was a sad state of affairs because the man who was believed to have made more than £100,000 from boxing, had his suits tailored at Saville Row, feasted on caviar and smoked only the best Havana cigars, fell from those giddy heights during the late 1940's and early `50's.

Although he had serious problems Boon was never a quitter and to try and make ends meet he continued to fight, but lost all but one of his last 12 contests. Heavy defeats in Canada, America, Honolulu and Australia led to the Board of Control taking away his licence for his own protection. In the end he was taking hidings purely for the money.

Boxing is littered with stories of men who fell from glamorous heights because they couldn't face up to and deal with realities of life outside the ring. Sadly the likeable Boon was a larger-than-life example of this hard truth. Yet it must never be forgotten that he was a legend of the British ring. He frequently figured in the world title equation for possible contests with Henry Armstrong, Lou Ambers, Marty Servo, Ike Williams and Tippy Larkin. Yet despite all the hype and newspaper talk none reached fruition leaving him and the fans bitterly disappointed.

In his private life, Wendy divorced him after seven years because of his playboy lifestyle and refusal to give up boxing. In 1952 he married stage designer, Corrine Cooper, and emigrated to Australia, but that also ended in divorce. On a happier note he remarried Wendy in 1966 and spent the rest of his life with her. Despite good intentions, Eric could never hold down a job for any length of time and consequently his financial problems persisted.

In order that the reader can fully understand and appreciate Eric Boon, I have told his story 'warts `n all.' In doing so I have attempted, as far as is humanly possible, to present a frank and honest account of his life. Whilst resisting the temptation to minimise the problems and temptations he encountered I have been anxious not to show him in a bad light. In fact the shortfalls contribute massively to his story if only to demonstrate the courage he showed in confronting them. Eric always accepted that he squandered his money and never sought to blame anyone but himself.

More than 30 years since his passing, Eric Boon remains a legend in the Fens and beyond. What he achieved in the ring is an important part of British boxing history. Researching his life has been a thoroughly enjoyable experience because not only have I traced many of his fights which did not appear on any previously published records, I have also discovered so much more about his life outside the ring. Such material, no matter how small, was essential to hopefully making his story more than one confined just to boxing.

I sincerely hope that my efforts have done Eric justice and rekindled memories of one of Cambridgeshire's greatest sporting heroes. My only regret is that I never saw him fight.

Bob Lonkhurst
Potters Bar - 2011

BORN TO BE A FIGHTER

The little railway track which meandered gently through the flat Cambridgeshire countryside has long since gone, but a welcoming ceremony which took place at one of the stations amid driving snow on a bitterly cold afternoon in December 1938 is very much part of local history. Situated in the rich agricultural region of the Fens, the small market town of Chatteris has never been renowned for producing a string of quality boxing champions. In the mid-1930's, however, one young man sprung to prominence from the local boxing club and developed into arguably the hardest punching lightweight in the history of British boxing. He was the subject of that ceremony.

As the 2.18 pm train ground slowly to a halt the stocky good looking local lad stepped proudly on to the platform clutching a gleaming Lonsdale belt. The Mayor, civic dignitaries and hundreds of local folk of all ages were there to greet him. Then, led by the town band, he was paraded through the narrow streets aboard a decorated coal lorry to a reception at the Empress Cinema in Park Street.

The previous evening, at the age of eighteen, Eric Boon had become the youngest man ever to win a British championship, and before reaching twenty would win a Lonsdale belt outright. In between times he was involved in one of the greatest fights ever seen in a British ring when he stopped Arthur Danahar in 14 rounds. Billed as 'The Fight of the Century' it certainly lived up to all expectations.

Although Boon had only celebrated his nineteenth birthday three months earlier and his challenger had not yet reached twenty-one, they smashed box office records. It became the first fight to be shown live on television and public interest was so great that it was also beamed live into three cinemas in the west end of London where capacity audiences paid exorbitant prices.

The public had clamoured for the fight for more than six months and although promoters battled to stage it there were always stumbling blocks. At one point it was claimed that a wealthy sportsman wanted to stage it at a plush London hotel, but this caused such an outcry among the public and media that the plans were shelved. Common sense eventually prevailed and shortly before 9 pm on 23 February 1939, Boon and Danahar climbed into the ring at Harringay Arena. Despite their tender ages they were sportsmen of the highest calibre - courteous, well mannered and mature beyond their years. Both had massive followings throughout Cambridgeshire and the east end of London. What happened during the ensuing hour confirmed the accuracy of the fight's billing and would ensure that it was talked about for decades to come.

*   *   *

Eric Cornelius Reginald Boon was born at 12 Burnsfield Street, Chatteris, the home of his grandmother, Ellen Stephenson, who was present at his birth on 30 December 1919. He had a sister, Brenda, who was just 12 months older. His father, Reg, was a serving soldier and although granted two days home leave he had to return to his unit leaving his wife Liz with two babies to look after and only £1 in her purse. She was therefore very much reliant on her mother with whom they lived.

Two years later, Reg, Liz and their two children moved into a council house at Fenton Road, Warboys a small village a few miles west of Chatteris. Reg, who by this time, had been discharged from the Army, took a job with a local blacksmith. Five years later they all moved back to Chatteris and into a small property at 11 Burnsfield Street opposite Liz's mother. Having learned the trade, especially how to shoe horses, Reg Boon set up his own blacksmiths forge just round the corner in Station Street. It was only a few yards from their home and neighbours frequently heard his wife shout to him from the bottom of their garden when his lunch was ready.

Reg was a friendly man who became extremely popular in the community, never refusing to help a neighbour. He quickly built up his business and with Chatteris being surrounded on all sides by rich agricultural land, he was rarely short of work.

From a very young age Eric spent hours at his father's forge and grew to love horses. When they moved back to Chatteris he went to King Edward Elementary School for junior and senior boys. Most days as soon as school was over he hot-footed it to the forge. Like most inquisitive youngsters he was often picking up tools and playing with them, but once he was big enough his father taught him how to pound the anvil with a hammer. This soon became a hobby for Eric.

Not long after starting at King Edward School, Eric became mischievous and was often playing practical jokes. This soon led to playground fights and it was not long before he was looked upon as a real little demon. There were problems in the street as well and on one occasion he and some mates put lighted fireworks into a post box in Chatteris town centre. It caught fire and the brigade was called to put it out.

Reg Boon was very strict with his children and thrashed Eric whenever he got into trouble, but it had no effect on him. There were many occasions when his sister Brenda tried to protect him from punishment by taking the blame herself. One day after getting a severe thrashing, Eric just smirked and swore at his father before running out into the street. It was at that point Reg realised he was wasting his time hitting his son. "I never hit him any more after that," he told a relative years later.

At school the headmaster, Mr Kidd, tried similar punishment and caned Eric when he believed it was warranted. Even at the age of ten the young Boon feared nobody and resisted violently one day when Mr Kidd attempted to cane him for fighting. A struggle ensured and the headmaster called upon two other male teachers to hold him down. After being caned Eric told them that the next time they treated him like that he would take each one on individually.

Although by this stage the youngster had the reputation of being a tearaway, his mother went to the school and asked why it had taken two teachers to hold him down while he was caned. Her talk with the headmaster calmed matters down somewhat, but the major problem with Eric was boredom which was the cause of many of his misdemeanours.

Shortly after the caning incident there was a change of headmaster at King Edward School, Mr Kidd being replaced by Mr Precious. Aware that Boon was a potential problem he took him to his office one day and had a long talk with him. In class Eric was an average student who loved sport, particularly football. He played at inside forward and captained the school team before he was eleven. His other interests were billiards, darts and fishing, but because he got bored easily he always took two rods with him in the hope of catching more fish. He loved the sport and was often seen sitting in the street outside his house repairing his nets.

The arrival of Mr Precious at King Edward School benefited Eric who came to like and respect him. By this time he had joined Chatteris Amateur Boxing Club and was gradually becoming a calmer boy. He even took an interest in the town band and learned to play an instrument at school.

*   *   *

Playground and street fights were a regular occurrence for Eric before he reached the age of eleven. Two particular incidents witnessed by responsible people, however, led to him eventually joining the local boxing club which would shape his life forever.

The first was when he was caught by a local 'Bobby', Police Constable John Larner, fighting with another boy in a Chatteris back alley. The officer broke it up and told them that if they wanted to fight they should join the boxing club.

A few weeks later, Arthur Binder, who ran the boxing club and lived on the Burnsfield Estate, was walking past King Edward School when he saw a fight taking place in the playground. At first he was concerned because one boy, who he knew to be a local bully, was taller and a year or two older than the other. Within a few seconds, however, his fears evaporated as the smaller boy showed that he knew how to take care of himself. He attacked the bully relentlessly before finally knocking him flat with a single punch.

The smaller of the two boys was Boon, and Arthur was convinced that he had tremendous natural talent. After a short chat about what had been going on he invited him to go along to a club training session one evening. Eric was thrilled and after school ran straight to his father's forge and told him. Despite the thrashings he had been given, Eric and his father had a good relationship. Reg never gave up on him and encouraged him to go along to the club and give it a try.

One of Boon's first trainers was PC Larner one of the greatest devotees to boxing in the district. He was a very tall man and had to go down on his knees to teach Eric the basics of the sport. The man who devoted most time to him, however, was Arthur Binder.

Born in 1898, Arthur was already highly respected in Chatteris having been a successful amateur boxer during the First World War. He was an effective and disciplined trainer who, in 1920, began an association with Chatteris Engineers, at the time one of the finest football teams for miles around. He was the ideal man to get to grips with Boon and instil discipline and self control into him. Although Eric had massive energy and enthusiasm for a scrap, Binder recognised that he had to be taught how to box and channel his abundance of aggression. Even in training his attitude was to try and knock out an opponent in double quick time. He only threw punches to the head and knew nothing about defence.

Despite the shortfalls, Arthur knew he had a tremendous young prospect on his hands, so he was not prepared to rush him. He knew all about his aggressive and mischievous nature and the dangers that may loom ahead. Controlling that aggression would do society a favour, so with patience and understanding he spent hours grooming Boon for what he hoped would be a successful ring career.

Eric respected Arthur for who he was and how he operated. He obeyed orders, trained diligently and never once looked like going

4

off the rails after joining the club. Unfortunately, patience was not one of Boon's virtues at this stage of his young life and he kept pleading to be given a real fight. The trainer, however, was having none of it because Eric was impetuous. If he lost his head in the ring all the hard work would be wasted and the likely outcome of him drifting back to the street and playground fights could become a reality. Gone also would be all the discipline that had been drilled into him. "Not until I think you are absolutely ready," Arthur always told him kindly.

After more than a year training at his local club, Boon had his first official schoolboy contest at St Ives Corn Exchange on 17 March 1932. It was promoted by another highly respected Chatteris man, Fred Green, in conjunction with St Ives Boxing Club. As a number of other Chatteris boxers were also in action two coach loads of fans travelled to support them.

Boon faced St Ives youngster, 'Boy' Marriott over six two-minute rounds, but lost on points. Arthur Binder and Fred Green worked in his corner and were both pleased with his effort despite the press later describing it as a tame bout. He remained controlled throughout, but did not have the skill of his more experienced opponent. During this period in time, particularly in Cambridgeshire and surrounding counties, schoolboy boxers were rarely referred to by their first names, the title 'Boy' being substituted instead. Consequently, from his first bout Eric was always referred to as 'Boy' Boon.

In his next contest at Huntingdon two weeks later, Eric showed a marked improvement beating local lad 'Boy' Rushton on points over three rounds. In doing so he impressed a local newspaper reporter who wrote: "'Boy' Boon from Chatteris has a style all to himself."

With his first victory behind him Boon was rewarded with a fight at the Crown Theatre, Chatteris on 24 June against 'Boy' Cross from Huntingdon. Promoted by Fred Green it was the first boxing show in the town for a very long time and consisted of both amateur and professional contests. Despite still being a raw novice, many locals had come to see Eric and he didn't disappoint them. Growing more confident with each fight he scored another points victory over three rounds in front of a full house.

Even at this early stage of his career the tuition Boon was receiving from Arthur Binder was clear for all to see. After just three contests he was developing into a promising young boxer largely because he had abandoned the reckless intent to knock each boy flat in the opening seconds. Instead, he used the ring intelligently and developed a jab which gave him superiority in his last two bouts. Furthermore, he was becoming a disciplined young sportsman rather than the potential tearaway many locals had feared. His only weakness was that he had a huge appetite with a special liking for chocolates and oranges. Even as a schoolboy boxer who started his career weighing only six stone he often ate a large sandwich just an hour or so before a fight. "A good meal always made me feel hungry," he remarked years later when talking about his childhood.

The important thing for Binder was to keep Eric busy. With Fred Green involved in regular local promotions he continued to progress well. The local press warmed to the youngster and covered all his contests with great enthusiasm. After his victory over Harold 'Boy' Marwood at Whittlesey British Legion Hall in March 1933, the *Peterborough Advertiser* report stated: "If 'Boy' Boon keeps this up he will go far."

The following month the *Cambridgeshire Times & March Gazette* published a photograph of him with four cups and three medals. By May he had won ten contests in a row since his losing debut 14 months earlier.

Apart from boxing, Eric also loved football. He had developed into a talented young player and apart from representing King Edward School on a regular basis he also played for the Cambridgeshire County Schools Under 14 team. He trained as hard for football as he did for boxing, cycling everywhere because he knew it was good for strengthening his legs.

In July that year he also excelled at King Edward School sports day held at Wenny Road sports ground. He won the senior boys 220 yards flat handicap race, the senior novelty race and came second at throwing the cricket ball. His only disappointment was being beaten in a semi-final of the pillow fight competition.

After a break during the summer the amateur boxing season got back into full swing in September 1933 and Boon was matched with Paddy 'Boy' Chilvers from Kings Lynn over four rounds at Chatteris. Although he held no such title he was billed as the Schoolboy Champion of Cambridgeshire. As though wanting to live up to that status he boxed brilliantly to win on points. When presenting the prizes, local council dignitary, Alderman Leonard Childs, described the contest as one of the best he had ever seen.

A return between the two was a natural and took place eight weeks later at Whittlesey British Legion Hall. The prizes were two silver cups donated by the St John's Ambulance Brigade. Eric was again in tremendous form and proved too powerful for Chilvers who was floored twice in the second round before being knocked out in the fourth by a right swing to the jaw. It was Boon's best win to date and received good coverage in the local papers, particularly the *Cambridgeshire Times* which printed another photograph to illustrate a large story about him. There were, however, a number of inaccuracies regarding his record, particularly that he had never been beaten in the ring and usually knocked out his opponents. Chilvers was in fact the first he had beaten inside the distance.

To the surprise of his followers, Boon suffered a rare defeat at the start of 1934. After an extremely competitive six two-minute rounds contest at Manea Village Hall, he was adjudged to have been outpointed by Fred Kerr, billed as the Schoolboy Champion of Ely. Eric was again described as Schoolboy Champion of Cambridgeshire as he was in his next fight at Whittlesey Village Hall two weeks later against 'Boy' Cole the Schoolboy Champion of Lincoln.

In what was a wonderful scrap between two enthusiastic youngsters Boon got the decision at the end of the six rounds. The excited crowd threw 'nobbins' into the ring at the final bell and it was later reported that each boy was handed about a pound collected from the canvas. This led to claims in some subsequent newspaper reports that Eric had turned professional despite the fact that he was still only fourteen. The misunderstanding arose because most promotions staged in the eastern counties were made up of amateur and professional contests. Reporters therefore became confused, finding it difficult to identify which was which unless they specifically sought clarification from the organisers.

Despite his setback against Fred Kerr, Eric continued to progress well and remained undefeated in his next nine contests at Manea, Whittlesey, Chatteris, Downham Market, Long Sutton and Warboys. By this time Reg Boon had joined forces with Fred Green and was involved in a number of the small hall promotions as was Curly Randall, an active professional from March. Despite their obscurity the venues were all packed to capacity because boxing had such a great following. The good press coverage Eric received ensured that he had plenty of support wherever he fought.

Boon's amateur career ended abruptly towards the end of 1934 after it was discovered that he took part in a fight on a boxing booth at Chatteris Fairground in Wenny Road. During the summer Sam Minto, a well known West Indian professional boxer, took his booth from Essex across country to Derbyshire stopping on route at villages throughout East Anglia, including Chatteris. Sam was a legend and Boon, who had just left school, could not resist issuing a challenge to face him over three rounds. It was mostly bravado, but full of confidence he boxed well and lasted the distance and afterwards collected the agreed sum of ten shillings (50p) for what was a 'no decision' contest.

There was a massive crowd at the fairground staged at Manor Park in Wenny Road and word soon got around about Eric going in the ring with Minto. Eventually it came to the notice of the amateur boxing authorities who, after an emergency meeting, notified the Chatteris Club that by fighting Minto the youngster had forfeited his amateur status.

Arthur Binder and Fred Green were furious, but knew the controlling body would not relent. Eric was devastated when they broke the news to him as he arrived at the club for training one night in November. The two men had been with him from the start and developed him from a raw playground scrapper into a promising young boxer with an effective and controlled style.

Not wanting Boon to revert to his old habits Binder and Green knew the importance of continuing to encourage and support him while they worked out what the future held for him. He needed to be kept occupied because having left school at the end of the summer term four months earlier he was a hyper-active youngster who never walked anywhere. Instead he even ran or raced about the streets on his battered old bicycle.

He had no prospect of work other than at his father's forge, but even that was only on a casual basis as and when he liked. He did try selling ice cream for a local shopkeeper by riding around Chatteris on a three-wheeled bike with a box attached to the front, but that job didn't last long because he was sacked for eating too much of the product he was supposed to sell.

Meanwhile, Boon left the amateur scene at the age of fourteen with an impressive record of just two defeats from 24 contests. At home his mother's sideboard was laden with cups and trophies of all shapes and sizes as a testimony of his success. He once remarked: "I think I must have begun swinging my fists in my cradle. Anyway, my mother says that when I was only five I was a holy terror among the other kids in the neighbourhood."

2

YOUNG PROFESSIONAL

The influence of Arthur Binder and Fred Green convinced Boon that he had a great future as a boxer. Despite the setback he was growing into a mature young man who was determined to carry on. He knew that his future lay with the professionals so on 22 November, just a few days after he was forced out of the amateurs, he went to a show at Peterborough Corn Exchange and issued a challenge to anyone in the town to fight him. It was something that required immense courage, but Eric had more than most kids of his age.

Although the issuing of challenges was a regular feature in boxing, the local press loved this one because Boon had already built up a large following in the region. In their enthusiasm to add spice to their stories, however, reporters again exaggerated Eric's success and the number of fights he had taken part in.

Boon's challenge was quickly accepted by young Peterborough professional, Doug Claxton, and they were matched over six two-minute rounds at the Corn Exchange on 13 December. In a thrilling contest Eric was cut over the right eye in round three and Claxton floored for a count of 'seven' in the final round. Still not fifteen years-of-age, Boon got the decision and received three shillings and sixpence (17.5p) for what was his first professional contest.

Shortly afterwards he accepted a challenge from Young Snowball, an ambitious youngster from Stamford. They met at Peterborough on 17 January 1935, and although no weights were disclosed it was billed as being at flyweight. During a hectic scrap Eric's punching power was the deciding factor forcing the referee to call a halt midway through the final round.

Arthur Binder was delighted with the steady start Eric had made to his paid career because he was continuing the progress he had shown in the amateurs. In his next contest against Ted Royal from Cambridge, whom he outpointed at St Ives Corn Exchange, on a show co-promoted by Fred Green, he showed excellent skills throughout the six rounds.

Described in the press as a Peterborough citizen, it was claimed that Boon would probably be selected to compete for an Eastern Counties championship in the near future. This, however, was yet another example of inaccurate reporting. Although the recently formed Area Council were keen to install champions at all weights, Boon was still only fifteen, and in accordance with the rules of the British Boxing Board of Control formed in 1929, should not have been fighting for pay. The fact that he did so was because with many promotions being made up of amateur and professional contests very few checks were carried out. Although he continued to box as 'Boy' Boon from Chatteris during the early stages of his professional career there were occasions when Eric was referred to as Eddie Boon, Roy Boon and Eric 'Boy' Boon. Apart from Peterborough there were also references to him coming from Cambridge, Hackney, and on one occasion Bristol, while official records always listed his first contest as being that against Young Snowball. Such errors never bothered Eric who was just happy to see regular reports of his fights in the local papers. Their accuracy didn't concern him.

Boon's next contest took place two weeks later on what was the first ever boxing show to be staged at Spalding Corn Exchange. It was promoted by George Stokes, a well known young promoter from Peterborough who held a British Boxing Board of Control licence. He ran a sports, fancy goods and fishing tackle shop at Church Street, and managed a number of local boxers including Young Green from Chatteris.

Stokes had been impressed by Boon's performances when he beat Doug Claxton and Young Snowball on his promotions at Peterborough and believed he would excite the fans at Spalding and, if all went according to plan, help draw bigger crowds to future promotions.

Eric didn't disappoint the promoter and battered Darkie Brian so heavily that the referee stopped the contest in the opening round. His performance really impressed top London referee, Jack Hart, who even at that stage believed he had the makings of a champion. Hart had also been at Peterborough the night Boon stopped Snowball and told him there were great opportunities in London for a lad who could punch like he did.

"Nothing doing," snapped Boon's father. "He's too young for that sort of thing."

On his return to London, Hart mentioned Eric to Jack Solomons, an aspiring young promoter who was staging two shows a week at the Devonshire Club at Hackney. He was always on the lookout for young talent and, trusting the referee's judgement, told him to keep his eye on Boon and let him know how he progressed.

Hart next saw Eric on 21 February 1939 at Spalding the night he stopped Darkie Brian more impressively than he had Snowball five weeks earlier. After the fight he took Arthur Binder aside and pleaded with him to let the youngster fight in London. Arthur was open-minded and together they tried to persuade Reg Boon to agree to Hart's proposal, but he still flatly refused. Hart shrugged his shoulders and, believing he was chasing a lost cause, walked away

10

and left the building. Eric, however, was too excited to just let it drop and chased after him. "Don't take any notice of my old man," he pleaded. "I'll be there - just tell me when and where." Hart grinned, and putting a hand on his shoulder said: "Okay son, next Sunday at the Devonshire Club."

The following day Hart contacted Solomons and told him of the developments, but warned him that Eric's father could be a stumbling block. The promoter was unconcerned and, confident that he could overcome any problems, immediately set about arranging a contest for his new young hope. Things didn't go according to plan because just seven days after hammering Darkie Brian, Boon suffered his first defeat as a professional. Against Jeff Smith from Wellingborough on George Stokes' next promotion at Peterborough Corn Exchange, he sustained an arm injury and was forced to retire after two rounds. Solomons was told of the situation, but as the injury was not serious he offered Eric a six-round contest on his Sunday afternoon show at the Devonshire Club on 10 March. His purse would be 30 shillings, a huge jump from what he had received for previous fights.

Arthur Binder delayed telling Eric's father about the arrangement, but on the Wednesday morning before the contest, a postman delivered a Devonshire Club poster to the Boon household at Burnsfield Street. Reg opened it and was shocked and angry at what he read. "Sunday boxing", he snapped. "Disgraceful."

His wife was also dismayed. "Look at this," she said, "six rounds contest - Young Higgins of Stepney versus 'Boy' Boon of Chatteris."

Both were strongly opposed to their son fighting in London and, being unaware of his agreement with Jack Hart, decided not to mention the poster to him. Eric, however, was in the next room and heard everything they said. Being a headstrong lad he had no intention of letting his parents wreck what he believed was a tremendous opportunity to progress his ring career.

On the morning of the fight he got up whilst his parents were still fast asleep, got dressed, packed his boxing kit into a bag and sneaked out of the house. Giving no serious thought to what he was actually doing, he then got on to his bicycle with the intention of riding all the way to London. On reaching a main road, however, common sense suddenly kicked in and he flagged down a passing lorry. On hearing where he was headed the driver hoisted him and his bicycle on to the back of the lorry which was laden with sacks of cabbages bound for Covent Garden market. When they were about halfway down the A1 Eric smiled to himself as a small saloon car flashed by. It was his father headed in the same direction.

The lorry driver dropped Eric off near Covent Garden and gave him directions to Hackney. It was still a few miles away so he pedalled as hard as he could determined not to be late for the most important fight of his career. He made it in good time, but was shocked to see his father standing outside the club.

After a few harsh words Reg Boon soon realised that nothing was going to stop his son going through with the fight. As they were talking Eric propped his bicycle against the wall of the Devonshire Club, but was sharply rebuked by a man who suddenly appeared from inside the building. "Hey you, take that thing away from there – who do you think you are?" he snapped.

It was Jack Solomons who, on fight days, had the habit of constantly walking in and out of the club willing the punters in. He had never met Boon or his father, but was taken aback by the youngster's response.

"I'm 'Boy' Boon," replied Eric, "I'm fighting here."

"Where have you come from?" asked Solomons staring at him with some amazement.

"Chatteris", replied Boon, "and I have to get back after the fight so I must have my bike handy."

The promoter was flabbergasted, but then remembered his conversations with Jack Hart.

"Chatteris, that must be in Cambridgeshire," continued Jack, "Do you mean to tell me you have cycled all the way here and now you are going to fight?"

"Well I did get a lift part of the way on a lorry," admitted Boon, "and I'm hoping to do the same going back unless my dad can get my bike in his car."

In the years that followed many stories were written about how Eric was supposed to have cycled all the way to the Devonshire Club and back. There were all kinds of variations as journalists sought to glamorise the courage and determination of the young fighter. Whenever he was interviewed Boon never admitted or denied what really occurred. Even in his autobiography, 'Jack Solomons Tells All', published in 1951, the promoter avoided revealing the true facts.

It was not until 1976 that Boon eventually admitted publically what had occurred. In an interview with Alan Hoby of the Sunday Express he said: "In fact that story is not quite accurate. I did leave Chatteris on the bike, but later I hopped a lift, bike and all, on a lorry. When we got near London I got off and cycled the rest of the way."

In reality, without the kindness of the lorry driver, Boon would never have reached the Devonshire Club in time to fight. Had that been the case Solomons may never have invited him back again and his career could have taken a different course.

Eric must have thought the world was against him after finally arriving at the club. Having been angrily confronted by his father and then Solomons, he got another earful once he got inside the building. "You're late," growled the whip, an angry individual who was unaware of how far he had travelled. "Hurry up and get ready, you'll be on before you know it," he continued as he ushered him towards the dressing rooms. He then forced a smile when he noticed the youngster was still wearing his cycle clips.

In view of what Jack Hart had told him Solomons was expecting great things from Boon, but by the time he got into the ring he was exhausted from his exploits since dawn. Despite the lift he had still cycled a long way and towards the end of the fight his legs were really aching. He managed only a draw with Young Higgins, six years his elder.

Although it was not the result he or Solomons wanted, the promoter wasn't too disappointed because in a close contest Eric had attacked throughout. In an attempt to snatch a dramatic victory he floored Higgins twice in the final round, but didn't have the power to finish it. Nevertheless, he created a good impression with the crowd, most of whom thought he deserved the decision. Many asked Solomons who he was and how he found him. They loved his raw, all-action style of fighting and their enthusiasm convinced Jack to feature him again as soon as possible. He therefore persuaded Eric and his father to sign a contract for six further contests under Devonshire Club Promotions within the next six months.

Also appearing on the Devonshire Club bill was another promising Chatteris boxer, Young Green, who won a 10 rounds contest on points. He was managed by George Stokes who also acted as a second for Boon in his fight against Higgins. Solomons was impressed with Green and reached agreement with his manager for a further series of bouts.

In view of the developing situation, Arthur Binder and Reg Boon took the view that Stokes should also manage Eric. He held Board of Control promoter and manager licences and was best placed to get him contests at a variety of venues and thereby enhance his reputation. Stokes accepted the proposal and after discussion with Solomons it was agreed that Boon and Green would appear on the same Devonshire Club Promotion bills which would enable them to travel the long distance together.

One of the first things Jack needed to do was ensure that Boon was licensed by the Board of Control, but knowing he wouldn't get a licence if he revealed his true age, Eric said he was sixteen.

Without asking too many questions Solomons completed an application form, although in error gave Boon's address as 16 Burnsfield Street. He promptly submitted it, together with the annual fee of five shillings, (25p) to the Board and Boon's licence was granted by the Eastern Counties Area Council on 25 March.

*　　*　　*

Two weeks after facing Young Higgins, Boon was back at the Devonshire Club and was outpointed over six rounds by Stan Yates of Kilburn who was 15 pounds heavier and much older than the Chatteris youngster. The contest only went ahead after a long argument between George Stokes and Jack Solomons because no replacement could be found at such a late stage.

Despite the obstacles he faced, Boon was extremely confident and, attacking from the opening bell, comfortably took the first two rounds. Yates then got on top and using his considerable advantages did enough to earn the decision. Boon, however, gave a good account of himself and among those whom he impressed was Leicester Manager, George Biddles, who handled British welterweight champion, Pat Butler. After the fight he tried to persuade Eric to sign with him, but he refused.

Eric's first victory at the Devonshire Club came two weeks later when he outpointed Teddy Softley from Poplar. Then, in what was his fourth contest at the venue within the space of six weeks, he knocked out 'Yorkie' Perkins in five rounds. His two-fisted punching thrilled the East End crowd.

The most natural fight for Boon at this stage was a return with Young Higgins, so Solomons staged it at the open air Mile End Arena on 2 June. It was originally set to take place two weeks earlier, but heavy rain caused the show to be postponed. Eric gained a comfortable decision after a good fight ensuring that his manager George Stokes had a successful afternoon. His other boxers, Fred Clements from Ely won on points and Young Green, who had won all of his four contests at the Devonshire Club, got a draw after 10 rounds.

14

Despite his tender age, Boon was attracting the attention of reporters from further afield than Chatteris and Peterborough. Whilst the local papers continued to publish short reports of his fights together with the occasional photograph, it was a story in a London weekly publication, *Sports Gazette*, in June 1935 which was the most interesting. Under the bold headline "Boy Boon, the Baby-Faced Battler who puts them away", a reporter wrote:

> Keep your eyes on 'Boy' Boon the cherubic faced baby of eight stone who has all the fight makeup of a future champion. The way he set about Young Higgins, a tough nut from Stepney, was good to see. Boon has always boxed with a bandaged left arm, but it does not appear to make any difference. He flails away with that left and it smashes home on the chin. How Higgins stood up as long as he did I do not know. Boon is a boxer with a bright future.

The bandage on Eric's left arm referred to in the report was worn merely as a precaution against injury like that which he sustained against Jeff Smith back in February. He wore it on several occasions, something that would not be permitted in modern times.

Returning to the Devonshire Club three weeks later, Boon scored a significant victory over Albert 'Boy' Bessell, one of the busiest flyweights around at the time. He had boxed at London venues on five occasions within the space of 14 days in early June, winning on each occasion, four by clean knock-outs. He even had two fights in one day, boxing at Mile End Arena in the afternoon of 16 June and Hammersmith the same evening.

The Devonshire Club was packed for the Sunday afternoon show with punters expecting fireworks from the two explosive youngsters. As so often happens, however, they were disappointed because with their reputations at stake both lads showed more caution than usual. The fight went the distance with Boon taking the decision, but he was mature enough to know that it was an important victory.

There was more disappointment for the club regulars when Boon surprisingly dropped a decision to 'Kid' Savage at the end of August. Although he was the better boxer, the Islington lad's strength and persistence throughout the contest earned him the decision after an intense battle. The defeat irritated Jack Solomons who knew there some were obstacles to overcome.

Jack was particularly annoyed with George Stokes who, in early August, had used Boon, Young Green and a number of other Peterborough boxers to make up a show at a grand fete at Grimsthorpe Castle in Lincolnshire. Although Eric emerged unscathed from his winning fight against Alf Eburne from Wembley, he and Green were still contracted to the Devonshire Club for one more fight.

Whilst he was convinced that Boon had the charisma and fighting style to become a success, Jack was concerned about the amount of travelling he did for each of his London fights. Despite scoring only one quick victory from his seven in London, the East End fans loved his exciting two-fisted style. Within a short space of time he had become immensely popular and even after he lost to Savage, the trade paper referred to him as "the clever boy who is so popular at the club."

Desperate to get his balance and reasoning right Solomons explained to Eric that if he was to fulfil his undoubted potential and become a club regular he needed to get further experience nearer to home. A round trip of about 150 miles was too far to expect a fifteen-years-old lad to travel to fight every two or three weeks. Consequently, with understanding on both sides it would be another eight months before Boon boxed at the Devonshire Club again.

*   *   *

The break from travelling to London appeared to benefit Eric because boxing at small arenas at Cambridge, Watford, Spalding and Norwich he scored 12 consecutive victories between October 1935 and March 1936, seven coming inside the distance. The first was a points decision over Charlie Smith (Apsley) at Cambridge Corn Exchange. It was then that he really began to show his power winning his next four fights by the short route.

At Cambridge on 25 November he floored Ginger Daniels (Newmarket) four times in the opening round. Only the bell saved him from being knocked out, and after he took another count early in round two the referee stepped in. Showing exceptional aggression it was as though Eric had a point to prove and at Watford Trade Union Hall nine days later he floored Charlie Smith twice in the second round before the fight was stopped. Six weeks earlier Charlie had taken him the distance without hitting the canvas.

Carrying his new-found punching power into 1936, the Chatteris youngster hammered Young Burbage (Islington) to the canvas four times before knocking him out in round four at Cambridge. At the same venue four weeks later he knocked out Terry Ellis (Chelmsford) in the opening round.

Local newspaper reporters were thrilled as Eric's career gained momentum. There were, however, still considerable inaccuracies and exaggerations regarding his record. One report claimed he had won all of his 27 contests inside the distance. Another, when covering his points victory over 'Smoker' Smith at Norwich Corn Hall, claimed it was his twenty-third consecutive victory with nine knockouts inside three rounds. The *Eastern Daily Press,* however, was spot on saying: "Boon created a good impression and more will be heard of him."

Two days before meeting Smith, Eric faced Tommy Herbert (Leicester) at Spalding Corn Exchange and won every round against an older and more experienced opponent. Throughout the fight he rained terrific blows to head and body, and frequently drove Herbert to the ropes, but the plucky Leicester man was still on his feet at the final bell. A report in the *Lincolnshire Free Press* described Boon as "a clever young boxer, full of confidence and should go far in the game."

Two more knockout victories followed as Boon crammed in fights in the Eastern Counties. At Spalding, in what was described as his first fight at bantamweight, he knocked out Fred Franklyn in four rounds. The local crowd really warmed to Eric who, just as he had against Herbert, threw himself into the attack from the opening bell. Franklyn, described as one of the best bantams in Lincolnshire, was unable to deal with Boon's heavy two-fisted attacks. He was floored for a count of 'three' in the opening round and 'seven' in the third before taking the full count in the fourth.

Billed as Roy Boon of Cambridge, Eric was back in action two days later at Norwich. His opponent, local boxer, Young Hawes, started confidently and floored him with a good right in the opening seconds. The Chatteris lad was up without a count, threw a vicious right to the jaw to send Hawes crashing backwards. His head struck the canvas heavily as he landed and was counted out in just 27 seconds. It would remain the quickest victory of Boon's career.

Eric was on a roll, but after stopping Young Griffo with a badly cut eye in the opening round at Norwich, he was surprisingly held to a draw by Billy Boyd (Dorrington) at Spalding five days later. With a sound defence, Boyd was by far the best opponent Boon had faced and the only time he was in trouble was during round four. The referee's decision was a fair reflection of the action-packed six-rounder and well received by the crowd.

Nine days later at Cambridge, Boon had his first 10 round contest facing old opponent Charlie Smith. He again struggled to land his big punches and had to be content with a points victory. Although he had not been beaten since his last contest at the Devonshire Club, Fred Green believed it was time to take on a more experienced manager and trainer.

His first move was to write to George Cook, the old heavyweight who, in his day, met most of the top men including Joe Beckett in 1922, Phil Scott (1926), Larry Gains (1933) and Jack Petersen in 1934 in unsuccessful challenges for the British Empire title. Having opened a new gym at the Prince of Wales Hotel at Abbey Road in North West London he placed an advert in *Boxing* offering six months free tuition to any aspiring youngster wanting to take up boxing as a career.

In his letter Green explained all about Boon's powerful punch, his success since he started boxing and the fact that he had reached the stage where he needed somebody to educate him on the finer points. Fred added that Eric was boxing at Cambridge Corn Exchange on 27 April and invited Cook to attend. If that was not possible they could visit him at his new gym or his home address at 109 Finchley Road. The letter was concluded by Green stating that Reg Boon would give his consent to George becoming Eric's manager and trainer if a satisfactory contract could be arranged. He mentioned the fact that they had turned down an approach from George Biddles.

Green also wrote to Jack Solomons who knew of Eric's successful run in the Eastern Counties. A few days later he received a response from Mike Milligan stating that Boon had been matched with Jackie Roberts of Wimbledon over eight rounds at the Devonshire Club on 15 April. In what was his first contest there since August the previous year the youngster made no mistake and produced a big right hand to knock out Roberts in the second round.

Full of confidence Boon returned to the small halls of the provinces with mixed success. Three days after beating Roberts he dropped a six rounds points decision at Spalding to Ginger Brant from Leicester, one of the best flyweights in the Midlands. There was nothing in it for three rounds, but Brant moved and counter-punched well, frustrating Eric's attempts to land heavy shots to the chin. The Leicester man, a late substitute for Tom Kelby of Derby who failed to appear, stuck to his task and earned the decision thereby inflicting the first defeat on Boon in 14 contests.

One of the great things about Eric was that even at the age of sixteen he never lost his determination for success. On 27 April, believing he would be boxing in front of George Cook, he put on a workmanlike performance to knock out substitute Sammy Baker in two rounds. The end came when he landed a hard right followed by a terrific left hook to the chin and Baker, an airman based at RAF Mildenhall, crashed to the floor. His head struck the canvas and he lay motionless as the count was tolled over him.

On the day of the fight Fred Green received a letter from George Cook stating that he was unable to get to Cambridge, but offered

Eric a gym trial against one of his boys. He said that provided he was good enough he would be interested in taking him on, but added that in view of his tender age he would require the right instruction to bring the best out of him. Fred saw that as a bit of a knock-back so he didn't mention it to Boon before he faced Baker.

By this time he was already booked to box at Peterborough Corn Exchange three days later against Bill Boyd who held him to a draw at Spalding five weeks previously. Eric was a quick learner and by fighting regularly against opponents of all ages and styles he had gained valuable experience. This showed against Boyd who he comfortably outpointed over six rounds in what was a marked improvement from their previous contest.

Boon's busy schedule was due to continue on 9 May on a show promoted by Spalding & Gedney Hill Boxing Club at the local Corn Exchange. He had been matched with Tom Kelby (Derby), but he again pulled out at short notice. When told by the promoter that he would face substitute, Tommy Herbert from Leicester, Eric flatly refused. His father and the Master of Ceremonies, Captain Saunders, tried to persuade him to change his mind because a large crowd had assembled at the venue where he had become very popular, but Eric stood firm. Although he had outpointed Herbert in a hard fight at the same venue three months earlier, he never gave a reason for his decision. It was a complete mystery as described in an article in the *Cambridgeshire Times* under the headline 'Spalding Boxing Sensation – Boon refuses to Fight'.

After a break of almost two months Boon was chosen to box in one of six contests featuring local boys at the City of Ely Amateur Sports Association annual show staged at the Paradise Recreation Ground on August Bank Holiday Monday. Also on the show was another Chatteris youngster, Roy Driver, who was having his professional debut. Like Eric, he had been a successful member of Chatteris ABC and the local newspaper published a photograph of him with 19 trophies he had won.

The show was a massive event breaking records both in attendance and competition entries. During the evening the band of the Cambridgeshire Regiment was an added attraction and the boxing organised by Cambridge promoter, Arthur Waller, proved to be a fitting finale to a great day.

Boon featured in the opening contest over four rounds against Jock Nicholls (Aberdeen) and received a tremendous welcome as he climbed into the ring. He then gave the big crowd what they wanted by taking control of the opening round and never letting up. Mixing boxing skill with aggression he remained calm throughout a thrilling contest. He demonstrated a good left jab and his powerful right swings frequently staggered Nicholls.

In the final round both lads went flat out, but the Scot was punished so heavily that he could hardly stand at the final bell. Boon won clearly and the reception he received on leaving the ring demonstrated his growing popularity in the Eastern Counties. Since being beaten by 'Kid' Savage at the Devonshire Club almost 12 months earlier he had lost only one of 17 contests and stopped or knocked out nine opponents all of whom were older than him. Throughout that time Jack Solomons had monitored his progress and was convinced that he was a more mature fighter and punching harder. It was time therefore to offer him more fights at the Devonshire Club on a regular basis.

3

THE DEVONSHIRE CLUB

Jack Solomons was a fishmonger by trade and ran a stall at Ridley Road Market, Dalston. As a youngster he boxed as 'Kid' Mears, but gave up after only three professional fights and decided his future in the sport would be on the safe side of the ropes. In 1931 he and two associates bought the lease of a derelict chapel situated at Brenthouse Road, off Mare Street in Hackney, just a couple of miles from his fish stall. By hard work and careful planning they developed it into what would become one of the most intimate boxing arenas in London. By May the following year it had developed rapidly and nine promotions were held there that month alone. Often referred to as the Devonshire Sporting Club it also had facilities for wrestling, darts, billiards, bridge and other social entertainment, and had a restaurant and fully licensed bar.

The first show at the new Devonshire Club was on 21 October 1934, but was poorly attended. Boxing at the venue was slow to catch on largely due to competition from established venues, the Whitechapel Pavilion and The Ring at Blackfriars. Solomons, however, wasn't to be denied and staged affordable value-for-money shows on Friday evenings and Sunday afternoons most weeks. They were generally made up of local talent, and in the early days spectators could watch a bill of four or five six round contests for as little as sevenpence (3 ½ p), in the balcony and one shilling (5p) ringside.

With the passing of time news spread regarding the quality of shows being staged at the Devonshire. Consequently, attendances swelled and within a year it was generally a full house. Youngsters from all over London and the provinces frequently turned up with their kit hoping to get a late substitute job. The atmosphere was like no other small arena in London because, with a capacity of no more than 450, the fans were crammed in shoulder to shoulder. Rows of seats stretched back from all sides of the ring and the balcony, which virtually overlooked the ring on three sides of the building, held eight rows of wooden benches. Many of the ringside seats had small arm attachments for fans to place their drinks and, between fights, waiters drifted about taking orders for rollmops, kippers and jellied eels. Solomons was no fool, and being a fishmonger, did everything possible to maximise his business.

The Devonshire was not the healthiest of environments on fight nights as thick clouds of cigarette, cigar and pipe smoke slowly drifted slowly towards the ceiling like a thick fog. In their excitement fans often knocked beer over each other prompting the occasional unofficial skirmish although generally problems were resolved quickly. Action in the tiny ring, no more than 14 feet square, always took centre stage.

The surge in popularity of the Devonshire Club was good for the development of boxing at grass roots level. Not only was it attractive and affordable to the working class fans, it became a nursery for the sport. Solomons was always looking for new young talent and kids arrived there from all over the country because he staged a lower standard of contests than the bigger arenas. Although he never staged anything more important than a Southern Area championship at the Devonshire, his enterprise was instrumental to him eventually becoming a major promoter.

Big fight nights in London during the 1920's and early 30's were generally social occasions when Lords and their Ladies occupied expensive seats at the big arenas. From such a show to one at the Devonshire Club was a far cry because whilst the entertainment served up to the gentry was often without thrills, that delivered in the East End was the real thing. There was no hiding place in the tiny ring with its blood stained canvas, and the club favourites were hailed as gladiators and cult heroes.

The crowd at the club demanded action and if a fighter dilly-dallied about he got a fruity rebuke. The first rule of the Devonshire was to come out fighting. Whilst patrons would not stand for brutality they made sure that the men in the ring gave value for money. Hard non-stop punching was their motto and "may the best man win." They had their favourites, men who sold the place out, yet they always saluted a gallant loser. Wherever he came from he was guaranteed generous applause and in many cases Solomons got him back for more fights.

This was the environment the young Eric Boon was introduced to when he first boxed at the club against Young Higgins in March 1935. Most lads of fifteen would have been terrified and never returned, but Eric was made of stern stuff. Despite coming from a quiet Fenland market town he was a tough aggressive youngster who feared nothing and nobody. He sucked up the tense smoky atmosphere and couldn't wait to get back there again.

Excited at what the future held Boon increased his training at Chatteris and, in particular, spent hours pounding the anvil at his father's forge. Although still only a teenager he became incredibly strong and fit, but most importantly he was developing punching power that was sheer dynamite.

Jack Solomons knew from his earlier dealings with Boon that he was ever eager to fight. Having had 17 contests in less than a year he knew that his attitude hadn't changed. He remained a huge talent, but because of his age the promoter knew things could go badly wrong if he was rushed too quickly. On the other hand he wanted to match him with opponents who would bring the best out of him and thereby aid his development. Solomons eventually decided the best man for the job was another Devonshire Club favourite, Len Ash, who had run up a string of victories there. It proved to be sound judgement because on 21 August the two went at each other like terriers throughout the eight rounds contest and it was Boon who got the decision.

Solomons was delighted and his next test for Eric was Charlie Wise of Poplar who, as Cyril Wiseman, won a national Junior Intermediate Championship in January 1935. He was considered to be one of the best second class bantamweights in London, and although he was only nineteen had the experience of over 100 amateur bouts behind him.

Wise pushed Eric all the way in a great eight-round scrap and the Chatteris lad's points victory was considered by some critics to be his finest at that stage of his career. Afterwards he was congratulated by former world flyweight champion Jimmy Wilde, a ringside guest of the promoter.

Boon suffered no ill effects from the bouts with Ash and Wise and after a few weeks rest scored two quick victories within three days. Bert Whall (Norwich), a claimant to the Eastern Counties bantamweight title in 1934, was stopped in two rounds, and Teddy Larkham (Brentford), also a well known footballer, was knocked out in 40 seconds of the first.

Meanwhile, the Sunday regulars at the Devonshire Club were clamouring for a return between Boon and Len Ash. Wanting Eric to get more rounds under his belt Solomons matched them over eight rounds in his top of the bill contest on 18 October. Ash, a Hackney barber who also boxed as 'Kid' Ballyer, was so confident of victory that he promised Solomons that he would give up boxing altogether if he failed. "No chance," retorted Boon when he heard. "He'll be lucky to last the distance this time."

The spirit between the two youngsters was incredible and the fight became the talk of the East End. On fight day the Devonshire was packed to its doors and hundreds more crowded outside while details of the action was relayed to them. At the end of eight hectic rounds Boon again got the decision and years later Solomons claimed that Ash kept his word and never fought again. Instead, he stuck to hairdressing.

Boon, meanwhile, went from strength to strength. In a period of less than two months after beating Ash the second time he took part in 11 contests, four of which were at the Devonshire Club. He drew two and won the rest, five of which were inside the distance. The more he fought the more powerful he became, but despite this there were concerns in some quarters about his lack of defence.

After he outpointed Jack Watkins (Muswell Hill) in a great scrap over eight rounds, a report in *Sports & Entertainment Gazette* stated:

> Boon is a fierce two-fisted fighter who can punch holes in any opponent, but this contest should have taught him that he won't go far unless he learns to box as well as he fights.

It was fair comment because having floored Watkins for counts of 'nine' in round two and 'three' in the third Eric then took as much punishment as he dished out in his attempts to finish it early. In the end only his great stamina got him home victorious.

After knocking out Teddy Vince at Bury St Edmunds the following day, Eric faced 'Young' Fred Dyer at Norwich in his third contest in just five days. Although conceding five pounds in weight, Dyer was by far the more experienced and puzzled Boon throughout the eight rounds. He was unable to land his big shots and many thought him fortunate to get a draw in what was described as one of the hardest fights of his career.

One of Boon's real assets was that whenever he failed to beat an opponent impressively he just took it in his stride. He trained hard and put in more hours pounding the anvil at his father's forge knowing that his punching power would increase as he matured and developed physically.

Although interspersed by distance fights there were still impressive stoppage victories as he fought with regularity. Bobby Lyons took a number of counts at Norwich before being knocked out in the fifth. Against Joe Page of Blackfriars, they shook hands, sparred briefly before Boon knocked his opponent out with a terrific right to the head in about 90 seconds.

At the Empress Hall, Earls Court, on 30 November, Boon's performance in knocking out the infinitely more experienced 'Young' Nat Williams (Liverpool) was described as the best of the evening. Right from the start Williams, who had years of experience, attempted to assert his superiority and skill, standing upright like a teacher trying to give his pupil a lesson. Eric, however, was confident and unfazed and soon conveyed the message that Williams couldn't teach him anything.

The Chatteris boy exhibited excellent talent, landing some beautiful punches from both hands and fought with rare judgement for a lad of such tender years. Midway through the fifth round he manoeuvred his opponent to the ropes and then brought up a peach of an uppercut which landed with full force to the point of the chin. Williams went down like a log and was counted out at full stretch. It was several minutes before he recovered.

Writing in *Sports Gazette,* Editor Isidore Green commented:

> Now this 'Boy' Boon is a good lad. He has a load of boxing assets and I was more than pleased to see him accomplish this latest feat for in the *Sports Gazette* I have constantly sung his praises. I have watched most of his fights at the Devonshire Club and have been impressed.

Within a year *Sports Gazette* changed its title to *Weekly Sporting Review* and, with the passing of time, Green constantly reminded readers that his was the first publication to bring Boon to notice as a prospect very early in his career at the Devonshire.

Jack Solomons was equally impressed with Boon's performance against Williams and afterwards told a group of reporters: "He is well on his way to championship honours."

Boon's performance against Williams earned him a fight on a big charity show at the Stadium Club, Holborn, organised by Charles Donmall, Secretary of the British Boxing Board of Control, in support of a testimonial for the famous referee Moss Deyong. Many dignitaries attended the seven-fight promotion topped by world flyweight champion, Benny Lynch. It was an honour for Eric to be included on the bill and proved that he already had the right connections.

Before the boxing commenced Lord Lonsdale presented Lynch with the first Lonsdale Belt issued by the British Boxing Board of Control. Several hundred pounds were raised in donations following an appeal from the ring by Sir Noel Curtis-Bennett, and items including a box of Lord Lonsdale's famous cigars and a puppy by champion greyhound Mick the Miller, were auctioned.

Boon's opponent in a lively four-round contest was George Cunningham (Bethnal Green). Although the East Ender put up a brave performance he could not check the non-stop attacks of his youthful opponent. Eric punched hard and accurately throughout, flooring Cunningham for a count of 'eight' in round three before taking a well earned points decision.

Also appearing in a winning contest on the Stadium Club bill was Harry 'Kid' Silver, a fifteen-years-old Jewish boy from St Georges. Born at Clapton, a very short distance from the Devonshire Club, he had made his professional debut at that venue six months earlier. He was trained by Mike Milligan who was Jack Solomons' right hand man at the club. After winning his first few contests, *Sports Gazette* described Silver as a 'boxing sensation' which Mike thought was a bit over the top. He insisted he would take the youngster along steadily for a while and not allow him to have more than one fight a month.

As assistant matchmaker, whip and trainer, Mike was responsible for the general running of proceedings at the Devonshire. It was always up to him to get busy when a billed boxer didn't turn up. Whenever things didn't go according to plan it was Milligan who was called upon to straighten them out or settle disputes. He was an extremely popular and capable character who knew the game inside out and was responsible in no small way for the success of the club.

Milligan had also been involved with Boon since he first boxed at the club and was responsible for making most of the arrangements by correspondence with Fred Green. He trained Eric whenever he stayed in London, and once the press realised their potential they predicted that Mike had the chance of two future champions in Silver and Boon.

Meanwhile, whilst being delighted at Boon's ring progress, Solomons was becoming concerned by the fact that he lived so far away from London. Although he sometimes stayed at the promoter's house at Clapton, Eric detested the capital. Rather than stay there after a fight he often spent half a crown of his purse money to persuade all-night lorry drivers to take him back to Chatteris. There were other occasions when he travelled home by train.

Solomons knew a prospect when he saw one and was convinced that Boon possessed all the ingredients needed to become a champion. Although he was still growing he had tremendous power in both hands, was developing good boxing skills and had incredible enthusiasm. He had rapidly become a Devonshire Club favourite and, although most regulars were East End folk from the Jewish community who didn't even know where Chatteris was, he often packed the place out. A good looking lad with thick black naturally wavy hair, old-timers described him as a breath of fresh air because they loved his crash-bang style.

Deciding that he would rather have Eric close at hand in the East End than 70 miles away in the Fens, Solomons travelled to Chatteris early in 1937 and had a meeting with his parents. He asked that the youngster be put under his personal management and be allowed to live with him and his wife at their home at 42 Jessan Avenue, Upper Clapton, a short distance from the Devonshire Club. Reg and Liz were reluctant to agree, pointing out that it was too big a step for a seventeen-years-old to take, but Eric pleaded with them to let him go. "If I don't make good I'll come back and work in the forge," he promised. His plea tipped the balance and, wanting the best for their son, his parents eventually relented. A contract was drawn up and from that point Solomons became responsible for making and agreeing all of his fights.

Jack still had to overcome the problem of Boon's dislike for London, but after some thought came to the conclusion that Harry 'Kid' Silver could be the person to resolve it. Although Eric had more ring experience, Harry was a streetwise London lad who knew his way around, particularly in the East End. He got the two lads together and his plan worked perfectly because being of a similar age, they hit it off almost immediately. They talked almost non-stop about boxing, did their morning runs together and trained in the gym under Mike Milligan. Silver showed Eric around, where he could eat cheaply and how to amuse himself at little expense.

Once the Chatteris lad found his feet and began to get used to life in the big city he wanted to spread his wings and visit the West End. Solomons wasn't too keen on the idea because he knew only too well how youngsters could be led astray, lose their discipline and consequently their dedication to boxing. He and Silver therefore put their heads together and pulled a fast one on Boon.

One night Silver suggested to Eric that they had a night on the town. Whilst showing him the bright spots of Hackney and Aldgate he managed to convince him that they were actually the West End. Mare Street had cinemas, cafes, pubs, the Town Hall and the Hackney Empire, and in those days was a great deal less harmful to a youngster than the bright lights of the West End in the late 'naughty thirties.' Although Boon enjoyed himself it wasn't exactly what he had expected so he gave up the idea of going to the West End again, at least for the time being.

*   *   *

Once Solomons had sole control over Boon's career he really put him to work, cramming five contests into the first four weeks of 1937. Quick victories over Al Church (rsc.6), Billy Bennett (ko.2), Billy Sheldon (ret.3) and Billy Griffiths (ko.1) demonstrated the youngster's incredible punching power. Church was given a real battering before it was stopped while Bennett was in trouble from body shots in the opening round and knocked out by a single right to the chin just 30 seconds into the second. "Smart work Boon" wrote the trade paper *Boxing*.

Against Billy Sheldon at the Devonshire Club, hefty punching played havoc with the Newcastle man's defence. After taking a count of 'eight' in round three he sustained a badly cut left eye which forced his retirement. That evening Solomons had invited a number of leading boxing correspondents to the club to watch the youngster he claimed had the punching power to knock out grown men. Boon didn't disappoint them or his new manager, putting on what was described as one of his best performances to date. Sheldon was one of the most experienced boxers in the north of England having faced many top men and beaten most of them. Boon was already being described as one of the heaviest hitting lightweights of his age in the history of British boxing. "He never lets up once his opponent is in trouble," wrote one weekly sports correspondent.

Apart from showing up well in front of the press boys, Boon was also given the best possible exposure by boxing on charity shows in London which were invariably attended by wealthy patrons. When he knocked out Billy Bennett at Holborn Stadium the event was in aid of the Booth Street Relief Institute and Stamford Hill Aid Society. Two weeks later Jack Solomons staged a testimonial evening at the Devonshire Club for the top class light-heavyweight, Archie Sexton, who had been forced to quit the ring after sustaining serious damage to an eye. A packed house gave Sexton a great reception and an appeal from the ring raised almost £200. Boon then faced Billy Griffiths of Wales and knocked him out midway through the opening round.

Boon's first taste of big arena boxing was when he appeared on the undercard of the Jack Petersen – Walter Neusel heavyweight fight at Harringay Arena on 1 February 1937. Because of his continued success and crowd appeal the shrewd Solomons contacted Britain's top promoter, Sydney Hulls. A deal was struck whereby Hulls would put Eric on some of his shows and Solomons would fix up the supporting bouts for Harringay promotions. The undercard for this show not only featured Boon, but also Harry 'Kid' Silver and three men who would later become opponents of the Chatteris man – Dave Crowley, George Reynolds and Norman Snow.

Content with the way things were progressing Solomons decided it was time Boon took on better class opposition. When he faced Mike Sullivan just a week after his Harringay debut it was his first 10-rounder. Sullivan was an experienced professional who gave Eric plenty to think about early on, but once the youngster found his range a vicious right to the jaw brought matters to an end in round four.

Eric continued to impress the critics with his tremendous power and was described in *Sporting Life* as 'the knock-out artist.' Other papers made reference to the fact that only a year earlier he was a flyweight, but had progressed so rapidly that he was now capable of knocking out lightweights.

Boon had filled out considerably during the past 12 months and by this time was a fully fledged lightweight. The constant strength building exercises at his father's forge had developed him considerably. Not only did he possess incredible power for a seventeen-year-old, but his biceps bulged and he had the shoulders of a middleweight.

Before a capacity crowd Eric battered Dave James from Wales throughout most of their eight rounds contest at Reading. The Welshman was bloodied in the third, took counts in the fourth, sixth and seventh rounds, only the bell saving him from a knockout on the latter two occasions. He was, nevertheless, extremely game and lasted the distance to lose widely on points. Harry Silver later boxed a competitive bout over four rounds and secured his 15th consecutive victory.

Satisfied that his man could look after himself against decent opposition, Jack Solomons agreed to Boon meeting Eastern Counties featherweight champion 'Chucky' Robinson over 10 rounds at Norwich the following week. On what was the first occasion where his official weight was reported, Eric scaled 9st 11 ½ giving him an advantage of seven and a half pounds. In a hard contest from start to finish Robinson's considerable experience helped him cope with Boon's power and extra weight. Although the Chatteris lad took a well earned points decision he could not put 'Chucky' on the floor despite landing plenty of hard shots from both hands.

Inside the distance victories over 'Spin' Anson (RAF) and Tony Butcher (Liverpool) followed in quick succession, but then Eric's long unbeaten run came to a surprise end at the Devonshire Club on 21 March 1937. He had been due to meet Tommy Dowlais of Tredegar, but when the Welshman failed to turn up Solomons installed Harry Brooks of St Georges as a last minute substitute.

Giving away almost a stone in weight Boon was at an immediate disadvantage against a strong, experienced old-stager who also had advantage of six inches in height and reach. When he retired after four rounds it was generally considered to be a wise decision as the fight had been scheduled for 10 rounds. The following day, however, press reports indicated that the Chatteris lad had been outclassed. Differing and controversial accounts left *Weekly Sporting Review* to print what it called 'the inside story' of Boon's defeat. Editor, Isidore Green, felt that people not present at the fight may well be led to believe that Eric was badly beaten. This was not so and in his report wrote:

> In fact he was doing very well against his much heavier opponent, and his heavier punching and youthful aggressiveness were

gradually overcoming the cagey ringcraft of the St Georges boxer. During a melee at close quarters in the fourth Boon cried out that he could not see. Brooks had apparently accidentally caught him in the right eye with a thumb. Water streamed from it and within a few moments the optic was almost closed.

The Devonshire Club management had for once showed bad judgement because there was no sense putting a great young prospect like Boon in against a man he could never realistically hope to knock over. Nevertheless, he gave it a great try leaping at Brooks in an attempt to score to the head. He did most of the forcing and although slightly ahead at the end found his opponent just too strong. "The pain from my eye was unbelievable," said Boon later. "I wanted to carry on, but knew I couldn't. I hate quitting."

Eric was extremely upset at the defeat after a long unbeaten sequence, especially as it was his first in London since August 1935. Jack Solomons added that it was the first time Boon had been stopped in 34 contests, but his estimate was wide of the mark. It was in fact 52 fights earlier that he last lost inside the distance, that being against Jeff Smith at Peterborough in February 1935. Another thing that Solomons didn't know was that Eric had damaged the same eye in training a few days earlier. He said nothing about it for fear of losing his purse money.

A few days before Boon faced Harry Brooks, Isidore Green met him on a train. Eric had just arrived in London from Chatteris and was on his way to the La Boheme gym in Mile End Road. At the time he believed he was fighting Nipper Whiting and asked the journalist what he knew about him. Although they had spoken briefly on previous occasions, Green was impressed by the maturity of the youngster and in his column on 20 March 1937 wrote:

> I liked Boon's boyish enthusiasm for the game because he is unlike many of the youngsters I know who, because they have won a fight or two, think themselves world champions. He spoke about his long run of successes in the same manner as a clerk might talk about his book-keeping.

Green predicted that in about a year or so, provided that Boon was not overworked, he would be a serious menace to most men at his weight. The defeat to Brooks did Eric no harm other than irritate him. He was not hurt and merely shrugged it off as a learning exercise and one of those things which occur in boxing. His next contest was in his home town of Chatteris on a big promotion staged by Jack Solomons and the Devonshire Club. Jack saw it, not only as a business venture, but a long overdue opportunity for locals to see how well Boon was developing. Townsfolk had followed his career closely, but many either couldn't afford to travel far afield to watch him or didn't have the means to do so. Consequently, over 600 excited fans packed into the Empress Cinema to see him make his first ring appearance in the town as a professional.

The cinema was chosen because there was no town hall or other building in the locality capable of accommodating the anticipated large crowd. With the ring erected on the stage where the screen hung, the show was a great success and described in the local press as the finest ever staged in Chatteris. Several well known boxing personalities made the journey to the Fenland town and autograph hunters were busy securing signatures. Jack Hart, the well known London referee who had first introduced Boon to Solomons, officiated throughout the programme. Three weeks earlier he had been in charge of the British heavyweight championship fight at Harringay between Tommy Farr and Ben Foord. Tiny Bostock, fancied by many critics to become the next British flyweight champion, sat at ringside. He had recently been headline news by issuing a challenge to Benny Lynch for a fight at £500 a side. The Master of Ceremonies was described in the press as "the famous Mr Buster from London." He was Buster Cohen, an extremely robust and jovial character with a huge reputation who had been the resident MC at the Devonshire Club since it opened.

Boon's opponent was George Bissett from London who claimed never to have been knocked out in 107 contests. From the opening bell, however, the young Chatteris favourite seemed intent on wrecking that proud record. Heavy punches over Bissett's heart and to the side of the head visibly shook him and he never seemed to recover. He went to the floor early in round two following a hefty smack in the eye. After starting to rise at the count of 'six' he dropped back to one knee, and with a helpless shake of the head told the referee he couldn't see. Hart continued to count and Boon was declared the winner by a knockout. It was a great achievement and by weighing in at 9st 8 ½ he was now a confirmed lightweight.

As Solomons continued to keep his young prospect busy he made sure that he faced men who would not fold easily. It proved to be absolutely the right tactic because by having almost a fight a week through April and May, Eric continued to rack up a good percentage of quick victories, and was also taken the distance by capable, experienced men.

By this time Solomons had strengthened his business relationship with Sydney Hulls and was officially installed as matchmaker for the supporting contests on all of his big London promotions. This was good news for Boon who was given a four rounds contest on another big Harringay bill on 15 April topped by Tommy Farr against former world heavyweight champion, Max Baer. His opponent was Angus McGregor, one of the best lightweights in Scotland. From the first bell they tore into each other and brought the huge crowd to its feet yelling with excitement during each round. The referee's decision of a draw was absolutely correct.

Solomons also planned to take Eric to Paris for a contest in May, but it didn't materialise. Instead quick victories over Jocker Johnson (rsc.5), Bobby Lyons (ko.1) and Ron Porter (rsc.4) thrilled the crowds and confirmed his incredible punching power. After the victory over Porter, *Weekly Sporting Review* commented:

> Boon will develop into a star of the first order if he maintains his present rate of progress. There is a wealth of talent in his work.

The contests Eric really learned from were those against seasoned campaigners Bob Barlow, George Kelly and Jack Lilley. He had to work extremely hard against all three and showed that he was much more than just a powerful two-fisted young brawler. Against Barlow over 10 rounds at Norwich it looked as though he would again win inside the distance as he crashed heavy left and right hooks through the Derby man's guard. Barlow took a count of 'nine' in round six, but then hit back well as Boon began to tire in what was a thriller from start to finish. The Chatteris boy only got the decision by virtue of his work rate in the early rounds.

A week later on a Friday night show at the Devonshire Club, Boon faced Irish lightweight champion, George Kelly, in his first contest over 12 rounds. It was his sternest test to date and the place was packed out. Kelly was also a big attraction and one of the busiest fighters around at the time having battled through a total of 30 rounds during the previous week alone. On paper Eric's task looked awesome, but despite being severely tested he confirmed his great promise and came through it with credit.

Kelly's experience and know-how were far superior to most of Boon's previous opponents. Often under severe pressure from two-fisted attacks he frequently pulled his young opponent up sharply with solid single shots to the head or under the heart. Yet he couldn't quite find the punching prowess of Boon who, despite getting tired during the last few rounds, still did enough to keep his nose in front and take the decision. George was a capable and willing rival and the press described the encounter as Boon's toughest since turning to the sport. 'Boon's Great Display' was the bold headline in the trade paper *Boxing*.

In the dressing room afterwards, Kelly told Jack Solomons that he had never been hit so hard. "When Boon hit me in the stomach with one right hand I felt like I'd been run over by a bus," he groaned.

The fight convinced Solomons that Eric was well and truly out of the novice class and two weeks later he topped the bill at the Devonshire Club in another 12-rounder. His opponent was Jack Lilley, an extremely clever ring general from Congleton and he only won by the narrowest margin. Had Jack possessed a really damaging punch Boon would have had greater problems. Although always attacking he was frequently made to miss and often out-jabbed. His best work usually came at close quarters with two-fisted attacks to the ribs which slowed his man down in the later rounds.

It was a great fight throughout with both men sustaining eye damage, Boon as early as round two and Lilley in the 11th. Only Eric's aggression and persistence over the final rounds secured him victory. Although he appeared to be feeling the pressure fighting experienced men who didn't crumble to his heavy punching, it was important that critics and fans remembered that he was still not eighteen. These were the contests where he learned the ring skills that were to set him up for the gruelling road which lay ahead. The fact that he packed out small arenas, particularly the Devonshire Club, was good business for Jack Solomons, but great credit had to be given to the promoter for his matchmaking skills. Both he and his young protégé were already on a climb to greatness.

*　　　*　　　*

No matter how good a boxer is, setbacks of one kind or another are almost inevitable. Despite having had a five week break from the ring, Boon suffered another when he faced Johnny Softley, a hard hitting youngster from Poplar over 12 rounds at the Devonshire Club on 2 July. He was the twin brother of Teddy Softley who Eric outpointed at the club in April 1935. They were tough boys trained by Dave 'Tatts' Phillips who, over the years, had worked with many good men in the East End including Jack Hyams, Jack 'Kid' Berg, Johnny Brown and Phil Lolosky.

Going into the fight Johnny had a record of 20 wins and 13 draws against 12 defeats and was seen by Solomons as the ideal man to test Boon. He turned professional in 1934 and boxed mainly in the East End. A testimony of his ability was that four weeks earlier he had knocked out Angus McGregor in nine rounds at Mile End, something Boon failed to do when he faced the Scot in April. Softley had been matched over 15 rounds on 12 occasions, three of which were against Bethnal Green strongman, Johnny Cunningham who he beat once and drew with in the other two.

Both boys set a fast pace from the start exchanging powerful blows at a rapid rate. Although Boon punched hard, Softley punched harder and in the early stages Eric must have realised that Johnny was one of the toughest men he had ever faced. There were times when Boon was forced to use his boxing skill and, instead of relying solely on his power, frequently scored with stiff left jabs to the face. Whenever they got to close quarters, however, both unloaded and scored heavily. The third round was particularly exciting and the packed Friday night crowd were on their feet cheering every rally.

Midway through the fight Boon appeared to be feeling the pace whereas Softley came out looking fresh at the start of each round. From the sixth he got on top throwing powerful uppercuts to the chin which shook the Chatteris boy. Eric, who was down briefly in this round, was caught repeatedly by solid hooks and threw very little back. He looked decidedly weak on his legs during the seventh and his corner sensibly retired him during the interval.

Although no excuses were made for the defeat, Eric had complained of pains in one leg when he arrived at the club earlier. Solomons immediately took him to a doctor at Mile End where he was given an injection to deaden the pain. There was no question of him pulling out of the fight, but Jack later claimed the leg gave way during the second round and Eric was fighting an uphill battle from then on.

The injury proved to be nothing serious, and not in the least discouraged by the setback Boon was back in the Devonshire Club ring two weeks later against another experienced man in Bryn Morris from Derby. He boxed steadily to take a good points decision and was careful not to get over enthusiastic about ending the fight early. Using excellent judgement he dealt effectively with an aggressive opponent who was intent on battering his way to victory. Regulars at the Devonshire found it strange that Boon didn't seem anxious to unload his heavy blows, but instead went about his work as though keen to improve his boxing skills. He used his left jab to good effect, followed up with equally accurate right crosses and steadied the Derby man with hurtful shots to all parts of the body. At the end Eric was a good winner, but Morris received a generous ovation for his full-bloodied effort.

On the same bill, Johnny Softley scored another impressive victory outpointing 'Tiger' Bert Ison over 12 rounds while Boon's close mate Harry 'Kid' Silver won in the first round.

In reality, the defeat Boon suffered against Softley did him good. Critics remarked that he didn't look his normal self, although there was no attempt to take anything away from Johnny. Boon made no excuses and, training hard under Mike Milligan, worked on his mistakes and weaknesses. Men like Softley, and Harry Brooks before him, made Eric a better and more compact fighter. They put him through difficult contests and as a result he would not be beaten again in 34 contests spread over more than three years.

4

THE LEARNING CONTINUES

Jack Solomons knew that, despite still being only a boy, Boon would fight anyone put in front of him. Whilst being extremely mature and courageous for his age there was, however, still a rawness about him which would be quickly exposed if he faced the top men too soon. The agreement therefore was that for the time being Jack would keep him busy against moderate to good opposition without taking any unnecessary chances. Most of those fights would be at the Devonshire Club.

By the time Eric reached his eighteenth birthday at the end of 1937 he had engaged in 33 contests in just 12 months. During that period he had graduated from being a six-round fighter to one who boxed regularly over 10 or 12 rounds, mostly of three minutes duration. After beating Bryn Morris in July he ran up a string of 11 inside the distance victories most of which were at the Devonshire. It was an incredible period which brought him to the notice of most of the established boxing writers.

Friday fight nights at the Devonshire Club were real value for money events and fans often queued for up to an hour to see the first rate thrillers Solomons and his able ally, Mike Milligan, lined up for them. There could have been few gamer men to fight at the club than Wilf Dexter from Nottingham, but the night he faced Boon, the Chatteris youngster was at his most powerful best.

Eric was in excellent condition, his punching and timing were perfect and he was far less erratic than in previous contests. His punching was effective from the start and although Dexter tried hard to trade punches and tire him out it was a hopeless task. Down for a count of 'eight' in round three, the Nottingham man carried on gamely until the referee called a halt in the seventh.

Two weeks later Solomons staged an eagerly awaited return between Boon and Charlie Wise described by *Weekly Sporting Review* as "the very essence of ring action." Since his points defeat to Boon a year earlier, Charlie had become another Devonshire Club favourite by virtue of his all action, whirlwind style. A few days before the fight *Weekly Sporting Review* predicted:

> The fans will not be disappointed when they see these two human machines in action at the Devonshire next week.

Although there was plenty of action Boon dealt easily with Wise's attacks and punished him when and where he liked. He was overwhelmingly superior on the night and the referee was right to call a halt during the third round. Charlie had at last met a man who was far too good for him. Some fans were disappointed that what had promised to be a cracker was in fact quite one-sided. Wise and his father, however, took exception to remarks made in one national newspaper and the matter eventually became the subject of a High Court case.

With his stock soaring Boon next featured in the main event at another Devonshire Club promotion at the Empress Cinema, Chatteris on 5 October. His opponent was Benny Thackeray from Leeds, a vastly experienced stylish boxer with a great reputation. Between 1931 and 1934 he fought Johnny King of Manchester on six occasions, winning two and drawing one. Johnny is still generally recognised as one of the best British bantamweights of all time having won the British title three times and also the British Empire championship

Interest in Boon had grown massively in the Fens since his last appearance at the venue six seeks earlier. With 700 fans packed inside, many more were turned away frustrated at being unable to see their young idol. Weighing 9st 11 ¼ Boon had an advantage of just over two pounds and, knowing the task he faced, set about Thackeray from the opening bell. The craggy faced man from Leeds showed good skill under pressure during the first three rounds, but had no answer when the local youngster caught up with him early in the fourth. A vicious right to the solar plexus sent Benny to the canvas for a count of 'nine' and within seconds of rising a similar punch put him down again. With agony etched across his face, he had no chance of beating the count. He had difficulty breathing and it was almost a minute before he could be moved to his stool. They were exceptional punches that Boon slammed into his opponent and one national newspaper reporter claimed they were similar to those developed by former world heavyweight champion, Bob Fitzsimmons, who was also a blacksmith.

Once again Eric had shown not only incredible power, but also great maturity. Having seen the effect that the first shot had on the experienced Thackeray, he wasted no time in landing another. His display had brought huge excitement to his home town and the fans gave him an incredible ovation as he left the ring. Hundreds of others waited outside in the street to greet him as he left the Empress Cinema. Jack Solomons was delighted with his charge and noted the crowd reaction. He knew that by featuring the lad he could sell out any venue at Chatteris whenever he chose.

Next up for Boon was a return with Bryn Morris who came in as a substitute for Frank Simms (Lincoln) at the Devonshire, but there was an unsatisfactory ending to this contest due partly to its duration. Announced by the MC as being over 12 rounds, Morris was clearly under the impression that he had been booked for ten. When the bell ended that round the referee was called to his corner and after a brief conversation with him and his seconds Boon was declared the winner on a retirement. As in their first scrap, Morris pushed Eric hard, but he dealt with it well. He received good press and writing in *Weekly Sporting Review,* Isidore Green said: "I was very impressed with Boon who is improving with every contest."

Boon was fortunate in that by this stage of his career, he sustained very few facial injuries. Consequently, he was able to box on a regular basis, and over the next seven weeks crammed in a further six contests. Two were at the Devonshire Club, two at Cambridge and one each at Chatteris and Bury St Edmunds, none of which went beyond three rounds.

Each victory served to swell the youngster's fan base and Jack Solomons the businessman was keen to capitalise. Due in no small part to Eric's continued success there was a huge boxing revival in Cambridge and surrounding districts. Sportsmen of the town therefore banded together and booked the Corn Exchange for a series of monthly promotions with a view to showing local talent and introducing prominent London based boxers. As Boon fell into both categories Solomons quickly became an interested party. Following discussion, agreement was reached that he and the Devonshire Club would organise contests in the same way they had done so successfully at Chatteris.

The Corn Exchange had been a happy hunting ground for Boon, and although he had not boxed there since April 1936, Solomons planned to use him in the main event on 25 October. The place was packed out and dignitaries, including the Mayor of Cambridge, were in attendance. With Mike Milligan acting as chief whip and general assistant, the show was a great success especially as Boon put on another great display. Although his original opponent, Wilf Dexter, pulled out at short notice and was replaced by fellow Nottingham fighter, Fred Thackeray, it made no difference to the ambitious youngster. Clearly intent on a quick finish he smashed his opponent to the canvas for three counts in the opening round. A similar explosive punch brought matters to a conclusion early in the second.

The organisers were delighted and four weeks later there was a massive attendance at the Corn Exchange when Eric again boxed in the main event. He faced a real task in Bob Rowlands from Sunderland, an experienced man who held victories over other Devonshire Club favourites Johnny Softly, Mick Carney, Con Flynn and another former Boon opponent, Angus McGregor. At first it was thought that Bob was a bit above Eric's class, but the youngster was not concerned and gladly agreed to take the fight.

Once again Boon was the sensation of the show. To the astonishment of the packed audience he knocked out Rowlands in the second round with a mighty right hook to the jaw. The power behind the blow was incredible for a lightweight not yet eighteen-years-old. It crashed home with such speed and force that the Sunderland man was rendered unconscious and had to receive lengthy medical attention. It was almost half an hour before he recovered. Proof of Boon's punching power was that it was later claimed that Rowlands had never previously been knocked out in over 100 fights.

It was yet another victory which particularly impressed Isidore Green who, in his column in *Weekly Sporting Review,* wrote:

> My Cambridge correspondent's remarks on 'Boy' Boon's wonderful victory on Monday makes me feel quite pleased. I am more convinced than ever that Boon is one of the finest lightweight prospects in the country. I was the very first to write about him and have encouraged him in all of his contests at the Devonshire Club and maintain that if he's carefully handled he will become champion.

The *Weekly Sporting Review* was one of Britain's fastest growing publications specialising particularly on boxing and show business. Being an ambitious young journalist Green got on extremely well with Boon, his close mate Harry Silver and their boss Solomons. Consequently he was often the first to know what was going on and wasted no time passing stories on to his readers.

Between the two Cambridge promotions Boon knocked out Harry McKenzie in two rounds at the Devonshire Club before returning to Chatteris on another promotion staged by Solomons and the club. He was again top of the bill, his opponent being Dave Wilding (Birmingham) another good young prospect whose successes included an eight rounds points decision over Eastern Area champion, Chucky Robinson. The fight created tremendous interest and for the second time in six weeks the Empress Cinema was sold out days in advance.

Unfortunately for the fans a fight involving Boon was again a short one because Wilding sustained a nasty gash above his right eye which forced the referee to intervene early in the second round. There had not been much action during the four minutes they were in the ring because with each respecting the other they took careful stock and took no chances. Boon got through his opponent's guard twice in the opening round, but early in the second was driven to the ropes by good shots. Typically, Eric responded in the only way he knew which was to immediately hit back. A hard right split Wilding's eyebrow and the contest was over.

In making the official announcement Master of Ceremonies, Buster Cohen, told the audience that Boon was unhappy about the ending and offered Wilding a return. He added that Eric was idolised in the East End, but was finding it difficult getting good fights in London because many boys with good reputations were not prepared to meet him. There were not many welters or even middleweights who could punch like him.

Buster was a rotund and thoroughly entertaining character and the Chatteris folk loved his charm and personality. He told them that Boon was being handled as a boxer should be. "I am certain that before many more months I will be honoured to introduce to Chatteris a lightweight champion," he told them. It was great stuff and bowing to all sides of the ring he received a huge ovation.

Boon wound up 1937 with two more quick victories within the space of three days, but paid a price. Whilst hammering Con Flynn, a useful fighter from Islington at the Devonshire Club, he badly injured his right hand. Punching extremely heavily he floored Flynn five times in less than three rounds before the fight was halted. Although a number of publications reported that the Islington man had either retired or been stopped, the official verdict was that he had been disqualified. This came about because during round three Boon was knocking Flynn all around the ring and eventually his chief second, George Carney, jumped in to stop it. As this was a flagrant breach of Board of Control rules the referee was left with no alternative but to disqualify Flynn. Although the verdict deprived Eric of another stoppage success on his record it was none the less a notable achievement because Flynn had beaten Leicester veteran Len Wickwar who, the night Boon beat Flynn, outpointed British lightweight champion, Jimmy Walsh.

As soon as the fight was over, Eric complained of excruciating pain in his right hand. Mike Milligan removed his glove and found that the hand was swollen and badly discoloured. A subsequent medical examination revealed two splintered bones and as a consequence Boon was advised to rest the hand for a month.

Eric, however, had no intention of resting because he was booked to fight Llew Thomas of Bargoed over 12 rounds at Bury St Edmunds three days later. The promoter of that fight, Wally Dakin, was at the Devonshire Club, and realising Boon's predicament Jack Solomons remarked: "Well Wally, there goes your top-liner, you unlucky devil."

Boon, who was on his way back to his dressing room, overheard the comment and stopping dead in his tracks said: "Of course I shall box Mr Dakin. I won't let you down."

Solomons couldn't believe what he was hearing. "But you can't fight with a hand like that," he snapped.

"Why not?" retorted Boon. "My left is still good. I'll knock the man out with that."

In those days medical supervision in boxing was nowhere near as stringent as in modern times. Nothing more was said about the subject and Boon travelled to Bury St Edmunds and fought Thomas as arranged. True to his word he knocked out the man from Wales with a left hook in round three after flooring him several times.

In his autobiography *"Jack Solomons Tells All"* published in 1951, the promoter claimed that the knockout arose partly because of the action of one of Boon's followers. The individual in question allegedly rushed to the ringside and called the referee's count in Thomas' ear. The only problem was that when he reached 'seven' the third man had already called 'out'.

*   *   *

Following strict medical advice to rest his injured hand for a month, Eric spent the Christmas period with his family at Chatteris, and also celebrated his eighteenth birthday. Like a true professional, however, he maintained his fitness by running several miles each day across the bleak Fenland lanes in all weathers. Boxing had become like a drug to him and he couldn't wait to get back into action. He didn't have to wait long because Jack Solomons, greatly encouraged by the success of his shows at Chatteris and Cambridge, decided to try and revive boxing at Ipswich.

By working closely with local promoter and matchmaker, Wally Dakin, it proved to be another successful venture and a large crowd, including many Devonshire Club regulars, packed into the local Corn Exchange on 13 January 1938 and saw an excellent evening of boxing.

The 10 rounds top of the bill contest featured the popular former Southern Area flyweight champion, Pat Palmer, with Boon in the chief supporting bout over eight rounds. When his original opponent, Bobby Burton (Leeds) pulled out, he faced a more difficult proposition in Alex 'Kid' Jackson, a well known Scottish boxer who had won his last 20 contests. He made his Devonshire Club debut on New Year's Eve and impressed the East End crowd with a fine 12 rounds points victory.

Both weighing 9st 11, they were well matched physically, although it wasn't long before the well-muscled Boon began to dominate the exchanges. He moved well, punched hard, albeit sparingly, and although he floored Jackson for a count of 'eight' with a right to the chin in round four and again with a similar punch in the fifth, he resisted taking unnecessary chances. Jackson stood up to his task well and his clever footwork and ringcraft saved him from further punishment. He actually took the initiative during the later stages as Boon looked content to go the full distance to take a well earned points decision. He was just happy to be back in the ring.

As Eric's right hand had given him no problems, Solomons wasted no time getting him back into regular action with four contests at the Devonshire Club in as many weeks. The youngster was in devastating form winning all by clean knockouts inside three rounds.

Just seven days after fighting at Ipswich, Boon faced George Reynolds (Wolverhampton), and despite conceding almost a stone in weight, he was sensational. Heavy left and right hooks to the jaw put Reynolds down for 'eight' in the opening round. On rising two similar punches sent him through the ropes for another long count. Determined to end matters quickly, Eric caught his man with a hard right to the chin which put him down for the count early in round two.

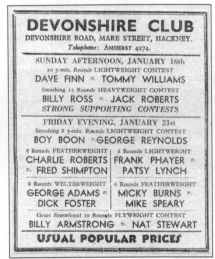

DEVONSHIRE CLUB
DEVONSHIRE ROAD, MARE STREET, HACKNEY.
Telephone: AMHERST 4274.

SUNDAY AFTERNOON, JANUARY 16th
10 3-min. Rounds LIGHTWEIGHT CONTEST
DAVE FINN *v.* TOMMY WILLIAMS
Smashing 12 Rounds HEAVYWEIGHT CONTEST
BILLY ROSS *v.* JACK ROBERTS
STRONG SUPPORTING CONTESTS

FRIDAY EVENING, JANUARY 21st
Smashing 8 3-min. Rounds LIGHTWEIGHT CONTEST
BOY BOON *v.* GEORGE REYNOLDS

| 8 Rounds FEATHERWEIGHT | 8 Rounds LIGHTWEIGHT |
| CHARLIE ROBERTS *v.* FRED SHIMPTON | FRANK PHAYER *v.* PATSY LYNCH |

| 8 Rounds WELTERWEIGHT | 6 Rounds FEATHERWEIGHT |
| GEORGE ADAMS *v.* DICK FOSTER | MICKY BURNS *v.* MIKE SPEARY |

Great Sensational 10 Rounds FLYWEIGHT CONTEST
BILLY ARMSTRONG *v.* NAT STEWART
USUAL POPULAR PRICES

Tommy Dowlais from Tredegar was given an even greater hiding being knocked out in the first round after having been floored five times. "A tremendous display of aggression by Boon" was how one publication described his victory.

The following week, on a show to raise much needed funds for the Jewish Maternity Home, Boon dropped Jack Hardiman (Smethwick) five times in the opening session of their eight three-minute rounds contest. Desperate to end matters, however, he became very erratic and his game opponent survived into the third before being knocked out. The packed house gave Eric a standing ovation as he left the ring.

Jamaican boxer, Dodo Williams, was Boon's next victim. In previous contests he had shown himself to be a smart boxer and only a few weeks earlier pushed Southern Area champion, Dick

Corbett to a close decision at Cambridge. Against Boon, however, he fared no better than those before him.

Getting in close from the opening bell, Boon stunned Williams with fast hurtful punches to head and body. Full of menacing intent, the only thing on his mind was an early finish. A right to the chin smashed Williams to the floor for a count of 'nine'. On rising he was driven to a neutral corner where another vicious right to the jaw put him down with no chance of beating the count. The Jamaican did not land a punch of consequence during the mere 90 seconds it lasted.

The victory brought more praise from one of Eric's greatest admirers, Isidore Green. In an enthusiastic, yet extremely descriptive report in *Weekly Sporting Review* he said:

> Boy Boon is indeed in smashing form these days. He continues to win his fights in the quickest and most decisive manner. For a fighter so young he has a remarkable punch. He has learned how to hit with the full force of his closed fist and his deliveries are accurate too, which is all very unfortunate for his opponents.
>
> Boon has discarded all ideas of fancy work. He goes in for the 'kill' immediately the bell has rung and forces his way towards his rival with his punch already set. There is no stopping him and he is attacking with a viciousness which leaves his opposition no room for retaliation.

Meanwhile, Eric took great interest in another young boxer, Fred Cotton from Barrow. He was regularly at ringside when Fred fought and on one occasion at the Devonshire Club in early 1938, went through a lot of emotion and even had tears in his eyes as his mate made a gallant effort to avoid defeat. Boon, Cotton and Harry 'Kid' Silver spent a lot of time together and became known as "The Three 'Kid' Musketeers."

*   *   *

Some weeks before the fight with Dodo Williams, Jack Solomons arranged for Boon to box a return with Johnny Softley on the big Jewish Sportsmen's Committee promotion at the Royal Albert Hall on 3 March. Eric had been itching for the contest for months because although he accepted that Johnny beat him fairly and squarely when they met back in July the previous year, he needed to set the record right if he was to progress up the lightweight ladder.

Realising the significance of the fight Solomons approached Nat Seller who ran a thriving boxing gym at 136 Whitechapel Road in the heart of the East End. "Nat, I want you to get Boon really fit for me," he said. "He's having a return with Johnny Softley at the Albert Hall and he's got to reverse the last decision."

Seller was an established trainer with a good pedigree. He started boxing at the age of eleven at his school in Watney Street, Stepney, and for the Boy's Brigade. He knew all about the great East End arenas such as the Whitechapel Pavilion, the Judean Club, Premierland and Wonderland where long fights were rewarded with half a crown and a cup of coffee.

Shortly after enlisting for National Service, the Provost Sergeant, an Army champion, persuaded him to box. He won army bantam and featherweight championships and was undefeated for three years before becoming an instructor with the Army Gymnastic Staff during the First World War. Back in civilian life he learned his training skills under Jack Goodwin who was recognised nationally as one of the best boxing coaches of all time.

Seller had been looking after fighters for 20 years. He was a recognised authority on physical culture who knew exactly how to make a boxer concentrate on his job. Since opening his La Boheme gym in October 1937 he had become respected throughout the East End for his discipline which was why Solomons persuaded him to take over Boon.

At the time Nat was training Harry Mizler for a British lightweight championship eliminator against Dave Crowley at the Royal Albert Hall on the same bill as Boon against Softley. Although he claimed never to have seen Eric fight he knew he was a great prospect and had no hesitation in agreeing to Solomons' request. It was the beginning of what would become a great boxer-trainer relationship although for Nat it would provide plenty of day-to-day headaches which only ceased when he stopped training Boon.

Nat really put Boon through his paces working alongside Frank Hough, Pat Palmer, Harry Silver and Mizler, all of whom were due to box on the Albert Hall promotion. Within a few days he put Eric in the ring to spar with Mizler and he gave Harry a real pounding. To the less knowledgeable observer he looked more like a title challenger than an eighteen-years-old youngster learning his trade.

Years later, Seller recalled what happened and said that the one thing which stood out in his memory above all others while running his East End gym was "the day Jack Solomons brought along a young lad by the name of Boon."

Eric made the weight nicely and went into the ring against Softley fitter than at any stage in his life. He was supported by a group of over 60 loyal fans who had travelled from Chatteris. They had obtained tickets through Fred Green who continued to maintain close contact with Boon and acted as an agent for him and the Devonshire Club.

All the hard work was worth it because once again Boon became the star of a big London promotion. National newspaper reporters at ringside to describe the main event were full of praise for the young man from Chatteris. In what was described as the best fight of the evening he rightly got the decision in an absolute thriller in which neither boy spared himself from start to finish. It was a testimony of Softley's toughness that he stood up to Eric's tremendous punching where so many others had failed. He rightly received a wonderful ovation for being a gallant loser.

The show was a great success with donations totalling over £1,400 being drawn from the audience following speeches by top boxing referee, Moss Deyong, and well known sportsman, Norman Laski. Top of the bill was the British lightweight championship eliminator between Dave Crowley and Harry Mizler both of whom would feature in the career of Boon.

Revenge for Eric was sweet and Jack Solomons described the fight with Softley as one of the greatest ever seen at the Royal Albert Hall. Up until that time he had always promoted his protégé as 'Boy' Boon, but realised this now had to change. Although he had only just turned eighteen, Eric was no longer a boy so for the next few fights he would be known as 'Roy' Boon. Some newspaper reports at later dates, however, claimed that this was due to a printing error on subsequent fight bills.

The success over Softley created another problem for Solomons because although he knew Eric needed to step up in class he was still afraid of rushing him too quickly. Boon was fearless and the greater his success rate the more confident he became. He would have taken on a world champion given half a chance. So when Dan Sullivan, who bought Jack Doyle out of the Army in 1932, proposed a contest with his boxer, Johnny Ward, Solomons immediately agreed. Although the Irishman had run up a string of victories Jack knew enough about him to believe he would be a good test for Boon without being unnecessarily dangerous.

The fight was set for 7 April at Harringay Arena on a Sydney Hulls promotion featuring British light-heavyweight champion, Jock McAvoy, defending his title against Len Harvey. Boon prepared for the fight at Chatteris and while there stayed with his parents as did his trainer Mike Milligan. At about 2 am during the night before the fight Mike was suddenly awoken by a rattling noise coming from the kitchen. Thinking it might be a burglar he got up, went downstairs where to his amazement he found Eric sitting at a table tucking into a plate full of pineapple and ice cream. Milligan was furious because he was constantly reminding the young boxer about his diet. "Don't worry," said Boon calmly, "I'm doing the fighting and I'll win."

Later that morning they left Chatteris for the weigh-in and arrived at Liverpool Street Station with plenty of time to spare. Concerned about Boon's weight, Mike hustled him into a chemist's shop and made him stand on a set of scales. To his horror Eric was two pounds over the weight stipulated for the fight. He didn't dare tell Jack Solomons, so with still an hour to go before the official weigh-in ceremony he reluctantly agreed to Boon's suggestion of going to a Turkish bath. Despite knowing the baths could leave his charge weak Mike saw no alternative, so they hailed a taxi and headed for the West End.

Milligan was so agitated that he spent more than 10 minutes in the steam room with Boon before he realised he was still fully dressed. Eric got the weight off without too much trouble and they went to the weigh-in with Solomons none the wiser. It would be difficult to find a more loyal and staunch supporter of Boon than Mike. He was a man who always visualised the youngster as a future champion and was quick to chastise any individual foolish enough to utter a detrimental remark in his direction. Years later when Boon's name was mentioned in conversation, Mike always turned to Solomons and said: "If only you knew what happened before the Johnny Ward fight."

Although Ward had a reputation of being something of a whirlwind, Boon never gave him time to settle. Heavy combination punches had the Irishman down three times in the opening round from what was described by one journalist as "the fiercest punching ever delivered by a boxer of Boon's age and weight." Ward was out on his feet and the referee intervened just as the bell sounded to end the round.

With a glint in his eyes Eric turned to Mike Milligan as they left the ring and cheekily said, "I told you I'd win – you worry too much." The trainer ignored the remark – he was just relieved that Boon had suffered no ill effects from using the Turkish bath. It turned out to be a good night for the Devonshire Club faithful with Harry Silver and Fred Cotton also winning their fights.

Despite his delight at Boon's dramatic victory Jack Solomons now faced an even greater dilemma. There was no question that the young boxer now had to be stepped up in class and with that in mind he went to see Sydney Hulls at his office in Shaftesbury Avenue. Although Eric had twice thrilled the crowds in minor bouts at Harringay, Hulls was not convinced that he was likely to become the world beater his manager was claiming. Jack even suggested that they matched Boon with British lightweight champion, Jimmy

Eric's parents, Reg and Liz, on their wedding day.

Boon with a collection of trophies won as a schoolboy.

Boon aged thirteen as a schoolboy boxer.

Boon (centre) with fellow members of Chatteris ABC.

King Edward School football team 1933. Boon (centre front row) was captain.

Eric, aged fifteen at 8 stone 2lbs.

Boon (right) and Harry 'Kid' Silver, visit a children's hospital at Manchester in August 1938.

Eric, in late December 1938, in the sports car given to him by Jack Solomons for beating Jimmy Walsh

Training at Ely for the fight with Crowley in December 1938.

Strength building at his father's forge before the Crowley fight.

Boon on the shoulders of Nat Seller (left) and Dick Gutteridge after beating Crowley at Harringay on 15th December 1938.

With his close friend and mentor, Mike
Milligan in 1939.

Milligan (right) was a regular passenger in Eric's sports car.

Boon (right) attacks Crowley at Harringay on 15th December 1938.

Boon and girlfriend Ollie Franks, leave Liverpool Street Station for Chatteris on 20th December 1938.

Chatteris Town Band lead the procession celebrating Boon's home -coming on 20th December 1938 as British champion.

Boon, surrounded by family and friends, aboard a decorated coal lorry leading to a reception at the Empress Cinema, Chatteris.

Boon stands between Jack Solomons and Harry 'Kid' Silver aboard the lorry surrounded by excited fans at Chatteris.

Crowds outside the Empress Cinema, Market Hill, Chatteris, celebrate Boon's return as British champion.

Boon, seated centre between his parents, at a tea party in his honour at Chatteris on 20th December 1938.

Walsh, in a non-title fight at catchweights for only a side stake which he would happily put up.

Still not convinced the cautious Hulls contacted the boxing correspondents of all national newspapers and advised them of Solomons' proposal. Every one of them opposed the idea and in their columns the following day were very critical of Boon saying that he should learn to walk before he could run. The fact that he had taken part in over 80 professional contests by this stage apparently counted for nothing. Yet it was another indication of Eric's maturity that he ignored the negative comments and just concentrated on training for his next contest, an eight-rounder against Matt Moran from Manchester at the Devonshire Club 10 days later.

The fight came about because Moran had created a great impression against Johnny Softley in his first appearance at the Devonshire. Although he lost on points over 10 rounds, he fought like a man of iron taking Softley's best shots without flinching. The more punishment he took the stronger he fought back. After the fight Jack Solomons went to Matt's dressing room and said: "If you will come back here in three weeks and box Eric Boon I will give you more money than you have ever had for a fight."

Although he agreed in principle, Moran knew it would be touch and go as to whether he would be fit. During the battle with Softley his gum shield fell out and a heavy punch badly split his tongue.

Fortunately, the injury healed quickly and he returned to the Hackney arena to face Boon in what was a fascinating clash.

Meanwhile, Jack Solomons was still keen to get Eric into the ring with Jimmy Walsh. Talks with Sydney Hulls had continued although the promoter remained somewhat apprehensive because of the negative response from the critics. Like Solomons, however, Hulls was a shrewd businessman and for the time being kept his options open.

A few days before the Moran fight Solomons told Isidore Green that it was important to move Boon up in class. "You can tell your readers that some big things are being fixed up for Boon," he said. "He's in big demand so watch out for surprises."

He then teased the journalist by producing an envelope from his pocket on which were written the names of Walsh and Danahar. When pressed as to whether they were prospective opponents Jack smiled and said it would not be policy to reveal further information. Green found it all very intriguing, but the speculation made great headlines for his popular publication.

Boon's fight with Matt Moran took place on a Sunday afternoon and the Devonshire Club was packed to capacity. Matt was a tough well-known booth fighter, and just prior to his fight with Johnny Softley had purchased his own boxing booth. Against Boon that toughness kept him going in what was a typical Devonshire Club fight, one where the crowd were on their feet throughout. The power the Chatteris boy put into his punches would have inflicted a knockout on most other men.

Boon looked set for an early victory when, after being surprised by a vicious right swing which caught him flush in the face, he slipped a similar delivery and smashed Matt to the floor for a count of 'eight.' Landing his most devastating punches Eric sent the Mancurian down three times in the second and again in the fifth, but couldn't knock him out. Moran took a fearful hammering for six rounds, but always came back for more, gallantly refusing to admit defeat.

The end eventually came in round seven when, with Moran virtually at a standstill, the referee mercifully intervened. It had been a tremendously brave performance which was greatly appreciated by the packed crowd. He was cheered all the way back to the dressing room, and shouts of "You're one game boy" and "Fantastic show mate," echoed around the smoky arena. Afterwards Jack Solomons presented Matt with the gloves he had worn. "Keep these," he said, "You've had them for seven rounds and earned them."

It was to be Moran's last official professional contest, but one he never forgot. In his excellent book, *'Matt Moran's Shamrock Gardens'* published in 1988, he said:

> I saw quite a few Stars of David whilst boxing Eric! He had me on the floor in the first, but I managed to box for another six. I took nearly as much punishment from ringsiders who were slapping me on the back as I climbed out of the ring.

The manner of Boon's victory over Moran demonstrated just how much he had progressed since losing to Johnny Softley back in July 1937. Apart from incredible power in both hands he had acquired good ring skills showing that he was on the verge of championship class. With that in mind there was no let-up by Jack Solomons in his efforts to push him forward. Immediately after the fight he told press representatives that he would do whatever he could to get Boon matched with Jimmy Walsh. "I happen to know there is a big County Show at Chatteris on 28 May," he remarked. "Just imagine it, Boon on his home ground against the British champion. What a setting."

On 27 April 1937, Eric accompanied his manager to the Stadium Club to help promote a contest against experienced Welsh champion, Boyo Rees, scheduled for 2 May. The Chatteris boy was introduced from the ring just prior to a contest between Arthur Danahar and Hal Cartwright, and on his behalf it was announced that he had challenged Danahar to a contest at 9st 9 for £200-a-side. Danahar, a former ABA lightweight champion, had only been a professional for six weeks, but was undefeated in four contests and already being tipped as a future champion. Following his victory over Cartwright it was announced that Boon's challenge had been accepted and that £250 was being held at the office of his promoters, the National Sporting Club.

Boon's fight against Boyo Rees the following week didn't last very long. After a minute of virtual inactivity Eric suddenly crossed a solid right to the chin and the Welshman fell to the floor. He was up at a count of 'two', but Boon was on him like a flash, driving heavy blows to head and body. A vicious left hook to the stomach opened Rees up for a right to the jaw which ended the fight. Even as Boyo was falling, Boon still landed several more rapid shots for good measure. Rees fell flat on his face and didn't move during the count.

In some respects the ending was a surprise because the sturdily built Rees, a man of great experience, was renowned for his gameness and ability to absorb punishment without flinching. A few weeks earlier he took a real battering from Arthur Danahar, but was never on the floor during the six rounds contest. Boon's shattering victory in just two minutes confirmed that, pound for pound, he was one of the hardest punchers in the country.

Afterwards Eric revealed that the fight nearly didn't go ahead. During the afternoon he had a temperature which looked like preventing him from going into the ring. By the evening, however, he was sufficiently improved thanks to a couple of doses of 'something' followed by a good sleep. "I knew I had to end it quickly," remarked Boon, "so I crammed everything I had into the first round."

The trade paper *Boxing* presented Boon with a Certificate of Merit describing his victory over Rees as the best performance of the week in the United Kingdom. A number of national newspaper critics were also mightily impressed with his showing, none more so than Geoffrey Simpson who, writing in the *Daily Mail*, said:

> ...fighting with a series of hooks to the jaw as destructive as any I have seen delivered by a boxer of his poundage. So well does he place his punches that he is likely to flatten any lightweight with it. A champion's title seems to await this youngster.

Boon had now won his last 21 contests within the space of just eight months, and 18 of those had come inside the distance, many against good class opposition, Bryn Morris, Alex Jackson and Johnny Softley being the only men to survive and hear the final bell. There was a sensation about many of those victories which contributed to bringing Eric very much into the public mind.

Solomons, to whom all credit was due, had planned a careful schedule in moving Boon up the fistic ladder without being over-ambitious, but following the destruction of Boyo Rees, was more convinced than ever that his charge needed a real test. With that in mind he met Sydney Hulls again immediately after the Rees fight and finally talked him into matching Boon with Jimmy Walsh.

Jack even suggested that the fight was staged in the open air at Chatteris where Eric had a massive following. It was this which finally convinced the promoter it was a huge money-spinning opportunity. Hulls duly contacted an agent based in the Fenland region and was advised that an annual agricultural show was being staged at Chatteris on 28 May. It would draw huge crowds from Cambridge, Ely, March and many surrounding districts, so, making sound business sense, the promoter made every effort to stage the fight on the same day. With Hulls and Solomons finally in agreement they drove to Chatteris to seek out a suitable venue.

5

A RAINY DAY IN CHATTERIS

Agreement was reached for the fight with Jimmy Walsh to be staged at the Chatteris Engineers football ground during the evening of the annual County Show. The contest made at 9st 12, was described as the biggest sporting event ever staged in the region, and tickets sold rapidly as soon as it was announced. Special late night trains were organised to serve all areas between Kings Lynn and Cambridge whilst agents for the Eastern Counties Bus Company took hundreds of bookings. Arrangements were therefore made to vastly increase bus services in all directions in and out of Chatteris to cope with the anticipated crowds. Hundreds of fans were also expected to travel from London where Boon had firmly established himself as one of the most popular fighters of the day.

It was the first time that Sydney Hulls had promoted in Cambridgeshire, but he was excited at the prospect. He knew it was not a fight for London because being a non-title event it would never have generated the same amount of revenue as in the Fens where Boon was already an idol. Eric's progress was the predominant sporting interest among Fenland fans many of whom stayed up late on the nights of his fights just to get the result.

On 19 May, accompanied by Jack Solomons and Tiny Bostock, Hulls travelled to Chatteris to finalise arrangements for the fight. Plans were made to accommodate a crowd of up to 10,000 of which 4,000 would be seated. Local stalwart and boxing promoter, Fred Green, was heavily involved in making local arrangements on behalf of Hulls. Later the same day the party moved to March where they had a press conference and luncheon at The Griffen Hotel. Hulls described Boon as "the biggest attraction in London today," and said they all anticipated a great fight.

"They are both great little boxers," he told a large group of excited reporters. "Nobody can say what will happen."

Asked about his future plans for Boon the promoter said that victory for the Chatteris lad would certainly upset arrangements for the Walsh-Dave Crowley championship contest set to take place at Liverpool four weeks later. He thought it quite possible that Eric could meet Crowley in an eliminator. He added that whatever occurred he was hoping to match Boon with Henry Armstrong, the American, who was due in Britain during June. "Even if Boon is beaten next week I still have plenty of fights in mind for him," said Hulls. "He will certainly be fighting again in Chatteris before long."

"I see no reason why we shouldn't run several first class shows there this summer," he continued. "We might also try March as well."

Questions were then raised about Eric's weight. This annoyed Solomons who said that he would probably scale about 9st 10 for Walsh or even make the lightweight limit. He quickly dispelled rumours that Boon was having weight problems and would probably have to move up to welterweight. "There is no truth whatsoever in those rumours," said Jack angrily.

Although the majority of critics believed Eric was too young to face Walsh who would be far too clever for him, others were suddenly hailing the Chatteris lad as a future world champion. Whilst this was all very flattering, it was a marked turn-around from comments made a few weeks earlier when the fight was first mooted. The manner of Boon's victory over Boyo Rees had in fact made some critics reassess his prospects because there was little doubt that he had the power to flatten most men of his weight provided he connected correctly. Much depended on whether Walsh would give him the opening.

Irrespective of what was written about him, Eric was a firm believer in his own strength and ability. He was fired with so much enthusiasm and youthful ambition that he didn't care what the newspapers thought. "I feel I can beat the world," he frequently remarked albeit in a relaxed and low-key manner. In those days he never asked who he was fighting, just when and where it was taking place. He had served his apprenticeship in the toughest school of all – the colourful Devonshire Club. There was nothing brash or cocky about him because he was sensible enough to know that he still had plenty to learn.

What was often overlooked by the critics was the fact that Boon was a good boxer as well as a destructive hitter. Unlike in his earlier days, he rarely wasted a punch. By keeping his elbows well tucked in the full weight of his body was behind each blow. Trained firstly by Arthur Binder, then Mike Milligan and Nat Seller, he had become an almost perfect fighting machine.

Boon's one round victories over such tough fighters as Johnny Ward and Boyo Rees naturally drew more attention to his punching power than his boxing skill. The fact was that his big punch would have been less effective without the skill to make openings for it. Against Ward and Rees he drew experienced men into traps and then caught them with terrific blows against which they had no chance.

Despite the concerns of the critics both men were happy when the fight was made. For Eric it was the step up in class to really test him, and for Walsh, who was due to defend his title against Dave

Crowley, it would provide a good warm-up. He saw no danger in taking on the Chatteris youngster whose reputation caused him no anxiety. He knew how to deal with this type of opponent and took the view that, if Eric's handlers were prepared to take the chance and the financial inducement was sufficiently attractive, he had no objection.

Boon carried out the bulk of his training for the fight under Nat Seller at the La Boheme gymnasium at Mile End. He was tremendously impressive and sparring partners, Bertie Brooks and Angus McGregor, with whom he drew at Harringay in April 1937, were given an extremely painful time. Harry Mizler, who had fought Walsh on three occasions, also engaged in light sparring with Eric and said he had never come across a more accurate and solid puncher. Brooks said that when Boon landed his right hand with force it left him feeling paralysed. "I felt as if I had been snapped in half," he told a reporter from *Weekly Sporting Review*.

Meanwhile, Walsh warmed up for the contest by knocking out Jim Cameron, a seasoned Glaswegian, in 80 seconds of the first round at Preston on 16 May. It was a clear warning to Boon that he meant business. Although the Chatteris faithful had installed their boy as a firm favourite, the manner of Jimmy's victory added fresh interest.

Walsh was born at Chester in 1913 and made his professional debut in 1931. He was a vastly experienced and accomplished campaigner who was a great favourite at Liverpool Stadium where he won the British lightweight championship in April 1936 by stopping Jack 'Kid' Berg in nine rounds. He successfully defended the title against another skilful man, Harry Mizler, in London six months later to become the first lightweight to win a new British Boxing Board of Control Lonsdale belt.

Sydney Hulls had hoped Walsh would complete his training at Chatteris, but he preferred to go to Ely away from all the hype and excitement. Accompanied by his manager, Tony Vairo, and sparring partner, Peter Clark from Birkenhead, he arrived there two days before the fight. He worked out at the headquarters of the local amateur boxing club where members weighing up to 11 stone were invited to spar a round or two with him. Local people warmed to Jimmy who willingly chatted to them and signed a host of autographs.

In the days leading up to the contest Chatteris was fight crazy and there was more excitement than if the local football club had been playing in a cup final. The little town was teeming with journalists from all over the country. All of the nationals were represented as were local papers from throughout Cambridgeshire and surrounding counties. They all wanted stories because any snip of information could be made into a headline. The fight had really captured public imagination and those close to the two boxers were sought out and asked for predictions as to how they expected it to go. "I'll make the bold statement that Boon will knock Walsh out in three rounds," remarked a confident Jack Solomons. "You have no idea the way he is punching."

Mike Milligan believed Boon would win in five rounds. "None of us are underestimating Walsh," he said, "but Boon will beat him. If we didn't think he was good enough we would never have made the match."

Nat Seller was more cautious, but remarked: "I think Boon has a wonderful chance. I have been in Harry Mizler's corner in each of his three fights with Walsh and can therefore say with authority to know something about Walsh's methods."

Boon himself was naturally full of confidence. "I won't let the Devonshire Club or the Chatteris folk down," he told a group of reporters. "I am going to win. I know Walsh is the champion and that's why I'll try harder than ever to beat him."

Walsh, his London agent Johnny Sharpe and manager Tony Vairo said very little other than that they were extremely confident. In their reports journalists made the inevitable comparisons between the two boxers. It was pointed out that Walsh never came close to knocking out Boyo Rees when they met on two occasions in 1936. On the other hand top men including Nel Tarleton, Ernie Roderick, Freddie Miller, Jack 'Kid' Berg and Mizler all failed to stop Walsh. It was intriguing stuff and added flavour to the battle ahead.

*　　　*　　　*

The County Show at Chatteris was staged by Cambridgeshire & Isle of Ely Agricultural Society and was one of the biggest annual events in the region. It was always regarded as a gala day and with the big fight scheduled to take place during the evening, an even bigger crowd than usual was expected. On the day, however, incessant rain which started at dawn, threatened to ruin both events. As the day passed there was no let-up in the weather and a postponement of the fight seemed inevitable.

Despite the conditions the County Show went ahead as planned, but the town was in turmoil as farmers, small-holders and agricultural fanciers swarmed in from miles around. Vehicles of every description lined the streets, pedestrians were milling about in droves, but despite them being saturated a real holiday atmosphere prevailed. Stalls selling a variety of merchandise were surrounded by customers. Police reserves teemed all over the place and music from the showground echoed around the town.

As the day passed conditions grew worse and the outlook gave rise to fears that the rain would have a serious effect on the financial state of the show. Those fears dispelled somewhat during the afternoon, however, when it was seen that a very large crowd had braved the weather to attend. The showground grandstand was full and hundreds of other people stood in inches of mud around the main enclosure and other areas of the field. The entertainment included exciting events such as a motor cycle football match by West Ham speedway riders and a display by members of the Army School of Physical Training at Aldershot. There was also a pony cabaret, parade of foxhounds, show jumping events and a massive firework display. The Chatteris Town Silver Band and the band of the Cambridgeshire Regiment played popular music throughout the day. Towards the end of the show drums of the regiment beat the retreat.

Meanwhile, Sydney Hulls and his associates were comfortably but anxiously settled in the warmth of The George Hotel hoping for a change in the weather. The George, a hostelry steeped in character and atmosphere, was the local headquarters for boxing. The licensees, Alexander and Constance Cameron, were keen followers of the sport and had turned an upstairs clubroom into a thriving gym. It was the place where fight folk gathered and on the occasion of the town's biggest ever contest it was packed from opening time.

Although the weigh-in took place at 2 pm, the promoter decided to wait another three hours before making a final decision. A number of London newspaper men were in close attendance listening to every comment Hulls made, and at the same time keeping in close touch with their editors. The fight was of great importance because it had all the makings of a huge story should Boon win in dramatic fashion.

Suddenly, at about 5 pm, somebody dashed into the hotel and told Hulls that there was a break in the clouds and the rain was easing. That was sufficient for him to put his plans into action. Everyone set off for the Engineers ground about half a mile from the town centre where the ring was hurriedly erected and an army of helpers arranged the seating. The standing enclosures were roped off and bales of straw rushed to the field by tractor and trailer to cover the rain sodden ground around the ringside and in the aisles between the seating. In addition to the existing football stand, two uncovered stands had been erected to ensure everyone got a good view. Everything was in place by the time the gates were due to open. Six hours earlier all that could be seen in the ground was a huge pile of chairs and a small herd of cows.

As word spread around the town that the fight would definitely go ahead, an endless stream of excited fans made their way to the venue. The only entrance to the field was a five-barred gate which was only partially opened so as to allow spectators to pass through in single file. A long orderly queue formed and by the time the preliminary bouts commenced at 8 pm about 6,000 were assembled inside.

*   *   *

Apart from concerns that the weather could cause the fight to be postponed, many fans from London had great difficulty actually reaching Chatteris. Although the rain fell heavily, five charabanc loads left the Devonshire Club at 2.30 pm. Ten times that number had wanted to go, but it was reported that the transport authorities refused to grant the necessary permission for more vehicles. For the fortunate ones the journey took four hours. Hundreds of other fans who travelled from Liverpool Street by rail were turned back when they reached Cambridge. Thunder, lightning and the risk of flooding prevented them using the branch line to Chatteris.

There were also some amusing situations, not least one which arose as a result of an article written in the *Daily Mirror* by John Thompson a few days earlier. In a delightfully descriptive, albeit tongue in cheek foreword to the fight, he described farmers from miles around "turning up in their wagons, gaitered, bob-hatted and sucking straws." The farmers, who obviously had no sense of humour, took offence and, early on the evening of the fight, a group of them arrived in Chatteris intent on confronting Thompson. Dressed in their Sunday suits and looking more like a Board of Directors at an annual meeting, they sought out Jack Solomons at a pub close to the venue and angrily asked him to point out the journalist.

Thompson was actually standing next to Jack at the bar, but being a shrewd East End boy, Solomons turned to him and said: "Say Bill, what time do you think John Thompson will get here." The reporter blushed and uneasily continued to sip his beer as Jack assured the irate farmers he would identify their target the moment he arrived.

Having prevented a potentially hostile situation, Solomons strolled out into the street to take another look at the weather. It had started to rain again and as he was contemplating that the fight still might be postponed, Sydney Hulls suddenly appeared looking rather agitated. "Where's the boy?" he enquired referring to Boon. "In the dressing room I presume," replied Solomons nonchalantly.

"No, he's not there," retorted Hulls, "I've just been there and nobody's seen him all evening. He's got to get changed quickly because I'm going to put the big fight on early before the weather gets too bad. The preliminaries are just going in."

Solomons went into a panic and sent people, including his brother Maxie, Barney Silver from the Devonshire Club and Nat Seller, to search the town centre, George Hotel, the forge and anywhere else Eric might have gone and forgotten the time. Trying to calm himself down, Jack lit a cigar and strolled to the main entrance of the venue. There, to his relief, was Boon sitting on top of the gate watching fans as they went in. "What the heck are you doing here?" snapped Solomons.

"I'm waiting for my pals," replied Eric softly and totally unconcerned. Jack then remembered that earlier Boon has asked if he could invite two old school mates to the fight and he had given him two tickets. They arrived just as Solomons was ordering his boxer to the dressing room to get ready. Relieved that Eric was alright, Jack relaxed, but didn't know half the story. He would have been horrified had he known what the youngster had actually been up to. What could have ended up in a disaster stemmed from Boon's fascination with motor cars.

It all started a year or so earlier when Eric fell in love with a sports car displayed in a showroom near Solomons' house. He spent hours staring at it and although by this time he had several hundred pounds in the bank, Jack flatly refused to let him buy it. "You'll have plenty of time to go gadding about in cars later on," he told him. "Right now all I want you to think about is fighting."

That's how it remained until the Jimmy Walsh fight was signed. Jack told Boon that victory would put him in line for a championship fight and as an extra incentive said he would buy him a present. "You can have anything you like," Solomons told him, "that's a promise."

"Okay guv'nor," said Boon, "buy me that sports car and I'll lick any champion in the world for you."

Nothing more was said until a couple of days before the fight when Solomons joined Boon at The George Hotel where he was winding up his training. Taking him aside Jack handed him a large envelope and said, "There you are Eric, it's all in the bag."

Boon opened the envelope to find the log book and keys for a sports car. He was flabbergasted and before he could say a word Solomons took him outside where the gleaming little car was parked. "You're going to win this fight Eric," he said with a smile, "and to prove how much I think you will win it there is your present already."

An incentive to win the fight was one thing, but Jack had overlooked the temptation he was putting in the youngster's way. With a few hours to spare after the weigh-in on the day of the fight, Eric was full of excitement and desire to get behind the wheel of the car. Without thinking about the possible consequences, he took the keys and went scorching around the local countryside.

It was Nat Seller who eventually discovered what he had been up to. Yet with the fight only an hour or so away, he resisted the temptation to chastise the youngster as he was about to face the biggest challenge of his life. Instead he remained calm, got Eric ready for the fight and agreed not to tell Solomons what had occurred.

*   *   *

It was one of the most discussed fights of modern times and despite the rain more than 7,000 people had crammed into the muddy Engineers ground by the time the main event was due. All evening a constant stream had trudged from the town's showground and taken up their positions throughout the preliminary contests.

Unprecedented scenes were witnessed in the rural streets as the large car parks in neighbouring fields steadily filled with vehicles of every description from ancient bangers to lordly Rolls Royces. In another of his extremely readable articles John Thompson had predicted "that a huge crowd would arrive on farm carts, lorries usually for carrying live stock, and battered old two-seaters making it the greatest day the town had ever known."

The efficient way in which the County Police handled the crowds must have gratified the Chief Constable, Captain J T Rivett-Carnach, who took a ringside seat alongside well known sportsmen from Peterborough, Whittlesey and other surrounding districts. Sir Malcolm Campbell was seated amongst leading boxers Jimmy Wilde, Dave Crowley, Eddie Phillips and Tiny Bostock.

Prolonged applause greeted British light-heavyweight champion, Len Harvey, as he was introduced from the ring by jovial Master of Ceremonies, Buster Cohen. Yet it was nothing to that which greeted Boon a few minutes later as he was carried from the dressing room on the shoulders of his seconds. Meanwhile, Jimmy Walsh had worn improvised gum boots over his boxing boots as he made his way along the rain sodden gangway to the ring.

Wearing a black dressing gown with his name embroidered on the back, Boon looked the calmest person in the ground as he awaited the start of the fight. It had been the same at the weigh-in some seven hours earlier when he appeared to have absolutely no doubts about the outcome. Despite the fact that it had been pouring with rain and the outlook for the evening was anything but cheerful, he treated the whole affair as a routine preparation for just another fight.

"See you tonight," said Walsh after they had been to the scales.

"Yes, I'll be there," was Eric's relaxed response.

With the start of the fight just seconds away, tension mounted all around the ground as referee, Jack Smith, called them together in the centre of the ring. Boon was icy cool as he listened to the official's instructions – Walsh was fidgety, anxious to get on with it.

Boon, who had made no secret of the fact that he wanted to win by a knockout, attacked from the opening bell. The reputation of the champion held no fears for him, and keeping up a two-fisted attack he seemed to take Walsh by surprise. Once he settled though, Jimmy brought his left jab into play making Eric miss badly.

Eventually Boon broke through and a swinging right caught Walsh on the chin. Eric was too wild as he followed up, but in backing away to avoid a powerful left, the champion slipped on the canvas. Pandemonium broke out as the home fans thought their man had caught him. Amid shouts of "Finish him boy," Boon threw wild punches from all angles, most of which were either blocked or missed. A couple of left hooks did get through and Jimmy was forced to hold for which he was cautioned by the referee.

Years later, Boon recalled those early moments of what then was the most important fight of his career:

> *....I felt good as I sat in my corner waiting for the bell. Opposite me sat the champion, but to me he was just another fighter. I was fit and strong, and there wasn't a doubt in my mind. We touched gloves, and Walsh, using the ring like the master craftsman he was, stabbed out a menacing, ramrod left. Then he came into me, blocking the vicious right I slung over. As we broke I hooked him with my left and the champ was down! It was only a slip, but it had taught Walsh that all the talk about the Boon punch hadn't been hot air, and he started to keep away. So the rounds went by with Jimmy pitting his skill and craft against my punch......*

The second round opened sensationally with Boon landing a vicious left hook to the head which shook the champion. Urged on by his cornermen, Eric went after his rival and scored with two more powerful left hooks. Walsh looked to be in trouble and whilst he cleverly prodded his left jab into Boon's face there was insufficient power to hold him off.

Jimmy was again shaken in round four as Boon thumped home powerful rights, one to the stomach and the other to the chin. Momentarily the champion looked in trouble, but regrouped before Eric landed again. He ducked another wild right swing and stopped Boon's rushes with a series of accurate jabs to the face.

During the middle rounds Walsh became more aggressive and looked to be controlling affairs with his jab. A good left steadied Boon in the sixth and although the champion was making it a close contest he couldn't afford to relax for a moment against the aggressive youngster. They showed great respect for each other and both were warned for holding after good punches thumped home.

Boon later recalled an incident at the end of round five when he took a vicious uppercut and weathered the round on groggy legs:

> *....and back in my corner Solomons, the super psychologist, began whispering words of encouragement. "Remember that car Eric," he said, "only five more pints of petrol and you're driving it away."*

As Eric continued to attack, Walsh received generous applause from the appreciative crowd for his defensive skills and clever riding of blows. Yet he couldn't keep Boon off for long as his power threatened to become the dominant factor. He later admitted that at that stage of the fight he began to feel the tide was turning against him.

It wasn't until round eight that Jimmy looked like getting on top when, for the first time, he became the aggressor. Cleverly manoeuvring Boon into position he whipped in a stinging left cross followed by a right making the Chatteris boy realise that the fight was far from over. A tremendous right uppercut whipped into the solar plexus clearly hurt him. His hands dropped and he tottered backwards only to be caught by a follow-up left and right to the jaw. A full bloodied right shook him to his boots forcing him to hold on desperately. They wrestled for a few seconds until Walsh pushed Eric off and went on the attack again. Although it was his worst round of the fight Boon had amazing stamina. He took everything Jimmy threw at him and at the bell was still swinging punches back.

As he slumped on his stool Jack Solomons immediately slapped the sponge on his head. "Feeling alright?" he asked quietly.

"Yes," muttered Boon.

"Did he hurt you?" Jack enquired.

"A bit," said Eric.

"Well that's all he's got," insisted Solomons. "He can't hit you any harder."

"Just one more thing Eric," said Jack as the boxer got off his stool. "I can just see you driving that car. Only two more pints of petrol. Now go out there and get him."

It was a feature of Boon that he always did as he was told before and during a fight. Despite the hammering he had taken in the previous round, he had extraordinary reserves of strength. During the interval he made a miraculous recovery and, heeding his manager's instructions, leapt from his corner at the bell to start round nine and set up a vicious attack driving Walsh across the ring before he could settle. Three times he battered the champion to the ropes with a succession of hooks from both hands, but each time Jimmy wriggled free before Eric could finish him.

As they came out for the final round it looked as though Walsh needed a knockout to win. The boxers didn't quite see it like that as they slugged it out toe-to-toe, both appearing to believe that everything rested on the final three minutes. Boon looked the fresher and, keeping up the pace and pressure of the previous round, gave more than he took. Urged on by his wildly enthusiastic army of fans he bustled Walsh around the ring and gave him no room to work. As the final bell sounded there was an apprehensive hush as referee, Jack Smith, totted up his score card. That hush rapidly developed into an almighty roar which could be heard for miles around as the third man moved towards Boon and raised his arm in victory.

Pandemonium broke out and hats were thrown into the air. There was a mad stampede towards the ring because everyone wanted to kiss and cuddle the local hero, but Jack Solomons, Mike Milligan and Nat Seller got to him first. They circled their man then hugged and kissed him before lifting their heads to the heavens as if saying an impassioned 'thank you' for answering their prayers. Then with a massive grin Solomons said: "Good boy Eric, I'll buy you a tankful of petrol as well."

Speaking breathlessly into the microphone, Boon thanked his supporters and said that he would do his best to try and bring the world title to Chatteris. More rapturous cheering followed because to those excited country folk Eric was already a champion without a title.

Mike Milligan, who had been actively involved in Boon's development since he became a regular at the Devonshire Club, promised himself that if his boxer was victorious he would carry him back to the dressing room on his shoulders. Mike kept that promise although he had to struggle desperately hard to 'claim' the youngster from dozens of fans who had the same idea. Eventually it was Mike who succeeded in 'leading in the winner' followed by an army of happy supporters.

Meanwhile, enough people had remained around the ringside to give promoter, Sydney Hulls, a special cheer when Master of Ceremonies, Buster Cohen, introduced him as "the man who made this fight possible for Chatteris."

Although it had been an extremely close contest, and some criticism was made over the decision, the majority of newspaper writers agreed that Boon was a worthy winner largely because he never allowed Walsh to settle. The champion was on the defensive for much of the fight and only his great ringcraft saved him from the full effects of Boon's undoubted power. The crowd, nevertheless, appreciated his contribution to a great fight and gave him a great ovation as he left the ring.

Meanwhile, Eric's mother who had been waiting tensely in a nearby lane, rushed to the ringside. "I just couldn't bear to watch it," she told John Thompson of the *Daily Mirror,* "but I could tell he was winning by the tremendous applause at the end of each round."

The result of the fight marked the end of a memorable day in Chatteris history as everyone forgot the dismal weather. As they made their way home along the dark country lanes there was singing and cheering, excited banter about their idol's performance and what he might achieve in the future. Fireworks flared from a fair in a nearby field to mark a great victory.

At a press conference after the fight Jack Solomons said: "Boon is amazing. All the kid was scared about was that the fight might be postponed. When he was resting this afternoon he heard a rumour that it was going to be put off on account of the rain. We couldn't get him to settle down until he'd visited the promoter's office and was assured that it would take place."

When he made that statement Jack had no idea of the antics Eric had got up to with his motor car.

The public response to Boon's victory over Walsh was incredible, and a couple of days later he contacted the *Cambridgeshire Times* explaining that he wanted to thank his supporters and townsfolk for their kindness and support. "I've had so many letters and telegrams of greetings and congratulations that I cannot answer them all," he said. "I wish to express my deep gratitude and thanks to everyone." The newspaper was happy to print his remarks.

BUILD-UP TO A TITLE

A few days after the Walsh fight Sydney Hulls announced that Boon would be in action again on 14 June at Harringay Arena. Top of the bill would be a final eliminator for Tommy Farr's British heavyweight title between Ben Foord and Eddie Phillips.

There was also talk of a possible contest with Arthur Danahar at Earls Court five weeks later which it was hoped would top a bill to aid a fund for old-time boxers. The Marquess of Queensberry, who was personally backing Danahar in the sum of £250, suggested forming a committee of newspaper reporters to select who should benefit from the fund. At the same time Tony Vairo, manager of Jimmy Walsh, issued a challenge to Boon for a return contest under championship conditions for a £500 side-stake. Eric's reaction was that Walsh would have to put his title on the line as well. That, however, was not possible in the immediate future because Jimmy was contracted to defend it against Dave Crowley at Liverpool on 22 June.

Meanwhile, George Biddles, mine host of the Star & Garter at Derby and manager of Leicester veteran, Len Wickwar, issued a winner-take-all challenge to Boon and any other lightweight contender. The only man to have beaten Wickwar in his last 15 contests was former world featherweight champion, Freddie Miller. Jack Solomons rightly avoided Len as he wanted Eric to start facing continentals in his progress towards a British title. His opponent for the Harringay bill was to be Belgian lightweight champion, Raymond Reynard.

Boon's victory over Jimmy Walsh earned him another Certificate of Merit awarded by 'Boxing'. At Solomons' invitation it was presented to him the following week in the ring at the Devonshire Club by the editor, Sidney Ackland, accompanied by members of his staff. The packed house gave Eric a rousing reception and this continued as further presentations were made to him by admirers. The highlight was a valuable gold watch from Jack Solomons' wife.

Due to an injury to Eddie Phillips, Boon's contest with Raymond Reynard was postponed for a week. In some respects this was fortunate for the Chatteris boxer because since his fight with Walsh he had been troubled by pain in his left arm. Examination revealed that a small bone was slightly out of position, but this was corrected by a session of manipulation.

More inconveniences followed when, a few hours before he was due in the ring, Reynard dropped a block of granite on his foot causing an injury which forced him to withdraw. Len Lemaux, a dockyard worker from Portsmouth, described as the Hampshire title holder, was a hastily found substitute. Unbeaten as a lightweight, he had won dozens of fights in the south of England and had recently issued a challenge to Boon and any other contenders for a contest over the championship distance for £100-a-side at 9st 7 to 9st 9. He was not considered to be an easy proposition for Eric.

Regarded as a genuine lightweight prospect, Lemaux had faced some of the hardest hitters at his weight, and in 174 amateur and professional contests had never been knocked out. Although he started confidently, he was soon under pressure and proved no match for the aggressive tactics of the heavy-hitting Chatteris man whose timing was far better than against Jimmy Walsh. A left hook sent Lemaux to the floor for a count of 'six' and he was still groggy when he rose. Within a few seconds Boon slammed home a magnificent right which was deadly and to the point of the chin. Landing with great force it sent the Portsmouth man spinning to the canvas in a dazed and bewildered state. He could only stare up at referee, Captain Davidson, who counted him out in just two minutes 40 seconds of the opening round.

Boon, at 9st 12, had a five pound weight advantage, but nevertheless continued to fulfil his considerable promise. Although the contest was over quickly, the packed Harringay crowd who had given him a great reception as he entered the ring, went wild with enthusiasm. Once again he had thrilled a big arena audience and his Fenland fans were not the only ones who believed he was destined for the top level.

Writing in the *Daily Mail*, Geoffrey Simpson predicted:

> With such irresistible power in his fists, Boon is a champion in the making if ever there was one. What a pity he's not a heavyweight.

Boon's most recent success prompted more challenges, not least from Joe Morris, the manager of Dick Corbett who held the British bantamweight title between 1931 and 1934. Morris spoke to Isidore Green one day at Mile End Arena and said he believed Dick could easily beat Boon and was prepared to back him in the sum of £50. During his early days in London, Eric had trained a lot alongside Dick with whom he became very friendly. The former champion imparted a great deal of information which helped him improve his skills tremendously. Although Green passed Morris' message on, Jack Solomons saw no benefit in such a fight.

During the same period John Harding, manager of the National Sporting Club, told Green that he was extremely irritated about the situation regarding a proposed contest between Boon and Arthur Danahar. "I have given the Boon camp every opportunity, but they have not shown any willingness," he remarked. "Solomons challenged Danahar to a fight at 9st 9 for £250-a-side. We accepted without hesitation and £250 has been lying in the offices of the National Sporting Club for six weeks."

Harding added that he notified Boon's connections to this effect and expected them to cover the amount and enter into negotiations to stage the fight. "But they have done nothing about it," he said angrily, adding that there were now other plans for Danahar.

Again Green was the messenger boy and asked Solomons if he had anything to say regarding Harding's statement. Jack said there was no question whatsoever of them wanting to back out of the fight. "The rules and regulations of the Board of Control state that all challenge money should be deposited with that body," he replied firmly. "The £250 which Harding claimed was at the NSC for six weeks was of no practical value in his office. It must be deposited at the Board. As soon as this has been done we will cover it and a fight will be arranged."

At the beginning of July, yet another challenge was issued to Boon, this time by Johnny Softley who wanted a fight at 9st 9 for £100-a-side. "I've beaten Boon once and he's beaten me once," he told *Weekly Sporting Review.* "He should give me the chance of a rubber meeting. My £100 is waiting if he will cover it."

Again Solomons saw no benefit in the fight and instead matched Eric with Billy Masters of Glasgow who had beaten Softley at the Devonshire Club earlier in the year. What looked a meaningful 10-rounder would take place at Mile End Arena on 24 July.

In the meantime Sydney Hulls was already seriously contemplating another open air show at Chatteris with hopes of better weather. He had expected a crowd of 10,000 for the Walsh fight and believed this could be bettered in the summer especially in view of Boon's continued success. He decided that the postponed fight between Boon and Belgian champion, Raymond Reynard, would make a perfect top of the bill contest. Arrangements were therefore set in motion for it to be staged at the Engineers football ground on 16 July, a Saturday evening.

Reynard was a credible opponent with a reputation of being extremely tough and aggressive. In his first appearance in a British ring he went very close to beating Harry Mizler, losing narrowly on points after an epic battle. He showed that he could take heavy punishment as well as dish it out. He had fought on a number of occasions at The Ring, Blackfriars, and always impressed regulars with his toughness.

Shortly after the fight was signed Boon issued a challenge to Dave Crowley who, the previous week, had taken the British lightweight title from Jimmy Walsh. There was, however, some doubt as to whether this would be accepted because his manager, Harry Levene, intimated before the Walsh fight that they would not meet Boon for at least six months unless it was at catchweights.

News of Boon's rise to fame had even reached the other side of the Atlantic and as a result he received an offer from promoter, Jack Kearns, for a tour of the United States taking in three contests which would earn him £2,400. Although everything was in the early stages Jack Solomons suggested that if the challenge to Crowley was accepted they would stay in England. If not they would leave for America in August. Before that, however, Eric expected to have two more fights, one of which was against Reynard.

*   *   *

Boon's training camp for the Reynard fight was set up at the King William IV public house at Chatteris where he trained hard under the watchful eye of Nat Seller. There were no frills about the gym which was at the top of a dark narrow staircase in an outbuilding. Pictures, cuttings and old fight bills were tacked to the walls, the smell of dry sweat lingered in the air and a small businesslike ring was installed at one end. The daily routine was crude but effective stuff with Eric stripped down to a slip and gym sweater. As he pounded a swinging bag stuffed with old clothes and weighing about half a hundredweight, Seller quietly whispered words of instruction and advice. Boon took everything on board, his determination and work rate being exceptional. He impressed members of the public and press representatives who were admitted to most sessions, particularly Joe Valencia who wrote for *Sporting Life* under the pseudonym 'Straight Left,' and Mike Milligan who had been a great influence on Eric since he first arrived at the Devonshire Club.

Several rounds on the bag were followed by a session on his back doing the severest of physical jerks after which he set about circling an iron bar suspended from the roof. The session concluded with Boon gasping and grunting as he lay face down on a long table with Nat Seller administering an intense massage. Seller explained to a group of local journalists that Eric always followed an ordinary routine of training and was subjected to common sense work. "An hour of actual ring work is worth a day on the punchball or bag," he told them. That was one of the secrets of Boon's success.

"A man who does too much bag work is likely to pull his punches," Nat continued, "and if he pulls them in the gymnasium he will pull them in the ring."

Eric had not been beaten since joining Seller at the beginning of the year. The trainer's methods were never inflexible and he always gave his boxers a day's rest when necessary, but he made every minute of the real work count. "I can assure you," he told his attentive audience, "that against Reynard, Eric will be as near to a fighting machine as anyone I have ever trained."

Because he was such a devastating puncher, Boon often had a shortage of sparring partners, and this fight was no exception. In training for Walsh he went through four groups in as many days despite wearing 16 ounce gloves. The problem was that he usually went flat out in gym sessions because he believed it was the only way to become a better fighter. "You learn nothing just going through the motions," he often remarked.

Despite his incredible aggression in the ring, Eric was just the opposite outside it. He was a quiet, modest and extremely polite young man, always happy and carefree, completely unspoiled by his rapid success and popularity. He had changed dramatically from the days of his early youth when he was verging on becoming a young tearaway. There were many things that contributed to his popularity, not least the fact that he lived simply, did not spend money extravagantly and openly stated that it was for Chatteris he wanted to win a world title. The local youngsters idolised him and whilst training for the Reynard fight he gave an open invitation to any of them to turn up at his gym at 3 pm any afternoon and he would help them train.

He was also extremely popular with the young ladies of Chatteris and many a pretty head was turned as he walked along the street. A few days before the Walsh fight Sydney Hulls told John Thompson of the *Daily Mirror* that there would be very few dry eyes amongst the local girls if Eric was beaten. He was the most sought after young bachelor in the town and they had been saving up for weeks to buy their tickets.

One of Eric's proudest possessions was the pair of gloves he wore against Jimmy Walsh. They hung in his bedroom over an enlarged photograph of him with Jack Solomons and Mike Milligan taken at Earls Court in 1936 after he knocked out Nat Williams. Everywhere in his home, cups, trophies, miniatures and framed photos were proudly displayed, yet despite his success which started when he was twelve, his mother hated boxing. She had only been to one of his fights and even then left before it was over. His sister Brenda, however, had often watched him fight although she never really approved of him being a professional.

As in the days before Eric's fight with Jimmy Walsh, Chatteris was full of expectancy as his date with Reynard approached. In the pubs, out on the streets and on local buses people talked about little else. It was another massive event for the little market town situated miles from the bustling city centres. Local promoter, Fred Green, a bus driver who lived at Station Road, contacted all of the local newspapers asking for any local boxers interested in appearing on the bill to contact him. Bobby Salisbury (Chatteris), Walter Redit (Soham), Harold Maywood (Peterborough) and George Gale (Whittlesey) had all been successful the night Boon triumphed over Walsh. Again there was great interest, and Redit, fellow Soham fighter, Ernie Price, and Tommy Windsor and Bill Boyd, both from Peterborough, were billed.

At a press conference at the King William IV just prior to the Reynard fight, Boon told reporters: "There is just one thing you can tell my friends and that is I hope the fight will be a good one. I hope I will not let my supporters down and naturally I hope I shall win."

Some light hearted moments followed the usual predictions and questions from reporters, particularly when one photographer thought it would be good to have a picture of Eric shoeing a horse. This appealed to Boon's sense of humour and without a moment's hesitation he whispered something to his father who immediately left the room. A few minutes later Reg returned to the pub with a large carthorse.

For the serious picture session everyone moved the short distance to Reg Boon's forge at Station Street where Eric had built up his phenomenal strength by using a heavy sledge hammer on the anvil. He gave them a demonstration and posed for whatever they wanted. The press boys loved the relaxed attitude of Boon and his handlers, and wrote that they were the most delightful people one could ever wish to meet. It was an atmosphere which had developed with time and there was plenty of banter in the training sessions as well. Yet one word, or even a stern look from Jack Solomons, who Eric always called 'The Guv'nor', and he was back to work again. It was hard to believe that he was still only eighteen.

Boon always claimed that he learned something from every fight, and in their stories before the Reynard fight reporters predicted he was likely to show real accuracy and better timing than before. His critics had often said that he missed with too many punches, but the answer was that when he hit his opponent it was with a 'slaggerer', a local expression for 'massive punch'.

*   *   *

Raymond Reynard arrived at Chatteris two days before the fight and completed his training at The George Hotel. He had been active in continental rings for eight years and it was claimed that he had never been knocked out in 300 amateur and professional contests. He had successfully defended his Belgian title on 11 occasions. In October 1936, he fought Vittorio Tamagnini for the vacant European lightweight title in Rome, but retired after seven rounds.

For the first time as a professional, Boon finally assumed his true first name. Known as 'Boy' throughout his early career, he had recently been referred to as 'Roy', but decided that now he was sufficiently well known he should adopt his real name for this fight and in future be referred to as Eric Boon.

Once again rain fell on Chatteris during the evening of a big fight, but not so heavily and prolonged as it had a couple of months earlier when Boon faced Jimmy Walsh. Despite this a crowd of more than 5,000 braved the elements demonstrating yet again the glowing admiration they had for their young idol. They buzzed with excitement as Reynard climbed into the ring, then massive cheers erupted as Boon followed on the back of Nat Seller.

Unfortunately, there was no roof above the ring, and although sawdust had been thrown over the canvas before the preliminary bouts got underway, conditions still looked wet and slippery. Another thick sprinkling was therefore made as Master of Ceremonies, Buster Cohen, introduced the boxers. He announced that at the official weigh-in, Boon scaled 9st 11 ¾ and Reynard 9st 13, a pound over the agreed limit, but being the sportsman he was Eric claimed no forfeit.

Looking deadly serious as the bell sounded for the start of the opening round Boon strode purposefully to the centre of the ring where they touched gloves. Reynard, obviously aware of his opponent's reputation, backed away with an air of apprehension about him. He pawed at Eric with a left jab, but the Chatteris lad stepped back and then in a flash attacked viciously forcing the Belgian to the ropes. A left hook crashed against the side of his head and a right swing which followed also found its target. Before Reynard could move another terrific left hook smashed into his right eye sending him crashing to the rain sodden canvas. There was stunned silence as referee, Jack Hart, started his count.

His legs and trunks plastered with wet sawdust, Reynard courageously pulled himself up against the ropes at 'nine' to avoid the first knockout of his long career. Blood streamed from a cut above his right eye and he was very unsteady on his feet. With Boon waiting to step in and finish it, he held his left arm across the

69

damaged eye and signalled to Mr Hart that he could not continue. It was all over in just 30 seconds.

As Eric acknowledged the cheers of his soaked, yet wildly enthusiastic fans, Reynard left the ring still needing some support from his seconds. Although their idol had won in sensational and convincing style many people were disappointed at the speed with which the fight ended. Even after the final bout of the evening some were still asking what really happened. The best answer probably came from Reynard himself who, back in his dressing room, told his manager: "I never saw it coming."

Meanwhile, a relaxed and composed Boon told reporters: "Dave Crowley is the boxer I would now like to meet especially now he has become the new champion. I am told I still have plenty to learn. I agree, but this is the only way one can learn. I am young and full of ambition, and ready to fight for the British title."

Tremendous praise was heaped on Boon following his latest success with large reports appearing in most of the nationals. A huge article appeared in the *Cambridgeshire Times* under the headline 'Wonder Boxer of the Year.'

Describing him as one of the greatest prospects Britain has ever had, a reporter for the *Sunday People* wrote: "Chatteris was an unknown town until Boon put it on the map with a series of non-stop victories."

An amusing story to emerge from the fight related to referee, Jack Hart who, it was claimed, was standing beside the press table puffing a cigar as the announcements were being made. The moment he was introduced he gently laid the cigar on the table, climbed into the ring, called the boxers together and gave them his final instructions. He then signalled to the timekeeper that he was ready for the fight to commence. Just over a minute later, after Boon had been declared the winner, Jack left the ring, returned to the press table and finished his cigar.

Immediately after the fight Jack Solomons confirmed that Boon's fight with Scottish lightweight contender, Billy Masters, scheduled for Mile End Arena the following Sunday, would go ahead as planned. Jack added that he had received a further communication from America offering Eric a fight with world lightweight champion, Lou Ambers, in September. This, however, appeared to be rather optimistic as Ambers was due to defend his title against Henry Armstrong in New York on 17 August.

Solomons told Jeff Barr of *Topical Times* that Sydney Hulls was deadly serious about staging a fight between Boon and Ambers at Harringay which seemed to indicate that those behind Eric thought he was unbeatable. Even when Barr pointed out that to have beaten Tony Canzoneri twice in world championship contests, Ambers was far superior to anyone Boon had faced, Solomons just laughed it off. "That really doesn't matter," he remarked with great assurance. "Boon will not only be on his feet at the end, but in all probability will have the crack American on the canvas for the full count."

Whether it was for the world title or not, Hulls and Solomons knew the fight would draw a huge gate and Solomons admitted that they had already worked out how much it would generate. He added that whilst defeat would not seriously affect Boon's future, victory would send his stock soaring on the world stage.

Barr was not convinced and urged caution because whilst Boon was the type of fighter to knock out anyone put in front of him, he was also one who could be outclassed by a world class opponent with a punch in his left glove. "I hope somebody will think first before jumping," he wrote in his column.

There was also the inevitable flurry of challenges to Boon just as there had been after he beat Jimmy Walsh. The most serious came from Beacontree lightweight, Jimmy Vaughan, for a fight at £200-a-side based mainly on the fact that he had beaten good American, Phil Zwick, who himself had previously defeated Walsh and Johnny McGrory. Vaughan's manager, Johnny Sharpe, made a separate challenge to Eric through the pages of *Boxing*. Neither were ever accepted.

Meanwhile, the possibility of a fight between Boon and Arthur Danahar continued to make the sports pages of national newspapers. Sydney Hulls offered a purse of £1,000 for the contest to take place at Harringay on condition that Danahar's backers deposited £250 with the Board of Control. Boon was willing to adopt the same course. Yet as each camp continued to blame each other for the lack of progress the fight seemed no nearer to taking place especially when John Harding stated that the National Sporting Club were in the process of staging a series of fights for Danahar.

* * *

Two days after his victory over Reynard, Eric went to the Embassy Theatre, Peterborough together with Jack Solomons and Nat Seller to see a variety show compered by Jack Doyle, the popular Irish heavyweight. Jack, who had not boxed since outpointing King Levinsky in April 1937, had developed a successful singing act backed by an exhibition of boxing training. During the show he recognised Boon in the audience and invited him to go on stage and say a few words. The Irishman congratulated him on his 30-second demolition of Reynard and the audience gave him such a wonderful reception that the theatre manager persuaded him to return on the Friday. He was billed as an added attraction and the theatre was packed to see him. After being introduced by Doyle, Eric gave a spirited exhibition of shadow boxing, ball punching and skipping.

After the show a *Cambridgeshire Times* reporter spoke to Doyle who said that he was very impressed by Eric's punch which was more powerful than anyone he had known of his weight. "He's a nice clean looking boy, very fast and there's every prospect of him becoming a world champion," said Jack. "I'm quite sure he will be if he's handled properly."

The theatre performance was light relief for Eric because just two days later he was back in the ring to face Billy Masters at the open air Mile End Arena. In reality, however, he should never have been there because the previous day he had three teeth extracted and the dentist left him in a very poor state. He was in severe pain and didn't sleep a wink the night before the fight. Jack Solomons was so concerned that he was on the verge of contacting the match-maker, Jack King, to call the fight off.

It was a rational argument by Jack because he was rightly concerned that punches to the head and mouth could leave Boon with permanent damage. Eric, however, would not hear of it and plenty of harsh words were exchanged between the two. Whilst the youngster's attitude typified his immense courage, it was one occasion where he was probably too brave for his own good.

Solomons eventually gave in, albeit very reluctantly, and they went to Mile End for the Sunday afternoon show. As Boon stood in his corner awaiting the start of the contest, he spotted his good friend, Isidore Green, sitting close by at ringside. "Are you okay Eric?" enquired the journalist. Boon opened his mouth and showed him the mess the dentist had left him in. Then with a nonchalant shrug of the shoulders said: "I couldn't let the Mile End crowd down, so after a lot of argument with my manager I decided to fulfil my engagement."

Nat Seller was not happy with his boxer's laid back attitude in the ring. "Concentrate," he snapped as he carefully slipped the gumshield into Eric's mouth. "You've got a job to do."

A crowd of record proportions had packed into every available standing space long before the fight started. Hundreds more climbed to vantage points including low roofs outside the arena. Boon was a massive attraction in the East End, a real hot-bed for boxing, and fans were told hours earlier that all seats had been sold.

Despite considerable pain and discomfort Boon gave further evidence of his crushing power as he disposed of Masters early in the second of a scheduled 10 rounds. Wading in with both fists flailing, he seemed over eager for an early finish, and Masters was able to cleverly block several hefty swings and duck under others. At the same time he scored well with several left jabs which brought a graze on Eric's nose.

The Chatteris man eased up briefly, but towards the end of the round landed a jolting short left jab followed by a heavy right to the chin. Masters fell to the floor and was only just on his feet when the count reached 'nine'.

Billy attacked at the start of the second, and after cleverly slipping a vicious left he connected with a good shot of his own which sent Boon halfway through the ropes. Predictably, the effect on Eric was immediate, and regaining his balance he unleashed his full battery of punches once again. After a close quarters attack he suddenly caught the Scot flush on the chin with a huge left hook sending him crashing on to his back. Masters was barely conscious as Boon looked down at him confident that he was another victim who had no chance of beating the count.

*   *   *

While Boon concentrated on his boxing, hardly a week went by without differing stories appearing in the press regarding him and Arthur Danahar. They were the two most talked about lightweights of the day, yet the fans really had no idea what was going on behind the scenes. Much depended on which newspaper they read.

At the beginning of August 1938 some reporters claimed that the two had still not been matched. The previous week, however, rumours were rife that they had definitely signed articles to meet on 20 August, yet details of the venue and promoter were not revealed.

Isidore Green of *Weekly Sporting Review* persisted in his attempts to discover what was going on, and spoke on a number of occasions to members of each camp. John Harding did go as far as to admit that he had tried to make the contest for 20 August, but nothing definite had materialised. He added that all of his conversations with Jack Solomons, who wanted the fight over 10 rounds at 9st 9, had been by telephone. "Solomons persisted in that, so I gave way," said Harding.

John told the journalist that he genuinely believed things would move ahead and even cancelled his holiday to Switzerland and put his staff on standby. When he tried to contact Solomons again he had gone on holiday. Harding claimed that in an attempt to keep things moving he then contacted Sydney Hulls and suggested a joint promotion. They spun a coin for choice of venue and when Hulls won he initially agreed to the proposal.

When Green spoke to Hulls he stated that he had offered Danahar a purse of £1,000 to fight Boon. He jumped at it, which was no surprise to the promoter who believed Arthur had not previously received more than £100 for a fight. It was Hulls intention to stage the contest at Harringay on 13 September as the chief support to a 12-rounder between top heavyweights Eddie Phillips and Jack Doyle.

Although, according to Hulls, Danahar appeared anxious to clinch a deal, efforts again fell through. The general consensus of opinion among critics was that the managers and promoters could not, or would not, reach agreement regarding the stipulated weight for the contest. The more cynical observers insisted that whilst the boxers were willing, their handlers didn't want the fight to take place for fear of the loser's reputation being in tatters. Defeat for either would undoubtedly result in huge financial losses. It was a fact that business always came before boxing in the battles between parties who controlled the fighters.

This view was supported to a certain extent by Joe Bromley who, writing in *Sporting Life,* believed the National Sporting Club, being quite aware of Danahar's box-office value, were not prepared to take any risks regarding his reputation. They had serious concerns as to whether he could still comfortably make 9st 9 and remain strong. Whilst there was no denying Arthur's considerable talent, the fact remained that he had still only had eight professional contests. He had not gone beyond eight rounds whereas Boon had proved he could do 10 or 12 easily, and at the top level as was shown against Walsh.

Negotiations had reached deadlock and it became obvious that until one side gave way over weight and distance a fight between the two seemed unlikely to materialise. Hulls did, however, try to persuade the Board of Control to show their authority and call for Boon and Danahar to meet for the Southern Area title. Again there was nothing doing and the Board even excluded both from eliminators for that championship.

* * *

Apart from appearing in two exhibition bouts at Sewards Paddock, Chatteris, in mid-August, Eric took a short break from the ring after beating Billy Masters. Often accompanied by Mike Milligan, he attended a number of small shows in the Eastern Counties including one at Haverhill where he was given a great reception. It was an open-air event organised by the local Rovers Support Club, and when introducing him from the ring promoter, Wally Dakin,

74

described Eric as "one of the greatest little fighters England has ever found in the last or present generations."

In acknowledging the introduction and reception, Milligan told the audience that plans were in hand to take Boon on a trip to America. They felt he could do well over there and if all went according to plan it was hoped he would eventually fight for the world title.

Back in London, Sydney Hulls was already trying to manoeuvre Eric into a world title contest much nearer to home. He cabled an offer to Henry Armstrong, who had taken the lightweight championship from Lou Ambers, to face Boon in Dublin. The inducement was a purse of £5,000 tax free, plus expenses for a party of four on a round trip from the United States. Despite much press speculation no acknowledgement was received which was probably just as well because the plans were too ambitious.

Armstrong was, pound-for-pound, one of the greatest fighters in the world. He won the world featherweight title in 1937, a year in which he was undefeated in 27 contests only one of which went the distance. In May the following year he added the welterweight crown by beating another great warrior, Barney Ross, and then three months later took the lightweight title from Ambers. By the time Hulls tried to match him with Boon he had taken part in over 100 contests in some of the toughest arenas in the States.

Hulls knew that given half a chance Eric would have jumped at the opportunity to fight Armstrong, yet apart from the money angle such a contest made no sense. If things went wrong it would almost certainly have destroyed the future of a wonderful young prospect. Whilst there was no denying Boon's exceptional power, he had failed to floor Jimmy Walsh or even come close to stopping him just three months earlier. Armstrong was in a different class. He was an all-time great who would probably have beaten him far too early in his career.

Although Hulls' proposals continued to make headline news the overall situation was best summed up by Jeff Barr in one of his articles in *Topical Times* when he remarked: "The sooner this ridiculous talk finishes the better."

Despite being as eager as a schoolboy to visit America, Boon himself was much more realistic and level-headed. "I do want to go to the States," he told Barr, "and I want to fight there, but whether I do so is another story. I could do with a few scraps with some of those preliminary guys and if I keep beating opponents with reputations in Britain then I should be able to do just as well over there."

As the interview continued Eric said he desperately wanted to fight Dave Crowley. "I believe I can lick him and I know his style of fighting would suit me," he remarked. "Jimmy Vaughan from Beacontree is yelling his head off to fight me for whatever is offered so, as far as I am concerned, the fight is on."

Outside the heavyweight division Boon was one of the most talked about fighters in Britain at this time. He had rapidly captured public imagination because he had all the elements of becoming a really top class fighter. Wherever he went people knew him and whatever he did the papers reported it. A typical example occurred one day during the summer when he drove to an open air show at Mile End Arena in his white sports car and everyone saluted him. Dressed in a smart grey-flannelled suit with a black pullover he looked the perfect model. During the show he followed Eddie Phillips into the ring and the roar that greeted Boon outdid that afforded to the popular heavyweight. It was an amazing spectacle considering he had yet to win a British title.

Writing in *Topical Times*, Jeff Barr remarked: "It reminded me of the cheering that used to greet Bombardier Billy Wells and Jimmy Wilde when they were Britain's greatest ring idols."

Barr had known Eric ever since he first put the gloves on as a junior at Chatteris Boxing Club. In his articles he recalled how the chubby, eager-eyed youngster used to question him eagerly about boxing problems. "But no matter how many I answered he was always ready to fire more at me," he wrote.

Their relationship was, in many ways, similar to that between Boon and Isidore Green. Consequently, Barr was often one of the first to hear small snippets of information which were unlikely to interest reporters from the nationals. He knew that even when Eric wasn't boxing, he went to countless small-hall shows throughout London and the Eastern Counties. He seemed to turn up everywhere which added to his immense popularity.

It was inevitable that the young Chatteris fighter often found himself in amusing situations and Barr loved revealing them. One related to another Sunday afternoon during the summer of 1938 when Eric attended a show at Mile End Arena. As was the custom during the interval, well known boxers stepped into the ring to be introduced to the crowd. Boon followed in his turn and as he ducked under the ropes, the well known Master of Ceremonies, who had announced him as a winner at Harringay a few nights earlier asked: "What's your name son?"

"Boy Boon," replied Eric in amazement.

"Oh yes, so it is" replied the embarrassed official.

During early August there was renewed gossip in the press about the likelihood of a fight between Boon and Danahar. Those claiming it would take place over eight rounds at 9st 12 were completely unfounded as Jeff Barr made clear in *Topical Times*:

> I can state quite definitely that nothing of the kind will happen. Boon will only fight Danahar at 9st 9 over 10 or more rounds, but not at 9st 12 over eight rounds.

With a fight against Henry Armstrong a non-starter and a trip to America on hold for the foreseeable future, Sydney Hulls concentrated on Boon's development on the domestic scene. His initial plan was to match him with Gustave Humery of France, remembered for his incredible fight with Harry Mizler at the Royal Albert Hall in October 1935. According to one sports correspondent "a scrap between Boon and Humery would draw like mustard plaster."

Hulls originally wanted the contest to take place on his big bill at Harringay Arena on 2 September, but when this had to be rescheduled negotiations with Humery fell through. With the date free the promoter hurriedly arranged a show at the White City Greyhound Stadium, Manchester for what would be his first promotion in the city. Boon, who according to Hulls, needed exposure in the north of England, was matched with Eric Dolby, a promising twenty-two-years-old from Derby, who had lost only five of 89 contests.

After doing his main training in Cambridgeshire, Eric travelled to Manchester a week before the fight and completed his preparations at the City gymnasium. He was accompanied by Nat Seller and Harry Silver and whilst there visited a Jewish hospital where they toured the wards, chatted to patients and were kept busy signing autographs.

The main event on the Manchester promotion was a heavyweight contest between Jack London and Al Delaney from Canada, but it was Boon who excited the fans most. Dolby, who was also a good footballer and had been offered professional terms with Derby County, was no match for the Chatteris lad whose punching power made the fans gasp. The Derby man was bludgeoned to the floor for three long counts in the opening round and did well to survive until the bell. Showing amazing courage he came out for round two looking fresh and boxed cleverly to keep the tenacious Boon at bay. The third round, however, proved to be the last as the Chatteris man, getting to close quarters, hooked heavily to the head with both hands. Dolby took three more counts before the referee intervened.

Boon, who at 9st 11 ½ had a weight advantage of two pounds, became such a hit that he was invited to appear on a big show at

Belle View on 31 October in aid of Manchester Victoria Jewish Memorial Hospital. He regarded it as an honour, but eventually commitments in London prevented him from taking part.

Next up for Boon was a contest with Mistos Grispos scheduled to take place at Harringay as the chief support to the twice postponed British heavyweight title eliminator between Eddie Phillips and Jack Doyle. A couple of weeks beforehand, however, Eric threatened to pull out when he discovered that his pal, Harry 'Kid' Silver was not on the bill. The two lads had become almost inseparable since they first met and had boxed many times on the same bills. Whenever Silver fought Boon won.

"That's made Eric superstitious," Jack Solomons told Isidore Green who had become fascinated by the situation. "When we told him that Silver wasn't on the Harringay bill he immediately replied that he wouldn't fight. He's very serious about it and it's quite definite that unless a place is found for Silver, Boon won't go on."

Green was so intrigued that he pursued Eric. "What if you went to America and Silver wasn't able to go?" he asked.

"Oh yes he would," replied Eric. "I would gladly pay his expenses just to have him with me."

The stance which Boon took worked because within a week Silver was matched over four rounds with Johnny Ryan. Hulls and Solomons regarded Eric as too big an asset to allow him to drop out of the Harringay bill.

Meanwhile, there was another strange occurrence during the build-up to that promotion. Tom Evans, for many years the trainer of Tommy Farr, was engaged to train Boon and Silver, and they worked at The Star & Garter gym at Windsor. Evans' appointment came as a great surprise, not least to Nat Seller who had trained the youngsters for the past 10 months. He insisted he had no notification from Jack Solomons and the first he knew about it was when he read it in the newspapers. "I look after Boon and Silver as if I were their father," Nat told Isidore Green with deep sincerity. "During the whole of that time they haven't lost a fight."

The whole thing was a mystery, and when asked for an explanation, Solomons said that he couldn't say anything as he didn't have a hand in it. There was yet another strange situation involving Boon on the day of the fight. After the weigh-in at 2 pm, Solomons took him back to his house at Clapton for a meal. When they had finished Eric said he wanted to go for a stroll before resting and promised to be back in about half an hour. He didn't return and the next time Jack saw him was when he turned up at Harringay Arena looking extremely tired and asking for a rub-down. Despite constant probing Solomons was never able to establish where he had been or what he had been up to.

During the build up to the fight Sydney Hulls issued a press bulletin stating that Grispos, the son of a wrestling booth proprietor, was the official lightweight champion of Greece and had a splendid record in continental rings. He was a strong two-fisted fighter who gave a good account of himself against Dave Crowley at Sheffield two months earlier before losing on points. Many spectators thought he should have got the decision so the promoter believed he was just the man to extend Boon.

It proved to be an accurate portrayal because Grispos showed that he was a skilful boxer and considerably more ring-wise than Boon. The manner in which he rode punches perplexed Eric as he strove desperately to put him away. The usual fireworks from Boon didn't materialise and the bout became scrappy and irritating. As early as the first minute Grispos was warned for a low blow. After giving further warnings, referee Moss Deyong, took him to his corner at the end of the round to have his instructions translated.

Although Grispos generally showed a desire to keep the fight clean, he continued to pick up mild rebukes from the referee for low blows and holding. It was clear that he had become wary of the official because frequently, after scoring with blows to the stomach, he looked in his direction to see if it was okay. When there was no reaction he shook Eric's glove as if thanking him for not complaining.

There were also several occasions when the Greek patted Boon on the head. His behaviour irritated many in the crowd who wanted to see aggression, not something like 'an old pal's act.'

As usual Boon took everything in his stride and once he realised that he was unable to score a knock-out he sensibly relied on his left jab to pile up the points. Although he was cut beneath the left eye in the seventh he ran out a clear points winner. There was some booing at the end, partly because of Grispos' tactics, but also out of frustration that Boon had failed to end the contest in his customary fashion. Afterwards, however, it was revealed that he had damaged his left thumb as early as the second round. Early reports indicated there was a fracture, but Solomons later confirmed it was only severe bruising.

In an interview in his dressing room, Grispos said through an interpreter, that whilst Boon had great punching power it was not as good as that of the Italian, Aldo Spaldi.

Solomons was convinced that there wasn't a lightweight in Europe capable of beating Boon, but the problem was that good continentals were reluctant to travel to London to fight him. Eric needed to be kept busy, but against durable men who would make him work and think. With that in mind he was matched with former Welsh light-weight champion, George Reynolds, over 10 rounds at Seymour Hall on 20 October. George had been a top amateur, winning the Welsh ABA bantamweight title in 1932 and the featherweight championship the following year. He claimed never to have been knocked out.

The fight was one of a number of big attractions organised to raise much needed funds for the Booth Street Relief Institute. Boon gave his ardent fans plenty to enthuse about by knocking out Reynolds after just 23 seconds of the second round. A left hook was followed by a vicious right to the chin which travelled only inches. It was a spectacular performance and confirmed that he was, without doubt, the hardest punching lightweight in the country.

7

A PRIVATE PROPOSAL

Immediately after Boon's victory over George Reynolds, Jack Solomons told the press that he was ready to face Dave Crowley on a winner-take-all basis provided the British title was at stake. "In addition I am prepared to support my man with a side-stake of £250," he added.

The National Sporting Club, meanwhile, were running weekly promotions at the Empress Hall, Earls Court, and during mid-October 1938, Boon, Crowley and Arthur Danahar were introduced from the ring. They were the three most talked about lightweights in the country and were there because Boon and Danahar were due to box at the venue on 31 October. There was no hint of rivalry between them as they smiled, shook hands warmly and engaged in friendly conversation.

As Boon and Danahar were natural contenders for Crowley's title, Solomons immediately agreed to John Harding's proposal to put them both on the same show. He billed it as 'an invitation to fanciers of the sport to go along and compare the two most promising lightweights in the country.' It proved to be a successful promotional gimmick and a crowd of 7,000 packed into the Empress Hall with hundreds more turned away.

In joint top of the bill contests both over 12 rounds, Boon faced strong, awkward Mac Perez billed as the lightweight champion of North Africa. Danahar faced a potentially easier target in Douglas Kestrell from Wales.

Boon, who had resumed training under Nat Seller, had a weight advantage of almost six pounds, but was unable to make it count as Perez, his face bearing the scars of many ring battles, gave him plenty of problems. Eric had never faced anybody so artful before. The African, obviously aware of Boon's reputation, devoted most of his energy to avoid being knocked out. He held on frequently, ducked low and used every tactic in the book to frustrate Eric whose inexperience showed against an opponent of this type. Referee, George Garrard, a former flyweight from Acton, warned Perez on a number of occasions during the first five rounds for illegal use of the head and ducking too low.

Frustrated at his inability to land a telling blow, Boon showed greater determination in the sixth, but as he pressed forward Perez literally ran away. Eric re-grouped and tried again, but as he closed in the African ducked so low that his head rammed into Boon's groin. The Chatteris man let out a loud yell and jumped around holding his protector before dropping to his knees. The referee, who at first appeared uncertain about what had occurred, started to count, but when Boon got to his feet, he cautioned the African before ordering them to box on.

Despite being in agony Boon lashed out wildly forcing Perez to defend desperately until the bell. Eric struggled to his corner to the sounds of booing from the crowd, and sat with his head between his knees throughout the interval.

Early in the seventh, after Boon's seconds had complained angrily about Perez continually ducking low, the referee issued yet another stern warning. Eric continued to attack, but most of his big punches missed their target. When he did eventually trap the African on the ropes a raised knee smashed into his groin. He collapsed to the floor writhing in agony whereupon Mr Garrard promptly disqualified Perez.

It was an unsatisfactory ending, but an inevitable one, and as Boon left the ring there was more booing from sections of the crowd. It was an uncalled for reaction because Eric's only failure was his inability to finish Perez in his accustomed style. The objectors were either extremely unsporting or seated too far away from the ring to have seen the agony the British boxer was in. One newspaper critic actually praised Boon for his performance saying: "he impressed me more than in many of his previous contests, yet had the regrettable experience of being booed. The fight was an education for him."

Later, as he lay in his dressing room crumpled up with pain and almost crying, Eric told a group of reporters: "I never knew there could be so much pain." He showed them his protector which bore a considerable dent.

Despite Boon's disappointing performance against Perez, Nat Seller was unconcerned and had no doubts about his potential. Writing in *Topical Times* he said:

> Although not a champion, Boon in my opinion is certain to win a title before he is very much older. I have trained him for some time now and he appears to be one of the few fighters who has nearly everything that goes to make a champion. He has a punch as hard as any lightweight in the country, boxing ability, trains hard and is always willing to take advice. No matter what I tell him he is always willing to carry out my instructions, and a boxer who is ready to learn has the first makings of a champion. A boxer crashing the headlines when he is very young is apt to get a swollen head. This, however, is not so with Boon. He is still the quiet lad, and if ever a boy had what it takes to make a champion it is Boon.

The idea of putting Boon and Danahar on the same bill was to try and show who was the better of the two. Their backers had hoped that both would rise to the occasion by trying to better each other which in turn would progress the chances of an early meeting between them. Danahar duly beat Douglas Kestrell in the opening round to convince his fans that he was the better of the two. In reality, however, their respective performances that night proved nothing other than to increase the pressure for them to meet.

Boxing experts were equally divided over their respective merits. There were challenges and counter challenges between their backers and supporters, and a lot of talk that led nowhere. The simple way to decide who was the better man was to put them into a ring and let them fight. It was such a ready-made contest that there was no reason why it should be continuously put off until one or the other faded out of the running.

Whilst the boxing public and critics clamoured for the fight, behind the scenes it was all about money, distance and where it should be staged. Solomons, who had close links to Sydney Hulls, wanted it to take place at Harringay, but having nurtured Danahar since he turned professional, the National Sporting Club sought to stage it at Earls Court. Yet what had become a promoter's dream reached deadlock because nobody was prepared to yield. Both parties knew that whoever staged it stood to make a fortune.

Despite his unsuccessful bid to promote the fight during the summer, Hulls had by no means lost interest. Having had Boon on four of his Harringay promotions and several more at other venues over the past 18 months he was well aware of his box office attraction and earning potential. With a long background of boxing organisation behind him, he stood as the leading promoter of the day. From a series of big fights at Crystal Palace, he became matchmaker at Wembley and packed that arena with stars from all parts of the world. Switching to Harringay he brought over Max Baer and his brother Buddy, Walter Neusel and Ben Foord as well as promoting British heavyweight champions Jack Petersen and Tommy Farr.

With Jack Solomons' help Hulls had obtained Boon's agreement to meet Danahar, but then met an obstacle when Jack suddenly felt he owed allegiance to John Harding and the National Sporting Club who were equally anxious to stage the fight at Earls Court. Despite a lot of haggling there seemed little prospect of it going ahead in the foreseeable future.

Suddenly, at the beginning of November 1938, there was another twist to the equation. It was claimed that an anonymous London sportsman was prepared to offer a purse of £1,250 to stage the fight at a plush hotel in the west end of London. Dramatic stories appeared in most of the national newspapers and London evening publications. Yet because no official press conference was ever called by the organisers, accounts differed greatly. There was a great deal of speculation and confusion which left the real boxing fans to rely on what the papers printed.

What did become clear, however, was that Joe Bromley of *Sporting Life* and Ben Bennison, boxing correspondent for the *London Evening Standard* were the only journalists really close to what was happening. Both claimed to have been present when contracts for the fight were signed. Whilst most reporters only ever referred to the London sportsman as being anonymous, John Thompson of the *Daily Mirror* named him as Mr M Burns who allegedly stated that his offer was for the fight to take place at either Olympia or the Royal Albert Hall. Two days later, however, the paper ran another story under the headline 'Danahar will fight Boon at secret party.'

From reports filed by Bromley and Bennison on 4 November it was revealed that a meeting was held at Sydney Hulls' office at 95 Shaftesbury Avenue the previous day and an announcement made that Boon and Danahar would meet over eight rounds at 9st 9 on 20 November. The fight would be under the auspices of the British Boxing Board of Control who would appoint a referee and other officials. Failure by either boxer to make the stipulated weight would result in a substantial financial forfeit.

The identity of the London sportsman and size of the purse were not revealed although it was made clear that both boxers would be handsomely rewarded in equal terms. Present were Hulls, Jack Solomons representing Boon, John Harding, Danahar, who was hurriedly brought from Bethnal Green, and the two journalists.

The announcement came as a complete shock to Bromley and Bennison because the public would have no involvement in the promotion. Only a handful of privileged people and selected friends of the sportsman would be present. Even the general press were expected to be excluded, but those who were invited would be asked not to publicise the result. It was the most amazing fight announcement of recent years and savoured the old Corinthian days when monied sportsmen put up purses for a private view of two great gladiators in combat.

There was a great deal of discussion before the articles were presented and although Solomons immediately signed on behalf of Boon, Danahar was allowed to take his contract to his home at Bethnal Green where his parents and the rest of his family were waiting to give their approval. "You see, I always tell them what I intend to do," he remarked.

Danahar returned to the office about half an hour later. "Give me a pen," he said excitedly, and then eagerly put his name to the contract.

"Look at that," said Hulls to his audience, "it just had to be done. Nothing could stop these boys fighting."

According to Joe Bromley, Danahar said his position had become uncomfortable because whenever he walked about in the East End people kept asking him when he was going to fight Boon. "I am anxious to meet Boon any time, anywhere," he remarked. When asked if he preferred the fight to take place in private the question was lost amid the discussion going on around him. He was then shepherded to the office door and disappeared.

Anxious to glean as much information as possible the reporter then spoke to Harding who insisted that he had vigorously protested against the procedure being adopted. He insisted it was against his advice that Danahar signed the contract for the fight to take place in private. In his opinion members of the National Sporting Club should have been given the opportunity to be present because it was their enthusiasm which had helped build up the Bethnal Green lad's prestige.

Solomons was equally outspoken on Boon's behalf saying that his charge had undergone similar questions from the public as Danahar. Whenever he went home to Chatteris he was repeatedly asked by local people when he was going to fight the Bethnal Green man.

In a subsequent interview with John Thompson of the *Daily Mirror,* Harding expressed his severe disapproval of the arrangements. "These young men have been paired for the benefit of very wealthy patrons of sport who will stage the contest at a private party," he remarked.

Harding added that he was going to ask Danahar to appear before the Directors of the National Sporting Club to explain his decision. "The club are not able to make a better offer than that which has already been made to the two men," he remarked, "but they can protest most strongly about the fight being allowed to go on in this way."

Ben Bennison also spoke to the main players and claimed that the fight was made by Sydney Hulls at the request of all parties. If this theory was true it was an obscure situation.

He asked Hulls why it was to be staged in private. "The explanation is simple," replied the promoter. "Boon, through his manager, Jack Solomons, prefers to fight under my direction at Harringay. Danahar feels that he is under such heavy obligation to the National Sporting Club that it would be unfair for them to fight at Harringay."

"Both are confident of victory," continued Hulls, "and since they are so determined to fight each other the only way was to put them in a private ring and let them hammer it out."

When pressed regarding the venue for the contest Hulls remained guarded. "I cannot name the rendezvous at the moment," he said. "The most I am at liberty to divulge is that the fight will be staged under the most desirable auspices at a place in the heart of the west end of London."

Jack Solomons told the gathering that Boon was prepared to bet £50 of his own money that he would win. "That's a bet," snapped Harding. "It will be the first I have ever had on a fight or fighter, but this is different. If Danahar wins it will go to him."

Harding continued his conversation with Ben Bennison saying: "I strongly object to the match being in private. It was essentially one for the National Sporting Club and one that an unlimited public wanted to see. Of course being manager of Danahar I can do no more than protest."

He added that Arthur felt that if he didn't accept the chance to fight Boon, he would have to confess to having no professional pride. "He has begged for this opportunity to prove that he can go one better than Boon and at the same time stake the strongest possible claim to fight Dave Crowley for the lightweight title," said Harding. "In the circumstances it is proper that the lad should be his own agent. For the club's part, we will see that he has the best possible preparation."

In one of his columns, Bennison claimed that he had to shoulder part of the responsibility for setting Boon and Danahar at war. He said that in an earlier article in the *Evening Standard* he had written that he was tired of all the challenges and counter challenges, and was opposed to them being nursed and coddled any longer. He added that to his recollection no similar fight had ever taken place in private.

Whilst everyone was still assembled at Hulls' offices, Boon telephoned from his Chatteris home and spoke to Solomons. "Everything alright guv'nor?" he asked.

"Yes," replied Jack.

"Good," said Boon, "I bought a parrot this afternoon."

There was laughter in the office when Jack related the comment. "That is Boon," said Jack with a smile. "He is more concerned about his parrot than what might happen when he fights young Danahar. He is just a simple lad."

*   *   *

It was not difficult to predict public response when the news broke. There was sheer anger because the fans, by their loyalty and through their pockets, had helped make Boon and Danahar the successful young men they were becoming. Ordinary people were adamant that the fight belonged to them not a privileged group of wealthy fanciers sitting in the comfort of a posh London hotel. It was a fight everyone had been clamouring for yet if the latest proposal went ahead those at grass roots level would be denied access to it.

Joe Bromley claimed to have seen the contracts which stipulated that the fight would be over eight rounds at 9st 9 at a well known hotel in the west end of London and would commence at 12.15 am on 21 November 1938. Other newspapers confidently predicted the venue was the banqueting room of the Grosvenor Hotel at Park Lane.

In Chatteris response to the news was immediate. A public meeting was hurriedly arranged because people were furious that potentially one of the greatest fights between two British boxers should be staged in private and only a privileged few paying up to 100 guineas to wine and dine should get the opportunity to watch it. This was a fight for the general public and they intended making the strongest possible protest that the working class people of Cambridgeshire and London were to be deprived of it.

Angry locals queued outside the Empress Cinema to sign a petition threatening to organise a march to the House of Commons. Banners hung across the streets of the town, one of which read 'This is our Fight.' Placards and posters were displayed on walls and in the windows of houses and shops. There were demonstrations outside Boon's house at Burnsfield Street. People told him in no uncertain terms that it was unfair of him to fight at a private venue where they couldn't cheer him on. Things became so heated that one group threatened that if they found out where the fight was taking place they would set fire to it.

Other protests took place across London and the Home Counties, and many boxing writers were eager to join in the outcry. They plastered their columns with indignation and rightly claimed that in the interest of boxing as a sport this private contest should not be allowed to take place.

Newspaper offices were inundated with calls from members of the public whilst others rang Jack Solomons and the National Sporting Club. In the East End crowds gathered outside Jack's fishmonger's shop at Ridley Road. The protesters made it clear that everything possible would be done to stop the fight taking place unless the public could see it. As the pressure mounted Sydney

Hulls was quoted as saying he was becoming worried about 'this little fight' as he rather naively called it.

Boon became so concerned about the situation that on the evening of 4 November he went to the Friday evening promotion at the Devonshire Club where he received a mixed reception. When the Master of Ceremonies told patrons of the proposed private fight uproar broke out. Regulars there who had watched Eric rise from obscurity to fame were so furious that he had to climb into the ring and speak to them. "I know how you must feel," said the youngster refusing to shirk his responsibilities, "and I know how you have helped me all through my career. I want you to know that I am behind you one hundred per cent in your demands to see this fight."

"I agreed to it because it seemed the only way I could get to fight Danahar," he continued, "and I am very keen to show that I am the better man."

There was absolute silence as Eric spoke, an indication of the respect the Devonshire regulars held for him. He received polite applause as he left the ring, and although there was still anger among the patrons over the general situation of the private fight, his maturity went a long way to calming the atmosphere in the club.

The mounting of public opinion clearly got to Sydney Hulls because during the same evening he issued a press statement in which he said he would have nothing to do with promoting the fight in private. "I am getting in touch with the sportsman who wished to stage it for his friends," he added, "and I am sure he will agree it would be unwise or unfair to run it in private. I am therefore calling a conference of leading writers on Monday (7 November) to discuss the position."

In what appeared to be a clear case of back-tracking Hulls added: "I have endeavoured to arrange the contest between these two youngsters in public for the past three months without success. When I made an offer two months ago for them to meet at Harringay only Boon accepted."

As the top promoter in the country Syd didn't need to justify his actions of having attempted to stage the contest earlier. It was perhaps a case of protesting too much especially as many ordinary people already believed the whole thing was a publicity stunt. When this was put to Hulls by a reporter from the *Daily Mail*, he denied it claiming that the private fight was a perfectly serious proposition.

The fact remained, however, that the 'wealthy man well known in sport' never came forward and remained anonymous throughout all the speculation. This caused some cynics to believe that it was in fact Hulls himself who was trying to stage the fight in private. He certainly had the connections and know-how, and it became public knowledge that all dealings took place at his office. If Hulls was the main person then it had to be assumed that Solomons and Harding were party to the plans despite their many statements to the press expressing their opposition.

The situation certainly made for great stories and the press boys were like bloodhounds with their constant probing and seeking comments from the main parties. When asked by Ben Bennison on 5 November what the current position was, Hulls gave yet another detailed response. "So far as I am concerned there is no change," he remarked. "It is imperative, however, that I should remove what appears to be a general misunderstanding in the matter. I did not want the boys to fight in private. I was just as emphatically against the idea as John Harding, but my hands were tied in the sense that the lads were offered the opportunity to have what they considered an overdue fight, and they insisted on taking it."

"I have discussed the situation with the Marquess of Queensberry, Sir Noel Curtis-Bennett and Mr Harding," continued Hulls. "We are agreed that if it is at all possible the contest should be in public. Boon and Danahar are indifferent as to where it is put on. I am only too ready to co-operate to have it in the open and naturally I want it at Harringay. The National Sporting Club still prefer to have it under their direction."

"As a result of last night's talks, however, I believe a way out will be found," added Hulls. "It is suggested that the newspaper boxing writers be called into conference and give their point of view and assistance. I shall try to meet common wishes as represented by thousands of protesters from different parts of the country against the private fight. For the moment I can only mark time and nurse a headache."

John Harding made it clear that the National Sporting Club would do all in its power to arrange the fight in a public ring. They believed that the desires of the public, the backbone of boxing, should be met. "On behalf of the club," said Harding, "we are given to understand by Mr Hulls that he will place an offer before his backer during the weekend. We have high hopes that Boon and Danahar will fight in public at prices within the average pocket."

Solomons also sought to justify his position by stating that, as Boon's manager, he had to consider the boxer's welfare. "Terms offered to me were exceptionally good," he said. "Yet the wealthy man who has my signature for the contest should listen to public demand and decide that the fight should take place at a public venue. I am prepared to take less money than that agreed upon provided the boys meet at the stipulated weight of 9st 9."

Throughout all the confusion and speculation Boon actually started training at Ely, but after a couple of days he received a telegram advising him that the fight had been postponed. When interviewed by the *Cambridgeshire Times* he said: "Danahar wanted to fight in private, but I wanted it in public. The people here in Chatteris have stood by me and I'm going to stand by them. I haven't forgotten how they came to see me fight Walsh in the pouring rain. I want to fight Danahar because it's got to be settled and it will come in time."

By 9 November the outbursts of enthusiasm, anger and frustration had died down. Boon was quoted in the nationals as saying that unless the fight was in public he would not go through with it. Solomons said he thoroughly agreed with him. The matter had reached stalemate and most people thought the whole affair would die a natural death. After three days of boxing sensation and somersault, a fight between Boon and Danahar seemed no nearer reaching fruition. The main players had become extremely quiet yet a lot of questions remained unanswered. The identity of the 'anonymous' sportsman, if he ever existed, was never revealed. It was reminiscent of an unsolved 'whodunnit'where the main culprit is never tracked down.

*   *   *

The well known old adage 'your sins will come back to haunt you' eventually appeared appropriate when considering who the anonymous sportsman was. In a series of articles in *Empire News* in 1950, the Marquess of Queensberry made reference to the proposed private fight between Boon and Danahar. He mentioned 'wild rumours doing the rounds about it being held in private for the edification of an unnamed multi-millionaire and a few choice friends.'

"Well I can reveal that Hulls and Harding were guaranteed that 1,000 rich sportsmen would pay 100 guineas each if a contest was staged privately at midnight in the ballroom of either the Grosvenor or Park Lane hotels. The offer was refused and Harringay was chosen," he declared.

Two years later in an article in the *Sunday People*, Sam Burns claimed it was in fact Sydney Hulls who wanted to stage the fight in private before a select audience at 25 guineas a seat. Burns claimed it was a publicity stunt, but Hulls abandoned his plans very quickly when there were protests from both the fans and media.

Both stories had a ring of truth about them although that of Burns appeared nearer the mark. To a certain extent the thoughts of the cynics back in 1938 were justified.

8

BRITISH CHAMPION AT EIGHTEEN

Following all the controversy over a fight between Boon and Danahar, challengers were queuing up to meet either. Jimmy Vaughan remained confident that he had the beating of both, and Phil Freeman, manager of Morrie Mack Promotions, told *Weekly Sporting Review* that a prominent London sportsman was prepared to wager £500 on Vaughan.

George Daly, the busy Blackfriars fighter, had moved back from welter to lightweight and told *Weekly Sporting Review*: "I wish they would give me the chance to fight Boon or Danahar."

Meanwhile, former British bantamweight champion, Dick Corbett, said he was ready to fight any leading lightweight in the country for just his training expenses. "I am prepared to meet Boon, Danahar or Crowley for just £20 which is all I would need for my preparation," he told the press. His manager, Joe Morris, confirmed that Corbett, who had recently won five contests, was sincere in his offer for fights at 9 st 9.

Behind the scenes, however, Sydney Hulls was working hard to make amends for the controversy he caused over the proposed private fight. During mid-November he called Jack Solomons to a meeting at his office and asked if he would allow Boon to meet Dave Crowley for the British title. Jack jumped at the chance and quickly agreed terms.

Knowing that Boon was dining at a West End restaurant that afternoon Solomons went straight there and broke the news to him. Eric was so excited that he jumped up from his table and rushed for the door. Fearful that he was leaving without paying his bill, a waiter gave chase and caught up with him as he reached the street. Jack quickly smoothed things over, paid what was owing and took his protégé away to start making plans to set up a training camp.

Hulls had already spoken with Crowley and his manager, Harry Levene, about the fight and got their agreement. When he told the press that the fight would take place at Harringay on 15 December, it was another bombshell and the biggest piece of boxing news in months. The promoter duly made application to the Board of Control for the contest to be for Crowley's British title and this was ratified by the Stewards at their next meeting.

No sooner had Hulls announced the fight he was reminded by several critics that, as a bantamweight, Crowley only lost on points to the great Panama Al Brown back in 1933. The following year he put fear into world featherweight champion, Freddie Miller, and in 1936 in New York drew with Mike Belloise who, seven weeks earlier had been named by the New York State Athletic Commission as world featherweight champion following his victory over Everette Rightmire. The achievement earned Crowley a world title shot three months later, but he was counted out in round nine following what many critics claimed was a blatantly low blow.

Although not as vocal as when Boon was matched with Jimmy Walsh, some critics questioned if he was ready for a man of Dave's quality and experience. Hulls hadn't the slightest doubt. Having seen Eric beat Walsh, and then Crowley take the title from Jimmy four weeks later he had no misgivings whatsoever.

The decision brought a deluge of protests from the managers of other title contenders. Danahar, Ronnie James, Johnny McGrory, who had beaten Crowley at catchweights, and area champions Jack Carrick and Jimmy Vaughan, were all extremely disappointed that Boon had been given a title shot ahead of them. Yet there could be no argument because Eric had every right to be considered as a serious challenger, and had any of the others been chosen instead the same protests would have arisen.

The Board of Control duly considered and rejected all of the complaints lodged with them. In an attempt to pacify the situation, however, the Stewards stipulated that the winner must waive the usual six month's grace afforded to a champion and face an officially recognised challenger. The fact was that the lightweight division was particularly strong and one of which British boxing could be proud. Unfortunately, it wasn't possible to please everyone.

From a public point of view the general situation was made even more interesting by an announcement that Danahar and McGrory would meet at Earls Court on 5 December. The press claimed that the winner would meet Boon or Crowley early in 1939. Yet for reasons which were never disclosed the contest did not take place.

Meanwhile, Crowley gave a number of press interviews in which he said he was delighted to be fighting Boon. "It's up to me to make as much out of the game as possible," he added. "While I am at the top a fight with Boon will pack any hall, and if only from the money point of view I'd jump at it."

As news of the fight spread messages of congratulations poured into Boon's home and there was a constant stream of callers at the little terraced cottage at Burnsfield Street. Men who had finished work in the fields stopped off on their way home to tell his parents how pleased they were that he was to get the chance to bring a British title to Chatteris.

Since his leap to fame just over a year earlier Eric had become a hero throughout East Anglia. Yet he was about the only person who didn't show any excitement at what was actually occurring. With characteristic calmness he regarded it as just another fight, a reaction very similar to that which he displayed when he was matched with Jimmy Walsh. In the local pubs and clubs, however, there was tremendous excitement as licensees opened subscription lists for the many fans who wanted to travel to London for the fight.

Boon set up his training camp at the headquarters of Ely Amateur Boxing Club and stayed at the nearby Bull Hotel. His bosom pal, Harry Silver, and trainer, Nat Seller, were with him from day one. Within a few days they were joined by Scottish lightweight, Angus McGregor, who was chosen as Boon's main sparring partner largely because of his performance when they boxed a draw at Harringay in April 1937. With a fine record of 32 victories from 35 contests, Angus was known for his skill and toughness. Seller believed he was just the man to push Boon during sparring.

"Boon will just suit me," said McGregor during a press interview. "I shall be able to know in exactly what class I stand after a session or two with him."

Eric trained diligently under the watchful eye of Seller in what was described by John Thompson in the *Daily Mirror* as "the strangest fight camp I have ever seen." The gymnasium was in an upper room of a building situated near to the Cathedral in the quiet and dignified city. On the walls hung examples of how fishermen's dreams often came true. Record breaking pike and perch, professionally stuffed and mounted in framed cases on the walls, maintained all of their original beauty.

As Boon went about his daily routines gaitered farming folk stood around the ring. They were some of the Chatteris lad's most ardent fans and many travelled miles just to watch him train. Instead of the quick cockney jargon of the usual hangers-on during a boxer's workouts, there was a slower more refined chatter of country folk. Most of them probably didn't know a great deal about the intricacies of the fight game, but they were nevertheless confident that their young hero had the ability to defeat most men put in front of him.

"What a little marvel he be," was a remark frequently heard in the camp as Eric went through his strenuous programme with Nat Seller barking instructions like a Regimental Sergeant Major. The assessments were spot on because Boon was a little marvel. Power, courage, determination and all round ability had propelled him into the justifiable position of title challenger just a few weeks before his nineteenth birthday.

The training camp attracted many outsiders to Ely and hardly a day passed without visits from a dozen or so reporters from different parts of the country. Photographers were in their element and Eric never disappointed them, posing for their shots after every session.

Boon was close friends with Jeff Barr, boxing correspondence for *Topical Times,* who had known him since he was a boy, and told him that his great ambition was to win the Lonsdale belt. "It's more tempting to me than the cash," he said. "In fact, I'd like to win one of those belts so I could give it to my mother as a present, this is if I win it outright which I am sure I can."

Boon made himself extremely popular in the city by his unassuming attitude. He signed autographs daily and happily chatted to fans and well-wishers in the gym and at his hotel. Passers by who called out to him in the street were always acknowledged with a cheerful smile and wave of the hand. He was extremely confident, but never cocky, and to a group who spoke to him outside the Bull Hotel one evening said: "I don't think fifteen rounds will be needed, but I am training to go it just in case."

Apart from sparring each afternoon Eric's preparation included bouts of shadow boxing, skipping, bag and speedball work and sessions of assorted floor exercises all of which intensified as he worked towards the week of the fight. At the end of each session he took a hot bath which was followed by vigorous massage from Nat Seller both in and out of the water.

His main source of recreation was several miles of horse riding most mornings, followed by mucking-out the stables which Seller encouraged for further exercise. Harry Silver was constantly at Boon's side. In the ring he was used for speed and during their hours of relaxation rode with him, taught him Yiddish and how to play the Jewish harp. Music was always high on their agenda and Eric also spent hours playing his accordion and mouth organ.

A few days after he had settled into the training camp, Jack Solomons took a party of London newspaper reporters to Ely to watch Boon do a workout. Although he was generally a great organiser Jack hadn't thought it necessary to warn Eric they were coming. On arriving at the camp he was told that he and Silver had gone for a bike ride to Soham about five miles away. Solomons was not happy and became even more irritated when the pair eventually returned on the back of a farmer's cart tired out and covered in dust. "Relax guv'nor," said Boon with a cheeky smile. "Give me a few minutes to get cleaned up and I'll do a workout for your friends."

After a quick wash, rub down and a couple of rounds shadow-boxing to warm up, he climbed into the ring and flattened three sparring partners in quick succession wearing 16 ounce gloves. The press boys loved it, but quickly realised that rumours about a shortage of spar mates were true.

The sheer aggression of Boon once he got inside the ropes was the cause of many a headache for his manager and trainer. Despite pleas from Solomons and Seller he found it almost impossible to ease up. Consequently, most of those engaged to work with him left after just a day or two. Although there were plenty of lightweights around, very few were prepared to risk a hiding in a training session for just a few quid.

Two weeks before the Crowley fight Eric had a couple of eventful gym sessions with Harry Vaughan who, in his time, had beaten some of the best men around including a number of Americans. He fought a great deal in Australia where Tommy Fielding of California and Russ Crutcher, a former Australian champion, failed to upset him.

Despite having quite an advantage in weight, Harry found Boon too much for him. During one session he had to pull out in the second round after taking a terrific body blow. When they eventually resumed Eric knocked him heavily into the ropes and had to be called off. Vaughan admitted to a group of newsmen that he had never met a man with such a powerful punch. "It will take a remarkably good fighter to beat Eric," he told a reporter from the *Cambridgeshire Times* once he had recovered.

Because of the constant difficulty with sparring partners there were concerns in London about Eric being able to make the championship weight. Rumours to this effect, however, were unfounded and as the day of the fight drew nearer he looked in excellent shape. Every day he performed more and more like a champion. His footwork improved and the general opinion of regulars who visited the training camp was that one good blow from his right hand would knock most men out.

Jack Solomons and Nat Seller both told the press they were extremely happy with their man's condition. The only concern had been when he suffered from a tonsil infection, but frequent spraying prevented it from affecting his natural aggression. It was a problem which had flared up before so an operation was predicted for the following spring.

With about a week to go before the fight Eric began to wind down the major part of his training. Hundreds of people crowded into his gym and were fortunate in that he got some sparring with Tiny Bostock, Con Flynn and Tony 'Kid' Shepherd. Bostock, who had beaten Small Montana, a former world feather-weight contender, at Manchester the previous year, and Flynn a veteran of over 100 fights, praised Boon's power of punch.

The following day a large party from London accompanied Sydney Hulls to the Fenland city to watch Eric train. After a last minute rush Nat Seller was fortunate to locate Walter Redit, the Eastern Counties champion, who had been one of Boon's most regular sparring partners. He stood up well and despite taking a lot of punishment fought back well during a vicious third round. "I've seen Crowley in several of his fights and also boxed him in the gym," Boon told his audience as he towelled the sweat from his body. "I've never let the guv'nor down and I don't intend to next week. I hope to knock Crowley out."

Yet as questions were continually fired at him the Chatteris youngster spoke with more interest about a trumpet he had just bought. "I love music," he enthused, "and it will help me relax."

Crowley trained at the famous Star & Garter gym at Windsor, and in an interview with Jeff Barr of *Topical Times*, his manager, Harry Levene, expressed confidence about the likely outcome. "Boon has a reputation for putting fighters on the floor," he said. "Well, Crowley is going to show Master Boon what it is like to get licked himself. We don't care who fights Crowley as long as the dough is there."

As the day of the fight drew closer the one thing troubling Boon was how to persuade his mother not to go to the fight. She had only seen him in the ring on one occasion and even then she had to leave because she couldn't bear the tension. This time, however, she desperately wanted to be present at what was his biggest fight. "But I really don't want her to see it," he remarked, "I know she will only get upset and think I'm being hurt when I am not."

* * *

When Boon climbed into the ring to face Crowley he was just 13 days short of his nineteenth birthday. He was there on merit yet many of the critics, just as they did when he was matched with Jimmy Walsh six months earlier, believed he would crash badly against the champion. They reasoned that despite his phenomenal progress he had not reached the stage to take on a man of Dave's vast experience.

Crowley was a fast, versatile and extremely crafty ring campaigner who, in almost 10 years, had boxed from fly to lightweight and taken part in over 180 contests. He had faced British and world champions and campaigned in America. Many top names appeared on his record including Harry Mizler, Cuthbert Taylor, Petey Sarron, Dick Corbett and Jimmy Walsh. The only thing Dave lacked was a destructive punch, but the critics believed his skills would offset the punching power of Boon.

Frank Butler, Sports Editor of the *News of the World*, was one of the most ardent critics. He told Jack Solomons face-to-face that he believed Boon had been over-matched. Whilst having great respect for Butler, Jack wasn't in the least bit concerned because the reporter had been equally critical when Eric was matched with Walsh. "Let me give you some advice Frank," said Solomons with a smile as they dined at the Bull Hotel, "Bet against Boon at your peril."

Most fans saw the fight as a fascinating match-up with the thunderous power of Boon challenging the champion's speed and years of experience. Opinions over the likely outcome differed greatly, and not surprisingly all betting on the contest was laid at evens or slightly odds on Crowley.That suited Boon who told reporters that he intended backing himself and added that if he could get odds of 5/4 he would wager a few pounds more. It would be only the third time he had risked money on his own ability to beat an opponent. The two previous occasions were against Johnny Softley at the Royal Albert Hall and Jimmy Walsh at Chatteris.

Huge numbers of tickets were sold in Chatteris and the surrounding districts, and two special trains and seven coaches were organised to take local fans to London. The first train would leave Chatteris at four o'clock on the afternoon of the fight and arrive back at about 4 am the next morning. For those who were unable to travel, however, there was great disappointment when they realised that the BBC had no plans to broadcast the fight over the radio.

After a final light workout, Boon travelled from Ely to London by train on the eve of the fight and received a wonderful welcome when he arrived at Liverpool Street station. A large crowd waving bells and rattles cheered excitedly and patted him on the back and shoulders as he made his way from the platform to a waiting car. Pressmen and photographers jostled to get close to him and his entourage.

Pausing briefly to address the crowd, Jack Solomons said: "After he's won we are all going back to the Devonshire Club to celebrate with an all-night party. I want all his friends and supporters to come along and join us." The possibility of defeat apparently hadn't occurred to Jack

After a good night's sleep at his manager's house at Clapton, Eric had a light breakfast, went for a gentle stroll and generally relaxed until going to the Board of Control offices at Dean Street for the weight-in at 2 pm. Crowley scaled 9st 7 lbs 10 oz, but there was slight concern when Boon was one ounce over the championship limit. In accordance with the Board rules he was allowed one hour to take it off, but after exercising in an adjoining room for just five minutes he returned and scaled exactly 9st 9. Commenting on the fact that Boon was an ounce overweight, Nat Seller told reporters: "He was well inside the weight at midday, but the private scales on which he was then weighed were inaccurate."

Both men looked extremely fit and relaxed. In answer to questions from a large group of reporters each expressed confidence over the eventual outcome of the fight. Then after posing for photographers they shook hands warmly and went their separate ways.

Neither man had ever been beaten at Harringay and the fight marked the first occasion when boxers below the light-heavyweight limit topped a bill at the great arena. Crowley and world featherweight champion, Petey Sarron, did share top billing with Buddy Baer and Jim Wilde in May 1937, but generally it was the heavyweights who were regarded as the main attraction by the boxing public.

Harringay was packed long before the main event was due and according to Peter Wilson, writing in the *Sunday Pictorial*, Boon was the calmest man there when his pal Harry Silver was boxing in a preliminary bout. The relationship between them was so close that he insisted on watching Harry's fight which was the second of the evening. Boon was due on fifth and although it didn't leave much time for him to get ready he sat at ringside just behind the press benches and kept up a quick fire deluge of advice throughout the fight.

When Harry left the ring as a winner Boon shepherded him carefully back to the dressing room as though he were the main attraction. Then with a minimum of fuss he proceeded to get ready for his own battle. As the fight got closer, everyone else became tense and edgy, but not Eric. He sat calmly on a stool playing his mouth organ which he took with him to every fight. That was Boon's makeup. He never got nervous and was always full of confidence. Since Silver became his pal his entire outlook changed.

The atmosphere generated inside Harringay Arena on fight nights was like nowhere else in the country and this one was no exception. With the preliminaries over the lights dimmed and a fanfare of trumpets greeted firstly Boon followed a few minutes later by the champion. It was chilling stuff as the spotlights followed them to the ring. Both looked in magnificent shape as they stripped off their gowns beneath the powerful ring lights, listened to the referee's final instructions and awaited the opening bell.

As expected Crowley took the initiative from the start, peppering his young challenger with a stream of left jabs. A pattern was quickly set because he was the champion and boxed like one. His tactics were based on skill and ringcraft, darting forward and pouring out jabs then moving away before Boon could respond. Whenever Eric attacked he was cleverly tied up at close quarters or made to miss badly. His powerful swings and hooks rarely found their target as Dave cleverly side-stepped or drew back out of range.

Crowley didn't let up and by the end of the opening round Boon had a bruise beneath his left eye. His cheek was badly swollen by the fifth and in round six it was cut and the eye virtually closed. The champion's left hand was proving to be a potent weapon.

Eric also had other problems to contend with because by the sixth his right hand had become badly bruised from wild punches landing high on Crowley's head. Despite increasing pain, however, he bravely disguised the injury to avoid giving his opponent greater encouragement.

Although Crowley won most of the early rounds, Boon did have moments of success albeit too infrequently. It was not until round three that he landed a punch of any significance and even then the champion took it well, moved away and was jabbing out his left with great accuracy at the bell.

Ignoring the persistence of Dave's jab in the fourth, Boon landed several good shots to the head and looked to be getting into the fight. When the champion almost plunged through the ropes Eric stood back allowing him to regain his balance. Crowley readily acknowledged his sportsmanship.

There were some vicious exchanges in round five during which more damage was inflicted to Boon's left eye. After taking two solid left jabs to the face he countered neatly with a crisp right which spun the champion completely around. Crowley knew what was coming next, and as Eric rushed forward swinging wildly, he tied him up and cleverly countered with solid shots from either hand.

Although the champion's jab dominated the middle rounds, Boon stayed in the fight by continuing to plough forward throwing his big punches in the hope that one would connect. Not once did he show any signs of frustration, and despite realising the immense task he faced, just got on with his job.

As the fight progressed, Eric's left eye deteriorated rapidly and by the end of round seven he couldn't see out of it. Fearful that the referee could intervene, his chief second, Dick Gutteridge, decided to act, and using a sterilised razor blade, nicked the huge purple lump. Once the skin was lacerated he leant forward and sucked out the suffused blood, a process he repeated between the ensuing rounds. Although some fans and critics were horrified, it was a procedure he and his twin brother Jack had carried out successfully with a number of lesser-known boxers.

Both men had moments and success in rounds nine and ten. Boon scored with good single shots to the head, but Crowley took them well and continued his amazing jab and move tactics as the challenger's eye continued to trouble him. Up until this point it had been a one-sided fight and many observers thought Jack Solomons had made huge mistake by allowing his young prospect to face the experienced champion. There was a wide gulf in skill levels and in reality Boon was being given a boxing lesson.

It was at this stage of the contest when most critics expected the youngster to tire thereby allowing Crowley to cruise to victory. On the press benches they wondered just how much Boon had left in the tank and how good his preparation had been.

The fact was that Nat Seller never sent a fighter into the ring short of fitness so, knowing he could go the distance without too much difficulty, Eric had paced himself well. He was still strong, full of fight and possessed an abundance of confidence. He banked everything on ceaseless attack and never sought shelter from the stabbing, biting left hand of the champion.

Undaunted by the pressure he was under his concentration level remained high and going into the last third of the fight he never gave up hope of landing one of his explosive punches.

Suddenly in round 11 the fight seemed to change course and led to Boon being rewarded for one of the most courageous displays seen in the ring for years. As Crowley backed away from solid lefts to head and body, Boon ignored the pain and crashed his damaged right hand deep into the champion's stomach sending him to the floor grimacing in pain. Badly hurt, he appealed desperately to the referee that the blow was low, but was ignored by Mr Thomas who counted to 'seven' before Dave rose.

Fighting like a true champion, Crowley kept the aggressive Boon at bay until the bell, but the feeling at ringside was that the fight was beginning to slip away from him. He had shown out that he had been hurt and it was well known that Boon never let a wounded man off the hook.

Crowley boxed well in round 12, skilfully avoiding all of Boon's ferocious attempts to bring the bout to a conclusion. Despite being unable to see out of one eye, the challenger was still strong and very dangerous, yet by using all his experience, Dave kept on his blind side and continued to work the jab.

The champion was first to land in the 13th, moving inside a wild swing from Boon and finding him with a good left. There was no respite, however, and sensing victory Boon slammed two lefts to the chin followed by a vicious right cross which sent Crowley reeling into the ropes. He was in serious trouble and before he could regroup another well timed right smashed against his chin sending him to the canvas for a count of 'nine'.

On rising Dave made his first real mistake of the contest by deciding to stand and fight Boon instead of using his skill and backing away from danger. There were not many men who could trade with the Chatteris lad and get away with it, and this was just what he wanted. Seeing an opening he crashed left and right hooks to Crowley's unprotected chin sending him heavily to the floor and almost out of the ring. Eyes glazed he listened to the count, but could do little about it. His head lolled weakly over the bottom rope as Mr Thomas reached 'ten'.

Before Dave could be carried to his corner the ring was invaded by about 50 supporters of Boon who had been driven almost crazy with excitement by his sudden and dramatic victory. There was pandemonium before Police could restore order and eject them. Then thunderous cheers echoed around the nostalgic arena as the glittering Lonsdale belt was strapped around the new champion's waist by Board of Control Chairman, Colonel Myddleton.

One person who was permitted to climb into the ring was Eric's mother. Although she travelled to London with the crowds from Chatteris it had been his express wish that she did not watch the fight. The original plan was that she would stay at Jack Solomons' house, but then it was decided it would be better for her to be with many others at the Devonshire Club. As the fight drew nearer, however, she insisted on being closer to the action so she was taken to Harringay where she sat in a waiting room.

As soon as the fight was over news of Eric's victory was conveyed to her at which point she rushed towards the ringside. Boon was proudly showing off the Lonsdale belt when he saw her among the crowd. Her visit had been kept secret from him, but he smiled and held the ropes apart for her to climb into the ring. Laughing and crying they hugged each other warmly and nobody could fail to see the pride in the little country lady's face.

A few minutes later there were unprecedented scenes outside Boon's dressing room as dozens of well wishers struggled to shake his hand. Once inside the new champion reached up and kissed a silver horseshoe which hung from the ceiling. On it was pinned a message: 'Good luck son from Mum and Dad.'

Whilst ecstatic over his victory, Eric was in great pain. His left eye completely closed and with a swelling the size of a plover's egg on his cheek, it throbbed and stung. His right hand was so swollen that Solomons had to cut the glove off with a pair of scissors.

Taking her eyes off her son for a moment, Eric's mother turned to the hoards of pressmen who had forced their way into the dressing room and said: "Thank you for all the encouragement you have given Sonny. I know it has helped him. I didn't come in to watch the fight, but when someone came and told me he had won I ran as hard as I could to see him. I couldn't wait any longer."

She had combined her trip with a shopping expedition which, as it turned out, was very fortunate. Whilst examining Eric's injuries one of his seconds remarked that a piece of raw steak would be good for his damaged eye. "I have some here," quipped his mother. After rummaging through her shopping bag she eventually produced a fine cut which was promptly laid across her son's cheek.

In his dressing room just along the corridor, Dave Crowley was in tears. "I can't believe it," he told a small group of reporters. "I won the first ten rounds. I've fought some of the greatest fighters and I get knocked out by a kid of eighteen. But I've got to admit it, I've never been hit so hard in my life."

For their pains Crowley, as champion, collected £1,300 while Boon added £500 to an already substantial bankroll with the prospect of plenty more to come.

There was to be no early night for the new champion because Jack Solomons had been so confident that he would beat Crowley that he had arranged for a party at the Devonshire Club afterwards. Press representatives and close friends of Boon were all invited to join members for what turned out to be a great occasion going on well into the early hours.

Not many people realised it at the time, but Boon had just become the youngest man to win a British title. When this was first announced there was some dispute because a number of critics believed that honour was held by Ted 'Kid' Lewis who, if records could be believed, was only seventeen when he beat Alec Lambert for the featherweight title in October 1913. Everything depended on whether Ted had disclosed his correct date of birth. This, however, was resolved when his biography, *Ted 'Kid' Lewis – His Life and Times,*' was published in 1990 and revealed his date of birth as 28 October 1893, thus confirming that he was almost twenty when he became champion.

Back in Chatteris, a huge crowd gathered outside the Police Station waiting to hear the result of the fight. Arrangements had been made to inform residents of the town and surrounding villages by launching rockets into the sky. Green ones would indicate that Boon had won, red ones that he had lost and in the unlikely event of a draw a white rocket would be sent up.

One of Eric's keenest fans, Police Inspector S P Bush, a resident of the town who had been to most of his fights, agreed to undertake the task. He had been unable to travel to Harringay because he was in charge of the night shift. So, from 9 pm that evening he sat inside the Police Station anxiously awaiting a call from London to say whether or not Chatteris had got its first professional boxing champion.

The crowd outside, which grew by the minute, became excited every time the telephone rang. When the result eventually came through they went mad with excitement. Flags were waved and people danced and cheered as the green rockets soared skywards. News spread rapidly through the town, and pub landlords did a roaring trade just before closing time as people topped up their glasses to toast their new champion.

*   *   *

Chatteris had no more colourful character than Eric Boon and his popularity was amazing considering his tender age. Yet much as he loved his home town he bided his time before returning. His damaged eye and badly bruised hand needed urgent medical treatment. The eye had been the greatest concern during the fight and many critics believed that only the prompt, albeit grotesque surgery, performed by Dick Gutteridge enabled him to continue and emerge victorious.

Dick's action, however, was not without its drawbacks because a fortnight later he was taken ill and rushed to the London Temperance Hospital where doctors diagnosed blood poisoning. Whether or not the complaint could be attributed to the Boon fight was a matter of conjecture, but the doctors certainly thought so. After recovering Dick vowed never to take such chances again.

Another reason for Boon delaying his return to Chatteris was because he wanted to spend some time with his girlfriend, Ollie Franks. They met soon after he moved to London and lived with Jack Solomons. Ollie was one of an American Vaudeville act, The Four Franks, who were very popular in the capital. She was only sixteen when they met, and years later Eric confessed that she was the first girl he fell for. "Ours was a real boy-meets-girl romance," he told a Sunday newspaper. "I was getting fifty bob a fight so it certainly wasn't my money she was after."

Ollie was well connected in London and introduced Boon to the fascinating and glamorous world of show business. He met and became friends with dozens of famous stage stars, but it was a bewildering and fast moving experience for a young country boy who had scarcely had time to get used to the goings-on in the big city. Ollie, however, was extremely confident in such circles and with him being a fighter she assumed he would be the same. Yet whenever she moved away from his side Eric often sat around feeling awkward and embarrassed, nervously sipping lemonade and wondering what to do with his hands and feet.

At first Jack Solomons was uncomfortable about the relationship and laid down a stringent set of ground rules. Training was always a priority, there was to be no drinking of alcohol and no late nights in the days leading up to a fight. Being a diligent trainer Eric generally conformed although once he found his feet on the social scene there were occasions when Solomons and Mike Milligan had to take him in hand.

Boon returned to Chatteris from London by train on 20 December, but not before acting as Santa Claus at a children's Christmas party at Hackney Wick. He was accompanied by Ollie Franks, Jack Solomons, Nat Seller and Mike Milligan and, waiting on the platform were his mother and father, grandmother and other members of his family. They were joined by Mr W E Seaton, JP, Chairman of Chatteris Urban District Council, Mr E M Keatinge, prospective Conservative candidate for the Isle of Ely and Inspector Bush the senior local police officer.

Long before his train was due a large crowd of local people gathered around the little grey station building to welcome the champion who had brought honour, not only to himself, but the town as a whole. Despite heavy snow falling everyone was in high spirits because nothing like this had ever occurred in Chatteris before. "Sports crazy, that's what we are," a station official told reporters.

The excitement increased dramatically when the 2.18 pm train finally came into sight, and the crowd surged forward as it pulled into the station. Boon's private compartment was easily recognisable by a large placard hanging in the window. The moment the train stopped a group of Police Officers moved forward to clear a passage so Eric's parents were able to greet him without interference.

Jack Solomons was the first to step from the train beaming broadly and smoking his customary cigar. He was followed by Nat Seller, Mike Milligan and Ollie Franks. Then after a short pause a huge cheer erupted as Boon, his right hand in plaster and still bearing facial scars of his battle with Crowley, jumped on to the platform where he was affectionately greeted by his parents, relatives and close friends. Tears of joy streamed down his mother's face as she kissed him firmly on the cheek and hugged him with pride.

After posing for photographs on the snow covered platform, the party were escorted across the railway line, through the dense crowds to a decorated coal lorry parked nearby. Women and girls pushed and hustled to kiss him, or even lay a loving hand on his arm or shoulder. Still not yet nineteen, the young fighter was a massive hit with the local ladies.

Once safely on board the lorry more photos were taken and then, led by the town band of which Eric was once a member, the party were driven slowly away from the station to the accompaniment of the tune 'See the conquering hero come.' Snow fell heavily as they made the short journey through narrow streets, decorated with flags and bunting, to the Empress Cinema in Park Street. Crowds that followed the procession were so great that it was as though the whole town had turned out.

The snow failed to dampen people's enthusiasm as Boon forced his way to the steps of the cinema where he was officially welcomed by the Chairman of Chatteris Urban District Council. There was a huge cheer when Mr Seaton said it was his privilege and duty on behalf of the people of Chatteris to welcome Eric home. Many people had known him since he was a very young boy, seen him progress in the ring as 'Boy' Boon, then later as 'Roy' Boon and now Eric Boon, lightweight champion of Great Britain.

"That wonderful punch of Eric's did not let him down," said Mr Seaton to more loud cheering, "and he has got to the position he occupies today through clean sportsmanship. Everyone is grateful to him because he has brought honour to the town to which he belongs."

Mr Seaton added that he wanted to pay special tribute to Arthur Binder who had trained Boon as a schoolboy during which time he won many trophies. "Hearty, hearty congratulations Eric," concluded Mr Seaton to more deafening cheers.

Mr E M Keatinge expressed his welcome and said that Eric had done more than anybody to put Chatteris on the map. He hoped he would continue to progress and keep it there for many years to come.

Alderman Leonard Childs said that he was very proud to endorse all that had been said. As President of the local boxing club he recalled presenting Eric with a trophy he had won in a local contest. Although at the time many people had thought he would go a long way, not many believed he would return to Chatteris at the age of eighteen as the lightweight champion of Great Britain.

In response to the speeches by the dignitaries, Jack Solomons thanked the crowd for their wonderful reception. He then called for three cheers for Fred Green, Boon's local agent, Nat Seller and

Mike Milligan, and an especially big one for Eric's parents. The crowd responded as only a close knit community could.

Next to step forward and take the microphone was Nat Seller who said that he had been a boxing trainer for 23 years. It gave him the greatest satisfaction to have trained a youngster of eighteen from a little town like Chatteris for a title.

Massive cheering then erupted as Boon casually stepped forward and faced the crowd which had continued to grow with every passing minute. Amplifiers relayed his simple but sincere speech to the frozen but undaunted crowd. Totally unspoiled by his success he said: "My job is to fight not talk, and I hope I fight a lot better than I talk. The next time I come home like this I hope it is as lightweight champion of the world."

The crowd loved that remark, but Boon hadn't finished. "I hope that whatever successes I achieve in the future I shall never forget my friends in the old home town," he continued.

Then to some amusement, and even a degree of disbelief, the young champion revealed that he had placed great belief in a mascot he had retained since he began his career. Originally a piece of wood nearly a foot long, he claimed he chewed it and chewed it until there were only a few inches left. At first people did not know what to believe. They looked at each other in amazement, some smiled, others just shrugged their shoulders, but then as Boon began to move from the cinema steps massive cheering and applause broke out again.

After a short reception with Council officials and other town dignitaries, Eric and his companions took a short walk through the falling snow to his home at Burnsfield Street. Streamers stretched from house to house, one bearing the single word 'Home' in bold lettering. At the front door a deputation of cheering children greeted him and he responded by presenting each with a Christmas stocking.

A celebration tea party and sing-song had been planned, but as the Boons' little terraced cottage was far too small to cater for the numbers invited, neighbours Florence and Herbert (Bertie) Barrett and their daughter Rita kindly offered to stage it at their detached house in nearby Station Street. Bertie had always been a strong supporter of Eric and went to many of his fights.

The event was extremely well organised with a maid in attendance to assist the hosts to keep proceedings moving. It lasted for almost two hours and guests included Arthur Binder, Fred and Mrs Green, Boon's mother, father, sister and grandfather, Jack Solomons, Sydney Hulls, Nat Seller and other members of the Devonshire Club team.

As soon as the party was over Eric went to a local barber's shop for a shave and haircut before getting ready for a dance and social in the town centre to celebrate his success. People cheered wildly when he arrived with members of his family. Smartly dressed in a grey suit he took to the dance floor with his mother and the music was instantly drowned by more cheering. The locals were to give him a night to remember.

9

CHAMPION IN DEMAND

Despite his intense training programme and the demanding fight with Crowley, there was little time for the new champion to put his feet up and relax. He was a young man in great demand, and the day after returning to Chatteris he was guest at an event at Peterborough where he was presented with a gold watch from admirers.

The next day he travelled to Liverpool where he presented prizes on behalf of Littlewoods Pools, and on 23 December was guest of honour at a plush event at the Devonshire Club where he was due to be officially presented with the Lonsdale belt. Unfortunately the belt was not available because, having been taken from him shortly after he received it in the ring, it was then sent to engravers who had been unable to complete the new inscription in time. Instead of receiving the newly engraved belt as planned Eric was presented with another gold watch by top jockey, Steve Donoghue, as a memento of his success.

During the evening Sydney Hulls announced that he was considering a return contest between Boon and Crowley. "I have had hundreds of letters from people asking me to stage another fight between them," he remarked. "There seems to be a difference of opinion as to who was leading on points when Crowley was knocked out."

Then, in what appeared to be a somewhat premature statement, Hulls said that Boon may get a shot at the world title. He proposed to make an offer to Henry Armstrong to travel to London in late February or early March to defend his title against the new British champion. Failing that he hoped to match Boon with Lou Ambers who lost the title to Armstrong in August.

Jack Solomons confirmed that Eric would be happy to face Crowley again. "Given the luck to fight with two sound eyes, he should win in quicker time," he said. "If not he will certainly prove his superior boxing ability." Jack added that there was one stipulation, that the Crowley camp must be prepared to strike a large side-bet on the result.

The following day, which was Christmas Eve, Eric was due back in Chatteris to give away his cousin, Miss Florrie May Stevenson, at her wedding to Grenadier Guardsman, Mr Oswald Bowers. Accompanied by Jack Solomons and Nat Seller he left London early in the morning, but heavy snow and poor road conditions delayed his arrival. He eventually reached the church as the photographs were about to be taken. After tendering his apologies he presented the bride with a cheque for £10 as a wedding present.

After winning the British title Boon was inundated with letters and telegrams of congratulation. The local postman often had to make a special trip to Burnsfield Street because he couldn't carry all the extra mail on his regular round. As it was not possible to answer all the letters individually, Eric's parents contacted the *Cambridgeshire Times* who agreed to print a message of appreciation.

As the new British champion, Boon did countless interviews for national and regional newspapers and magazines. He was in constant demand for guest appearances, and in early January 1939, was interviewed on the popular BBC radio programme 'Monday Night at Seven.' Listeners were impressed by his clear and natural voice, and when asked by the presenter, Brian Michie, what his greatest ambition was, he replied: "To make the Lonsdale belt my own property."

A few days later he was a guest at a boxing promotion at Wisbech Corn Exchange and was kept busy autographing programmes for admirers. At one point during the evening Eric was called into the ring by Master of Ceremonies, Alec Shuker, who told the packed house that he had attended the show as a mark of respect for the support given to him by local people when he fought Crowley. To thunderous applause and cheering, the MC said that he hoped the next time Eric was introduced from a Wisbech ring it would be as a world champion.

Another distinguished visitor to the show was Johnny Cuthbert who, in 1930, won a National Sporting Club Challenge Belt outright at featherweight. He and Boon spent a great deal of time together, and onlookers claimed that Johnny was giving Eric valuable advice for a forthcoming fight with Arthur Danahar.

On 15 January 1939, Eric was belatedly publically presented with the Lonsdale belt. It took place at the Prince of Wales Theatre in the west end of London at a charity concert in aid of the Metropolitan Hospital.

Two days later, he was called to give evidence at the Kings Bench Division of the High Court in London in a libel action brought by Cyril Wiseman and his father against Mirror Newspapers. The action was over the contents of an article in the *Daily Mirror* on 4 February 1938 headlined "So this is Boxing." It referred to the scandal of a boxer who was punch drunk, and the plaintiffs claimed it referred to Wiseman who boxed as a professional under the name Charlie Wise. The newspaper denied the words referred to the

Wisemans and pleaded that they were true and fair comment on a matter of public interest.

Mr J D Cassell, KC, Counsel for the Wisemans, told the court that between 1934 and 1936 Charlie won 26 and lost eight of his amateur contests. He won 12 cups and 12 medals. As a professional he had a good career and by 31 January 1938 had won 44 bouts including one in which he deputised for Eric Boon. He had lost 10 and drawn three. Counsel for the newspaper group suggested that Wiseman had an injury to the brain on the third cranial nerve, but it did not prevent him from getting into the Army.

Boon was called to give evidence on the second day of the action and stated that he boxed Wise twice, both at the Devonshire Club. In September 1936 he beat him on points over eight rounds and 12 months later stopped him in three. Eric claimed to have had 200 fights and lost only six which, if records are accurate, was an exaggeration. He confirmed that Charlie once deputised for him in a contest at the Devonshire.

"Was it a very good fight?" asked Mr Cassells.

"Very good for Wise, but not for the other fellow," replied Boon.

Mr Cassells: "I suppose the same could be said of the 194 of the 200 people you have fought?"

"There was nothing wrong about Charlie's style of fighting," said Boon. "By the time I met him in September 1937 I had knocked out quite a few opponents in the first round. Wise stood up to me for three rounds and gave me a lot of trouble, but the referee stopped the contest."

Mr Cassells said: "It has been suggested that Wise was so dazed that he was fighting in a corner of the ring where you were not."

"If he was doing that then I don't know what I was doing," replied Boon amid laughter.

In cross-examination Eric said that he landed a good blow on Wise in the first round, but it did not daze him for the rest of the fight. He denied that he, Boon, suggested to the referee that he should stop the contest.

Again, the account given by Boon was questionable and contradicted a report of the fight in the trade paper *"Boxing"* which said:

> Boy Boon (Chatteris), looking as fit as we have ever seen him, gave a tremendous display of punching to beat Charlie Wise (Poplar) in the third round of a bout set for eight (3 min) rounds. Walking straight in, Boon hit with such power as to have Wise badly staggered before the first was ended. Wise was punched all round the ring to be finally sent down for 'seven' in the second, and Boon on one occasion looked towards the referee as though appealing for him to stop things. Fortunately, matters were not allowed to go

far in the next, as after Wise had been dropped by a smashing right
to the chin, the closure was applied.

The hearing lasted four days at the end of which judgement was
given in favour of the plaintiffs, and Wise and his father were each
awarded £1,500.

*   *   *

Boon had also become involved in one of the strangest wagers in
boxing since the old Corinthian days. During early December 1938,
whilst he was preparing to meet Dave Crowley, film actor Bruce
Seton issued a challenge to him. The situation arose during a
discussion about boxing. At one point, the actor asked friends who
they thought was the most powerful puncher in England at the
time. One was convinced it was Boon, stating that there were no
more than half a dozen lightweights capable of lasting more than a
few rounds with him.

Bruce disagreed saying that in his opinion anyone could last three
minutes with a man of his own weight provided he went into the
ring with the sole intention of survival. His brother, Sir Alexander
Seton, allegedly leaned across the table and said: "What do you
mean by anybody? Do you mean that you or I could manage it, or
are you referring to professional boxers?"

Having learned to box at the Army Officers College at Sandhurst,
Bruce was certain he could manage it. To make things more
interesting he was prepared to bet his brother a new set of
bagpipes that he could last three minutes in the ring with Boon
provided his sole purpose was survival. The wager was accepted
and sealed in traditional fashion by driving into a table two Skean-
Dhus, daggers worn in Highlanders stockings.

Boxing writer, Terry Leigh-Lye was handling Bruce Seton's
publicity at the time and one day, whilst having a drink with
another journalist, casually mentioned the bet. The man promptly
rushed to a nearby telephone and within a couple of hours the west
end of London was plastered with newspaper posters which read:
"Actor – Peer's Amazing Boxing Bet."

Leigh-Lye promptly contacted Boon and Jack Solomons and
explained the situation. Jack loved it and hurriedly organised a
dinner at the fashionable Kempinski's restaurant in Mayfair which
was also attended by Seton and Sydney Hulls. Midway through the
meal cameramen from a number of national newspapers burst into
the restaurant to photograph Boon and Seton supposedly signing a
contract. Rumours spread that the one round contest would take
place at a London gymnasium early in 1939. It never did because

the whole thing was a massive publicity stunt which proved very beneficial to Bruce Seton. He and Boon became very close friends and remained so for years to come.

*   *   *

In the days immediately following Boon's victory over Crowley, challenges were made thick and fast. The first came from Johnny Sharpe on behalf of Jimmy Vaughan. Still anxious for a rubber match with the new champion was Johnny Softley who had given Crowley a hard fight and recently beaten Greek champion, Mitsos Grispos.

Another interested party was Jeff Dickson who, a few years earlier, had been the top promoter in London. He was living and promoting in Paris and, recognizing Boon as a massive attraction, contacted Jack Solomons with a view to featuring him on a show in the French capital.

Meanwhile, the National Sporting Club made an offer of £1,500 for Boon to face Arthur Danahar at Earls Court, and Arthur personally wrote to the Board of Control asking that they recognised his claims to a title fight. The National Sporting Club offer was quickly followed by one of £1,700 from a large Jewish charity organisation. Then a few days later Captain A Bell made an offer of £2,000 on behalf of The Ring, Blackfriars for Boon to face Danahar in London during the last week of January 1939.

All of this activity put immense pressure on Sydney Hulls who desperately wanted to stage what had rapidly become the most attractive pairing in British boxing. Quickly abandoning all thoughts of a return with Crowley, he called representatives of Boon and Danahar to a meeting at his office on 29 December. After three hours of hard discussion nothing was agreed so the meeting was adjourned until the following day.

Eventually, after more than six hours of tense, and often heated negotiation, it was finally agreed that the fight would take place at Harringay on 23 February. Application would be made to the Board of Control for the contest to be recognised as for Boon's title. Articles were drawn up and signed in the presence of the Marquess of Queensberry and everything ended in smiles. The meeting concluded with Boon and Danahar agreeing to a side-bet on the fight of £100 before shaking hands and wishing each other the best of luck.

Later that day Boon had a meeting with press reporters. Still bearing a trace of the eye injury received against Crowley, he said: "I am very glad of this opportunity to fight Danahar and I sincerely hope the Board will allow me to stake my title. I do not want to hide it in cotton wool because anyone who thinks he can take it from me should have the chance to do so."

Winning the British championship elevated Boon into the world rankings compiled by the National Boxing Association. The champion, Henry Armstrong, Lou Ambers and Pedro Montanez were the only men ahead of him. The fight with Danahar was even greater news and the *Cambridgeshire Times* duly ran a lengthy story about it under the bold headline 'Fight of the Century."

Despite all the excitement, things were far from settled and in early January 1939 the Stewards of the British Boxing Board of Control held a special meeting to discuss a number of objections to the fight. Arguments had been put forward by representatives of other leading contenders, in particular Ronnie James, Jimmy Vaughan and Jack Carrick.

In a letter to the Board, Johnny Sharpe, the manager of Vaughan, insisted yet again that his man should be considered as the leading contender. He pointed out that Danahar had yet to box more than eight rounds and had never entered the ring at 9st 9. Vaughan's backer was still prepared to put up a side-stake of any amount up to £500. Sharpe attended the meeting and strongly reiterated what he had said in the letter.

Harry Levene attended on behalf of Dave Crowley. He told the Stewards that whilst he did not in any way object to the contest between Boon and Danahar, the winner should defend against Crowley and not Ronnie James who had been installed as the leading contender.

Boon and Jack Solomons were called before the Stewards to discuss an outstanding contract to face former Welsh champion, Boyo Rees, at Mountain Ash on 30 January. It had been due to take place on Boxing Day, but was rescheduled due to the injuries Eric sustained against Crowley. Arrangements were originally made back in mid-November which some members of the press considered strange because only six months earlier Boon had flattened the Welshman in the opening round. Connections of Rees, however, insisted it was a lucky punch which beat their man and it was at their instigation the return was arranged.

Extremely concerned about the soundness of Eric's hands, Solomons and Hulls tried everything to get the Rees fight put off until he had faced Danahar. They offered the Mountain Ash promoter, Bert James, the father of Ronnie, a substantial sum to release Boon from his contract and also promised Rees a fight on the Harringay bill. Both were rejected and the promoter made a formal complaint to the Board of Control. After a lengthy discussion the Stewards ruled that Boon must complete the contract with Bert

James before appearing in any other contest. When told of the decision, Boon was unconcerned. "If that's how the cat jumps, Boyo Rees can have all that's coming to him," he remarked with predictable calmness.

A discussion then took place regarding the injuries Boon had sustained in the fight with Crowley. Eric agreed for his injured hand to be examined at regular intervals by Board of Control appointed medical officers, Dr Marlin and Mr Ivor Black. After considering all aspects and objections put before them, the Stewards sanctioned the contest between Boon and Danahar as being for Eric's British lightweight title. In announcing their decision they stipulated that the champion must defend the title against the winner of an eliminating series between the other four. Vaughan was matched with Carrick, the Northern champion, while James was ordered to meet Crowley. The two winners would then meet in a final eliminator to take place by 15 April. Boon and Danahar both agreed to waive the six months grace normally afforded to a champion.

The decision angered Johnny Sharpe. "What's the good of having Southern Area and Northern Area champions if they are overlooked when it comes to finding a challenger for a title," he told the press.

In reality his argument was a valid one because on lack of experience alone Danahar could never have been recognised as the leading contender. Yet Sharpe had been in the game long enough to know that money talks. Boon against any of the other contenders would never generate the interest and revenue a fight between him and Danahar would because it was by far the biggest attraction out there.

The immediate problem facing Hulls and Solomons was to ensure that Boon didn't aggravate his damaged hand. They would have liked more time to allow it to heal, but in view of the Stewards decision, this was not an option. Boon himself took a positive view by putting the situation out of his mind and concentrating on his training. Nothing seemed to worry him or knock him out of his stride. He just carried on without a care in the world.

Becoming British champion two weeks before his nineteenth birthday could have sent many a youngster off the rails. An urge to live it up and spend money lavishly would not have been unnatural, but this was not for Boon. His only present to himself was a brand new sporting shotgun.

When journalist Arthur Helliwell visited him at The George Hotel as he trained to fight Rees, the gun had just been delivered. Fresh from its wrapping it stood gleaming like a trophy in the corner of the gym. Eric's eyes continuously strayed towards it as they stood talking, and he was itching to get his hands on it. "It's a smasher isn't it?" he remarked proudly with boyish enthusiasm.

114

"How does it feel to be champion?" asked the journalist.

"Oh, I don't know," replied Boon nonchalantly as he prodded away at a swinging punch bag. "I don't think about it that much."

It was a typical Boon response because the limelight held no attraction for him. Everything had happened so quickly, but back in Chatteris he remained the young man who grew up there. 'Our Eric' or 'Sonny' as the locals called him, was just happy with his new gun.

Boon travelled to Cardiff the day before the fight with Rees accompanied by Jack Solomons, Sydney Hulls and a contingent of Eastenders, mostly from the Devonshire Club. Although the boxer was extremely confident, Solomons had concerns about his right hand which was still prone to swelling. He and Hulls both knew that any further damage would mean another delay in staging the bout with Danahar.

Despite Boon holding a one round victory over Rees, the Welshman had to be taken seriously. He was a vastly experienced man who first won the Welsh title in 1935 with a 15 rounds points decision over Nobby Baker, lost it to George Reynolds in his second defence in 1935, but regained it with another 15 rounds success in April 1938. He later relinquished it.

According to William E. Allen, Boxing Editor of the *South Wales Echo,* Boyo was in his best shape since he was Welsh champion. He was hitting with tremendous power and critics expected him to give Boon plenty of trouble. He was determined not to suffer the indignation of being knocked out early again. Rees, however, was not without his problems because only a few weeks earlier fire had completely destroyed his house and all the contents. The contest was therefore the most important of his career. It was a huge attraction in South Wales and many reporters and photographers were present at the lunchtime weigh-in at Cardiff. Looking extremely fit and confident both men were inside the stipulated weight of 9st 12.

"I have trained hard for this fight and think I can put up a good show against Boon," Rees told the *South Wales Echo.* "This contest means a lot to me for I am fighting for my wife and home. If I lose it will not be for the want of trying. All I ask for is that all my friends turn up at Mountain Ash to give me a lift out of this fresh disaster."

Boon had little to say other than express his confidence. "I did it before and I can do it again," he remarked dourly before leaving the venue with his entourage.

Before the fight rumours were rife that extra padding was to be used to protect Boon's suspect right hand. To ensure that the rules were strictly adhered to, Norman Rees, the brother of Boyo, carefully observed the taping of Eric's hands in the dressing room. As no particular precautions were taken it was an indication that the British champion had no problems.

Things didn't go well for Rees in what the *South Wales Echo* described as a fiasco. From the opening bell Boon tore into him and floored him five times for long counts in the first round. Forced to defend desperately the man from Abercwmboi was cautioned for holding within 30 seconds. He could not hold off the determined attacks of the Chatteris champion and was still on the floor when the bell sounded to save him from another humiliating knockout.

Overmatched and outpunched, Rees showed great courage in round two keeping Boon at bay with good left leads. The punishment he took in the first round, however, soon took its toll. Punching with all his power, Eric drove a hard left to the temple which dazed the Welshman and before he could recover a vicious right to the jaw sent him crashing to the canvas. Although he pluckily scrambled to his feet at 'nine' referee, Mr C B Thomas, stepped in as Boyo was in no condition to defend himself.

"Yes, Boon is some puncher," said Rees afterwards. "He's the hardest hitter I've met, and I've met a few."

The outcome of the fight was sheer relief for Jack Solomons and Sydney Hulls especially as the first three knock downs Boon scored were all with his right hand. Each connected flush on the chin as did the one which finished the contest. When his gloves were removed there was no sign of bruising or swelling meaning that preparations for the Danahar fight could proceed without delay.

*   *   *

Back in London news of Eric's victory reached the National Sporting Club. When an announcement was made there were huge cheers from relieved patrons, many of whom thought he was taking an unnecessary risk so close to the Danahar fight. Despite the intense activity in his life, Boon took it all in his stride. He fulfilled most engagements offered to him and even did the occasional exhibition. The injuries to his eye and hand sustained during the Crowley fight healed well, and within a few days of beating Rees he returned to Ely with Nat Seller to commence preparations for his title defence against Danahar.

Angus McGregor was again engaged as his main sparring partner and was joined by Arthur Elmore (Kettering), brothers George and Pat Howard from Finsbury Park, and Harry 'Kid' Silver who, apart from being used for speed, was the champion's constant companion.

116

Strong and durable, McGregor did the bulk of the ring work. He made Eric work, helped him to considerably tighten his defence and altogether made him alive to his faults. There was great mutual respect between the two and Jack Solomons described Angus as "the ideal sparring partner."

Danahar, meanwhile, set up his training camp at Brighton under the guidance of Arthur Goodwin, a vastly experienced man who, the previous year, had trained Peter Kane for his fight against Jackie Jurich to win the world flyweight title. His sparring partners were Tommy Hyams (Kings Cross), Mac Perez, who had fought Boon three months earlier, Lefty Flynn, Jack Carrick and Jerry Costello. He was also accompanied by his brothers Albert and Alf. Knowing what he was up against in Boon, Arthur worked extremely hard and gave them all a difficult time. Their only respite was when he decided to go fishing.

In what was clearly a promotional gimmick, Boon and Danahar both appeared at Earls Court on 6 February and boxed in exhibition bouts. Boon did three rounds with Silver and Danahar did likewise with Lefty Flynn. Eric's powerful physique stood out in contrast to the lanky figure of Danahar who looked tense and nervous. Eric also caught the eye with his speed and high spirits although both were careful not to give anything away.

As the training progressed Boon's camp was packed every day with onlookers, and once his preparations reached their peak regulars were convinced he was punching harder than ever. On 14 February Jack Solomons and Sydney Hulls accompanied a group of about 20 journalists to Ely to watch the champion in a complete workout. They were not disappointed because it was hard and entertaining.

Angus McGregor was first to work with Boon and stood up to him well. Then to demonstrate that he could take a good shot, Eric dropped his guard and allowed the Scot to hit him as he pleased. Angus, however, was not prepared for the rapid left hook which shot out at the end of it all.

A round of light sparring with middleweight George Howard followed, but there was nothing light about the next session when his brother Pat climbed into the ring. Boon chased him throughout the three minutes and landed many of his vicious body shots. Light punches to the head shook Howard despite him wearing a head guard.

In the final session with Arthur Elmore, Boon really got warmed up, and a terrific right uppercut had his spar-mate completely bemused. After allowing him a few seconds to recover, Eric then hammered him to the ropes and opened up until Nat Seller shouted "stop" to save Arthur from getting badly hurt. There was a real buzz amongst the spectators as Boon left the ring and started his exercises. Skipping, punchbag work, ball-punching and shadow boxing formed the rest of the champion's afternoon routine.

Having learned well from his manager, Eric knew how to put on a show and the press boys loved it. Once his training was over they jostled for position and threw questions at him about the fight ahead. Confidently predicting he would win by a knockout within six rounds, Boon justified his prediction by stating that Boyo Rees had gone the distance with Danahar and some observers considered he was unlucky not to have got the decision. "Jim Cameron put Danahar down for 'nine' before getting knocked out," said Eric who then described how Jimmy Walsh had easily beaten Cameron.

"On form I should easily beat Danahar," he continued, "because as you know he has not been more than eight rounds."

Despite the confident mood within the camp it had not been all plain sailing. After the Crowley fight Eric's weight had shot up to 10st 5 and Nat Seller's job was to get him down to 9st 9. Apart from that there were also concerns that his damaged right hand may not have healed as well as at first thought. Solomons sensed there was a niggle during the press workout so he returned to Ely the following day. On looking at the hand he said: "It's no good Eric, we'll have to call the fight off."

"Put off nothing," snapped Boon. "I'm expected to fight Danahar and it's got to be done."

"Alright," said Jack, "have it your own way," but at that point he immediately cleared all the sparring partners out of the gym with the exception of Harry Silver. For the last week or so all Boon did was skipping, shadow-boxing and floor exercises. Whenever outsiders asked how the hand was he replied: "Fine."

Eric's relaxation at the camp usually took the form of shooting rabbits on local farms, cycling, playing darts, billiards and his musical instruments. This time, however, horse riding was strictly banned because Solomons and Seller were not prepared to allow him to take unnecessary risks ahead of such a massive engagement.

Occasional trips away from the camp also provided light relief. At one stage, with preparations well on course, Seller gave Eric a day off after he and Silver received an invitation to visit Isleworth Film Studios. There they were greeted by McLean Rogers who was directing a British film entitled 'It's No Use Crying'. They were given the red carpet treatment, being shown around the sets, introduced to members of the cast and given inside information about the film business. There was even talk that Boon could star in a movie about boxing which could be specially written for him if he beat Danahar. Before leaving he and Silver delighted their hosts by giving an exhibition and showing off their boxing skills.

Eric and his pal also visited a Jewish orphanage at West Norwood one Sunday afternoon in early February. The children made a tremendous fuss of them and both worked extremely hard signing autographs. Eric adored children and got real pleasure from playing with them. He had visited many hospitals, taking patients small gifts and generally trying to spread a little happiness. At Norwood he spoke to every child individually and was reluctant to leave.

*   *   *

Hopes of a fight between Boon and Danahar had been discussed for many months in newspapers and periodicals, and as the day of reckoning approached there was talk of little else in Chatteris and the east end of London. Although it meant very little outside the United Kingdom, it was such a tremendous attraction that sports writers ran out of adjectives and superlatives. The situation was incredible considering Boon, the champion, had just turned nineteen and his challenger was only a year older.

Despite their incredible popularity and ability, the two lads were dissimilar in almost every way. Boon was short, chunky and extremely muscular, an aggressive counter-punching country boy with devastating power in both hands. The son of a blacksmith, he had learned his trade in the small halls of the East End and around the Eastern Counties.

Danahar, who was London born and bred, came from a big fighting family. His grandfather and great grandfather were both bare-knuckle fighters, his father, Albert, and two uncles, Tom and Dave were also fighters, Dave having taken part in the last bare-knuckle fight at the National Sporting Club. Arthur also had five brothers all of whom had boxed.

The Bethnal Green youngster started boxing at a very young age and having reached the finals of schoolboy and London Federation of Boys Club championships, he graduated to senior amateur level. It was there that he really came to notice by winning the 1937 ABA lightweight title. He turned professional under the wing of the gentlemanly John Harding and the rich supporters of the National Sporting Club and boxed almost exclusively on their promotions at the Empress Hall, Earls Court.

Tall and slim, Danahar was an upright, textbook boxer, but lacked the power of Boon. With only 14 paid contests behind him, he was far less experienced than the champion whose total was approaching 100. A high percentage of Eric's victories had come inside the distance.

119

Enormous stamina, dogged courage in the face of adversity and a stubborn never-say-die attitude which invariably resulted in him scoring a knockout or stoppage, had made Boon the greatest box-office attraction Britain had seen in the lower ranks for years. Yet it was only after he so dramatically disposed of Dave Crowley that Jack Solomons was in a position to command the larger percentage of any purse with Danahar. Only 12 months earlier he was pleased to get a payday of £80.

As the day of the fight drew nearer fans in London were divided over who they supported. Coming from Bethnal Green should have given Danahar a clear edge, but Eric had built up a massive fan base in the capital as a result of his many thrilling performances at the Devonshire Club.

Despite the interest the contest had generated, a number of critics felt that Danahar was too inexperienced and had not beaten enough top-class men to warrant meeting Boon for the title. Having never boxed beyond eight rounds there were doubts about his stamina over the gruelling championship course of 15 rounds with a man as strong and rough as Boon. Such theories just added to the intrigue.

The way the contest had captured public imagination was eloquently summed up by veteran columnist, Trevor Wignall, the most widely read of British sports writers. On the morning of the fight, in his column in the *Daily Express,* he said:

> It is more than 40 years since I first walked into a booth to watch men raise their gloved fists. I have travelled and seen much since then. I have looked on champions as they rose to the heights, and as they fell. Isn't it odd that I think of tonight's contest between Eric Boon and Arthur Danahar as one of the most remarkable in my experience. It is remarkable because the couple are still almost of schoolboy age. They are not yet celebrated outside this country yet they have caused more talk, created more discussion and been the means of selling more tickets than any other lads of their poundage in the whole history of British boxing.

Many other fine stories were written before and after the fight because the rivalry of the two young men had captured public imagination to an equal extent. Those stories demonstrated the sheer magnitude of the event and how it had captured such a massive audience.

10

BATTLE OF THE CENTURY

Securing the Boon-Danahar fight was a massive success for Sydney Hulls who, when officially announcing it, stated that the purse would be the largest ever paid to lightweights. In order to cater for every level of fan he fixed a wide range of ticket prices at seven levels from six shillings up to five guineas. As soon as it was announced that the fight would take place at Harringay there was a huge demand. The cheaper ones sold out within days and after less than two weeks only those priced at five guineas remained.

In Cambridgeshire twice as many tickets were sold than for the Crowley fight and more would have gone had they been available. They couldn't be printed fast enough. Eventually the five guinea ones were in such demand that some changed hands at least three times before finally fetching up to £20 each. The day before the fight a count at the promoter's office revealed that just 27 tickets were left so it was decided that 'full house' notices were displayed before the doors opened.

Not for years had a fight generated so much argument and debate, and it was estimated that at least £30,000 had been wagered on the outcome. National Sporting Club members alone were said to have laid as much as £5,000 in bets on their protégé. Jack Solomons told John Thompson of the *Daily Mirror* that he knew of two bets each of £1,000 being laid at evens. Much of the overall situation arose because of the outcry created by the proposed private fight several months earlier. The more that was disclosed, the clearer it became that Hulls had been the brains behind the scheme, with Solomons and John Harding party to it. They were without doubt three of the shrewdest showmen in the business.

During the afternoon of the fight hundreds of Boon's supporters from Wisbech, Ely, March and Chatteris travelled to London aboard special excursion trains. One even had a placard attached to the front of the engine with the message 'Good Luck Boon' in large lettering. Many others made the journey by road.

Chatteris was abuzz with excitement. As Sydney Hulls had eventually reached agreement with the BBC for the fight to be broadcast live from Harringay on London and some regional wavelengths, most people planned to be near a wireless set as fight time approached. A few days earlier the promoter had refused to allow it because he regarded the corporation's offer of 75 guineas as ridiculous.

Every effort was made to help local people on what was considered one of the biggest nights in the town's history. Farm labourers were allowed to finish work early and most pubs in the town were full by mid-evening. Police were asked to install a television set at their local station, but this was rejected on the grounds that local interest might interfere with officers work. Instead a set was displayed in the window of Messrs J W Munns and Sons shop at West Park Street by Cambridge & District Radio, representatives for Ekco Wireless.

Boon wound up his training at Ely on the eve of the fight and then gave a lengthy interview to a reporter from the *London Evening News* who asked him what he thought about fame and how it affected his life. "Of course I think it is a good thing to be a great champion," he replied, "but I can honestly say it hasn't made any difference to my life yet. I mean it hasn't made any difference to my way of living. It can't with a boxer."

It was hard to believe that Eric only turned nineteen less than two months earlier. On the eve of the most important fight of his life he was totally relaxed as he gave a mature and educated account of the dedication required in his sport, the fitness levels that had to be reached and maintained, and the loneliness that sometimes crept in. "A boxer's life is like no other," he remarked. "He does only a little bit of work in the ring itself. His gymnasium is his office and that is where he does his real work to keep fit all the time. That means his life is always disciplined."

"Because a boxer's life is short," he continued, "he has to make his pile of money in a few years. I have my own clear plans and know exactly what I want to do with the money I earn and how to live the rest of my life after the retirement age."

Boon made it clear that he was happy in the gym and ring, and because he liked the actual work, fame as such didn't bother him. "My life is simple really," he added. They were the words of a lad with a clear vision, who had obviously given a great deal of thought to his future. Not those of a youngster who left school at the age of fourteen with no qualifications or a trade to turn to. Boxing had rescued him from becoming a tearaway or possibly worse.

During the course of the interview, which was published on the day of his fight with Danahar, there was a knock on the door of his gym at Ely. It was a postman with the afternoon delivery of mail. There were several letters for Eric and as he opened them a broad smile of delight lit up his face. "Look at that," he exclaimed, "A letter from Alex Henshaw. We've never met, but he's written to wish me luck and say how sorry he is that he cannot get to the fight. Now that does mean something to me. That really is one of the nice things fame brings to a champion."

Born at Peterborough in 1912, Henshaw was a celebrated pilot whose achievements were frequently headline news. In 1937 he won the inaugural London to Isle of Man air race in atrocious weather, and the following year at the age of twenty-five, won the Kings Cup setting an average speed of 236 mph, a record that still stands.

Henshaw was a real hero to Boon, and whilst training for the Danahar fight he read every report he could lay his hands on about the pilot's record-breaking solo flight from England to South Africa and back which commenced on 5 February. Later in the interview he referred to the letter again, revealing just how much it meant to him. "It's grand to get letters like the one from Alex Henshaw," he remarked. "It's satisfying to me to know I have got somewhere, made a position for myself and put myself in the way of living the sort of life I always hoped to be able to live."

*   *   *

Full of youthful enthusiasm, Boon had wanted to drive to London for the fight, but Solomons was having none of it. He regarded it as too much of a risk so, late on the afternoon before the fight, they travelled by train from Ely to Liverpool Street where a large crowd of fans had gathered to greet them. Eric spent the night at Solomons' house at Clapton where they sat up until gone midnight talking and playing cards. After eventually retiring to bed Boon was allowed to sleep through until mid-morning.

By that time Danahar was strolling along the Brighton seafront with his father, trainer and sparring partners to loosen up before travelling to London for the weigh-in. He had become extremely popular in the south coast town and chatting to a local reporter who joined them said: "I'm feeling fine. It's going to be a splendid fight I'm sure and believe me I am going to win."

Nat Seller arrived at Jack Solomons' house at 6 am. Jack was already up and dressed while Boon slumbered peacefully. They woke him at about 10 o'clock and after a light breakfast went for a brisk walk. Arriving back at Solomons' house they were greeted by groups of friends and well-wishers. Telegrams poured in at the rate of about a dozen a minute from all over the country wishing Eric success.

Mike Milligan and Solomons' brother, Maxie, had also arrived and everyone was amazed at Boon's composure. "I can recall him sitting in the parlour listening to the wireless without a care in the world," Seller recalled years later. "After letting him have a musical half-hour we sat and listened to Jack's analysis of the forthcoming fight."

The weigh-in took place at the Board of Control offices at Dean Street, Soho, at 2 pm. The street outside was crowded with fans clamouring to get a close-up view of the two fighters. Inside it was just as chaotic with rooms crammed to capacity with officials, reporters and photographers.

ERIC BOON		ARTHUR DANAHAR
19.	AGE	20.
5ft 4in.	HEIGHT	5ft 8in.
9st 9lb.	WEIGHT	9st 9lb.
15in.	NECK	15½in.
66in.	REACH	71in.
36in.	CHEST (NORMAL)	35in.
39in.	CHEST (EXPANDED)	37½in.
28in.	WAIST	28½in.
14in.	BICEPS	13in.
11½in.	FOREARM	11in.
20½in.	THIGH	18½in.
14½in.	CALF	13½in.
10in.	ANKLE	8½in.
7in.	WRIST	7in.

Looking fit and confident both men were inside the championship limit, Boon scaling 9st 8 ½ and his challenger a quarter of a pound lighter. After posing for photographs they sportingly shook hands and wished each other luck before going their separate ways to while away the final hours before battle. In the street outside there were very contrasting scenes as the crowds surged around Boon when he left the Board offices. Very few appeared to notice Danahar. Meanwhile tense excitement prevailed inside and outside the Board offices as unofficial discussions took place between fringe groups over who would win.

Solomons, Boon and the rest of their party went to a nearby restaurant for lunch after which they returned to Jack's house where there was plenty of company. The streams of telegrams and good wishes continued to pour in and the telephone rang every few seconds. Throughout all of it Mrs Solomons was kept busy making tea for visitors while the boys played cards until it was time to leave for the fight with Solomons' plan of campaign firmly in mind.

From early evening the scenes around Harringay were astounding. The streets were jammed solid as thousands of fans queued to get into the arena while others streamed out of cars and charabancs which had travelled from Cambridgeshire bringing hundreds of Boon's admirers from Chatteris and surrounding villages. Ticket holders had to force their way through hundreds of disappointed fans to get inside.

Both boxers arrived early and relaxed in their dressing rooms while others around them became tense and edgy. Danahar was a cool as a cucumber as he chatted to the Marquess of Queensberry who was there to give the National Sporting Club protégé support and encouragement. "The worst thing that can happen my lord is that I lose the verdict," he remarked, "but I am sure of one thing, that win or lose, Eric and I will give the customers a fight they will remember."

Along the corridor Boon was his usual calm self as he sat playing his mouth organ, and even had a game of darts before his hands were taped. He didn't care who he was going in against and earlier, when asked by a reporter if he would like to fight Henry Armstrong, replied: "I'll fight Joe Louis if the money is good."

Harringay Arena was packed to the rafters as trumpets heralded the boxers to the ring. Powerful spotlights picked them out as they slowly made the long walk to the ring through the aisles of cheering fans. Glamorous women sat in ringside seats alongside their dinner-jacketed escorts, the aroma of cigar smoke filled the air. This was the big fight scene of the late 1930's and they didn't come much bigger than this one.

Danahar was first to make his entrance followed by his retinue of attendants including his father and brother, seconds Arthur Goodwin, Sam Burns and George Carney. John Harding was in close pursuit. There was no trace of nerves as he climbed through the ropes to a rousing reception and shouts of "Good Luck Arthur."

It was all of three minutes before Boon appeared followed closely by Nat Seller, Mike Milligan, Jack and Maxie Solomons, Jack and Dick Gutteridge. His reception was no less generous, and in true sporting fashion he walked straight across the ring and shook Danahar firmly by the hand. Then, amid deafening cheering, referee W Barrington Dalby, called them to the centre of the ring, uttered the briefest of final instructions before sending them back to their corners to await the opening bell.

The atmosphere was electric as they came out for the first round and Boon wasted no time forcing the challenger to the ropes where he smashed two left hooks to the jaw. It was typical Boon aggression and left Danahar in no doubt what to expect. Using his height and reach advantages to the full, Arthur soon found his range with a stream of accurate left jabs to the face to which the champion had no defence. When Eric landed a good right to the chin Danahar forced him back with more jabs. It was a fine opening by both men, raw aggression against boxing skill, and the crowd roared their approval at the bell.

Although Boon forced the pace, the challenger continued his boxing lesson in round two. Stinging left jabs halted the Chatteris man each time he charged forward and a sharp right brought up a swelling beneath his left eye. Arthur was beginning to really fancy it and even opened up with both hands on one occasion as Boon advanced. It was another good round for the Bethnal Green man.

There was more of the same in the third as Danahar continued to box with delightful skill and accuracy. Whenever Boon unleashed his big shots Arthur cleverly backed away from danger although at one point he was staggered by a vicious left hook. He took it well, but when forced to hold on he was cautioned by the referee. Apart from being outboxed, Eric sustained an injury to his right hand when a wild punch caught his opponent high on the head.

Boon was always looking to land big single shots to head or body, but by using the ring well Danahar continued piling up the points in the fourth. When he slipped to the canvas during mid-round Eric sportingly held out a glove to help him up, but in his excitement Arthur ignored it and caught the champion off guard with a solid right to the chin. Amid loud booing from his army of fans, Boon smirked and went for him like a tiger, but Danahar hit back. They stood toe-to-toe in the centre of the ring exchanging solid punches with incredible fury and by the end of the round Boon's left eye was badly marked and swelling rapidly. During the interval the referee went to the corner and took a cursory look at it, but was waved away by the seconds.

Although many of Eric's fans were becoming slightly concerned they knew he had been in a similar situation against Crowley, but still battled on to victory. Jack Solomons always maintained that Danahar would tire because he had never gone beyond eight rounds. "Son, it's going to be tough for you at the start," he told Eric in the dressing room before the fight. "You will be taking a lot of punches and they will hurt, but if you hang on in there for eight rounds he will tire and then you can get that wallop of yours working."

During the interval after the fourth round Arthur Goodwin angrily admonished his fighter for disobeying strict orders to box. Meanwhile, the Marquess of Queensberry asked John Harding how he thought the fight was going. "If Danahar will only stand away and box instead of fighting, he is going to win," he said with some apprehension, "but if he continues to mix it Boon will knock him out."

Eric was quickly off his stool for the fifth as though intent on ending the fight. He attacked with venom, but again Danahar's immense skill nullified the power. He controlled matters with his jab and also landed a number of right crosses causing further damage to Boon's left eye. The fight had settled into a pattern of boxer against fighter and at this stage the boxer was very much in control.

As round six commenced Boon again shot out with both fists flying, but Arthur made him miss badly. He even went after the champion and at one point it looked as though Eric was tiring. Boon, however, showed that he also possessed skill as he cleverly avoided the challenger's attack and smashed a terrific left to the chin. Danahar was hurt, but used his skill to avoid further trouble.

Determined to grind his challenger down, Boon began round seven throwing big punches from all angles. The occasional shot did find its target, but in making openings Eric had to take the stinging rapier-like jabs Danahar continued to pump out with great accuracy. It was doubtful whether the champion had won a round by this stage. With his left eye now completely closed and blood dripping from his nose it looked like Danahar's fight.

There was massive betting at the ringside and although the odds varied, many were still being struck at evens. Despite being a long way behind, people knew Boon could still turn it around with a single punch. John Harding knew this too and during the interval following the seventh pleaded with Danahar to stop mixing it. "Use your jab," he implored, "you've won every round so far. Just stick to what you do best."

Throughout the build-up to the fight Jack Solomons had constantly reminded Boon that Arthur had never gone beyond eight rounds. In the opposite corner he urged his battered fighter to increase the pressure and take control. "Remember, eight rounds, he's already beginning to tire," he whispered. It was like a gramophone record playing over and over again. Despite the punches he was taking, Eric's response was always the same: "It's alright guv'nor, I'll catch him in a minute." Boon never doubted that and the thought of losing never entered his mind.

With his manager's instructions still ringing in his ears, he stormed from his corner at the bell for round eight. He met Danahar head-to-head and banged home some terrific punches with both hands. His combinations were vicious and accurate, left-right-left, they all sapped the challenger's stamina.

Arthur tried desperately to use the ring, but Boon stayed with him. It was his turn now, and halfway through the round he took control of the fight for the first time. A savage right over Danahar's almost rigid left jab landed flush on the chin. It staggered him and as he tried to grab, Boon shoved him away and another right crashed against the chin sending Arthur heavily to the floor in a heap. He rose at 'nine', tried to hold, but Eric shouldered him away and went for the kill. He swung the trusty right and knocked the challenger flat on his back.

Again he gamely rose at 'nine', hung on desperately only to be forced back by the referee. There was to be no let up. Boon strode forward and four consecutive swings rattled against Arthur's unprotected chin. He was badly shaken and it seemed that the fight was over. Amazingly, Danahar tried to hit back and held on until the bell which almost certainly saved him from defeat. It had been the worst round of his so far unblemished professional career. Had the fight been over eight rounds his arm would have been raised as the winner, yet all of his good work had been torn apart in a matter of seconds. He was in terrible trouble because there were still seven rounds to go.

Having tottered to his corner, and slumped on to his stool Arthur got a real ear-bashing from Harding who again implored him to box instead of mixing it. "I'm tired Mr Harding," he muttered. "My legs don't want to go on so I'm going to try and knock him out." It was not the most sensible response to make to an animated cornerman.

The crowd were in a frenzy as the bell sounded for round nine. Sensing victory, Boon attacked furiously, and although he could only see out of one eye, he rocked Danahar with two vicious lefts to the jaw. Still feeling the effects of the hammering he received in the previous round, Arthur clinched and mauled at every opportunity much to the displeasure of the referee who again sternly lectured him.

Despite looking hurt and confused the challenger was far from finished and fought back gamely. As Boon became over-anxious and somewhat careless in his attempts to finish it, Arthur caught him with a beautiful short right to the chin. Although he wasn't badly hurt Eric sagged to a sitting position on the bottom rope and then started to rise at the count of 'four'. Excited by his success, Danahar struck Boon with another punch while his knee was still on the canvas. The crowd booed their disapproval and the champion's handlers screamed protests from the corner. Being the sportsman he was, Eric made no attempt to milk the situation and just smirked before going after his opponent with bad intentions. Fancying his chances even more, Danahar faced up to him and went toe-to-toe until the bell when Mr Dalby followed him to his corner and severely admonished him over the illegal blow.

The 10th was another competitive round in which Danahar seemed to have a new lease of life. After Boon landed a powerful uppercut, the Bethnal Green man again ignored the advice of his corner and waded in throwing right hooks. It was real street-fighting stuff with neither prepared to give an inch as they traded blows at a rapid pace. Suddenly two tremendous punches from Boon crashed against Danahar's chin and had him groggy, but still he hit back. He forced the champion to the ropes with a series of jabs and just before the end of the round landed three solid rights on Eric's already closed left eye. There was pandemonium in the crowd as the seemingly beaten challenger was back in the fight. As Boon returned to his corner with blood dripping from his nose and mouth he knew that the fight was far from over.

The crowd were divided as to who was ahead at this stage. There were concerns in the minds of the handlers in both corners because they knew it could still go either way. Could Boon's eye hold out? Would the referee stop the fight and if so in whose favour? Boon had the power, Arthur had the skill, but who was the stronger? It was still there to be won and lost, and the tension was incredible.

Both men looked weary as they came out for round 11, but Boon looked the more determined. He went straight into the attack catching Danahar with heavy swings to the jaw. Only the challenger's beautiful boxing kept him in the fight. Eric was still looking for the big shots and in the dying seconds of the round let go a familiar combination. A wicked left hook beneath the ribs brought Arthur's guard down leaving an opening for left and right hooks to the chin. Danahar sank to the floor, but with the count at 'two' the bell saved him. Slumped on his stool he was given an illegal dose of brandy to try and liven him up. He didn't know where he was as his seconds worked feverishly to clear his head.

Boon was not without his problems and his left eye was a terrible mess as they commenced the 12th. Peering through the right he pounded Danahar with everything he had because he was well aware that the referee could call a halt at any moment. Although he still hit back, Arthur was very weak and Boon knew it. A left-right combination sent the challenger crashing to the floor. Glassy eyed and breathing heavily, he dragged himself up at 'nine' only to face another vicious onslaught. He was determined not to quit, but another accurate right hook bludgeoned him to the floor again. Showing the most incredible gameness the Bethnal Green man clambered to his feet as Mr Dalby tolled 'nine', and staggering and swaying along the ropes, his great fighting heart kept him upright until the bell.

Arthur was completely sold out and nobody would have blamed him if he had quit at that stage. Yet bravery and family honour made him rise from his stool and go out for the 13th. For a few moments he valiantly attempted to box the champion off. He landed a sharp right to Boon's closed eye, poked out a few left jabs, but there was no longer any power behind them. Eric, however, was still strong and grimly determined to bring matters to a close. As he left his corner at the bell Solomons had reminded him that it was in this round that he stopped Crowley to win the championship two months earlier. Although he couldn't quite repeat that feat he did succeed in pounding Danahar to the canvas for three counts of 'nine' as a result of fierce two-fisted attacks.

Danahar's courage was immense, probably as great as any man who has ever set foot inside the ring. Yet it was painful to watch. He had done everything asked of him, gone well beyond the call of duty and nobody wanted to see him badly hurt. He was weakening rapidly and whenever he tried to clinch Boon shoved him off with ease and continued the pounding. The audience were stunned by his display of raw courage and many were screaming for the referee to stop it. Their pleas fell on deaf ears.

After Danahar rose from the third knock-down, Boon waded in and fired a mighty two-fisted barrage of punches. Some landed, others missed as the challenger reeled again the ropes desperately trying to protect himself. Again the bell came to his rescue whereupon Boon, out of sheer respect and admiration for his opponent, stepped forward and patted his face with his gloves before returning to his corner.

As Arthur turned unsteadily towards his corner there were more calls for the contest to be stopped. There were others, however, who believed that if he could fiddle his way through the last couple of rounds he might still nick the decision. His handlers thought so as well and there was no question of them pulling him out.

In the opposite corner Jack Solomons read the situation in exactly the same way and implored Boon to go out and finish it. "Close the show," he yelled as Eric stood up from his stool to await the bell.

Visibly weak on his legs Danahar bravely went out for the 14th, but Boon tore into him throwing punches from all angles. It was sheer brute force. A vicious right slammed against Arthur's chin sending him careering into the ropes and on to the floor where he laid in a helpless heap. As if by instinct he dragged himself to his feet yet again as the count reached 'nine'. It was like an action replay of what had occurred so many times before.

Glassy-eyed with mouth agape, he stood swaying defensively against the ropes, arms hanging limply at his sides. As the aggressive Boon hovered waiting to move in and finish it, referee Barrington Dalby finally stepped between them and signalled it was all over. It was a merciful, albeit belated end to one of the greatest fights ever seen in a British ring. Yet as a top class referee, Dalby should have stopped it much earlier and saved Arthur from the brutal hiding he took. The consequences could have been extremely grave and left a lasting stain on British boxing.

Harringay rocked to its foundations as the capacity crowd rose to salute two splendid warriors. The applause was relentless and lasted for several minutes. It had been a fight of breathless uncertainty from the first bell and Boon had finally retained his title against an opponent of exceptional skill and bravery. Whilst displaying his own brand of courage Eric could be thankful he possessed that bit extra. It was his incredible strength, punching power and, above all, sheer determination which enabled him to finally emerge victorious.

There were remarkable scenes in the ring as Boon's seconds rushed at him and lifted him shoulder high before the Lonsdale belt was strapped around his waist for the second time in two months. The crowd then quietened for a few moments as Eric took the MC's microphone with one hand and raised the other as he was about to address them. "I have had quite a few fights in my time," he said, "but I have never met a gamer boy than Danahar. I hope now to win the lightweight championship of the world."

With one eye closed, his face and body still splashed with blood, Boon left the ring to delirious cheers from his delighted fans. The journey back to the dressing room was arduous as his handlers struggled to protect him from the hysterical mob wanting to congratulate him. The crowd swayed dangerously as hundreds of hands grabbed his gloves and affectionately slapped his back and shoulders. Many excited fans pushed their way towards the dressing room and were only prevented from getting inside by a group of police officers linking arms in front of the door.

Once in the safety of the dressing room, Eric slumped into a chair and grinned with satisfaction as his seconds carefully unlaced his gloves. "That was some fight," he muttered through bruised and twisted lips as blood still dripped from his nose, "but I enjoyed every minute of it."

He was a very weary young man and moved to a couch where he stretched his aching limbs as Nat Seller skilfully massaged and kneaded the tiredness from them. His face was a hideous mess and his right hand badly swollen, yet with the tumult and cheering still echoing from the arena, he was completely relaxed. When members of the press crowded into the dressing room the first thing he did was to pay tribute to his opponent. "Danahar was wonderfully plucky," Eric told them with sincerity. "He gave me a very hard fight and I hope he is alright."

Boon was a reporter's dream because he rarely pushed them away. He had forged close friendships with a number of them, particularly Isidore Green, Jeff Barr and Frank Butler. They knew that whatever they asked he would give them answers. Yet after a fight like this one they expected it to take some time.

"I knew I could do it," he told them quietly as he laid back on the couch. "Like Crowley, Danahar was too clever for me in the early rounds, but that didn't worry me. I knew I would catch him in the end just as I did Crowley."

"Goodness knows how many lefts Danahar landed," he continued. "For round after round he peppered my face with them – beautiful straight punches with a kick in every one."

Boon's father and grandfather were at ringside for the fight, Reg having closed his blacksmiths forge early and travelled to London wearing his famous grey cap. It took them an age to struggle through the crowd clamouring to try and get into the champion's dressing room and when they eventually got inside the press boys were in full swing. As most recognised them, the questioning was put on hold and they were politely afforded access.

"Nice work son," said Reg Boon emotionally as he proudly embraced him. Then, as he hugged his father and grandfather, Eric faced the large gathering and said: "It's the world title I'm after now."

Through the shrewdness of Jack Solomons, Boon chose to go on a percentage of the gate and was rewarded with a purse of £2,765. A further £450 was added from television contracts.

In contrast to the champion's injuries Danahar was virtually unmarked, his hair barely ruffled, although his face was drained of colour and legs weak. His purse was a mere £500 and there was nothing from television. Despite that he took defeat in true Cockney fashion. "Did I put up a good show? Were the crowds satisfied?" he asked reporters who stood beside him with notebooks at the ready.

"I began to feel tired in the tenth round," he continued. "I had never gone more than eight rounds before in my life, but it is all good experience isn't it? I must hope for better luck next time."

Outside his dressing room young girls wept, but as he left he smilingly assured them he was okay. "I did my best," he said, "I couldn't do any more. I would love a return."

Referee, Barrington Dalby, was one of the few people permitted entry to the dressing rooms after the fight. His mission was to congratulate both men and thank them for their incredible sportsmanship. "Those kids were the bravest winner and loser I have ever handled," he told reporters. "I consider myself very fortunate to have been third man in the ring with two such splendid warriors."

Another visitor to Boon's dressing room was Danahar's mother who had gone to Harringay on the back of a motor cycle. Despite her bitter disappointment at seeing the hiding her son took she composed herself and made her way along the packed corridor. Once inside she walked straight up to Eric and kissed him on the cheek. "Congratulations," she said softly, "I am Danahar's mother." Boon smiled warmly, gave her a hug and thanked her for coming. "Good luck son" she muttered as she turned to leave, "you are a great fighter."

It was wonderful sportsmanship, so typical of the whole Danahar family who all agreed that Eric was the better man on the night. They became good friends and showed him tremendous respect for years to come.

*   *   *

It was originally planned that Boon's mother, Liz, would lead a contingent of more than 1,000 fans from Chatteris, but hating to watch him fight, she pulled out. Instead she watched the contest on television in the living room of a friend's house. During the early rounds when her son was out-punched by Danahar she turned away and often left the room. It was too much to bear, but as the bout changed course and Eric got on top she took more notice and jumped about excitedly as the Lonsdale belt was strapped around his waist. Even then she still told her friend she hated to see him fight.

As with Boon's fight with Dave Crowley, a green rocket was fired from the back yard of Chatteris Police Station to tell people in remote parts of the Fens about his success. Because the fight was broadcast the whole town knew the result in minutes and the High Street was the scene of great celebrations. Local landlords did a roaring trade in the short while until closing time.

The night was also a triumph for television because the magnitude of the event was such that it became the first professional fight to be shown live to a British television audience. Although the production of television sets was in its infancy, the few privileged to own them were able to watch the fight from start to finish.

It was also transmitted live to three London cinemas, the Pavilion at Marble Arch, Monseigner News Theatre also at Marble Arch and the Tatler in Charing Cross Road. Thousands of excited fans queued for several hours to get seats at one guinea each and there were a number of hostile scenes caused by queue-jumping. Events at the Monseigner were particularly ugly.

Despite the theatre seating only 400 a crowd of about 3,000 gathered outside blocking the pavement and bringing traffic on the roadway to a halt. When the doors eventually opened attendants were swept aside as those at the head of the crowd stormed into the theatre. A number of genuine patrons were knocked to the floor as people without tickets fought to get seats.

Unable to control the situation the management telephoned police and within minutes twelve constables ringed the box office fighting back intruders. As they struggled to keep order more squads in police vans were rushed to the theatre and started ejecting the 100 or so who had got in without paying. Once the situation was under control legitimate ticket holders began filing to their seats. Meanwhile, outside in the street officers struggled to keep order and many people had to be pushed away when they refused to believe that no seats were available.

Transmission of the fight was on the whole good. The picture was shown on large screens measuring 15 feet by 12 having been reproduced from one of only six inches square enabling viewers to watch the fighters at life size.

After the showing at the Marble Arch Pavilion, Isidore Ostrer, Chairman of British-Gaumont, told the press that the experiment had been so successful that all British-Gaumont cinemas in the country would be equipped with televisors. What was regarded as an extremely important development in the progress of television was an idea originally put forward by John Harding. With the backing of the Marquess of Queensberry it eventually went ahead through the cooperation of Sydney Hulls, the British-Gaumont Picture Corporation and the BBC.

For television purposes the ring ropes had to be pale yellow instead of white in order to show up clearly on the screens. A huge battery of lights was suspended above the ring which made the boxers and the referee feel as though they were in a tropical country. It was an entirely new experience for everyone, but the whole future of television in the cinema, particularly in relation to sport, rested on the experiment.

Much was written about the event, with many publications incorrectly stating that it was the first fight to be televised into British homes. Although very few sets existed at the time, Archie Sexton and Laurie Raiteri boxed an exhibition at Broadcasting House in London in August 1933, which was the first bout to be shown on television. In November 1936, three other exhibition bouts were televised. Boon against Danahar was the first professional contest that viewing audiences watched.

*   *   *

One of Danahar's cornermen for the fight with Boon was Sam Burns, and during 1952 he wrote an extraordinary article in the *Sunday People* regarding matters that went on behind the scenes. He claimed that Arthur did not have a manager and consequently was not aware of the terms Boon was getting. After hearing whispers when he arrived at Harringay on the evening of the fight, he became agitated.

The first question Danahar asked was why Boon was getting £3,000 and he was only getting £500. Nobody seemed prepared to answer and at first Arthur didn't quibble. Suddenly the dressing room door opened and in walked an official from the BBC who was in charge of the television arrangements. "What's going on?" asked Danahar. "Who's copping for all this camera stuff?"

According to Burns nobody seemed willing to answer the questions, but Danahar insisted. "I want my whack from this TV programme or I'm not going through with the fight." Burns claimed that they tried to reason with him, but before they got very far the dressing room door opened again and the Whip shouted "You're on now Arthur."

Danahar didn't hesitate and snapped: "I'm not. I'm not fighting."

According to Burns, he stepped in at that point, and with gentle persuasion, told Arthur he believed that a lot of money which could have gone to him had gone elsewhere. Danahar realised that Burns wasn't trying to kid him and asked: "Well what can I do then Sam?"

"You can do this," insisted Burns, "get out there and give the fight of your life. Can you hear the roar? The crowds are waiting for you Arthur. They have paid their cash and if you back down now they won't blame you. The people who have upset you, they will blame you for the let down."

In his account of events, Burns claimed he said: "Alright, the title's waiting in the ring if you can take it. Get in there and win it and then you can talk real money." Ten seconds later Arthur was walking towards the ring and the fight was on.

If things occurred as Burns described it was kept remarkably quiet because no journalist ever made reference to it. It didn't appear to affect Danahar's performance in the ring, and there was no apparent falling out between him and the National Sporting Club. Even stranger was the fact that both the Marquess of Queensberry and John Harding were in the dressing room, yet Danahar supposedly chose to have the conversation with one of his seconds instead.

*　　　*　　　*

Four days after their epic contest, glowing tributes were paid to Boon and Danahar at a National Sporting Club promotion at Earls Court at which both were guests. To great applause the two young fighters entered the ring with club chairman, Admiral Sir Lionel Halsey, who told the audience he could not have been prouder of Danahar if he had won the title. "He fought with courage, determination and the best of British sportsmanship," said Sir Lionel to loud applause. "These two boys whose combined ages do not total forty have restored the glamour to British boxing."

Turning to Boon, Sir Lionel referred to him as a worthy champion who displayed marvellous grit and courage. "With one eye closed and your right hand broken, you battled on with true British bulldog spirit turning a losing fight into a winning one. You are the greatest fighter in the country." He confirmed that Eric would be a guest at the National Sporting Club on 2 March.

There were even greater cheers when Boon, smartly dressed in a dinner suit, stepped forward and took the microphone. "Ladies and gentlemen," said the champion, "I want to say how proud I feel at this honour. Arthur Danahar is the greatest fighter I have ever met. I would much rather have lost the title to him than anyone else. He was a most wonderful rival and I wish him the best of luck."

"As a token of my regard for the wonderful fight he gave me," continued Eric, "I have great pleasure in presenting him with this silver cigarette case." It bore the inscription 'To a great fighter, Arthur Danahar – from Eric Boon – 23 February 1939.'

On receiving the gift, Danahar took the microphone and said: "Ladies and gentlemen, I thank you. Boon is a great champion, and I wish him every success when he fights a third time for the Lonsdale belt. I hope he makes it his own property."

Warmth radiated from the two young fighters as they stood in the centre of the ring, arms around each other acknowledging yet another rousing ovation. Earlier, they had chatted for a long while in the entrance to the main hall. They laughed and joked and discussed all manner of things. It was hard to believe that only a few nights earlier they had almost knocked the life out of each other. They were like two bosom pals, and those privileged to see them together witnessed genuine friendship and sportsmanship as they talked with spontaneous and natural enthusiasm.

Their fight set many records, another being the fact that never before had two young men below the age of twenty-one ever fought for a British title. It more than lived up to its billing and was reported in every newspaper in the United Kingdom and many others beyond those shores. It was one of the great sporting events of the 20th century that would remain engraved in the memory of everyone who saw it. Never was there a more gallant loser than Arthur Danahar and nor was a champion more magnificent in defence of his title than Boon who was a wholehearted admirer of his opponent.

The following day was spent in contrasting styles. While Danahar chose to relax with a few hours fishing, Boon was called to Westminster Magistrates Court to answer a speeding summons. The only sour note to arise from the contest was when the Board of Control received reports from its inspectors and the referee regarding the conduct of the cornermen of each boxer during the contest. At a special meeting the Stewards decided that Jack Solomons be cautioned and informed that he would be held responsible should there by a repetition of such conduct on any future occasion. It was also agreed that letters be sent to the trainers of Boon and Danahar, Nat Seller and Arthur Goodwin respectively, informing them that a serious view would be taken of any unruly conduct in the corner at any future contest at which they were present or were the trainers of the boxers in question.

*   *   *

In less than a year, Boon had battled his way from being a £10-a-fight boxer to the highest paid lightweight ever to fight in Britain. Two days after beating Danahar he drew his wages, five one pound notes, from Solomons who, some while earlier had set up a joint bank account into which he paid all of Eric's purse money and the boxer withdrew the same amount each week. Before he beat Crowley it was £3.10 shillings, but was given a 30 shillings rise for winning the title. The rest remained in the bank as an investment for him and it had been that way since shortly after Jack became his manager.

There were sometimes occasions when Boon found himself in debt at the end of a week. "I could do with another ten bob guv'nor," he would tell Solomons hopefully. "I owe it to somebody."

"That's too bad," Jack would reply with a grin as he counted out the one pound notes. "You had better go steady this week and pay them back out of this."

There was even an occasion when Eric wanted to give his father £100 to improve his forge, but even then Solomons refused to allow him to touch his savings. He lent him the money out of his own pocket and arranged for it to be repaid out of the champion's next purse.

Boon owed a great deal to Solomons when he was a youngster. In and out of the ring he carefully nurtured his protégé, keeping him sane and unspoilt at a time when he could have run wild with a few thousand pounds burning a hole in his pocket.

11

LOVE, COURTS, AMERICA AND THE STAGE

During the early hours of the morning following the fight with Danahar, Jack Solomons took Boon to two London hospitals. At Moorfields in City Road an examination revealed a burst blood vessel beneath his damaged left eye. Treatment was the application of two leeches to the inflamed area in an attempt to reduce the swelling. It was an ancient, but well-established practice in which the small reptiles, reportedly imported from France at the retail price of one shilling each, would bite a hole in the skin and suck the blood of the patient. Provided the blood vessels had been broken this would draw the loose blood from the affected area thereby diminishing the contusion. Eric was told that even after it had fully healed he would need a long rest to avoid further and possibly more serious damage.

Boon and Solomons then attended the Metropolitan Hospital at Kingsland Road, Dalston where, on their arrival a nurse called out to the casualty doctor: "Here's a boxer with a black eye."

The doctor in question had been at the fight and, on recognising Eric, congratulated him on his performance as he examined his injured right hand. An x-ray revealed a compound fracture of the second knuckle whereupon he was advised that it would need a complete rest. Although his hand was damaged as early as the third round, it was with a right to the jaw that the champion effectively ended the fight.

It was dawn before Boon and Solomons returned to Jack's home where the young boxer slept until about 11am. At breakfast he looked more like the loser of a fight than a winner. His left eye was completely closed, a huge wad of dressing across the cheek was held in place by a length of sticking plaster stretching from the bridge of his nose to the neck, and small bruises and grazes were visible on other parts of his face.

Despite his appearance Eric spent a couple of hours doing press interviews before making a brief appearance at Westminster Magistrates Court to answer a speeding charge. Solomons told reporters from three London evening papers that it would be at least three months before Eric would be fit to box again. He revealed that in the meantime a trip to America had been arranged for him.

As his right hand was heavily bandaged Boon shook hands with his left when introduced to reporters. Small bruises and grazes marked his face and the thick dressing failed to hide the injury to his left eye. "I felt the hand go in the third," he remarked. "After the fifth it was so bad that I could hardly bear it. It hurt every time I hit Danahar and it was as though needles were being pushed into my hand."

The account of events demonstrated his immense courage because he disguised the injury so well that neither Danahar nor his cornermen were aware he had a problem. Explaining the damaged eye, Eric said he was never really concerned. "I got one like this when I fought Crowley," he remarked with a cheeky smile, "so I reckon I am used to it."

"Everyone was saying that Danahar was the better boxer, but I was the better fighter," he continued. "I just knew I could beat him, but he was better than I thought he would be. I must say I have never met anyone quite so game. It was a wonderful fight."

Boon explained that he would be glad to get back home to the country. "I am not so fond of London," he remarked, "but still it hasn't done me so bad has it?"

At a press conference at the National Sporting Club, John Harding told reporters: "Danahar has no excuses to make. He didn't think the referee should have stopped the fight when he did, but there is no doubt about it that after the tenth round his legs would not hold him up."

Harding added that after a good rest, Arthur would campaign at welterweight and to that end a challenge was issued to Boon for a return over 10 rounds with a side-stake of £1,000. They wanted the fight to take place in three months. Some newspaper reporters even predicted it could be added to the Tommy Farr – Red Burman bill at Harringay on 13 April, although this contradicted reports from both camps regarding the boxers needing long rests.

Later that evening the largest attendance ever packed into the Devonshire Club expecting Boon to put in an appearance to celebrate his latest success. Although the champion had desperately wanted to be there to thank his army of East End supporters who regarded him as a local lad, Solomons had sent him home for what he hoped would be a few days rest.

"We want Boon," was the spontaneous chant from the crowd who were getting impatient at not seeing their hero.

"You can't `ave `im," retorted the rotund Buster Cohen who had climbed into the ring to conduct the evening's proceedings. After explaining the situation he went on to pay tribute to both Boon and Danahar. "Boy Boon thinks the world of Arthur," added Buster, "and we also want him to know the esteem that we here at the Devonshire also hold for him."

Concluding his speech Cohen said: "The Devonshire has made boxing history by making 'Boy' Boon." Rapturous cheers greeted the statement.

* * *

Boon left Liverpool Street station on the 4.45 pm train for Ely where he arrived almost unnoticed. Despite the bandaging to his right hand he collected his car and drove home. His parents weren't expecting him, but when he knocked at their door in Burnsfield Street the Lonsdale Belt was strapped around his waist and he held a horseshoe in either hand. One was the first he ever made at his father's forge when he was fifteen. The other was a good luck symbol which had been sent to Harringay by a friend with a sprig of white heather attached to it. Both hung in his dressing room before and during the fight.

"Hello mum," said Eric as he walked through the door. "I thought I would come home for a few days."

After a slap-up meal and long chat with his parents, Eric was ready for bed. He slept soundly until midway through Saturday morning when his mother insisted that he had a good breakfast. A busy schedule lay ahead of him and after going for a haircut he had a meeting at The George Hotel with reporters from two Sunday newspapers. Their main interest was not the fight with Danahar, but details of Eric's latest love affair.

By this time his romance with Ollie Franks was over. Whilst he was in training to meet Danahar she disappeared – not even a letter of explanation or even a telephone call to say goodbye. At least that's what he thought at the time. It wasn't until much later that he discovered she sent him a telegram saying she had been called back to the United States urgently. The reason he didn't receive it was because Jack Solomons intercepted it and tore it up. He had a champion worth a potential £100,000 to look after and decided he should concentrate solely on fighting and forget about girls.

Although Eric saw a lot of Ollie when he was in London, he was also showing considerable interest in another young lady, Joan Byers, an attractive eighteen-years-old hairdresser from Littleport who he first met about a year earlier. She had been at the Danahar fight and there were rumours that they were about to become engaged "I met her at a dance," Boon told a reporter from the *Sunday Graphic,* "and we fell in love, but don't run away with the idea I'm getting married soon."

The Sunday papers thrive on stories of romance, and despite the tender ages of the couple, this one was no exception. Any young lady seen in Boon's company would become headline news, so he told them what they wanted to hear. "I don't suppose we will marry for a year or so," he continued, "but she is my only girl friend. When I come back from America we are going to announce our engagement."

Desperate to meet the new lady in Eric's life, the reporters accompanied him to Littleport where she lived. Joan, a stunning brunette, insisted that despite what Boon had said, and rumours which surrounded their relationship, they had no imminent plans to become engaged. "We are still very young," she said clutching his arm. "I shall miss him terribly when he goes to America, but I suppose it will soon pass. My greatest wish is that Eric realises his ambition of gaining the world championship."

Boon confirmed that his priority was to win a world title. "That is going to occupy all my time until I have got it in the bag," he said. "There will be enough time for romance after that. At present fighting is the most romantic thing in the world for me. It is going to remain so until I am right up the top of the tree."

He said that another of his ambitions was to grow tulips and daffodils, and planned to use his purse money to purchase land. "Boon tulips and Chatteris daffodils, it sounds great doesn't it?" he remarked. The idea was solely his own and, as it turned out, was very much a fantasy which would never take off.

Continuing his hectic schedule, Eric drove from Littleport to the nearby Ely Corn Exchange to honour an invitation to attend an amateur boxing promotion. He was introduced from the ring by Major Gordon Fowler who, addressing the packed audience, said: "He is our champion, not only the lightweight champion of England, but one who we think will be champion of the world."

Eric smiled and waved as he acknowledged the tumultuous cheers, but quickly jumped from the ring when there were shouts of "speech". It was his cue to leave the arena and, accompanied by Miss Byers, drove back to Chatteris where, together with his mother, father, sister and friends went to the Empress Cinema and watched the film of his fight with Danahar.

*　　　*　　　*

Jack Solomons' gift of an open-top sports car to Eric was, with hindsight, not the most sensible object to give an eighteen-years-old country boy. It became like a magnet to him and he drove it at every possible opportunity no matter where he was. Whenever he was staying at Chatteris he spent much of his spare time racing around the Fenland lanes often taking local boys for rides. It was his pride and joy, but unfortunately it wasn't long before he fell foul of

Harry 'Kid' Silver (left), Jack Solomons and Eric
Boon.

Jack Solomons (left), Arthur Danahar. Mike Milligan, Boon and Nat Seller in the ring after "The Fight of the Century" at Harringay on 23rd February 1939.

Solomons and Harry 'Kid' Silver examine Boon's hands after the Danahar fight.

Boon with girlfriend, Joan Byers, after the Danahar fight.

Boon is handed a hearty meal by Mum, Liz, watched by sister, Brenda.

Eric plays the family piano at The Manor, Doddington watched by a refugee.

Harry 'Kid' Silver (left), Sydney Hulls, Boon and Jack Solomons on board the liner Queen Mary bound for New York in March 1939.

Boon (left) with Harry 'Kid' Silver.

Boon (left) playfully spars with Daily Mirror boxing correspondent Peter Wilson.

Boon (right) with former British heavyweight
champion, Tommy Farr, at a charity function in
London during May 1939.

Rehearsing the script for a TV play of
Boon's life story. From the left are Ernest
Maxim, Rae Johnson, Boon and fiancé,
Wendy Elliott.

Boon floors Johnny
McGrory at Peterborough
on 28th June 1939.

Training at Joe Bloom's
gym in London in early
1940 for a fight with Jack
'Kid' Berg from which he
withdrew.

Working on the rowing machine at Joe
Bloom's gym in February 1940.

Boon married actress , Wendy Elliott, at St Albans Church,
Golders Green, on 17th April 1940.

Boon (right) is held back by referee, Mr. C B Thomas, after flooring Jack 'Kid' Berg with a low blow at the London Coliseum on 21st April 1941.

Boon is disqualified by the referee as Berg is tended to whilst lying on the canvas.

the law for violating the road traffic laws. He also had his share of minor accidents.

On 2 February 1939, Boon was summoned to appear at Littleport Magistrates Court for failing to conform to a road traffic sign at Common Lane nine days earlier. When he failed to appear the case was heard in his absence.

Police Constable Armstrong told the court that at 2.25 pm on 5 January 1939 he was on duty in Littleport High Street when he saw a motor car being driven from Common Lane towards the High Street. The vehicle failed to conform to a halt sign and turned left into the main road at about 25 mph. Boon was the driver and when stopped and told of the offence he replied: "I didn't know there was a sign there." The Magistrates found the case proved and the boxer was fined £1.

Eric's next court appearance was on 24 February, the day after his encounter with Danahar. At Westminster Magistrates Court he pleaded guilty to a summons of exceeding the speed limit on Chelsea Embankment on 6 February. It was claimed that he was doing 42 mph on a 30 mph road. Asked by the Magistrate, Mr Ronald Powell, if he had taken his driving licence to court, Boon replied: "No sir."

"Why not?" asked the Magistrate.

"My manager had the summons and didn't want to give it to me because he was afraid it would upset me before my fight," replied Eric.

The case was adjourned until 3 March to allow him to produce the licence. On that date he was fined £2 and his licence endorsed.

Another case against Boon was heard at Ely Magistrates Court on 2 March, and again he failed to appear. A summons alleged that he drove without due care and attention. Superintendent Wells told the court that Police had received no communication from Boon and asked for the case to proceed in his absence. The Magistrates agreed.

It was alleged that at 10 pm on 10 February 1939, Boon drove his car out of a side street at Ely directly into the path of a fire engine which was travelling along a main street and had the right of way. The fire engine, which was not on a call but taking local firemen home from their annual supper, was forced to swerve to avoid a collision. Had another vehicle been travelling in the opposite direction a serious head-on accident could have occurred.

When spoken to by a Police Constable who witnessed the incident, Boon allegedly said: "No, I didn't hear or see the fire engine and I don't think I was driving that fast."

The Magistrates found him guilty and he was fined £5 and his licence endorsed. Eric's failure to attend court was probably due to the fact that he was in London as a guest at the National Sporting Club the same evening. A presentation of a gold cigarette case was made to him by Sir Noel Curtis-Bennett at the club's Piccadilly headquarters as an appreciation of his fight with Danahar.

*   *   *

Boon's success in the ring was life-changing and he attracted plenty of attention from people unconnected with boxing. He and Danahar became the subjects of a Brylcream advert which covered a quarter of a page in all editions of *The Star* and *London Evening News* on the day of their fight. Eric's potential for acting was also recognised, particularly by Bruce Seton with whom he had become good friends. The actor planned to produce a film in which Eric, Harry Silver and Nat Seller would play leading roles.

Writing in *Topical Times,* Jeff Barr, revealed that the champion had photographed perfectly at a secret film test and revealed:

> When Boon returns from America I can tell you exclusively that he will burst into a new light and become a film star. A story which has already been written for him called 'Tiger of the Fens' will feature actor Bruce Seton. The story will start with a blacksmith and there is to be a great fight outside the smithy featuring Seton and Boon.

Also on the champion's agenda was the trip to America which Jack Solomons organised ahead of the Danahar fight. There were no plans for Boon to fight there, just visits to the top gyms, study American training methods and have a look at some of the top lightweights. An added bonus was that Harry Silver would accompany him.

A trip to America with his best pal was just another of Eric's dreams come true. It had always been the custom of British champions to want to cross the Atlantic and he was no exception. A few years earlier when he was becoming an idol at the Devonshire Club he often went for walks around the London Docks with Silver, Jack Solomons and his brother Maxie. Full of enthusiasm and pipe dreams he often used to say: "Come on fellas, how about getting on a boat to America. They can't do any more than make us work our way." Although the others laughed and carried on walking, Eric was deadly serious.

Despite knowing about the proposed trip before he fought Danahar, nothing was conclusive as far as Boon was concerned.

Answering questions from reporters after a training session at Ely a week before the fight he said: "I don't know definitely whether I shall be going. It depends on how the fight goes and that's all the more reason why I want to beat Danahar."

Being a master of kidology, Solomons had dangled another carrot just like he did when he promised Eric his sports car if he beat Jimmy Walsh. A trip to America if he beat Danahar was another huge incentive for the youngster and it worked.

Boon was absolutely thrilled when he finally realised his dream had become reality. "Isn't it grand," he remarked to a reporter from the *Cambridgeshire Times.* "Here I am only nineteen and in the big money already with a trip to America coming to me. I have been wanting to go there since I was a kid blowing the bellows at my father's forge. Now I am going to see Madison Square Garden."

With the number of fights he had behind him, Eric was considered to be one of the most experienced fighters of his age in the world. He confirmed that he wanted to fight Henry Armstrong for the world title as soon as it could be arranged. He had studied films of the champion and was confident that he had an answer to everything the American could throw at him. "What I want to do now is bring the world title to Britain if only to show the world that British youngsters are not the decadent weaklings that some of the old fellows make us out to be," he remarked.

The party for the American trip consisted of Jack Solomons and Sydney Hulls together with their wives, Boon and Silver. Hulls had some business to tie up with Red Burman ahead of the fight with Tommy Farr, but his priority was to try and sell Boon to the American promoters. Most importantly, he wanted to set up a possible world title fight for the Chatteris youngster, although he was adamant that if it was to be against Armstrong it would have to be in London.

When they were about to board the liner Queen Mary at Southampton on 5 March, Hulls discovered he had forgotten his passport. After some discussion with customs officials he telephoned his fifteen-years-old son who located it, took it to Heston Aerodrome where a private plane, chartered by Hulls over the phone, was waiting. The document was then flown to Cherbourg where it was handed to an official who took it aboard the Queen Mary when she docked.

The trip which lasted just over three weeks, was a wonderful experience for Boon. His eyes were really opened because the fight game in America was so different to that back home. Although the group spent a lot of time sight-seeing, they visited some of the major gymnasiums and arenas, particularly in New York, and attended a number of boxing promotions. Within hours of arriving they were guests at ringside at a show featuring lightweight contender, Pedro Montanez, who knocked out Jack 'Kid' Berg in five rounds.

They also attended a promotion at St Louis where Henry Armstrong was defending his world welterweight title against Lew Feldman. The idea was to let Boon see the great champion in the flesh, but he was disappointed when Henry ended the contest in the opening round.

They also met many leading personalities on the American fight scene, in particular, Mike Jacobs, the top promoter of the time. He had received good reports about Boon and wanted to feature him on one of his shows. That, however, remained a consideration for the future because also on their agenda was an appointment with a leading bone specialist for a second opinion about Boon's right hand. A further x-ray confirmed a compound fracture of the second knuckle which meant he would be out of action for at least another three months.

Not a man to waste time and lose an opportunity, Hulls immediately made a telephone call to a contact in London and completed provisional arrangements for a vaudeville engagement for Boon. It would keep him occupied for several weeks after they returned home.

Eric was so excited about the set-up in America that he just wished he was fit enough to get a fight there and then. Silver, however, could not resist an offer of a contest and on 22 March stopped Jimmy Cogman in the fifth of a six-rounder at Newark, New Jersey. Solomons and Boon worked in his corner.

The party arrived back at Southampton on 29 March to find a group of newspaper reporters gathered at the quayside anxious to hear of developments on the other side of the Atlantic. Solomons told them that Eric may return in about six weeks depending on how his hand healed. "Boon has an offer to fight the winner of the Henry Armstrong-Lou Ambers world lightweight title fight which takes place on 9 August," he told them. "He was also offered Armstrong for the welterweight title, but we refused that because we don't want him to fight above his weight at this stage."

Whilst they were away Dick Corbett issued another challenge to Boon for a fight at 9st 9 or 9st 10 for £250-a-side which would be deposited with the Board of Control on Eric's acceptance. His manager, Joe Morris, told the press that more money would be wagered on a contest between them than had been with that between Boon and Danahar. There were also further suggestions that Boon might have a return with Danahar at 10 stone over 10 rounds at Harringay on 13 April. The feeling was that the main event between Tommy Farr and Red Burman was unlikely to fill the arena and an attractive supporting contest was badly needed. When this was put to Solomons, he flatly denied it. "I have already said that Boon will not fight for at least three months," he snapped, "and that is final."

*　　*　　*

Once he was back in England, Boon commenced rehearsals for a musical vaudeville act, plans for which were well advanced before he went to America. Knowing that he would be out of action for some time Hulls and Solomons were anxious to keep him occupied and at the same time earn some money. Hulls had close connections with a number of leading personalities in the entertainment business and, together with Solomons, joined forces with producer, Sir Oswald Stoll, to organise the act.

Knowing that Eric could play musical instruments, particularly the accordion and mouth organ, an elaborate music hall type act was designed for him. In many ways it was similar to acts staged by a number of great champions in the past.

The setting was a boxing ring in which Eric would perform training exercises and routines to music, dance and play the harmonica, trumpet and accordion. During rehearsals he showed a natural talent for music although he was not satisfied he had mastered the accordion. Never a quitter, Boon took it home and practised for hours. He also learned some intricate tap-dancing steps.

The rehearsals required a high level of concentration and were far removed from anything Eric had experienced before. In order to maintain his enthusiasm and keep his mind fresh he therefore took breaks and often strolled to nearby boxing gyms. One day he walked into Joe Bloom's place near Covent Garden and bumped into Arthur Danahar who was training for a fight with Harry Craster on the Farr – Burman bill at Harringay the following week.

"Hello Arthur, how's things?" asked Eric.

"Fine," replied Danahar, all smiles. "How did you like America?"

They then entered into a lengthy conversation much to the amazement of delighted onlookers. Despite their epic battle less than two months earlier the two youngsters had become good friends largely out of the tremendous respect they had for each other.

Boon's vaudeville show opened at the London Coliseum on 10 April with a matinee and two evening performances. These were followed by a week at the Hackney Empire, another week at The

Empire, Shepherds Bush, then a three week tour of the provinces with shows at Portsmouth, Bristol and Manchester.

Introduced to the London Coliseum audience by event sponsor, Fred Curran, himself a well known music hall performer of days gone by, Boon looked magnificent. Glowing with confidence from the moment he walked on stage there was not the slightest doubt about the success of his act. He carried a presence which many a seasoned artiste would have craved. He was not in the least bit awed by the fact that he was making his first vaudeville appearance at one of the largest and most famous theatres in the country. Furthermore, the audience there had a reputation of being one of the most critical in the world of entertainment. Yet Eric took his bow with a smile that oozed the most precious gift of all in the variety profession – personality.

Everyone who knew Boon, or who had watched him perform in the ring, acknowledged that he was a remarkable young man. To him a fight was just a job of work to be done. Yet he had an amazing aptitude to adjust to entirely new surroundings, matters completely alien from his regular profession. Had he been ordered to drive a train or go hop-picking he would have adapted easily and gone about the task with enthusiasm and thoroughness leaving not the slightest opening for criticism.

Going on stage for the first time was no different. He showed no nerves whatsoever and despite facing an audience strangely contrasting from the usual fight crowd, he relished it. With the sublime confidence of an experienced actor he proceeded with the first part of his act. Exhibiting incredible speed and precision he gave a professional demonstration of shadow boxing followed by a series of body exercises which revealed him as one of the most perfect specimens of athletic youth the country had ever seen. Ladies in the audience gasped at his finely toned muscles.

After a short pause, Eric's supporting cast, the Chatteris Lovelies, a group of eight attractive beautifully developed young ladies dressed in sporting white blouses and shorts, ran on to the stage. To musical accompaniment they danced around him and he kept in perfect time with them as he pounded a punch-ball. The act had been faultlessly rehearsed and was a revelation to those who only knew Boon as a boxer.

As the champion took his bow and left the stage he was replaced by Buster Cohen immaculately dressed in a Saville Row double-breasted dinner suit and bow tie. One of London's great characters, Buster boomed out an enthralling description of Boon's wonderful achievements in the ring. "At seventeen years of age," he roared with passion and enthusiasm, "Eric Boon was signed up to meet the British lightweight champion, Jimmy Walsh. Critics were not afraid to say that he was over-matched, but ladies and gentlemen, as you are all aware, Boon beat the champion."

Continuing his narration, Buster told how Boon knocked out Dave Crowley to become British champion, beat Boyo Rees in two rounds and how he successfully defended his title in that remarkable contest with Arthur Danahar. He recalled the handicaps he overcame to pull through and win with indomitable British courage and determination.

There was absolute silence as Buster recounted the spectacular progress of the young British champion. Reaching out to his audience with the ease and freedom of a born speaker, he emphasised the right things at the right time. It was great stuff, and in the four and a half minutes he was given to tell his story he did Eric proud. The applause was long, but dignified, unlike the wild scenes of celebration which generally followed the champion's ring successes.

Boon and the Lovelies then returned to the stage, this time with skipping ropes. The music struck up in quick tempo and the champion, with four girls on either side, gave a perfect display of rope skipping with the Lovelies keeping excellent time. As the girls gradually faded into the wings the stage lights dimmed creating a striking effect and all the audience could see were Boon's illuminated boxing boots performing a series of most intricate steps.

As the spectacular feature ended, Buster Cohen re-emerged to introduce Eric's pal, Harry 'Kid' Silver, who was to box three exhibition rounds with the champion. The Chatteris Lovelies, two at each corner, formed the rope posts and seconded the boxers in what was described as "a novel and attractive tit-bit."

Boon and Silver gave an exciting exhibition of gymnasium boxing accompanied by encouraging shouts from the Lovelies. "Hook him Eric" and "upper-cut him Harry," they yelled. Even the audience joined in as though the fight was for real. Although Nat Seller and Mike Milligan were close at hand, they were not needed because the ladies performed the seconds' duties with adequate skill.

The curtain fell as the two boys hurled blows at each other with great speed. The act had lasted for just over 20 minutes with Boon in full action most of the time. It was clean, novel and refreshing stuff throughout and the sustained applause at the conclusion set the seal on its success. It was originally intended that the highlight of the show would be for Eric to dance, sing and play his musical instruments, but due to time limits that piece had to be deleted.

At the conclusion of his third and final performance, Boon was visited in his dressing room by Isidore Green who, as Editor of *Weekly Sporting Review*, had spent the whole day with him during rehearsal. In one of his columns he described the boxer as "an amazing youngster."

Green's impressions of Boon as a fighter had been well documented, but this was something very different and he was quick to pen his feelings. "I've never met anyone so cool, adept and so ready to acquaint himself to something new as this nineteen-year-old wonder boy," he wrote.

"It was grand," Eric told his friend with a warm, but tired smile. "I enjoyed every moment of it and would love to go on again right now."

Jack Solomons was immensely proud of his charge. "He doesn't care for anybody or anything," he told the journalist. "The kid's got no nerves at all. He learns things in a minute. Fred Curran didn't have the slightest trouble with him at rehearsals. He did what he was told and did it well. He realised he was topping the bill at the Coliseum and made up his mind to put on a show worthy of the house. Well, I'm sure you're satisfied he hasn't let anyone down."

The performances at the Coliseum were only the start and after a week at the Hackney Empire followed by a further week at The Empire, Shepherds Bush, he took his act to the provinces.

At Bristol Hippodrome during the week commencing 1 May, he did two shows a night starting at 6.30 pm and 8.45 pm. His act was supported by other stars including jugglers, musicians and comedians, in what was described as an all-laughter evening of comedy.

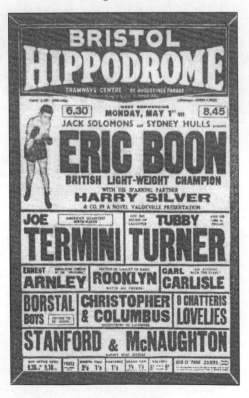

Whilst at Bristol, Eric followed in the footsteps of Jack Petersen and Tommy Farr by attending a greyhound race meeting at Eastville Stadium. There he presented a silver goblet trophy to the owner of Legal Fleece, winner of the Graded Handicap Kennel Stakes. Then to great applause from all sides of the stadium, he was paraded around the track followed by Jack Solomons displaying the Lonsdale belt.

On his final day in the city, Boon returned to Eastville Stadium because local boxing promoter, Captain Peter Prince-Cox, had arranged for him to kick off the association football match between Bristol Rovers and Newport County.

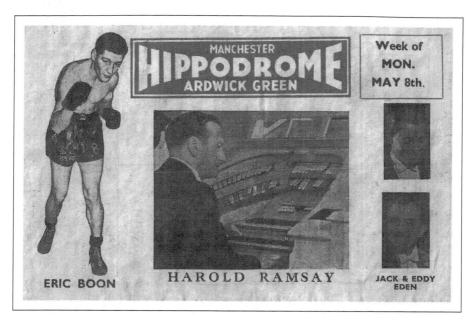

ERIC BOON   HAROLD RAMSAY   JACK & EDDY EDEN

The following week, Boon's act moved to the Manchester Hippodrome at Ardwick Green. Advertisements displayed in the city described it as a "Novel Vaudeville Presentation" by Jack Solomons and Sydney Hulls. As at previous venues Eric, together with a full supporting variety cast, appeared before sell-out audiences every evening throughout the week. Local newspapers heaped praise on the British champion, one report in the *Manchester Evening News* saying:

> Eric Boon had the eight Chatteris Lovelies to help him in his act, but he didn't even need them. Hitting out at the punchball, exercising so that the audience could see every muscle in his body move in perfect time with the music, skipping and sparring with his partner, Harry Silver, Boon provided a turn that was pleasing to watch.

Reviews of the act were incredible and as a result Boon was inundated with offers of engagements right up until the end of the year. Jack Solomons, however, refused to accept any dates beyond 8 May because there was the possibility of a fight for the champion in June.

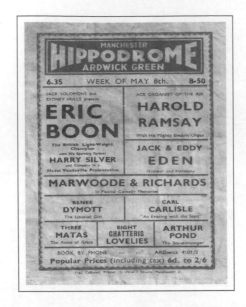

The success of the vaudeville tour confirmed just how popular Eric was in all parts of the country. Wherever he went, venues were sold out and it made no difference whether he was fighting or performing on the stage. People just wanted to see this talented and personable young man in the flesh. He didn't let them down and, taking everything in his stride, signed autographs at the stage door and gave countless interviews to the press. Wherever he went his act became headline news albeit in a field far removed from anything which had gone before.

12

TICKING OVER

The vaudeville tour proved extremely successful for a variety of reasons not least the fact that it kept Boon in the spotlight at a crucial stage of his career. It also gave his injured hand the vital weeks needed for it to heal properly and at the same time ensured that he remained reasonably fit.

A lot had been going on during his enforced lay-off from the ring with Hulls and Solomons working overtime in an attempt to secure a programme of meaningful fights for him. High on their agenda was a world title contest, and with Henry Armstrong due to defend his welterweight crown against Ernie Roderick at Harringay on 25 May, one consideration was for Boon to meet the winner.

There were also plans to take Eric back to America. In an exclusive interview with *Weekly Sporting Review,* Solomons stated that Boon and Harry Silver would box on a bill at Toronto in early June and then move to the States where Eric would have fights in Chicago, New York and New Jersey. Provided he was successful he would have a world title contest in New York before the end of the year.

Jack added that he and Hulls had deliberated over the proposals for more than a week and decided to accept what was on offer. They had been in regular contact with American promoter, Mike Jacobs, and a contract had been signed to that effect. "It was impossible to refuse the offers that were made especially with the guarantee of a world title fight for Boon," he told Isidore Green. "There is little opportunity in London at the moment for our boys to fit in really big fights."

It had also been hoped to stage a super-show at Earls Court Exhibition Centre at the end of May or early June, but this became impossible because it would clash with the Armstrong – Roderick fight and a proposed return between Len Harvey and John Henry Lewis in early June. "We are assured of a busy time in the States," continued Solomons, "and the purses are of a size we could never get in England."

Meanwhile, at a meeting during mid-May, the Stewards of the British Boxing Board of Control decided that the managers of Boon and Dave Crowley would be given one month to arrange a return contest for Boon's lightweight title. This arose because the eliminating series they ordered at a meeting of 5 January had not been completed by the stipulated date. The Stewards therefore exercised their right to nominate one of the four men originally selected to box in the eliminators, and they chose Crowley. He had recently beaten Ronnie James in one eliminator, albeit by disqualification amid uproar. Although Jack Carrick had beaten Jimmy Vaughan the Stewards considered Crowley was the man best qualified to challenge Boon.

The Board's decision created a difficult situation for Hulls because although he would have preferred to stage Boon's title defences, he wasn't really interested in this fight. He took the view that it wasn't a particularly attractive pairing and would therefore be difficult to sell to the public. He knew, however, that if Eric failed to defend the title as ordered by the Board it was extremely likely that it would be declared vacant especially as there were a number of others anxious to get a shot at it.

Surprisingly, no other promoters showed serious interest in staging the fight due largely to the fact that most believed that when Boon defended his title he would, in all probability, do so on a Hulls promotion. There was also a lot of speculation about the overall fitness of the two boxers, Boon having had eye problems and both suffering hand injuries.

There were all manner of rumours concerning Eric's immediate future with most national newspapers carrying conflicting stories and predictions. There were suggestions that he may give up the lightweight title and concentrate on the welters because he was filling out. Another claimed there were plans for him to fight former world lightweight champion, Tony Canzoneri, at Wembley and after that sail for America. What did become clear was that despite all the hype about the fights for him in Toronto and the States, nothing definite had been finalised in that respect.

Even Boon appeared to be in the dark about his immediate future. As soon as his vaudeville tour was over he got straight back into training as a matter of course. Using the facilities of Wisbech Amateur Boxing Club his immediate priority was to get fully fit and lose a few pounds. Composed and unconcerned he told local reporters that although there was a lot going on behind the scenes, nothing definite had been agreed. "I just do the fighting," he remarked. "I leave all the other stuff to my manager. I just have to make sure I'm ready for whatever they arrange."

He said that he hoped his next few fights would be at Peterborough United football ground and that one of them would be against Dave Crowley. "If plans come to fruition," he continued, "I intend to set up a permanent camp here at Wisbech, but accept that the final decision will rest with my manager and trainer."

Once word got around that Eric was training at Wisbech, crowds flocked to the little gym at Hill Street each day. Unfortunately, it was not big enough to accommodate everyone, but those lucky enough to get in paid a small entrance fee which the champion asked be donated to the amateur club.

Boon was usually accompanied by a close friend, Ted Shilling, a young Chatteris man who was suffering from a severe illness. Another companion was Police Constable John Larner who had been one of his first tutors.

After a couple of days basic training, the champion started sparring, and used the ring with Eddie Steventon and Ted Welfar. Once he got back into his stride regulars were impressed with his speed of punch and incredible power. His right hand looked sound and he used it with confidence. Although nothing definite had been arranged for him he trained with zest and appetite, and was more than ready for whoever was put in front of him.

Boon was also kept busy making guest appearances, amongst them a visit to Wormwood Scrubs Prison in West London. Before an audience of 150 borstal boys he and Arthur Danahar boxed exhibitions with sparring partners. They were accompanied by Jack Solomons, Sydney Hulls, and John Harding who wanted Eric to box on a super-show he was planning to stage in Monte Carlo during August.

Other London engagements for Eric included being at ringside on 25 May for the Henry Armstrong – Ernie Roderick fight and presenting trophies at a function organised by the *Sunday Pictorial* newspaper for its annual darts competition.

The day after going to Harringay, Boon was guest at a boxing promotion at the Embassy Theatre, Peterborough, and during the course of the evening worked in the corner of Welsh boxer, Dan Gillespie, who was beaten in three rounds by promising Whittlesey youngster, George Gale.

Deafening cheers greeted Eric as he arrived at the venue with promoter, Jack Bancroft, and again later when he stepped into the ring. Master of Ceremonies, Patsy Haygate, told the packed audience that Boon had issued a challenge to Armstrong for a fight for the world lightweight title. It was also announced that his next contest would be at Peterborough against former British featherweight champion, Johnny McGrory.

In a subsequent press statement Sydney Hulls stated that the proposed trip to America for Boon was off. Instead he would meet McGrory in a non-title affair over 12 rounds at 9st 12. It would be staged in the open-air at the 40,000 capacity Peterborough United football stadium on 28 June during the Peterborough Agricultural Show and Newmarket Race Week when huge crowds were expected. The town was in easy reach of Chatteris and held fond memories for Eric because it was there he began his professional career.

Boon's first public appearance in a British ring since his meeting with Danahar was on Whit Monday afternoon, 29 May, on a show promoted by Sydney Hulls at Alexandra Palace football ground. The weather was glorious and the chance to see him back in action drew a huge crowd. He didn't disappoint them displaying all his skill and aggression whilst boxing three exhibition bouts with Notting Hill boxers, Wally Davis and Billy Cannon, and Bobby Lyons from Walworth. There was also a lightweight competition and other fights including an eight-rounder in which Harry 'Kid' Silver outpointed Tom Thomas from Wales.

A few days later Boon was the principal attraction at Ipswich Co-operative Society annual fete which featured a big boxing show at Alexandra Park. A crowd of over 5,000 watched him box a lively three rounds exhibition with Harry Silver.

Interest in Boon was so great that four separate articles about him appeared in the 26 May edition of the *Cambridgeshire Times*. Wherever he went and whatever he did it was reported, the stories often bringing smiles to readers faces. Jack Solomons told of an occasion when Eric was due to have his tonsils removed. As he had previously promised to box an exhibition for a London hospital, Jack telephoned the organiser and explained about the operation, but was persuaded to take Eric along so that one of their specialists could examine him. Jack agreed and after a short but thorough check the doctor said there was nothing wrong with the tonsils. Boon was delighted and promptly changed into his boxing kit and went ahead with the exhibition.

Eric frequently told journalists close to him that Solomons was the greatest manager in the world. He explained how he left everything in his hands, trusted him implicitly and couldn't draw a penny from his bank account unless Jack put his signature on a cheque. He sent the boxer £5 every week which he believed was adequate for his needs. At the beginning of June 1939, however, Solomons got a shock when he received a telegram at his home saying: "Send another fiver – stop – broke again – stop – your best fighter." On this occasion Jack obliged.

Despite the sudden surge in activity a possible encounter with Henry Armstrong dominated the sports papers of the nationals. Although Armstrong was committed to a lightweight title defence against Lou Ambers in New York on 22 August, Hulls was convinced it was a fight he would win. Looking beyond it he had several discussions with the champion's manager, Eddie Meade, and offered to put up a purse of £10,000 for Henry to defend against Boon in September. "In my opinion the fight would draw the biggest crowd ever seen at a boxing match in this country," Hulls told reporters. He said that his plan was to stage it in the open-air at the Arsenal football stadium in North London.

Before returning to the States, Meade told the press that they were very interested in the offer. "I know Henry wants to come back to England for another fight," he added, "and provided he retains his title against Ambers he would be willing to return and give Boon a crack."

The press were divided about Boon's chances should the fight materialise. A number of critics thought he had a good puncher's chance of victory, but writing in *Topical Times,* Jeff Barr was strongly against it, commenting: "It may result in killing off a great prospect."

That view was supported to a certain extent by Jack Solomons who was clearly not keen on Hulls' proposals. He said that having seen Armstrong's performance against Roderick at welterweight he thought Eric was crazy to even think of facing the champion. Boon disagreed with his manager and was confident his punching power would prove decisive. "I could beat Armstrong easier than I did Crowley and Danahar, "he remarked. "He hasn't any defence. He is just my ticket and I'm convinced I could knock him out.

As if incensed at the doubts being cast on his ability to beat Armstrong, Boon issued a challenge to Roderick for a fight at 10st 4 for a £1,000 side-stake. When there was no response he repeated the challenge a few weeks later. He reasoned that if he could beat the Liverpool man more decisively than Armstrong did it would more than justify him taking the fight.

In reality, Eric was treading a dangerous path because against Armstrong, Roderick proved that he was a genuine world class welterweight. He was much bigger than Boon who, despite his undoubted ability, had not yet reached that level. He needed to heed Jeff Barr's advice because if he faced Roderick he could take a beating at domestic level and all plans for the future would be destroyed.

Meanwhile, Dave Crowley started stoking up interest in another meeting with Boon as ordered by the Board of Control. He too was occupied with matters outside the ring having been cast in the role of a boxer in a movie 'The Night of Fire' being filmed at Denham and featuring Ralph Richardson and Diana Wynyard. In a press interview Dave said he was confident of victory and was willing to cover any amount Eric was prepared to lay down as a side-stake. Boon responded by saying he believed he would beat Crowley easier than in their first fight.

*　　　*　　　*

Boon continued to train at Wisbech which was in easy reach of his home at Chatteris. In doing so it meant he was in constant demand for personal appearances locally one of which was at a grass track motor cycle race meeting at Wisbech. It was the first time he had ever watched the sport and his attendance drew the largest crowd at the track that season. Although he also had another engagement which prevented him staying for the whole meeting, he did watch a race for a cup he had donated. It was for the Eric Boon Scratch Race which provided the spice of the afternoon's sport as, during the heats, riders continued to clip seconds off the record for the four lap race leading up to the final.

By early June, Jack Solomons and Nat Seller had become concerned by the social demands being placed on their man. Needing him to be in top condition when he faced Johnny McGrory, they took him away from the comforts and temptations of East Anglia to Southend-on-Sea where they set up a training camp at a new gym attached to the Alexandra Hotel. Eric loved the place and bubbled over with enthusiasm as he sparred daily with George Howard, Johnny Clark and Private Scott, a young soldier who was in camp at nearby Shoeburyness.

Residents and guests at the hotel loved Boon because he was so natural and unspoiled by his rapid success. He amused his admirers one day when he arrived at the gym for a workout in front of the press. After signing some autographs he strolled over to the punchbag and, as he chatted to reporters, scrawled the name Johnny McGrory on it in block capital letters. A few minutes later he hammered it for all he was worth.

Amongst the visitors to the gym that day was Dave Crowley, and onlookers were delighted to see the cordial feeling that existed between him and Eric. They happily posed for photographs and joked together before the champion commenced training.

"Do you want me to leave Eric?" asked Crowley as Boon set about his work.

"No, you stay Dave," replied Boon with a cheeky grin, "you might learn something."

In general conversation Crowley made no secret of the fact that he relished a return with Eric. Negotiations to stage it were well underway and it was hoped it would take place in late September or early October. Boon was aware that if the fight went ahead as planned victory would put him into the record books as the boxer who won a Lonsdale belt outright in the quickest period of time. It would beat the long-standing record held by Jim Higgins who won three bantamweight championship contests between 23 February 1920 and 31 January 1921. It was one of Eric's many ambitions.

Apart from training at Southend, Boon also gave exhibitions at a nearby holiday camp. Hundreds turned out to watch him and no matter where he went his popularity was incredible. It was something normally only associated with good quality heavyweights.

The compassionate side of the young Chatteris boxer also became evident when it was discovered that he had taken his friend, Ted Shilling, to stay with him at the hotel. In view of Ted's medical condition, Eric decided a couple of weeks sea air would be good for him. He also arranged for him to have a ringside seat at the McGrory fight after which he would pay for him to go on another two-week holiday.

Another kind gesture by Boon was to arrange for 30 Chatteris schoolboys and six teachers to have seats at the fight at his expense. They all attended his old school, King Edward, and his gesture was a true indication of his nature. He loved children as Jack Solomons and Sydney Hulls discovered one day when they drove to Chatteris to see him. On arrival at Eric's house they were told he had gone for a short walk so, having plenty of time on their hands, they decided to walk along the road in the direction he had gone. They hadn't got far when they came across a group of seven or eight youngsters pulling Eric along in a soapbox on wheels. "Hello guv'nor," he said laughingly, "I wasn't expecting you up here today. Jump in and we'll give you a ride."

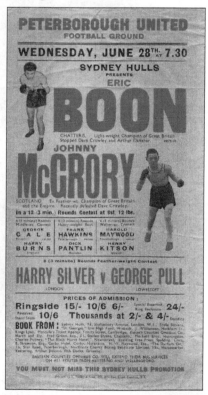

Meanwhile, the fight with McGrory was creating tremendous interest in Peterborough, Chatteris and surrounding districts. Having been out of action for almost four months people were clamouring to see Boon in the ring again and with that in mind Hulls catered for them all. Special ringside seats were priced at 24 shillings, reserved stand seats at ten shillings and sixpence with thousands at two and four shillings for standing customers. Plans were made to run special trains, motor coaches and buses from towns and villages from miles around especially Sleaford, Spalding, Lincoln, Boston, Skegness, Sandy and St Neots where there had been huge demands for tickets.

McGrory was a solid opponent who had only been stopped five times in 77 contests since turning professional in 1933 and was therefore expected to give Boon a thorough test. He was a former British featherweight champion having taken the title from Nel Tarleton at Liverpool in 1936. Later that year he became British Empire champion by outpointing Willie Smith in Johannesburg. Weight problems forced him to relinquish both titles without defending them, but he proved to be a formidable opponent in the higher division. Having outpointed Dave Crowley and Jack Carrick in 1938, he was considered one of the best lightweights in the country. Although he had won only three of his last eight contests many critics thought he was worthy of a direct shot at Boon's title especially as there was a growing belief that the champion needed to tighten his defence.

On the day of the fight the scenes in Peterborough were amazing. It was like cup final day as trains, buses, cars and charabancs from all parts of East Anglia brought thousands of fans to the town for what was the biggest fight ever staged there. The weigh-in took place at 1 pm at the very crowded Bell & Oak public house, and although the weights were not announced, both men were said to be inside the stipulated limit of 9st 12. Boon, who was accompanied by Jack Solomons and Mike Milligan, looked much heavier and more muscular than his opponent.

Organisation for the promotion was first class, the ring having been erected during the day by local men using local timber. Upwards of 90 police officers and special constables were on duty inside the ground and were backed up by 40 St John's Ambulance personnel and members of the Ladies Nursing Division. Even the weather held fine although there was a cloudy sky and stiff wind.

As Eric relaxed in his dressing room before the fight he had a surprise visitor, Mr Precious, who had been his headmaster at King Edward School, and one of the few people ever to have given him a thrashing. Having followed his former pupil's boxing career closely, he was there as a fan to wish him good luck.

"Eric was one of the very few boys I ever had to cane," he told an interested reporter. "His offence was in connection with a snowball he threw at a teacher which narrowly missed his head. Apart from that he was a perfectly well behaved and rather shy boy."

There were an estimated 18,000 fans inside the ground when, at 9.10 pm, McGrory, clad in a flame red dressing gown, marched from the dressing room to the ring. He was given a great ovation by the crowd which was swelled by several thousand Scots from the Corby area. Boon followed a few minutes later accompanied by his team of handlers all wearing their familiar white polo-necked sweaters with ERIC BOON – CHATTERIS emblazoned in scarlet across their backs. A fanfare of trumpets, which blasted from overhead amplifiers, greeted his arrival.

Hundreds more fans filled the windows of virtually every property with a view of the ground. Many others perched on every conceivable vantage point up to a quarter of a mile away armed with field-glasses, binoculars and home-made periscopes. Even an old watchtower became an unofficial grandstand. The scenes were incredible, the like of which had never been witnessed before at a boxing promotion in the region.

Boon looked very much the champion as he stood quietly in his corner awaiting the introductions. He was relaxed and confident as he waved and smiled to friends and supporters seated at ringside. Amongst them were his father and an attractive young lady who the press referred to as his fiancée, but didn't name her. Eric was odds-on favourite to win inside five rounds, but those odds shortened to three rounds after they peeled off their dressing gowns and revealed their respective physiques. Sadly the contest didn't live up to expectations.

Once it was underway Boon was quickly into his stride and looked as though he would secure an early victory. He floored McGrory for a count of 'eight' in the opening round, but after that never really put him under any pressure. His performance was disappointing and he lacked the power and accuracy displayed against Danahar. He appeared sluggish and did not appear to have regained his top form. McGrory avoided the champion's wild swings with ease and in the fifth took the fight to Boon who almost fell through the ropes while attempting to avoid a vicious counter-attack.

In the sixth Eric shook McGrory with a rare vicious left hook to the body, but was thwarted in his attempts to follow up. In round eight he finally began to show his true form when he forced the Scot to give ground after taking a hard right uppercut followed by a barrage of heavy shots to head and body. It was his first significant success since the opening round and laid the foundation for victory.

Boon started round nine in whirlwind fashion. After stalking McGrory around the ring he eventually nailed him with a left hook followed by a vicious right to the point of the chin. The Scot crashed to the canvas, but as he rose Eric drove a powerful left hook deep into the stomach. In obvious pain Johnny sank to the floor in a neutral corner writhing in agony and nearly fell out of the ring. His seconds jumped to the edge of the canvas screaming furiously that the blow was low, but referee Moss Deyong ignored them and counted McGrory out.

Still protesting bitterly about the final blow, trainer Pat Reilly, and the boxer's father, John McGrory, rushed into the ring and dragged their stricken fighter back to his corner where he was massaged. It was several minutes before he could be lifted down the ring steps and carried to his dressing room where he was examined and treated by a doctor.

McGrory was still in pain half an hour later when members of the press were admitted. Despite his cornermen's anger, he made no complaint about the legitimacy of the blow or Boon's sportsmanship. "Eric is a clean fighter," he remarked," and I'd love to meet him again."

Boon got a mixed reception as he left the ring. Although his fans cheered wildly, there was loud booing from those who supported the Scot and others seated a distance from the ringside. The crowd reaction upset Eric because throughout the contest he had shown great sportsmanship. Despite being well below his best he had made the pace and had the better of each round. McGrory was already in bad shape before the contest ended. In the eyes of the majority of critics and ringside observers the final blow was legal so the crowd reaction was uncalled for.

There was no denying that Boon's general performance for seven rounds was at best only average. In post-fight discussions, however, it was claimed that immediately after the weigh-in he had eaten a heavy meal consisting of two plates of stewed steak and vegetables followed by a large basket of strawberries with a generous portion of cream. If this was true only one conclusion could be drawn and that was that he had struggled to make the stipulated weight of 9st 12.

After returning home McGrory gave an interview to Jeff Barr of *Topical Times* and explained his feelings in greater detail. "I have not the slightest doubt I was hit low," he said. "No doubt it was an accident, but it put me out of action. I want to meet Boon again as soon as possible, anywhere, London, Glasgow, Chatteris or Peterborough. He's a strong lad with a good punch, but I think he is greatly overrated."

During the morning following the fight Jack Solomons announced that Eric would have another contest before defending his title against Dave Crowley. A challenge had been received from Leicester veteran, Len Wickwar, who had been at the McGrory fight and was unimpressed by Boon's performance. Through his manager Eric quickly agreed terms, and Sydney Hulls immediately travelled to Leicester and arranged to stage the fight at The Tigers rugby ground on 17 July. It would be over 12 rounds at 9st 12.

Wickwar was a legend in Leicester and despite being only twenty-six- years-of-age had won more than 400 of his 458 contests. No fighter in Britain had been busier. He had held Midlands Area titles at fly, bantam, feather and lightweight. Having faced most of the leading 9st 9 men, he was regarded as one of the best in the country at that weight. His best performance was undoubtedly when he outpointed British champion, Jimmy Walsh, in 1937.

Despite Boon eventually getting the job done against McGrory, Hulls and Solomons were far from happy with his performance. He needed to sharpen up before facing Crowley again which is why they agreed to take on Wickwar. He was a tough, experienced campaigner who they anticipated would give the champion plenty to think about and wouldn't get knocked over easily.

In view of the controversy surrounding the end of the McGrory fight, Hulls wrote to Dr R A Simpson, the medical officer in attendance at the Peterborough promotion and asked for details of his findings. In response the doctor confirmed that he saw Johnny in his dressing room immediately after the contest. He complained of considerable pain to the left lower side of his abdomen which radiated along the groin.

"I examined his abdomen," wrote Dr Simpson, "but could find no physical signs that would have justified my saying he had sustained a blow in that region below the level of the belt."

Because of the vehement reaction of McGrory's seconds and that of quite a large section of the audience, Hulls decided to go public with the doctor's response. He sent copies of his letter together with his own observations to the Editors of the *Peterborough Advertiser* and *Cambridgeshire Times* newspapers. Boon had always been regarded as a clean fighter and a model professional, and the promoter made it abundantly clear that he would take whatever steps necessary to defend that reputation and ensure it remained intact.

*   *   *

Boon trained at Ely for the fight with Wickwar and considerable adjustments were made to his training schedule. Previously, it had been confined to the gym where the main features had always been work with his trainers and sparring partners. He had never seriously bothered with roadwork in the generally accepted sense. Instead he had been in the habit of just strolling or trotting along the country roads around Ely.

Unfortunately, his situation had become more difficult because sparring partners were not interested even at £2 a day which was an extremely good rate. Eric's reputation in the gym was proving too much and even those who helped him for the Crowley and Danahar fights rarely stayed more than a few days. They weren't prepared to take any more doses of his vicious punching. Whilst training to meet McGrory the only men willing to get into the ring with him were welterweights and he came to the conclusion that it made him slow. Nat Seller therefore decided that the preparations for Wickwar would include more commitment to roadwork and less activity in the gym.

Boon started by running two mile stints each morning before breakfast and as his fitness increased the distances became as much as six or seven miles. At a press interview at his training camp one afternoon he admitted being amazed at the benefits derived from road running. It was an incredible statement considering the number of fights he'd had.

Despite there being very little sparring large crowds still visited the gym each day to watch Eric doing his skipping, shadow boxing, bag work and floor exercises. People just wanted the opportunity to get close to him. Regulars thought he was in the peak of condition and couldn't help admiring his wonderful physique. "If only he was a heavyweight," one local was heard to remark.

The fight with Wickwar was another tremendous attraction and Hulls expected a virtual sell-out. A few days beforehand he rented a small shop in Leicester town centre which he used as a booking office, and as an extra attraction displayed Boon's Lonsdale belt in the front window. On the evening of the fight they closed early, but nobody bothered to remove the belt. It was an amazing situation which did not escape the eyes of the press.

Writing in *Topical Times,* Jeff Barr said: "When I passed the window at midnight the streets of Leicester were entirely deserted and I paused to admire the belt. Had I been a less honest person I could have smashed the window and snatched the beautiful trophy."

Interest in the fight built up massively as the day of reckoning approached. Fans wanting details contacted the *Leicester Evening Mail* from as far afield as Newark, Derby, Birmingham and Nottingham. That had never happened before, not even when heavyweight favourites Reggie Meen and Larry Gains were at their peak.

Accompanied by Nat Seller and Harry Silver, Boon travelled from Ely the evening before the fight and stayed at The Victoria Hotel. The moment he arrived he checked his weight, but caused some anxiety by being one pound over the stipulated 9st 12. Although it

164

was quickly removed by a visit to a local Turkish bath, rumours had circulated for several days that he would never be strong again at lightweight.

The weigh-in was scheduled to take place at The Victoria Hotel at 1 pm on the day of the fight, but just as the parties were gathering Sydney Hulls received a message from the Board of Control stating that it did not comply with Board rules. It was therefore put back until 1.30 pm.

Once proceedings got underway Wickwar stepped on to the scales, but the arm did not move. Boon quickly followed whereupon the Leicester man protested causing Eric to go to the scales a second time. When his weight was called as being "under 9st 12", Len withdrew his protest. It was a puzzling situation and reporters from local and national newspapers were curious to know exactly what the problem had been. No explanation was forthcoming.

When asked for a prediction for the fight Boon calmly expressed his determination to win by a knockout. Standing beside him, Wickwar just smiled. He was completely unruffled and regarded it merely as another evening's work.

Thousands of fans descended on Leicester several hours before the boxing programme was due to commence. Whilst there was a massive local interest, parties from all over the Midlands made the journey and special trains brought many more from throughout East Anglia particularly Chatteris, Somersham, St Ives, March, Wisbech and Kings Lynn. Another large contingent made their way from London.

During late afternoon wet weather and strong winds set in and contributed to a nasty accident at the venue as the ring was being erected. One man was injured and several others had narrow escapes when steel scaffolding poles slipped and fell. He was taken to Leicester Infirmary with a head injury but not detained. The heavy rain persisted for several hours and during a preliminary contest it became so heavy that about 5,000 fans made a dash from their seats to take shelter in the stands. Police officers who tried to stop them were swept aside and several people were knocked to the ground and injured.

Those who remained in their ringside seats were saturated, but by the time the main event was due an estimated 14,000 were inside the ground. The atrocious weather failed to dampen their enthusiasm and they were rewarded with an absorbing contest.

Despite an old cut reopening under his left eye early in the fight, Boon soon took command. Although many were wild and out of range, his vicious right swings gave Wickwar plenty to think about

165

and he found it hard to get going. Despite this it was not until midway through round five that Eric exploded his right hook accurately and with full force. A huge shot to the chin sent the Leicester man crashing to the canvas for a count of 'nine'. On regaining his feet he recovered well and had Boon under pressure at the bell.

Wickwar had an added incentive to put on a good display because if he did so Hulls had promised he would be given a fight against one of the leading lightweight contenders the night Boon defended his title against Crowley. Yet being the wholehearted fighter he was Eric never gave up trying to end the fight early, but the experienced Leicester man showed great skill and courage to ensure that many of the champion's big shots hit thin air. He exposed Boon's limitations as a boxer and it began to look as though he may last the full 12 rounds. The way he absorbed a number of heavy punches caused some observers to wonder if Eric had lost some of his power.

In round nine Wickwar began to dictate matters for the first time and drove Boon to the ropes with a fusillade of jabs and hooks to the body. Then, as so often happened with Boon, his power suddenly became the deciding factor. Breaking away from a clinch, Len momentarily dropped his guard and the Chatteris man seized the opportunity he had been waiting for. A vicious accurate right travelled only a few inches before crashing against Wickwar's unprotected chin with incredible force. He fell face downwards on the canvas with no hope of rising. Referee, Jack Hart's count was a formality. It was a sudden and dramatic end to an interesting contest and Len had to be carried back to his corner. It was several minutes before he recovered.

Despite having gone into the contest following the most unusual training spell of his career, Boon fought much better than he did against McGrory, but still didn't escape unscathed. Apart from the cut reopening beneath his left eye he also sustained further damage to his suspect right hand. Back in the dressing room he was in so much pain that it was several minutes before his glove could be cut off. It revealed that the knuckle was badly swollen and a doctor who examined him advised complete rest for several weeks. "We were so afraid of this trouble that his training consisted entirely of shadow boxing, skipping and running," said Jack Solomons. "He never touched a punch bag at all, but the hand still swelled up in the second round tonight."

At first Boon played down the injury because within a few hours the whole team were due to attend a party he had organised at their hotel to celebrate Harry 'Kid' Silver's eighteenth birthday. Harry had also enjoyed victory on the Leicester bill, knocking out Jim Wellard in the fifth round. Another successful man was Tiny Bostock who beat Sammy Reynolds in the seventh, but he became extremely embarrassed at the party when Boon called upon him to sing. Tiny, a non-smoking teetotaller who went to church regularly, was a wonderful singer and people loudly cheered his rendering of 'Two Eyes of Blue.'

Although Eric had insisted that he had no immediate plans for treatment to his hand other than rest, it soon became obvious that the injury was serious. During the party he was in so much pain that he was unable to perform the task of cutting Silver's birthday cake. The party went on well into the early hours and Boon didn't rise until about 11 am. When he walked into the lounge of his hotel he was surprised to find Wickwar waiting for him. At first they acknowledged each other rather sheepishly, but then Eric smiled and said: "Well you don't look so bad."

Both had considerable swelling around their eyes and while chatting they were joined by Hulls and Solomons followed closely by a reporter and photographer from the *Leicester Evening Mail.* "Let's have a look at your hand," said Hulls. Boon held up his right fist which revealed swelling and redness around the first two knuckles. "I'm afraid a bone might have gone," he said ruefully while touching the fingers gently.

"You should get it x-rayed at once," warned Hulls.

"I'll take you to the infirmary Eric," offered Wickwar.

The worried champion readily agreed thereby creating the spectacle of a fighter whose hopes of victory had been shattered by one punch, taking the man responsible to hospital for treatment. Such compassion could only happen in boxing. Before they went Len joined Eric for a late breakfast where they talked boxing and held an inquest on their fight.

"My hand went in the second round, but I had to keep using it," said Boon. "Every time I touched you the pain shot up my arm."

Turning to other members of the group, Wickwar said: "He hit me twice on the left eye and then came the other punch, but I'm afraid I don't remember that. Eric is a terrific hitter, I must hand it to him."

Refreshed, the two fighters set off for Leicester Infirmary and Len was even present during the x-ray examination which revealed that no bones were broken. There was severe bruising especially in the area around the knuckle of the right fore-finger. It was a recurrence of an old injury so Hulls and Solomons accepted the advice of the doctor that Eric should not fight for at least two months. It was devastating news and to some extent dampened all the excitement of the previous evening.

Before they left Leicester two days after the fight, Solomons said that Boon would be seen by a specialist in London, and if necessary he would receive further treatment in America. Jack obtained a report from a consultant at Leicester Infirmary which said:

> On examining your x-ray I see evidence of what are probably two old fractures at the base of the fingers. These are probably due to injuries you received in previous contests. If you have plates taken in America we can send you this one for comparison. Anyway, I should advise you to get an opinion.

The fight had been a massive event for Leicester and the following day a photograph was published in the *Evening Mail* of Wickwar looking at Boon's damaged hand. Both were smartly dressed in two-piece suits with Jack Solomons standing between them. Meanwhile, Len's manager, George Biddles, said that the city wanted to see a return between them and hoped it could be made at 9st 9 when he was confident the outcome would be different.

There was to be more bad news for Boon because while he was having his hand x-rayed, the Isle of Ely Education Committee held a monthly meeting at March County Hall. One item on the agenda was an application submitted by Eric requesting permission to use the gymnasium of Cromwell School at Chatteris for training after school hours. Serious concerns were raised by some members who felt there was a danger of the school becoming more than just a venue where he could train. Because of his immense popularity large crowds always gathered to watch him prepare for fights. It was therefore visualised that if permission was granted the school would in effect become open to the public. This was not acceptable and, after a long discussion, Boon's application was rejected.

13

INJURIES, POSTPONEMENTS AND WAR

The injury to Boon's right hand meant that he faced another lay-off from the ring. It was extremely frustrating because talks to stage the return with Dave Crowley were well advanced and although nothing definite had been agreed it was hoped the fight could have taken place in late August.

There were also approaches from other parties on the domestic scene which would have guaranteed Eric good purses. A syndicate of London businessmen were prepared to offer a purse of £2,000 for him to defend his title against Benny Caplan of St Georges provided he beat Ronnie James at Swansea on 31 July.

The day after Boon defeated Len Wickwar, Alec Creamer, an enterprising Clydeside promoter, stated that he wanted to stage a contest between Boon and Scottish champion, Ginger Stewart, in Glasgow during September. He was assuming that the lightweight title would be at stake because he did not envisage Eric losing it to Crowley.

Creamer claimed that Stewart, who was also aged nineteen, was a fully-fledged lightweight who could punch just as hard as Boon and was probably a better boxer. He had lost only three of more than 40 contests since turning professional in 1936. The promoter said a fight between the two would draw a bigger crowd in Scotland because in the south people would not realise what the champion was up against. Creamer believed that at least £7,000 would be taken at the box office thereby making good money for the boxers, the Board of Control and himself. Despite his approaches neither Sydney Hulls or Jack Solomons showed any interest in his proposal.

Another challenge came from Kings Cross lightweight, Tommy Hyams, who considered he had more chance than anyone on the long list of challengers. "Boon is just made for me," he remarked. "My style would cause him more trouble than any lightweight in the country. I am convinced I could lick him."

Despite the period of inactivity facing him there was no chance of Boon idling away his time. He was a young man who needed to be kept constantly active so although he couldn't use his right hand he kept fit by running and doing gym exercises most days. He was determined to be fit and ready for action the moment he was given the all clear.

Having made good progress by early August, Eric agreed to take part in some exhibition bouts the first of which were at a boxing fair staged at Chatteris Auction Yard. A large crowd turned out to see the programme organised by Chatteris Amateur Boxing Club in association with Wisbech which provided several of the boxers. The highlight of the evening was provided by Boon who was greeted with wild cheering as he climbed into the ring. After doing three entertaining rounds with Harry Silver he gave a training demonstration which delighted the crowd. He then called for a volunteer to box a round with him. At first nobody seemed too keen, but eventually a local man, Jack Martin, climbed into the ring. Not content after one round he asked to stay on for another, and although he gave up before the finish he earned generous applause from the appreciative audience.

The following Saturday, 16 August, Boon and Silver gave a sparkling display over three rounds at Butlin's Open Air Sports Stadium at Skegness before a crowd of over 5,000. Again, Eric followed the exhibition with an entertaining display of his training schedule. The event was part of a new promotional venture by Sydney Hulls in which the main event was a heavyweight contest between Welsh champion, George James, who lost on points to Tom Reddington from Salford. James was seconded by Tommy Farr who was introduced to the crowd along with former world flyweight champion, Jimmy Wilde. Despite these two being massive names in boxing it was Boon who received the loudest cheers.

By mid-August, Hulls was satisfied that Boon's hand had healed satisfactorily. Having received regular check-ups by a specialist in London, the British champion was advised that as the fluid had disappeared from the injured area he could resume serious training. "It will be great to be able to punch again without red hot pains shooting up my arm," he cheerfully told a *Cambridgeshire Times* reporter.

Once Boon was given the all clear, Hulls resumed negotiations with Crowley's camp and after agreement was reached he announced that the fight would take place at the Empress Hall, Earls Court, on 25 September. A few days later he stated that in the event of Boon successfully defending the title he wanted to match him with Tony Canzoneri in London before the end of the year. It was a suggestion that had been floated in the press for several months, but not everyone was in favour of it. Writing in *Topical Times,* Jeff Barr insisted it was a fight which should be banned. "It would be an uneven gamble," he wrote, "and I am surprised at the shrewd Sydney Hulls suggesting such a match unless he is thinking of the publicity that goes with it."

Canzoneri had been a great lightweight, but at the age of thirty-one was washed up as far as world title affairs were concerned. He had been one of the hardest hitting men in his division nine years earlier, and in 1931 knocked out Jack 'Kid' Berg in three rounds when Jack was at the height of his career.

Barr called upon the Board of Control to ban a fight between Boon and Canzoneri because even if Eric won in spectacular style he would gain no prestige in Britain or America. On the other hand the Americans would be amused if Tony flattened Boon because it would ensure that he never got a world title shot.

A few weeks later Ronnie James was being hailed as one of the best lightweights in the world. He was seen by many critics as the man most likely to give Eric problems domestically and was much more of a threat than Crowley. On 30 July he knocked out Benny Caplan in two rounds at Swansea to score his fifth consecutive inside the distance victory since being disqualified against Dave in April. There were so many possibilities for Boon yet there were also plenty of stumbling blocks.

Whatever the situation the Chatteris man was a sports writers dream and some publications even made comparisons between him and Jack Doyle as to who was the greatest attraction. Boon could always draw big crowds because the fans knew they were guaranteed to see great punching. Even if he was only boxing an exhibition his presence was enough to swell the attendance dramatically.

At this stage of his career he had a better chin than Doyle, but being a heavyweight gave Jack the edge. It was, nevertheless, a tremendous compliment for a nineteen-year-old lightweight to be compared to a man who had drawn crowds in excess of 70,000.

Boon's value as a money-spinner was recognised by the fact that in his two championship contests record receipts for the lightweight division were smashed. When he beat Crowley in December 1938 more than £4,000 was taken, a record for the division. For the Danahar fight amazing figures of almost £13,000 were recorded.

Since becoming a successful young professional Eric had built a rapport with most members of the sporting press, but was closer to Jeff Barr and Isidore Green than all of the others. Both had known him from the start of his career and consequently he revealed more to them about what was going on than to any of the others.

One day in late August, Barr travelled from Chatteris to London with Boon who had a meeting with Hulls and Solomons. The reporter said there had been doubts in his mind for several months over a number of factors. Could he make 9st 9 comfortably, was his right hand sound and had the cut under his left eye healed properly? Grinning in his familiar boyish manner, Eric assured his friend that he was fine on all counts adding that he expected to knock out Crowley with the right hand.

Another of Eric's attributes was his tremendous sense of humour. He was one of the most carefree boxers around and always full of fun. During a few days holiday on the Essex coast at the beginning of August he sent a comic picture postcard to Sydney Hulls. It showed a golfer with a large 'L' plate hanging around his neck, and Eric's larconic message read: "You may be a good promoter, but golfers – I've shot `em! Your best headache – 10st 13 ½."

*   *   *

At 11 am on Sunday 3 September 1939 the Second World War was declared. Subsequent restrictions imposed by the government included the closing of all cinemas, theatres and other places of entertainment until further notice, and the prohibition of sports gatherings. Consequently, a number of attractive boxing promotions, including that involving the Boon – Crowley fight, would probably have to be postponed.

Unaware of the announcement, Eric was attending an event at Butlin's Holiday Camp at Clacton organised as part of a massive effort to raise £350,000 urgently needed by the Great Ormond Street Hospital for Sick Children. He was there to make a personal appeal on behalf of the hospital which at that time offered treatment to thousands of sick children from all parts of Great Britain each year. Entrance was one shilling which included the use of the tennis court, putting greens and swimming pool. All proceeds went to the hospital.

Boon received rapturous applause when he made his short, but impassioned speech, and throughout his stay at the camp he was in constant demand for autographs. It was only later in the day that he became aware of the critical world situation.

Within two weeks Eric was one of a number of top boxers to appear on the first Army boxing show of the war staged as entertainment for the troops by John Harding and Sydney Hulls at an undisclosed camp in the South of England. The programme consisted of three regimental bouts and a number of exhibitions featuring professionals Jock McAvoy, Arthur Danahar, Jack 'Kid' Berg, Harry Groves, Dave Crowley and Boon, who did his three rounds with regular spar mate, Harry Silver.

Not only was Eric brilliant in his exhibition which was described as the highlight of the show, but he also excelled in a training display. His skipping alone was said to be worth travelling miles to see and he really impressed onlookers most of whom were troops

172

due to leave Britain for active service elsewhere. For a lad of his weight, Boon did his stuff in a rhythmic and almost dainty fashion.

Just two weeks before it was due to take place the fight between Boon and Crowley was officially postponed due to government restrictions. It was a tragedy because although the Empress Hall was not as big as Harringay there had been a massive demand for tickets. Hulls had reckoned that a crowd of 10,000 would pay in excess of £10,000 to see the contest and by the end of August that prediction looked on course. All seats priced at six and twelve shillings had been sold and those at 18 shillings were going rapidly.

Both boxers were bitterly disappointed because despite the outbreak of war they had continued to train hard. Crowley's camp was at the Alexandra Hotel, Southend-on-Sea, while Boon alternated between Ely, where he spent a lot of time horse riding, and Chatteris where Solomons had a special gym created for him at the Palace Theatre where he did public workouts. His greatest disappointment on hearing that the fight had been postponed was the fact that he had set his mind on winning a Lonsdale belt in record time. Once he stopped serious training he and Harry Silver spent a lot of their spare time fishing and shooting.

Unaware of how long government restrictions would remain in force, Hulls and Solomons continued to try and plan Boon's career. Jack sent a cable to General Phelan of the New York State Athletic Commission asking that the British champion be recognised as the official challenger to Lou Ambers who had taken the world lightweight title from Henry Armstrong. Solomons said he was absolutely confident that his man had the beating of the new champion and was prepared to lay down a side-stake of £1,000 on Boon's behalf. Firstly, however, Eric had to beat Crowley again.

The possibility of a meeting with Ambers was a more realistic proposition for Boon than a fight with Armstrong. On hearing the news Jeff Barr travelled to Chatteris and saw Eric at his new gym. He looked really fit and relaxed, and said: "After I've beaten Crowley I will fight Ambers for nothing because I am certain my punch will bring the world title to England."

Although the war restrictions were causing complications it had been expected that agreement would be reached for the fight with Crowley to take place in London on 7 October. Hulls, however, faced real obstacles due to the reduced revenue which a fight was subjected to during war time. He therefore had to make adjustments to his original financial arrangements, in particular offering the two boxers reduced terms. Although Jack Solomons readily agreed on behalf of Boon, Harry Levene, the manager of

Crowley, insisted on a percentage of the gate rather than a guaranteed purse.

With the talks in deadlock, Jack 'Kid' Berg, who had been keeping himself in shape, issued challenges to Ernie Roderick and Boon. "I am almost a welterweight," he remarked, "but I could get near to a suitable poundage for Boon." Another offer, described as a record purse for Ireland, was made for Eric to meet Irish lightweight champion, Al Little, on 4 November. Jack Solomons told the *Peterborough Advertiser* that the offer was so attractive he had to seriously consider it.

Hulls wasn't interested in Berg, but conceived the idea of bringing in Ronnie James as a substitute for Crowley. It would be seen as an attractive fight by the boxing public especially as the Welshman had been the subject of a number of favourable stories in the media regarding his undoubted ability. Anxious to keep things moving, the promoter wrote to the Board of Control with his proposals, and also asked if permission would be granted for Boon to challenge Ernie Roderick for the welterweight title. Levene was furious and made a complaint to the Board. On reviewing the situation the Stewards agreed with Levene and ruled that Boon would not be permitted to take part in any British championship contest until he had defended his title against Crowley.

Board General Secretary, Charles Donmall, wrote to Hulls advising him of the decision and asked that he informed the Board by return if he had abandoned the idea of staging a Boon – Crowley contest. A copy of the communication was sent to the press because the Stewards regarded it as a matter of sufficient public interest.

Initially, out of sheer frustration, Hulls declared that he was no longer interested in promoting the fight. After a short cooling off period, however, the parties resumed talks and agreement was eventually reached for the fight to take place at Harringay. Yet there was still a lot of work to do because the authorities were still discussing the question of how many people would be admitted to the arena in compliance with the Police Emergency Regulations. At first a provisional date was set for 21 October, but that was later changed to 27 October. It was not until the middle of October that the Police finally agreed that the fight could take place on 4 November. Preliminary contests would commence at 2.30 pm with Boon and Crowley entering the ring one hour later.

Part of the problem for the delay and change of dates was because Hulls wanted the attendance limit increased. He argued that the stipulated one of 4,000 was not an economical proposition. Eventually, the authorities relented and the promoter was told he could cater for 5,000 whereupon he priced tickets from 12 shillings to 50 shillings ringside.

Throughout all the difficulties the two boxers continued training hard in the hope that matters would eventually be resolved. Crowley moved from Southend-on-Sea to Joe Bloom's gym at Earlham Street near Covent Garden and a few weeks later to the Star & Garter at Windsor where he worked under Len Harvey's old mentor, Wally May.

Boon, who by this time was ranked at number three in the world lightweight ratings, switched between Chatteris and London where he was able to get some sparring. He was delighted when the date was finally set because he still had high hopes of beating Jim Higgins record.

One day during early October he broke with training and went with Jack Solomons to watch Dave Crowley fight at Northampton. After Dave had stopped Griff Williams of Wales in five rounds, Boon said it was the best he had seen him box, and a left hook which floored Williams in the fifth was the hardest shot he had ever seen him throw.

"Nice work Davey," shouted Eric as Crowley left the ring. "A good punch that one."

"Sure," replied Dave, "the crowd are going to see a real scrap when we get together."

Solomons was also full of praise for Crowley and a few days later told Jeff Barr that his form would only serve to make Boon more determined. He amused the journalist when he told of how they had a bet as they left the arena after the fight. "I bet Eric that I could reach London in under three hours in the blackout," said Jack. "He jumped at the offer of an even half a crown saying that I wouldn't make it."

He then described how he put his foot down and reached their destination 10 minutes inside the limit. "It almost broke Eric's heart," continued Solomons. "He was so certain I wouldn't make it, and believe me I made him cough up that half crown."

Boon certainly got a kick out of life and Solomons kept Barr entertained with printable stories about him. Another related to a day when a Policeman in Chatteris saw Eric walking through the town and called over to him. "I want to speak to you because there was a light showing in your bedroom last night. You must be more careful."

"It was only a candlelight," replied Eric.

"I dare say," said the officer, "but you must have a smaller light."

"Very well," promised Boon, "I'll light half a candle in future."

Solomons was a fishmonger and usually purchased his stock in bulk at trade prices. He told Barr about a day when he took Boon with him to a fish market out in the countryside. When they arrived there he told Eric he had some business to attend to and ordered him to join a queue and buy two boxes of kippers for him. Boon obeyed his master without question and stood in line to await his turn to be served.

Solomons, meanwhile, arranged for a photographer to take a picture of him before sidling up to the market people and persuaded them to refuse to serve Eric as he was a boxer not a fishmonger. Everything went according to plan and Boon was ushered away, but his usually serene temper rose when he saw Jack and a group of porters hiding behind a cart laughing at his embarrassing predicament.

Barr was with Eric one day when he did an exhibition at a military camp. He was a tremendous hit with the troops, and the non-commissioned officers asked if they could give him a small present as a way of thanking him. Boon replied: "Yes, I would like one of your caps."

Without further ado he was presented with a Scottish Glengarry and one of the officers also gave him an emblem of his rank. Eric was as delighted as if he had been given a gold watch.

*   *   *

During the weeks leading up to the Crowley fight there was an atmosphere of quiet confidence in Boon's camp at Chatteris. He continued to put plenty of hard work into his preparation which consisted mainly of road work every morning followed by vigorous work-outs at the gym during the afternoons. There was still no sparring, but he worked overtime on the punchbags, speed balls and doing a series of floor exercises. When Sydney Hulls took a party of reporters to the gym they were impressed with what they saw and most believed Boon was punching harder than ever.

In an interview with the *Peterborough Advertiser,* Eric said that despite all the upheaval he was fit and ready to go and couldn't wait to get the fight on. When asked about the likely outcome he remarked: "It won't last as long this time. I don't underestimate Crowley, he's a good man, but," he added with a broad smile, "I've got to win that belt, I've got no braces."

During his preparations, Eric always found time to give words of advice to his friend Ray Buddle, a local light-heavyweight who also trained at his camp. Having turned professional only two months earlier he was raw, but promising, and loved being around Boon.

"Imagine it's a man and hit it like that," said Boon one afternoon as he drove punches into the heavy bag with extreme force. "Be confident and remember when you are in the ring that the other chap has no-one to help him any more than you have."

Between training sessions, Eric often treated local children to film shows using a luxurious cinematograph he was the proud owner of. He hired comic films and the kids treated him as though he was Father Christmas. He was a real hero and they all knew who he was and exactly what he did. "Are you going to knock him out?" they would often ask him. There would be many tears shed if he was beaten by Crowley.

It was also revealed that Eric and his parents had a thirteen-years-old refugee from Vienna living with them at Chatteris. One day between training he took the boy to London for a special treat, and local people remarked that the youngster looked upon him as a god.

During the period when the fight was still on hold due to war restrictions, Boon entered into an agreement with promoter, Captain Prince-Cox, to appear at the Bannister Stadium Sportsdrome, Southampton, on 28 October. He was to box two exhibitions on a show topped by former British welterweight champion, Dave McCleave, against up and coming youngster, Freddie Mills. Boon's pal, Harry Silver, would feature in a six-rounder.

In the meantime, the Crowley fight was finally rescheduled for 4 November just seven days later. Somewhat surprisingly Jack Solomons still allowed Eric to travel all the way from Chatteris to Southampton.

Although he had always acted with good vision and common sense regarding his young charge, on this occasion he undoubtedly exercised poor judgement. Not only did he and Eric travel the long journey by car in perilous times, there also had to be the possibility that the champion could get injured which is exactly what happened. As so often occurs in life, fate duly played its hand.

Boon sparred a round each with local boxers Harry Rashleigh and Eric Thompson and despite wearing 16 ounce gloves he caught both with hard shots to the chin which ended their involvement. He followed the exhibitions with displays of shadow boxing, skipping and ground exercises.

With the show being on a Saturday afternoon a huge crowd was in attendance and the promoter believed that Boon's presence swelled it by at least 2,000. He had a compelling personality and they cheered him enthusiastically throughout his performance. As he left the ring many wished him good luck in his forthcoming fight with Crowley. By this time, however, Eric knew he had a problem with his right hand having suddenly felt an all too familiar pain during one of the exhibitions. He quietly mentioned it to Solomons immediately after his training display, but they agreed to keep it

177

quiet in the hope that the damage was not serious. Throughout the weekend, however, Eric was in severe pain so early on the Monday morning he was taken to hospital where an x-ray revealed he had splintered the knuckle he injured back in the summer. Solomons immediately notified Sydney Hulls who was furious because it would mean yet another postponement of the fight with Crowley.

Hulls notified the Board of Control whereupon the Stewards ordered that Boon's hand must be examined by one of their appointed medical officers, Dr Malin. He concluded that Eric would not be fit to box on 4 November and requested further x-rays in order that he could determine how long the injury would take to heal and when Boon would be fit to resume training.

There were only four days to go when the promoter announced that the fight was off. The press had a field day describing the contest as the most ill-fated one boxing had known for years. A range of stories were published as to why the latest postponement had come about. Some mischievous reporters claimed that Boon was having weight problems and the injury story was just a cover. Part of the reason for this assumption was because Eric had persisted in issuing challenges to Ernie Roderick for a welterweight title fight. Even after sustaining his latest injury he offered a side-bet of £500.

Solomons also came in for criticism for allowing Boon to take part in the exhibition bouts. He rejected this saying that they had entered into an agreement while the Crowley fight was still in the air. Eric's presence had been heavily advertised and as a result heavy bookings had been made by fans wanting to see him. The Southampton promoter would have been in an awful mess if he had not turned up. He stressed that nobody was sure when a new date for the Crowley fight could be fixed so arrangements went ahead to accommodate Boon.

Jack insisted that he saw nothing wrong with going through with the exhibition bouts which could serve as a useful workout and pointed out that the injury was sheer bad luck. It could just as easily have been sustained in the gym.

As most of the press stories were wide of the mark Hulls wrote a detailed explanation of the facts in the programme for his matinee promotion at the Stadium Club on 6 November. As the matter was of great public interest it was reproduced in full in *Boxing* two days later.

Without realising it Hulls created another problem for himself when he instructed the Master of Ceremonies to announce that the Boon-Crowley fight would go ahead at Harringay on 4 December. This was a concern to Dr Malin who was the Board of Control medical officer at the Stadium Club promotion that afternoon. In an earlier discussion with the promoter he had said that in his opinion it was unlikely that Boon would be fit by that date.

Dr Malin submitted a report to the Board and both he and Hulls were called to a meeting. In answer to questions from the Stewards the doctor confirmed that he could not say when Eric would be fit until he had seen further x-ray plates of the hand after bandaging had been removed.

Hulls said that if Boon's hand healed as expected he wanted to stage the contest on either 2 or 9 of December. Harringay Arena was available on both dates and a large number of his regular clients were anxious to purchase tickets. It was a delicate situation and after a lengthy discussion the Stewards decided to monitor Boon's progress. They left it open for Hulls to make his own arrangements regarding rescheduling the fight.

The overall situation, however, was tense because a great deal of bitterness had developed between the parties, particularly Hulls and the Board of Control. Although Boon eventually got clearance to fight, there was a serious lack of communication and no sooner had Hulls confirmed that the fight with Crowley would go ahead on 9 December, another obstacle faced him.

In mid-November it was announced that the Board of Control, in association with the National Sporting Club, had 'organised and produced' for the Marquess of Queensberry, an all-star boxing programme in aid of the Lord Mayor of London's Fund for the British Red Cross. It was to take place at Earls Court on 27 November and top of the bill was a contest between Dave Crowley and Jimmy Vaughan.

Hulls was furious because after all the postponements of the championship contest between Boon and Crowley which the Board ordered, there had been no consultation with him. An injury to Dave would mean yet another setback. Furthermore, the chief support at Earls Court was to be a heavyweight contest between Tom Reddington and Tommy Martin which Hulls had already secured for his Harringay show.

The most infuriating aspect as far as Hulls was concerned was that the Board, having over 3,000 licensed boxers, could easily have put together an attractive show for Earls Court without risking those due to appear on his promotion at Harringay just two weeks later.

The press were quick to speculate on the situation especially when Board of Control Secretary, Charles Donmall, said he had nothing to say when asked for a statement. Frank Butler, writing in the *Daily Express* on 13 November, predicted the threat of a rebellion against the Board. Hulls and Solomons had formed a solid axis and were believed to be planning to stage unlicensed shows at theatres in London and the provinces. If they did break away, Boon and a group of other top boxers could follow.

Solomons, who was having his own difficulties with the Board over the extension of his licence for the Devonshire Club, was the perfect ally for Hulls. Not only was he the manager of Boon, he was also the agent for Tom Reddington. Consequently, the problems over the Earls Court bill were eventually resolved following delicate, and at times, tense negotiations.

Nevertheless, it remained a stressful time for Hulls because he was still experiencing difficulties with the authorities over crowd restrictions at Harringay. Because he was limited to only 5,000, he had to dispense with tickets priced at six shillings usually purchased by working class fans who could not afford to pay the higher prices. To be sure of making a profit he wanted a crowd of 7,000 and was prepared to do a deal with the Police.

As Harringay was an accredited air-raid shelter for 7,000 people who could be accommodated there safely the promoter promised that if he were allowed the additional 2,000 he was prepared to admit an additional 1,000 uniformed servicemen free of charge. The authorities, however, would not relent.

The press were very supportive of Hulls, arguing that he was being victimised at a time when Police were preparing to extend the limit for football crowds in the Metropolitan area beyond 15,000. Boon against Crowley was a massive fight which the public wanted, and even in wartime Hulls and Solomons were doing everything possible to keep boxing alive in the capital. They deserved better consideration instead of being victims of rigid enforcement of a senseless regulation.

Meanwhile, Boon hit out at the critics and doubters when he climbed into the ring one afternoon at the Devonshire Club. Genial Master of Ceremonies, Buster Cohen, made the opening for him saying: "Gentlemen, you have heard many rumours concerning the postponement of the Boon – Crowley fight. Some say Eric could not make the weight while others declared the bookings were bad. Well, there is a young man here who might be able to throw some light on the subject."

Eric was given a standing ovation as Buster called him into the ring. Calmly and politely he immediately removed any doubts about being able to make 9st 9. Then, holding up his bandaged right hand, he said: "I read that Crowley declared that he fought me last time with two bad hands. Is that any just reason why I should fight him with a damaged hand?"

The Chatteris youngster had an array of loyal supporters at the Devonshire Club and they cheered him to a man. They knew he was genuinely injured and if he said there were no problems with his weight that was good enough for them.

Throughout all the uncertainty, Boon never stopped light training. He was a determined and dedicated young professional fully intent on being ready when the day of reckoning with Crowley eventually arrived. During mid-November he moved from his training quarters at Chatteris to Leek in Staffordshire where Tiny Bostock had a fine private gym. Although Eric preferred the comforts of his home town he decided to try a change in the hope it might change his luck.

Bostock's gym was situated in easy reach of beautiful countryside and really suited him whenever he prepared for fights. The 'man about town' disposition of Boon, however, did not take the solitude to heart. Apart from having to cope with the blackout he felt utterly miserable amid the bleakness, isolation and rain, so within a few days he telephoned Jack Solomons. "This place may be okay for a hermit," he groaned when Jack answered the phone, "but I'll go cuckoo if I stay here much longer. You don't want me crazy before I beat Crowley do you?"

Determined to keep his young charge happy Jack told him to pack his bags and catch the next train back to London. Within 24 hours he was happily working back at his Chatteris quarters. Each day he was visited by an osteopath who administered treatment to his right hand and assessed the recovery. Knowing that the Board of Control were monitoring the situation, Solomons took no chances. Yet when he suggested that Boon travelled to London for a medical examination the Board refused to allow him to leave Chatteris because of the concerns about his weight. The Stewards reasoned that all the time at his disposal should be used to enable him to comfortably reach the lightweight limit.

Another prickly situation developed, but the Board eventually agreed for Dr Malin to travel to Chatteris on the condition that Solomons arranged and paid for a car to take him. On 1 December, after observing Boon working on the punchbag and conducting a thorough examination of his right hand, the doctor pronounced him fit to box. The only remaining concern was that when given a check-weigh Eric was 10st 1. Although he was down to 9st 12 ¼ five days later the Stewards were still concerned enough to direct that both boxers had check-weighs the day before the fight

Topical Times reporter, Jeff Barr, had been concerned about Eric's weight for some time based purely on the fact that he was a growing youngster. He and a number of other critics expressed concerns as to how long he could continue to make the lightweight limit and remain strong. Solomons disagreed, and when the matter

181

was raised at a press conference a week before the fight he said: "What people don't understand is that Boon dries out two pounds."

Jack admitted that the champion still had three pounds to shift, but gave an amusing explanation. He said that the previous week Eric had eaten two chops, peas and cauliflower for lunch, drank two cups of tea and a glass of orange juice. When his mother's back was turned he sneaked a bowl of fruit salad and ice cream. People who knew Boon had no doubts that the story was true because tales frequently leaked out about his love of food.

Solomons remained confident that his man would comfortably make 9st 9 by the day of the fight and remain strong because the whole team were adopting a thoroughly professional approach to the situation. In the gym, Nat Seller worked Boon hard and sent daily bulletins to Sydney Hulls regarding his weight. On the eve of the fight, however, there were still plenty of doubters because when Eric did a workout at Chatteris the previous day he was kept as far away from onlookers as possible.

Meanwhile, Harry Silver narrowly escaped serious injury when he was involved in a motor accident in London. He had arranged to take his girlfriend to the pictures, but as it was a wet night decided to use a large greengrocer's van he drove to market each morning. As he was driving home during the blackout a pedestrian flashed a torch in his face completely blinding his vision. Harry swerved violently and although he avoided hitting the pedestrian, he crashed into an obelisk. He was taken to hospital with leg injuries, but they were not serious enough to affect his boxing career. His girlfriend was less fortunate, sustaining facial injuries necessitating five stitches and her nose was put in plaster.

Boon was not told about Harry's accident until the extent of his injuries were known. Had he become aware that his great pal was in hospital he would have broken training to be at his side. Nothing would have stopped him, and with the Crowley fight only a few days away it was not a risk Solomons was prepared to take.

WHERE IS THE BELT?

For weeks stories predicting that Boon was struggling to make the lightweight limit had been splashed across the sports pages of most national newspapers. The champion therefore astonished everyone, except those really close to him, when he scaled 9st 7 ¾ at the official weigh-in.

Both men had passed medical examinations at the Stadium Club the previous day so there was relief for everyone when the day of the fight finally arrived. Crowley had been bitterly disappointed each time it was called off and with so many setbacks he began to have serious doubts as to whether it would ever take place. He had trained hard for several months and claimed to be at his fittest for more than two years. "I've never been beaten twice by the same man," he told Frank Butler of the *Daily Express*. "I always beat them the second time."

Boon was equally confident that he would emerge victorious again without getting his eye damaged in the process and revealed that he had backed himself to win a considerable amount of money.

Because of the danger of air raids the fight took place on a Saturday afternoon and was the first for a championship since the outbreak of war. Despite Sydney Hulls efforts to increase crowd capacity, he suffered a huge financial loss. The vast expanses of the great arena looked almost bare and it was estimated that no more than 3,000 turned up. Those who did, however, were privileged to see two superb boxers in one of the cleanest fights ever seen in a British ring. Their sportsmanship was incredible.

The fight started at a rapid pace with both men attacking viciously. They went toe-to-toe almost immediately, but Boon's power soon began to dominate and he won three of the first four rounds. A good left hook drove Crowley into a corner and although he jabbed and used the ring well, Boon ended the opening session with two good shots to the body.

There was a wariness about Crowley early in the second, but as the round progressed he gradually brought his boxing skills into play. Suddenly, as he moved forward and threw a left jab, the champion edged slightly to his right and countered with a vicious right which caught his opponent flush in the face. Dave staggered and his knees dipped to the canvas, but almost immediately he pulled himself upright and tried to fight back. Although Boon briefly tried to finish it, Crowley jabbed him and the champion chose to box on the retreat for the remaining seconds of the round.

Dave started round three with renewed confidence throwing a stream of jabs to Boon's head. Moving well there was more alertness about him as he avoided most of the champion's efforts to land big single shots. A good right opened a cut above Eric's left eye and a swelling developed beneath it.

There was huge mutual respect between the two which was highlighted by an extraordinary display of courtesy on the ropes when both apologised for offences which were not apparent to most ringsiders. Crowley clearly won the round, and although Boon scored with heavy single punches there was not the usual buzz and aggression in his work.

The fight really warmed up in the fourth with Crowley moving confidently forward jabbing out his left with great accuracy. Boon, relaxed and patient, seemed content to let him dictate proceedings, but then stopped him in his tracks with a solid straight left. Dave smiled and moved away, but the champion was looking to end it. Then, as so often happened with Boon, he became wild and many punches just hit thin air allowing Dave to contain him until the bell.

The fifth was an even round with Boon cleverly avoiding Crowley's jab, but doing very little work himself. It became messy with a lot of close-quarter mauling where neither man landed a punch of note. By this stage of the fight it was noticeable that Eric was using his right sparingly although when it landed made the challenger gasp.

Things livened up again in the sixth during which Boon landed a vicious right to the head which had the crowd yelling. Crowley, however, was untroubled and replied with a volley of punches to the head. Although the champion shook him with a solid left hook to the body, Crowley won the round with a late burst of accurate jabs.

There was very little in it as they came out for round seven. Crowley was into a good rhythm with his jab, and his ringcraft was excellent. Suddenly and unexpectedly, however, this ill-fated fight took an unfortunate twist. Dave caught Boon with a sharp jab followed by a right cross, but the champion stood his ground and drove him to the ropes where he unleashed three heavy rights. With great courage Crowley managed to work his way free, but as they clinched in the centre of the ring Boon threw another solid right. It caught Dave solidly on the shoulder causing him to fall back into a clinch.

Having worked up a good head of steam, Boon was anxious to bring the fight to an end and appeared to throw his challenger to the floor. Satisfied that his actions were legal, referee Jack Smith, belatedly picked up the count at 'three'.

Crowley meanwhile was a pitiful figure squatting in the centre of the ring, his right foot twisted beneath his body. He could barely move and with tears streaming down his face motioned mutely to his foot to indicate to his corner that he could not continue.

The referee's count had barely reached 'ten' when Boon's posse of excited cornermen scrambled through the ropes to embrace him. Eric was more controlled because although he had won and brought great delight to his fans, the victory had been achieved in a very disappointing way.

The crowd were absolutely stunned with many people bemused as to what had really occurred. It was an unhappy situation for everyone concerned. It had been an intriguing battle while it lasted with Crowley using all his skill and experience to pile up the points. The way he came back fighting after being stunned in round two was a testimony of his great fighting heart.

With a sick wife and a three-week-old baby daughter at home, the blackness of despair must have overwhelmed the former champion. Yet despite the agony and frustration of the situation, the heart of the man rebelled. Against all the pain he summoned up a twisted smile as Boon stood over him offering a gloved hand and broken words of sympathy.

Eric rose to equal heights in those moments of stress, and snatching the microphone from Master of Ceremonies, Pat Regan, he addressed the crowd. "I am very sorry about it all," he said with genuine emotion. "I wanted to win, but I would not have had it happen this way. I wish Dave Crowley better luck next time – he deserves a good break."

There was no display of joy from the champion when his arm was raised in victory because he felt no satisfaction at winning the way he did. He had won the Lonsdale belt outright in 11 months and 24 days before reaching the age of twenty, but he had not beaten Jim Higgins' long standing record.

Crowley smiled at his conqueror as he was carried to his corner where he beckoned to Regan who handed him the microphone as he slumped on his stool. Then with a superhuman effort he overcame his disappointment and apologised to the crowd, many of whom had pushed their way to the ringside to try and find out what had happened.

"Please forgive me," he said, "I am quite alright, but my ankle gave way. You can see I am not out of breath at all. It was such a fine fight and I thought I was winning."

The crowd cheered him loudly because there, in the hardest of all sports, were two young contestants apologising to their audience for what was a disappointing ending to a hugely competitive fight. It demonstrated what great sporting personalities they were. With typical professionalism they had overcome all the misfortunes which had occurred since Sydney Hulls first tried to stage their rematch.

Even then the problems weren't over because there was an inexcusable blunder by the Board of Control in not producing the Lonsdale belt which, by his victory, Boon had won outright.

"Where's the belt?" came shouts from all parts of the thinly populated arena when all the confusion surrounding the ending was over. Amid the shouts, Eric strolled around the ring looking about him and waiting for the customary presentation by a senior Board official. Much to his disappointment there was no such ceremony because instead of being at Harringay the belt was locked away in a vault miles from London for safe keeping throughout the duration of the war.

Earlier that week it had been carefully stated by the Board that should Boon win the fight he would be presented with a gold and enamelled replica of the Lonsdale belt which would be worth £250. The original would then continue in circulation. This was in fact against all the intentions of the belts in the minds of Lord Lonsdale and the committee of the old National Sporting Club. Those who won it outright received it with the names of past champions engraved on separate medallions.

Jack Solomons reacted angrily when he realised the situation and remonstrated with Board officials in front of ringside patrons. Quite properly the officials were not prepared to become involved in an altercation in public.

Meanwhile, Boon was devastated and burst into tears the moment he reached his dressing room. "Why didn't they give me the belt?" he asked Solomons the moment he returned.

Unable to contain his anger at seeing his young fighter so upset, Jack promptly did an about turn and headed back to the ringside. With a section of the crowd still chanting their dissatisfaction, he demanded an explanation from the Board officials.

In an attempt to calm the situation, the Steward in charge, Mr A Van Gelder, and General Secretary, Charles Donmall, went with Solomons to Boon's dressing room where there was a violent exchange of words. Van Gelder explained that the Board considered it safer to leave the belt in a vault rather than take it to the arena.

By this time a number of press reporters had gained access to the champion's dressing room and they grasped at every word. Donmall added that the belt was the property of the Board and Boon would receive a replica. Unfortunately, it had not been completed in time. This infuriated Solomons even further and a tense verbal battle raged between him and Donmall.

As the argument continued, Boon quietly got dressed, slipped out of the dressing room and left for Chatteris with friends. He didn't get involved in the argument and, despite his bitter disappointment, left it to his manager to sort out.

Solomons had still not calmed down when, two days later he stormed into the Board of Control offices at Soho waving a newspaper placard. *Daily Express* reporter, John McAdam, went with him as a witness. Again there were heated words between him and Donmall because Jack insisted that he was only prepared to speak to the Chairman, Colonel Myddleton.

In an attempt to defuse the situation, Myddleton said it was a new Board rule that only replicas would be given to outright winners. The days of the old battle-scarred belts were over so Boon shouldn't worry. The one he would get would be exactly the same as that held by the Board and of identical value.

"Alright," snapped Solomons, "if that's the case why not give this belt to Boon and the new one to the next champion?"

It was a reasonable question because as he remarked: "How many champions do actually win a belt outright – very few!"

Refusing to be drawn into a lengthy argument all the Chairman would say was that a new belt had been ordered and it would be handed to Eric as soon as possible. Not believing what he had been told about a new rule, Solomons left the Board offices and promptly issued a statement to the press in which he was highly critical of the regulatory body.

Jack knew the press were on his side because that morning most nationals published stories about the belt scenario. The majority were generally critical of the Board. Never before could experienced reporters recall an occasion when the winner was not presented with the belt in the ring after a championship contest. It was pointed out that if the Board feared for its safety why had this very belt spent three months in a public house and on another occasion displayed for several days in a shop window. Public opinion was also against the Board because people believed that they had an obligation even if the belt had been taken back from the champion afterwards.

With the situation clearly getting out of hand, Donmall issued a statement in which he said that the original belt was one of eight made to the Board's order three years earlier. He continued by stating that any boxer winning three championship contests at a particular weight was entitled to receive a replica of that belt and to the same value. It was this particular aspect which Solomons so bitterly disputed.

"Our lightweight belt was at stake for the first time in October 1936 and was won by Jimmy Walsh," said Donmall. "Later, Dave Crowley had it and passed it on to temporary possession of Boon. The present champion scored a second victory against Danahar and now he has secured a third success a replica has been ordered for him. It will bear the names of all the winners to date."

Although the statement went some way to appeasing the media, that was far from the end of matters. A few days later Solomons received a letter from the Board requiring him to appear before the Stewards on 20 December to explain his behaviour at their offices and also his outbursts at ringside after the fight.

*   *   *

The unfortunate ending to the Boon – Crowley fight raised serious concerns about Dave's overall fitness. Although it was discreetly kept from the press, he had strained an achilles tendon in training the week before. This was confirmed by his manager, Harry Levene, who revealed after the fight that the boxer received treatment at St Thomas' Hospital and that his trainer, Wally May, had also worked on him. "We all thought the leg would stand up to the strain," Levene told the press, "but it seems we were wrong."

He claimed that during the fight Dave staggered off balance and threw his whole weight on the injury. The damaged tendon just gave way. It was a pure accident and no criticism was levelled at Boon who was considered to be as clean a fighter as could be found in British rings. Levene stated that they wanted another fight with Boon in about five weeks time, declaring that it would draw a far greater crowd than the last one.

There were also concerns about Boon because, according to John McAdam, the champion's cornermen gloated to ringside reporters as they ushered their man from the ring that "he had done it with only one hand." Although Eric had been declared fit by a Board of Control doctor, naive and unprofessional comments were made by individuals close to him that he sustained a new injury to his right hand during the latter stages of training. It was also claimed that further damage occurred during the fight and that he had difficulty shaking hands with Crowley at the end.

In a subsequent interview with *Topical Times,* Mike Milligan explained that Boon suffered indescribable agony after landing the big right which wobbled Crowley in round two. Nobody except his cornermen knew what he was going through for the rest of the fight. When he dropped his hands in the fifth it was not carelessness, but because his whole body vibrated with pain. He could not raise them in self-defence. "Boon is the most courageous fighter in the world," said Milligan. "He won't give in unless he drops from sheer exhaustion. He has the heart of a lion – what a game boy – what a heart!"

Mike spoke with fervent admiration because if anyone knew Boon it was him. He had been like a father to him ever since his early days at the Devonshire Club, and it was a well known fact that wherever Eric went Mike was usually with him as was Harry Silver. He insisted that it would be at least four months before Eric could box again because his hand was in such a bad state.

Writing in the *Daily Herald*, James Butler advised Boon to take 12 months rest before his hand damage became irreversible. As Eric was scheduled for enlistment in the Royal Air Force in the near future he believed it would give him the perfect opportunity otherwise he would face early retirement from the ring. Butler was also concerned about Boon's weight and although he had a pound to spare against Crowley he did not appear to be as strong and aggressive as he was a year earlier.

Other media reports concluded that neither Boon nor Crowley had any right to be in the ring because they were not fit enough to take part in a championship contest. This heaped more pressure on the Board of Control and after reviewing the information before them the Stewards ordered Crowley and Harry Levene to appear before them on 20 December. That meeting at the Board was unparalled in the history of boxing and resulted in Hulls and Solomons resigning their respective positions as promoter and manager. What transpired was a revolt against the Board by Hulls, as the leading promoter, supported by Solomons, Levene and Dan Sullivan all of whom were prominent managers. All returned their licences and declared themselves no longer bound by the rules of the Board.

The trouble arose when the Board set themselves up as promoters to run the Red Cross tournament at Earls Court the previous month and sought to take boxers from contests already announced by Hulls for his Harringay show featuring Boon and Crowley. Hulls was called to the meeting over matters arising from that situation and promptly resigned.

He was followed by Solomons who had been called to explain his conduct over the Lonsdale belt situation following Boon's defeat of Crowley. As his actions had been heavily publicised Jack asked for the press to be present during the hearing of his case. Although his request was refused the Chairman offered him an adjournment to

189

seek legal representation and call members of the press as witnesses. He refused the offer and resigned. A press statement was subsequently issued by the Board that his resignation had been accepted.

Dave Crowley and Harry Levene were interviewed regarding the injury to Crowley which brought his contest with Boon to a conclusion. After full consideration of the facts before them the Stewards concluded that Dave was justified in taking part in the contest. A press statement was issued to this effect.

In a further discussion the Stewards agreed that Boon, having won three lightweight championship contests under the Board of Control jurisdiction, be the recipient of a Lord Lonsdale belt and, in accordance with Board regulations, be entitled to a pension of £1 a week on reaching the age of fifty.

Although Eric was not called to any of the meetings, events of that afternoon would have a marked effect on his career and change the face of boxing. Hulls and Solomons stated publically that they intended to stage unlicensed promotions, Jack twice a week at the Devonshire Club and Hulls at arenas throughout the United Kingdom. Boon, as a Board of Control licence holder, would risk immediate suspension if he worked with them.

*   *   *

Following the successful defence of his title, Boon was in great demand for public appearances. A week later he attended an amateur show promoted by popular Finsbury Park middleweight, George Howard, at Adelphi House in The Strand. Accompanied by Jack Solomons, he presented George with a certificate of merit awarded by *Boxing* for his recent fine victory over Dick Turpin.

On another occasion Boon visited a RAF Bomber Station in East Anglia where he gave a training exhibition and donated a silver challenge cup to the squadron boxing section. He was always willing to do work to help the troops and war cause. Despite wanting to keep the gloves he wore to win the Lonsdale belt outright, he donated them for auction, as did Crowley. The two pairs fetched a total of 30 guineas which went towards providing sports equipment for British troops.

On 17 December, a Sunday, Eric and Arthur Danahar faced each other again on a snooker table at Thurstons Club in London. It was part of a golf and snooker event in aid of the Red Cross in which Henry Cotton partnered Joe Davis against Archie Crampton and Tom Newman. Boon volunteered to replace jockey, Gordon Richards, who had been involved in a car accident, and Danahar willingly accepted an invitation to play him.

The following day, Boon topped a variety bill at the Embassy Theatre, Peterborough. Presented by Sydney Hulls and Jack Solomons, it was a reproduction of the vaudeville show in which he and Harry Silver had performed so successfully at theatres around the country earlier in the year.

The compere was Frank Curren and supporting acts included D'Alba described as 'the television girl', and well known BBC vocal act, Olive and Isidore Carlton. In advertising the event, Solomons asked that any young boxers wanting to spar with Boon gave their names and addresses to the box office at the Embassy.

The show ran for four days to packed houses and the champion was inundated with requests for autographs and interviews with the local press. One topic of interest was a challenge from Dave Crowley for a third contest with a side-stake of £250. Dave had said that despite being knocked out by Boon on two occasions, he still thought he was the better man.

"It would be no sort of victory to knock him out again," said Boon. "I have nothing to gain. I want to meet Henry Armstrong for the championship of the world. I know I can beat him, not only beat him, but knock him out. I should like to meet him over here, but it really makes no difference because I am ready for him."

Although Boon had continually sustained hand and face injuries in the ring many local people believed that he was fortunate not to have been incapacitated as a result of motor accidents. There had been a number of occasions when he had minor shunts with other vehicles, one of which occurred at Haddenham when he was in collision with a large lorry belonging to local firm, Messrs H T Setchell. Nobody was injured, but Eric's car was slightly damaged and the fact that he was the driver the incident received coverage in local newspapers.

His most serious accident, however, occurred in December 1939 at Mepal Viaduct when he struck a seventeen-year-old youngster who was on his way to chapel. Police and a doctor were summoned to the scene and after receiving initial treatment for his injuries the young man was taken to Addenbrookes Hospital at Cambridge suffering from a fracture to his left leg. Eric escaped unscathed.

15

CAREER IN JEOPARDY

Following the political turmoil between his manager, promoter and the Board of Control, Boon sensibly remained out of the way at Chatteris and kept a low profile. He received tremendous support back in the Fens because local people were justifiably angry about the Lonsdale belt situation. Being mature and level headed, Eric soon got over his disappointment and enjoyed a period of celebration at his home throughout Christmas and the New Year. Not only had he become the youngest boxer to win a Lonsdale belt outright, but he also celebrated his twentieth birthday on 30 December. With his sister, Brenda, reaching twenty-one just seven days later, the family made sure it was a time to savour because they all knew Eric could be called for National Service at any time.

This was a situation that worried Harry Silver because he believed the war would separate him from his bosom pal. Although he was only nineteen, Harry didn't want to wait for his age group to be called up so he and Eric spoke with Jack Solomons hoping something could be done. Jack wrote to the RAF Recruiting Officer at Cambridge asking if Silver could join up at the same time as Boon. Although he explained in great detail that apart from being active professional boxers, they were inseparable pals, it was all to no avail.

Meanwhile, the popularity of Boon was recognised by people in the music business and in early January 1940 he was lauded in a three verse song with refrain to a marching tune. "Boonie, Wonderful Boon" was written by Rose Broughton with music by James Morrell and published by Arthur H. Stockwell Ltd of London EC4. The sheet music went on sale at local music shops and newsagents.

Back in London a further meeting was held between Hulls, Solomons and the Board of Control Stewards. Although it was hoped that their differences could be resolved peacefully, there was no softening of attitudes. Bad feeling had become too deeply rooted and consequently the meeting broke up without achieving anything.

By this stage Hulls had arranged to promote regular shows at the Stadium Club, the first of which took place on New Year's Day. Solomons quickly followed suit by putting on two shows a week at the Devonshire Club with all the windows blacked out.

Hulls first promotion drew the wrath of the Southern Area Council at their first meeting of the New Year when a number of boxers, trainers and managers who were involved had their licences suspended. The promoter responded by telling the press that he wasn't in the least bit concerned by the action. He added that he intended staging further shows at 11 venues in various parts of the country during the coming weeks. He even put Boon's career in jeopardy by announcing that he would box an exhibition bout with local lightweight, Frankie McAvoy, at Colston Hall, Bristol, on 15 January. James Butler of the *Daily Herald* believed that if the bout went ahead it could cost Boon his title. Hulls, however, remained unconcerned telling the journalist that Eric was the star turn who the Bristol public wanted to see. Jack Solomons adopted a similar attitude stating that Eric would not be fighting seriously until his injured hand was completely sound.

Hulls and Solomons also organised another series of vaudeville shows for Boon. Those at Peterborough before Christmas had been a huge success so while he was out of ring action he could earn handsomely from the stage. He was joined by Harry Silver, Nat Seller, Mike Milligan and Buster Cohen, and the act was described as being even better than when it was first produced at the London Coliseum the previous year.

In a show at the Theatre Royal, Aldershot, one night in early January, however, there was a unique and dramatic occurrence. Boon invited members of the audience to the stage to spar with him and was surprised at how many took up the offer. At the end of the first house a soldier approached Eric and asked if he could spar with him during the second performance. He said that he was bringing a lot of his mates from his regiment so Boon agreed.

The first sparring partner was a lightweight and they boxed a fast, entertaining session in the friendliest of spirits. The soldier followed and, egged on by the yells of his mates in the audience, he tore into Boon in the opening round. He was a burley fellow over six feet tall and weighing almost 13 stone and despite Eric warning him to take it easy he lashed out with full force and chased him all over the stage.

As the second round commenced Mike Milligan, who was watching from the wings, saw the look on Boon's face and, turning to Buster Cohen, said: "It's off here Buster."

Mike knew Eric better than most and with the soldier showing no signs of easing up Boon decided to teach him a lesson. Steadying himself, he met his charging 'opponent' with a couple of light left jabs and then smashed over one of his specialist right hooks. The soldier crashed to the floor, but rose after about 10 seconds only to be floored again by another solid shot. This time he was flat on his back and out cold.

The audience watched in amazement, but on realising the soldier was attempting to take a liberty, heartily approved of the manner in which he was despatched. It was more reminiscent of the crude goings on in a boxing booth than vaudeville entertainment on a theatre stage.

When he recovered the soldier apologised to Boon and promised he would never try to be so clever again. The following night he was in the audience with a group of friends and when Eric went on stage he was one of the first to stand up and give him a good hand. Then, within hearing of many in the house, shouted, "There is the greatest fighter in the world. He's got a punch like Joe Louis and blimey, I ought to know."

Whilst at Aldershot, Boon took time out between shows to entertain troops at the local army camp. A couple of days later he went down with a severe dose of influenza, and on returning to Chatteris was advised by his doctor to spend at least a week in bed. In some ways the timing of the illness was fortunate because it meant he wasn't able to appear on Sydney Hulls unlicensed shows at Bristol.

Although Hulls tried to get Tommy Farr as a replacement to fill the top spot, he claimed to have been shaken up in a car skid the previous day. There was great disappointment on the night of the show because most people in the packed house were there to see Boon. In a statement on behalf of the promoter, it was optimistically announced that Eric would box in the city as soon as he was fit.

Among the visitors to Eric's house during his illness was Harry Silver who made his bedroom look like a fruit shop. One day whilst he was laid up Boon found the strength to get to the telephone and call Jack Solomons. "I'm dead ill guv'nor," he mumbled in a husky voice. "I can't move a step so can you send me a few quid?"

Although Jack was concerned about his young champion's wellbeing, he burst out laughing at the request. "What the hell do you want money for?" he asked.

"Nothing really guv'nor," replied Boon, "but I'm broke and I'll feel a lot better if I've got a few quid handy."

*   *   *

On 7 February a discussion took place at the Board of Control offices regarding the presentation of the Lonsdale belt to Boon at a National Sporting Club promotion at Earls Court five days later. Charles Donmall sent him a telegram to this effect, but the following day a response was received from Messrs Chatterton & Company, Solicitors, declining the offer.

Boon was still angry with the Board and, after a series of telephone conversations, a solicitor's clerk visited their offices on 10 February. After delivering an authorisation and receipt signed by the boxer, he was handed the Lonsdale belt which he took to Sydney Hulls' office where a meeting had been arranged. Eric was there together with Hulls, Solomons and a reporter from *Boxing*. Excitedly, he opened the brown paper parcel to find that he had finally got his hands on the shining new belt. "They must have polished it up," he said cheekily as he strapped it around his waist.

The belt had his name neatly engraved on it as the outright winner thereby bringing the whole unpleasant business to a conclusion. Despite all the massive publicity surrounding the original problems, only a few lines appeared in the national press once it was resolved.

That night Boon was honoured by the townsfolk of Chatteris at a function at the Palace Ballroom. Presentations were made to him of a writing desk, chair and fountain pen in recognition of the distinction he had brought upon himself and Chatteris by winning the Lonsdale belt outright. Local people including tradesmen, farmers, policemen and errand boys had all contributed what they could afford to the organising committee. They were extremely proud of the youngster who put their little Fenland town on the map. Despite the fame and riches that had come his way, Eric never changed his personality. He was a friend to many people and they were determined he should be honoured.

The ceremony was presided over by Alderman Leonard Childs, and he was joined on the stage by Eric's parents, Arthur Binder, the Rev. J.C. Hawthorne, Vicar of Chatteris and members of Chatteris Urban District Council. Over 200 people attended and proceeds from the event were donated to a charity for the comforts of local men serving in the armed forces.

Alderman Childs said the gathering was unique in the history of Chatteris. People had come together to honour a fellow townsman, not only for the wonderful things he had achieved in sport, but because he had made the world realise that there was such a place called Chatteris. "A few years ago it was always said that Chatteris was a place near March," he remarked, "but now it was where Eric Boon comes from."

"Greater than any of Eric's achievements," continued the Alderman, "is that in spite of all the praise he has received and all the publicity which has been given to him, he still remains the boy who came from the Chatteris Amateur Boxing Club."

The speaker described highlights in Boon's career, but recalled a specific incident when a reporter from a national daily newspaper called at his house for an interview. He wasn't in, but after a stroll around the nearby streets the reporter found Eric playing marbles with a group of boys.

Alderman Childs concluded by saying that everyone present wished Boon all the best for the future and thanked him for all that he had done for Chatteris. They looked forward to the time when they could refer to him as a world champion. Loud and enthusiastic applause greeted the champion as he stepped forward to accept the presentation.

There was a ripple of amusement when Eric told the audience that he did not deserve all the praise because he did not suppose there was anyone present whose back door he had not kicked in at some time or other. "I cannot find words to express myself as I would like to," he said, "but I do thank you for this wonderful presentation. I would like to thank all of my friends who have believed in me and followed me for eight years. I hope to go to America soon to fight Henry Armstrong, and if I do I can assure you I shall do my best to bring back the welterweight championship of the world.

*   *   *

In London, the Marquess of Queensberry and John Harding, who was still licensed by the Board of Control, started promotions again at the Empress Hall in aid of the Red Cross. This meant that boxers were no longer dependent on Hulls and Solomons for work. Furthermore, there was less likelihood of them losing their licences.

Hulls realised that something had to be done and gave Jack Solomons, as his matchmaker, one week to prepare a big fight programme in opposition to Harding's plans. It was just the opportunity Jack wanted, and to ensure the show was a sell-out he made a mouth-watering contest between Boon and former world champion, Jack 'Kid' Berg.

Although well past his best, Berg was still a great favourite and on 26 January faced Harry Davis of Bethnal Green in one of the fiercest fights seen at the Devonshire Club for a long time. The doors were closed half of an hour before boxing was due to commence and hundreds more fans were locked outside. When trouble flared, Police had to be called to disperse them.

The chief supporting contest between East End youngsters, Harry 'Kid' Silver and Harry Lazar, looked none the less attractive. Regular performers at the Devonshire, both had huge followings and Solomons had been wanting to match them for several months.

The fight between Boon and Berg was made over 15 rounds and scheduled to take place at the Empress Hall, Earls Court on 29 February, and after some argument agreement was reached for it to be at 10st 7. Asked by a reporter for *Weekly Sporting Review* why the fight was over the championship limit, Hulls remarked: "Don't you know? It's for the rebels championship."

By agreeing to the fight Boon appeared to have come out in the open as a willing participant on an unlicensed promotion. Up until this point no other British champion had actively taken the side of the rebels, but the press were convinced that should Eric go through with the fight against Berg, the Board of Control were sure to strip him of his title.

"They probably will," Solomons told James Butler. "In fact we are expecting them to make that move. If they do declare the lightweight title vacant I will invite the leading boxing writers to say against whom Boon should have defended his title."

At his promotion at the Stadium Club on 29 January, Hulls announced details of future shows he intended to stage. He said he planned to use Boon, Berg and Tommy Farr as the principals, and added that he was prepared to give Ronnie James the chance to press his claims for a title fight against Boon.

That night Eric and Harry Silver boxed an exhibition in aid of St Dunstans which was brought to the attention of the Southern Area Council. When contacted by James Butler the following day, Board Secretary, Charles Donmall, said it was for the Area Council to decide if Boon had infringed Board regulations. As the promotion was made up primarily of bouts between stable lads, it did not require a Board licence.

Donmall added that the Board had been asked to appoint officials because permission had been given for two professional boxers to take part. When it was subsequently discovered that Master of Ceremonies, Pat Regan, was a suspended licence holder, they withdrew the officials.

*　　　*　　　*

Following his illness Boon had remained at home for a couple of weeks and spent most of his time relaxing by shooting and driving in the countryside. Once the fight with Berg was agreed he moved back to London and got into condition at Joe Bloom's gym near Covent Garden. Within a couple of weeks he looked in great shape and his presence attracted large crowds, although Bloom, being a strict disciplinarian, allowed only a selected few inside.

During the course of his preparation Boon estimated that he would weigh about 10 stone against Berg, but insisted that he would continue to fight at lightweight. Jack Solomons agreed and during a press conference said: "Eric is still a lightweight. After he has fought Berg I will make his next match at 9st 12. He will then have two more fights and wait until June when his six month's grace will have expired. By that time he will be ready to defend his title."

It was an ambitious statement, but Jack appeared to have overlooked two major obstacles. As Eric had registered for National Service on 17 February he was due to be called up at any time and once that happened the military authorities would decide his future. Furthermore, the Board of Control would be unlikely to sanction a title defence should Eric box on any unlicensed promotions.

Berg, meanwhile, set up his training camp at Windsor and reports indicated that he was preparing harder than for any fight since he returned from America six months earlier. He had been an idol in the East End for many years and was thrilling fight fans when Boon was still a small boy playing about at his father's forge. Many people in the East End were convinced that Jack's ringcraft and vast experience would be sufficient to keep the fighting enthusiasm of Boon at bay. The bookies, however, disagreed and made Eric a strong odds-on favourite. Although most of the sports writers agreed with the bookies, Berg really fancied his chances. "I'm in condition," he told Geoffrey Simpson of the *Daily Mail.* "I stay alright and I flatter myself that I know more about the game than Boon."

In another interview with James Butler, Berg said he believed Eric's style would suit him. "If Boon believes he's going to win quickly he will be greatly surprised," he remarked.

Advance bookings went exceptionally well with over £2,300 being taken within a week of the contest being announced. The fans wanted it, the press boys loved it and their stories brightened the gloom of war in the weeks leading up to it. Everything looked set for a fantastic fight yet nobody was prepared for the bombshell Boon would drop the day before it was due to take place.

Eric clearly had every intention of going through with the fight because he trained vigorously and was very upbeat when interviewed by the press. He told everyone who went to see him that he felt certain of beating Berg and even hinted at future plans towards the British welterweight title.

Neither Hulls nor Solomons had any doubts about Boon facing Berg. He was at the Devonshire Club on Sunday 25 February and boxed an exhibition at the Stadium Club the following afternoon.

On each occasion he appeared to be on his usual friendly and jocular terms with Solomons, Mike Milligan and others who had nursed him through his ring career.

One surprising feature of Boon's training for the Berg fight, however, was the absence of Nat Seller who had prepared him for each of his championship contests. Without any apparent explanation Eric had taken on Eddie Edgar, and Seller was known to be very upset by the chain of events. Yet despite the change, Boon looked in magnificent condition and with just three days to go was brimming with confidence. "I feel as strong as a lion," he told James Butler after 10 rounds of sparring and a rigorous session of ball punching and skipping. Asked if he had seen Berg in action he replied: "Yes, he's a bit of a whirlwind, but I think my big punch will slow him down."

On the eve of the fight, however, Sydney Hulls received a letter from a firm of solicitors acting for Boon stating that it would be impossible for him to go through with it. A few days earlier rumours had been widespread that the fight would be called off and if that happened hundreds within the gambling fraternity stood to lose a huge amount of money.

Boon told Frank Butler of the *Daily Express* that difficulties arose the previous week when he contracted German Measles. He had a temperature of 102 degrees and his doctor ordered him to bed. "So I said I would not fight Berg," said Eric. "This got out amongst the betting boys who must have taken exception because I received mysterious phone calls threatening to beat me up if I refused to fight."

"I was told that a razor gang would be waiting for Fred Curran at whose house I have been staying," continued Boon. "They were going to get him, my trainer, Eddie Edgar, and myself."

Boon explained that as he felt under pressure to go through with the fight, he continued to train. "Then after thinking the whole affair over I became angry at the thought of betting gangs trying to force me into the fight. So I am calling the whole thing off," he remarked.

As soon as he heard what was going on Reg Boon moved to London to support his son. He went everywhere with him and, acting like a bodyguard, stayed by his side throughout the night. Contrary to their expectations, nobody approached Eric or made any further threats.

Nobody knew what to believe because all sorts of rumours were being banded about. Reporters from most of the national papers were digging around like ferrets trying to get at the truth and when their stories were published they read like chapters from a 'whodunnit.'

The sensational remark "Razor Gangs Threaten Boon" was one bold headline while the back page of another national newspaper was headed "Boon Fight Sensation."

Despite all the dramatic theories it soon became clear that the Board of Control were using Boon as a weapon against Hulls and Solomons who had developed a total disregard for their regulations and authority. The bitterness between the parties was deep and Charles Donmall adopted the view that they needed to be taught a lesson.

Matters came to a head on the eve of the fight when Boon received a letter from the Board in which he was told that if he went ahead with the fight against Berg he would be in breach of regulations. The letter clearly had the desired effect because the first thing Eric did was to telephone Hulls and explain that he was pulling out. The situation was not helped by the fact that Boon's relationship with Solomons had begun to turn sour. Although he had continued to train for the fight there were rumours that he had become dissatisfied with his financial arrangements.

James Butler was a vastly experienced journalist who was close to all of the parties. In an attempt to get a jump ahead of other newsmen he went to Hulls' office at Shaftesbury Avenue where he found the promoter involved in a tense discussion with Solomons. Butler was told about Eric's telephone call and that he had gone to see Donmall at the Board of Control offices a short distance away in Soho.

Anxious to stay close to developments the reporter hot-footed it to the Dean Street headquarters where he bumped into Boon's new trainer, Eddie Edgar, in a corridor on the second floor. "Where is Boon?" asked Butler. Acting dumb, Edgar said he wasn't sure, but not believing him Butler decided to wait. There was an uneasy silence for a few minutes and then a door to the main office opened and Donmall appeared. "Will you come in Eddie?" he said addressing Edgar.

Butler's suspicions were aroused even further when, a short while later, he saw some shadowy figures pass the glass panel of the door. He darted downstairs and into the street where he saw three men running away. He chased after them and discovered it was Boon, his father and Edgar.

Although Frank was a journalist for whom Eric had the greatest respect, he flatly refused to disclose what had been discussed in the Board offices. The reporter told him bluntly that it was believed he had pulled out of the fight. "The matter is in the hands of my lawyer," is all Boon would say.

Butler quickly returned to Hulls' office and asked Jack Solomons for his version of events. Jack admitted that the relationship between him and Boon had become strained due to money. He explained that the first hint of disruption arose about two weeks earlier when Boon withdrew several hundred pounds from the bank and used it to purchase a new car and other luxury items. "Since then he has been asking me to hand over about £2,500 which is owed to him," said Solomons. "It represents the balance of his earnings and is at the bank in our joint names."

Solomons told Butler that he reluctantly consented to Boon's request, but said he would hand the money to Hulls who would pay it to him after he had fought Berg. "But this suggestion evidently didn't appeal to him because he didn't want it tied up," remarked Jack who insisted that his idea had always been to keep the money in trust.

"Remember I brought him along from a six-round fighter to a British champion so naturally I feel very upset by his attitude," continued Solomons. "I have him under contract and I will keep him to it."

Boon had frequently referred to Solomons as "the man who gave me my greatest chance, always giving me a square deal and a man to whom I owe most of my success." He had uttered similar remarks to Hulls, and everyone who knew of their close relationship were astonished at the amazing split. Many in the press believed Boon was duty-bound to stick by Hulls and Solomons and should not on any account let them down because in the past he had received scrupulously fair treatment.

Later the same day Vivian J. Williams & Company, Solicitors acting on behalf of Boon, issued a statement to the press which read:

> This morning Mr Boon received a communication from the British Boxing Board of Control referring to the tournament at Earls Court tomorrow and pointed out "that as the person not holding a promoter's licence should you appear you will break Regulation 17, para 7." In consequence of that communication Mr Boon cannot appear at this tournament otherwise he feels he will be jeopardising his title and his future.

At 3 pm that afternoon a letter from Boon's solicitor was delivered by hand to Hulls' office. It read:

> We have been consulted by Mr Eric Boon with reference to the agreement alleged to have been made on our client's behalf by Mr Jack Solomons and yourself relating to the appearance of our client in a boxing tournament at the Empress Stadium, Earls Court on Thursday, 29th.

201

Our client has instructed us to inform you that this agreement was not made with the consent of himself or his father, and in fact, was in direct opposition to his own wishes. Furthermore, owing to the circumstances which have occurred between our client, Mr Jack Solomons and the British Boxing Board of Control, our client is of the opinion that Mr Solomons has broken the agreement by which Mr Solomons was appointed as our client's manager.

In addition our client has this morning received a communication from the British Boxing Board of Control in consequence of which it becomes impossible for our client to appear in the boxing tournament above referred to.

Hulls was perplexed and could not understand the amazing turn of events. He met with Boon, explained the seriousness of his predicament and appealed with him to fight, but Eric was adamant. "I cannot fight," he said repeatedly.

In a desperate attempt to turn things around Hulls and Solomons consulted their lawyers, but were advised that if Boon boxed on an unlicensed show the Board, by their own rules, would have no alternative but to suspend him as they had already done with a number of other licence holders. Hulls, who had suffered more than his share of headaches in recent months, accepted that Eric had been given strong advice not to go through with the fight.

As almost 5,000 tickets had been sold, Hulls was determined to go through with the show and at very late notice managed to get Sergeant Eddie Ryan to replace Boon against Berg. Highlight of the evening was an enthralling contest in which seventeen-years-old Harry Lazar from Aldgate outpointed Harry 'Kid' Silver over 10 rounds.

A couple of days later Lazar's manager, Alf Jacobs, issued a challenge to Boon for a fight at 9st 9 for £500 a side. The challenge seemed rather premature especially as Jacobs told the press that under no circumstances would he allow Lazar to box more than eight rounds. Harry's father, Ike Lazar, however, told *Weekly Sporting Review* that the challenge to Boon for a fight at 9st 9 was made to get their own back on him because when the fight with Silver was being negotiated Eric kept advising Silver to get it at 9st 3. "We rather resented Boon's interference," he remarked. "The match was entirely up to us to fix and although Boon was Silver's best pal, he had no right to butt in. As you know they fought at 9st 9, so to get our own back on Boon we issued a challenge to meet Harry at that weight, but if Boon ever makes that again I'll eat a sandbag."

*   *   *

The press hailed Boon's decision to pull out of the fight with Berg as a victory for the Board of Control over the so called rebels, Hulls and Solomons. Although details of what was said during his meeting with Donmall were never publicly revealed by either party, the general feeling was that Eric was left in no doubt as to what would happen if he boxed on an unlicensed show, particularly for Hulls and Solomons. Boon was a proud champion and, as his Lonsdale belt meant the world to him, he adopted the only sensible course.

The dispute between the Board of Control, Hulls and Solomons continued to fester and in doing so caused great difficulty to many licence holders. With Hulls being one of the most powerful and influential boxing figures in the country, it was a problem that needed resolving. The Board eventually accepted this and in April 1940 reinstated him as a licensed promoter, but steadfastly refused to allow Solomons back. Defiant as ever Jack went his own way and continued to stage unlicensed shows at the Devonshire Club until it was bombed later that year. The last show at the nostalgic old arena was on 19 May.

16

SO WHAT REALLY HAPPENED?

Whilst it was clear that the Board of Control, and Charles Donmall in particular, used Boon to get at Solomons for his unacceptable behaviour, there was much more to the overall situation than was ever made public. "A lot more will be heard about this," a close ally of Boon told Isidore Green, "and believe me it won't make pleasant publicity."

Forced to keep quiet, at least for the time being, Green stated that he could not reveal intimate details of behind-the-scenes activity to which he was privy. In *Weekly Sporting Review* at the beginning of March he wrote:

> I can, for the moment, relate the story in a non-committal manner, but the mystery remains why the Board of Control, or Boon himself for that matter, did not step in the moment the match was made, or at the latest when posters went up, and convey to Sydney Hulls that some kind of action was likely. It was always possible that as Hulls was no longer a member of the Board that problems were likely to arise over the promotion.

Two weeks earlier Green had revealed that he had obtained a startling piece of information concerning outside elements who were trying to influence Boon's boxing career behind Jack Solomons' back. There were allegations of double-crossing being attempted, but Boon had played the game and told his manager what was going on. For his part, Jack had apparently taken steps to rid his boxer of the unwanted pressure. In his column of 1 March, Green wrote:

> It would have been a wonderful story for any newspaper. Disclosures of this nature would have made the public blink with amazement, but I could see no real purpose being served by the publication of the story in these columns so I decided to withhold it.

In the days following the split between Boon and Solomons a variety of stories did the rounds. Some very ugly things were said about them both, but most was just malicious gossip. Despite being sworn to secrecy over certain matters Green was not prepared to just let the matter drop. After a short cooling off period he decided to try again and had long talks with Boon, Solomons and Hulls in an attempt to get at the real truth.

The man who said least was Hulls. He was reluctant to commit himself to the facts, but what he did say he made Green pledge not to use it for publication. Solomons had more to say, but again the journalist was sworn to secrecy. "It would not be advisable to print it at this stage," he wrote in *Weekly Sporting Review.*

Jack did say that despite what had occurred he bore Boon no malice. He believed the boxer had been influenced by certain parties "who he will be glad to get away from eventually."

Green badly needed another interview with Boon, but having been highly critical of him in an earlier article in *Weekly Sporting Review*, did not expect much cooperation. Knowing Eric was performing his vaudeville act at the Kilburn Empire, he turned up without warning one evening in mid-March. After the show he was shown to the champion's crowded dressing room and to his surprise was given a warm welcome when announced.

Boon knew why the journalist was there and by a series of diplomatic manoeuvres the room gradually cleared leaving only Boon, Fred Curran and Eddie Edgar with Green. "Well Eric," said Green, "the whole world is saying things about you and Jack Solomons so let's have the truth, the whole truth and nothing but the truth from you yourself."

At first the boxer eyed Green rather suspiciously, but then smiled and said: "If I was to tell you the whole truth I'm afraid I'd surprise you and even shock you. Anyway it isn't the right time to say too much. I could tell you a hell of a lot, but it mustn't go to print just yet."

At that point Fred Curran interrupted, "My god, there's a lot to be said now and a lot that's going to be said later too," he remarked sternly. "Eric is right, we've got to go carefully about what we say at the moment, and if we tell you anything and ask you to keep certain terms in strict confidence, we hope you will understand."

"I had every reason for backing out of the fight," insisted Boon, "and with all due respect to Jack Solomons, the most important thing was I didn't want to prejudice my Lonsdale belt and my championship by boxing for a rebel promotion."

"A good many people told me, and you were one of them, that my duty was to have stood by Hulls and Solomons no matter whether they were rebels or not," continued Eric. "Maybe, but the British Boxing Board of Control is, after all said and done, the British Boxing Board of Control, and they have all the powers and all the say in the running of boxing. If I had stepped into the ring against Berg that night there was every possibility that my belt would have been taken away from me and I would have been robbed of all my chances of fighting for a title again in the future."

"But Eric, you must have known these consequences when you agreed to the fight," argued Green. "Didn't you actually train for the fight? Up until three days before it was due, didn't you appear in the ring at the Stadium Club, and didn't the Master of Ceremonies announce to the crowd present that you were ready for the contest with Berg the following Tuesday?"

The reply Green received stunned him and in his article in *Weekly Sporting Review* on 16 March he stated that he wished there was a law which permitted him to print it. He claimed it was a revelation which knocked the bottom out of anything else he was expecting, but it made him realise that Boon had been involved in some extremely embarrassing business over which at that time he had no control.

"Tell me Eric, have you got any ill feelings towards Jack Solomons?" asked Green.

"Emphatically no," replied Boon. "I have always found him a decent fellow, but I am very, very annoyed at his obstinacy in refusing to release my money. I know I shall get it alright and I know that every penny I have earned in the boxing game will be handed over to me."

"I am not so keen on some of the hangers-on and I didn't like the way that some of those fellows ordered me around and offered me their advice," continued Eric, "but you can say quite openly in the *Sporting Review* that Jack Solomons treated me, apart from this recent quarrel I've had over the money, like a toff. When all this business is over I hope to be on friendly terms with him again."

Boon's remarks seemed to refute many of the ill-founded rumours that would have led the public to believe that he and his manager were at daggers drawn. One was that the champion was under a new manager, and Green put forward the name of a particular individual and asked Eric if it was true.

"There is absolutely no truth in that whatsoever," retorted Boon. "People have been saying things which at best are pure guesswork and you can tell your readers that no other manager is conducting my affairs."

Boon also denied that he had fallen out with many of his friends at the Devonshire Club. "All I know is that what I have done is in my best interests," he remarked. "Yes I admit I have had several arguments with some of the Devonshire Club heads, but I am not 'Boy' Boon any more. I am Eric Boon and I couldn't tolerate being treated like a kid all my life. Jack Solomons looked after me sensibly and I did all that he told me, but I couldn't stand the outside influences."

Fred Curren made it clear that he was only interested in Boon's vaudeville arrangements and was in no way connected with his boxing affairs. Fred was more direct in his comments and said that there had been a number of occasions when he couldn't help being a spectator to what was going on behind the backs of Boon, Solomons, Hulls and others leading up to the split. He said Eric was quite within his rights to adopt the attitude he did.

"The last thing I wanted to do was let Solomons or the public down," said Boon. "I had to consider the position from every angle, but the damage was done by a certain element which, in its anxiety to go ahead with its plans, gave me the least consideration. Better advice prevailed and I accepted it. If only the public knew the real facts."

Green then asked Boon if there was any truth in a story that he had been threatened by a mob who would razor him if he failed to fight Berg. At that point Eddie Edgar interrupted and said he had been threatened and was compelled to seek Police protection. "I don't know what they wanted of me," he remarked. "I wasn't concerned with the controversy, I am just a workman. I was asked to do a job and I accepted. Nothing else concerned me. Eric approached me to train him. I didn't ask any questions because I was just glad of the opportunity to earn a few honest pounds. Why should I have been threatened?"

Boon, however, did not treat the reporter's question very seriously although he did admit that he heard that a certain mob had been formed to 'do' him. Although it annoyed him at the time he treated it as hot air. He made it abundantly clear to Green that he did not in any way associate Solomons with the threats. "Jack would not have any part of that business I am sure," he told Green. "I have a good idea who was responsible for this dirty business, but let's forget it."

Earlier in the evening, whilst watching the show, Green noted the absence of some of Boon's colleagues who had appeared in previous performances. In particular, Harry Silver did not box the usual exhibition, his place being taken by Johnny Ryan from Kilburn. Lew 'Buster' Cohen's role as Master of Ceremonies was filled by Fred Curran who was also responsible for the production. Eddie Edgar took the place of Nat Seller. Mike Milligan was not there either and Devonshire Club regulars, who had filled the dressing room in every town where the act was performed, were also missing.

In answer to questions from the journalist, Boon insisted that the recent troubles had in no way affected his friendship either Silver or Seller. "Nat is an innocent party," said Boon, "but in view of my split with Solomons I was compelled to dispense with his services."

Before Green and Boon parted company Eric hinted that he could be involved in a really important contest in the not too distant future. "If this fight comes off you will have plenty to write about," he said with a wink and a smile. He then shook hands with Green and asked him to convey his regards to his East End friends. "They will judge me in a different light when the real truth comes out," he remarked.

Green was very close to Boon and knew him even better than seasoned national newspaper reporters like James Butler and his son Frank. Eric revealed things which he didn't tell anyone else, but in doing so would not permit Green to publish them. The young journalist knew that whilst Boon was loyal to Solomons, he was an impressionable young man who had attracted the attention of undesirable hangers-on. Sadly, that was a feature of the fight game and Green had to live with the frustration of missing out on a major exclusive. Had he published everything he knew, he would have left his friend open to danger, so instead he wrote a lengthy article headlined, *"Boon's own Story* which appeared in *Weekly Sporting Review* on 16 March.

A few weeks later Jack Solomons praised the publication, and in particular Isidore Green, for what he described as the fairest and least biased of all the stories written about the affair. "Yours was without doubt the outstanding story of many that were published," he remarked, "and I should like you to express my appreciation of it to your readers."

Jack was so gratified that he purchased 300 copies of the paper which he distributed amongst his friends and the sporting populus of Chatteris in order that they could read the real cause of the breakaway by Boon.

*   *   *

The proposed contest between Boon and Berg threw up problems of another kind for *Daily Express* sports writer, John McAdam. He was strongly opposed to the fight and in a radio broadcast to the armed forces on 24 February was rather damming of Berg.

> Speaking of older men, why just as soon as he had drawn his old-aged pension, next Thursday 'Kid' Berg will totter along to Earls Court to fight Eric Boon, the British champion, and the only one of the top-notchers to stick to his reputation. After that fight Berg is almost certain to start thinking of a better way of earning his living.

In a High Court action on 25 September 1940, Berg was awarded £500 damages for the alleged slander. McAdam appealed and in the High Court on 4 March 1941 that appeal was allowed.

*   *   *

The day after the fight with Berg was called off, Boon received a telephone call from Swansea promoter, Bert James, wanting to open negotiations for him to defend his lightweight title against Ronnie James at the Veitch Field during May. Having split from Solomons, Eric decided to handle his own affairs so in order to get away from all the recent acrimony, he caught the first available train to West Wales.

There was another incentive for the champion to make the trip because by this time there were conflicting reports that he had become engaged to Miss Wendy Elliott, a blonde musical comedy actress, who was playing the leading role in 'No, No, Nanette' at the Swansea Empire.

One report claimed that they had planned to officially announce their engagement immediately after the Berg fight. At first Eric denied the suggestions and Wendy supported him telling curious journalists that there were some obstacles to overcome. "We can't marry before Eric joins the RAF," she remarked.

Wendy's mother expressed the view that they were both too young to marry and believed it would be wrong for her daughter to sacrifice a career which she started when she was only twelve. "They've only known each other for about nine weeks," she told a correspondent for a woman's magazine. "Wendy has not the slightest interest in boxing and until she met Eric had never had a boyfriend."

Boon first met Wendy while involved with his vaudeville production at Peterborough just before Christmas. She was rehearsing for pantomime which would take over at the theatre at the conclusion of his engagement and he claimed that the moment they met it was love at first sight. Despite their respective occupations proving a hindrance their relationship developed rapidly. Wendy had been in Swansea for more than two weeks when Eric joined her and word soon got around that they were an item. The following day the *Swansea Evening Post* carried a picture of them viewing trophies to be fought for on an amateur boxing show at Mannesmann Hall in aid of St Dunstans & Swansea Boys Clubs. Wendy was described as the boxer's fiancee.

On 4 March, Boon sat ringside with Bert James and watched Ronnie James knock out Joe Stark of Egham in eight rounds. It had been hoped to announce that a contest between Boon and James had been agreed, but weight problems and his impending call-up for National Service had become a stumbling block.

As soon as Wendy's musical engagement at Swansea reached its conclusion, she and Eric returned to London and were frequently in the headlines. They attended a performance of 'Moonshine' at the Vaudeville Theatre in the Strand where Boon was given dancing lessons by the production dance manager, John Jackson. He was later photographed holding his Lonsdale belt with the principal of the show, actress Sylvia Marriott.

A few days later the couple were guests on the popular BBC radio programme, 'In Town Tonight', which had been revived after an absence of almost a year. In answer to a question from the presenter, Wendy replied: "Yes, it's quite true, Eric and I are definitely engaged."

When asked if the champion had finally taken the count, she said: "Yes, and I hope it's a long count, the only one I ever want to hear."

Although she still had further musical engagements to fulfil, Wendy said they hoped to get married on or before 6 May which was her twentieth birthday. Everything changed quickly, however, when Eric received a letter ordering him to attend the Recruiting Centre at RAF Uxbridge on 27 March. After undergoing a routine service medical examination he was added to the official reserve list to await call-up. The sudden reality of events regarding Eric's impending enlistment with the Royal Air Force, however, melted Wendy's mother's objections to their getting married and the occasion was brought forward to 17 April.

Boon spent the eve of his wedding in London with a group of friends, among them several of his favourite newspaper reporters who were anxious to know of his future plans. He told them that after a short honeymoon he would join the RAF as a physical training instructor, but plans for he and Wendy to set up home together had been upset by the war. "Perhaps I shall get leave for a fight or two," he added, "but I'll definitely be resuming my boxing career after the war and, as my own manager, I hope my new partner will help."

The wedding took place at St Albans Church, Golders Green, and Boon, accompanied by his best man, Eddie Edgar, arrived half an hour before the bride. Crowds cheered as Wendy stepped from her car wearing a white lace gown and long veil. She was escorted up the aisle by her uncle, Mr Elliott Makeham, who gave her away, and was attended by her actress sister, Claudine Elliott. A number of well known names from sport and show business were in the congregation including England international footballer, Eddie Hapgood, but the only boxer was Harry 'Kid' Silver. As they left the church following the ceremony, Eric and Wendy were greeted by a line of news cameras. Afterwards they attended a reception organised by the bride's mother at their home at 36 Hamilton Road, Golders Green, before setting off for their honeymoon at Bournemouth. On their return they lived with Wendy's mother because with Eric about to be called up for National Service it was impractical to try and find a home of their own during wartime.

*   *   *

A few days earlier, American promoter, Mike Jacobs, was reported as saying that Boon would fight Henry Armstrong for the world welterweight title in New York in June. At his wedding, Eric played dumb and told James Butler, who was there as a guest, that he knew nothing about it. "At the moment I am more concerned with my service duties than fight offers," he remarked.

Jacobs, however, claimed the fight was made by cable and that Boon had signed a contract. When told about this Eric said his only contract was to marry his fiancée Wendy Elliott.

Despite Boon's denials, just a week after his wedding, it was established that he had applied for a visa in order to fight Armstrong in America. On 24 April, Frank Butler was told by Passport Office that the application was being considered, but not yet granted.

A Reuter message from New York stated that Boon had cabled Jacobs saying that he was leaving England the same day. The report added that he proposed to fly to Lisbon where he would either board a liner to the United States or travel there by clipper. Press enquiries confirmed that he had applied to go to Lisbon.

It was an intriguing story because everyone involved clearly overlooked the fact that by the date of the proposed fight Boon would be firmly under the command of the Royal Air Force and unlikely to have been granted the necessary leave. Yet despite all the confusion there was substance to the story because on 19 April the British Boxing Board of Control received a cablegram from John J Phelan, Chairman of the New York State Athletic Commission regarding the possibility of Boon fighting for the world welterweight title. They confirmed this to the press and stated that it was being considered.

According to Reuter, Mike Jacobs claimed that Boon had already cabled acceptance of the terms offered. It was added, however, that the National Boxing Association of America (NBA) had promptly refused to sanction such a contest as being for the world championship. Frank Butler fully supported such a decision highlighting the fact that Boon, a British lightweight champion, had not even beaten a third-rate welter. Whilst the Board of Control may well have granted him authority there remained the obvious criticism that Ernie Roderick and every other ranked British welterweight should have priority over him.

The cross talk between London and New York dragged on and a few days later the *Daily Express* received a cable in which Mike Jacobs insisted that everything had been fixed for Boon to fight Armstrong in New Jersey on 10 June where the contest would be recognised as for the world title. The Passport Office in London, however, insisted that nothing had yet been agreed for Eric.

Frank Butler was firmly of the opinion that the fight would not take place especially as Jack Solomons, who was still Boon's unofficial manager, claimed to know nothing of the alleged proposals. Jack refused to say anything else because of a pending legal action against Boon.

Butler caught up with Eric a few days after he returned from his honeymoon. Despite his previous denials about a possible contest in America, the champion said he wasn't very optimistic about getting his permit to travel there. "I shall of course go if I get a passport," he said, "but I am a little doubtful of that."

Eric's assumption proved to be correct because on 30 April his passport application was refused thereby ending what hope he had of fighting for a world title in America. On the positive side, however, there were signs that his partnership with Jack Solomons may be about to flourish again.

Three days earlier Isidore Green went to Wally May's gym at Earlham Street near Covent Garden. He was the only pressman there having a received a private telephone call from Boon the previous evening. As he arrived, Eric greeted him with a broad smile saying: "What a story I've got for the *Sporting Review*."

At that moment Nat Seller walked in whereupon Boon went and changed into his gym gear and began pounding the heavy bag. Nat took off his coat and, with stop watch in hand, eyed Eric closely as he put him through his paces. He was back as the champion's trainer.

During the course of the training session Jack Solomons arrived and Green noticed that there was a lot of nodding and winking between the parties. The moment Boon finished training he and Jack went into an office where they engaged in a lengthy conversation. The young journalist was fascinated, but despite his careful probing nobody would say anything. What it was all about was to remain a secret, at least for the time being. "If you are the shrewd guy I think you are, you will put two and two together," remarked Solomons as he was about to leave the gym.

Up until that point whenever there were rumours of Boon being lined up for a fight, all Jack would say was that he had been advised by his solicitor not to make any comment regarding his position with the Board of Control or the Devonshire Club because of an impending legal action with the boxer.

The next day, 28 April 1940, the Devonshire Club, having been re-licensed by the Board, staged its first official promotion for several months. Regulars there were shocked when Boon arrived with his new wife, Wendy, and sat in booked seats alongside Solomons and Mike Milligan. It was his first visit to the club since problems arose between him and Jack, but as they all sat chatting happily and watching the entire show it was clear that their troubles were behind them. The threat of lawsuits were a thing of the past

Despite probing from inquisitive reporters very little was revealed because neither party was prepared to cause further offence to the other. In reality, the bond between them was too strong not to be patched up. It was later admitted, however, that agreement had been reached that licence holders requiring Boon's services made arrangements through the unlicensed Solomons.

Within a few days the rift between Boon and Hulls had also been healed which was pleasing. So many threats had been made by the opposing parties about how they would blow the fight game apart if matters reached the law courts. It became almost sickening to continually hear the underhanded talk and rumours that swept through the sport.

Hulls, who had been re-licensed by the Board of Control, was quick to tell the press that a fight between Boon and Ronnie James would definitely be staged in mid-June either in Cardiff, Swansea or London. Although Boon had earlier told Frank Butler that it was unlikely that such a contest would take place for at least a year, the promoter insisted that negotiations were proceeding.

The Board had by this time installed James as the official contender for Boon's title, although the Stewards were doubtful if it would ever take place. Hulls, nevertheless, pushed forward with his plans and in May travelled to Wales with Tommy Farr with a view to staging the fight at Cardiff City football ground. The promoter badly wanted to show Boon off in South Wales where he had a number of commitments during the summer. Having only recently got his Board of Control promoter's licence back, Hulls sprang another surprise when he stated that he hoped to stage a bout between Boon and Jack 'Kid' Berg for charity during mid-May. Whilst they were ambitious plans, the promoter appeared to have overlooked the fact that there was little likelihood of Eric being able to meet such commitments. His immediate future would be determined by the Royal Air Force.

NATIONAL SERVICE

Boon's last public appearance before joining the Royal Air Force was on Monday 13 May 1940 when he attended an evening boxing show staged by Sydney Hulls at Fair Meadow, Chatteris. All contests featured local boxers and during the interval he was introduced from the ring together with former world flyweight champion, Jimmy Wilde. Eric then agreed to act as referee for the next bout which was a comedy act between Londoners, Kid Nitram and Ginger Crew. He pair went at each other from the start and their unorthodox methods greatly amused the crowd. Boon smiled throughout and generally let them get on with it before raising both their hands at the end of three rounds.

Two days later the British champion reported back to RAF Uxbridge to commence his national service. The sudden call-up unfortunately prevented him from boxing a three-rounds exhibition bout with Harry Silver at the Devonshire Club on 16 May at a benefit night for resident Master of Ceremonies, Buster Cohen.

As Aircraftsman 2nd Class, (Service No 919473) he was transferred to 99 Squadron training pool at RAF Manston, Kent, a few days later. He remained there undergoing initial training until 21 June when he moved to the school of physical training at Uxbridge where he underwent a seven week course to become an instructor. On completion he returned to his squadron.

Like most top level professional boxers called up for military service, Boon was afforded every facility to train and maintain his fitness once he had completed the basic training. With the standard of equipment far superior to that he had become accustomed to in civilian life, he devoted much of his spare time to a regular training schedule at his base gymnasium.

Knowing that Eric would be granted privileges not afforded to general conscripts, Sydney Hulls was anxious to get him back into the ring as soon as possible. As no progress had been made by mid-June regarding a possible fight with Ronnie James, the promoter announced that he planned to match Boon with Welsh welterweight champion, Taffy Williams, from Swansea on an open-air show that summer. This drew immediate criticism from the press because earlier in the month Williams had been knocked out in two rounds by Ernie Roderick.

Hulls, however, had no intention of giving up because of his commitments in South Wales, particularly at Abertillery where he intended staging a big charity show on which he planned to use Boon in the main event.

By July the Luftwaffe had begun bombing raids over London and South East England and boxing had become almost non-existent in the capital, but Hulls was confident the sport would flourish in the provinces. He therefore made further trips to South Wales and eventually announced that Boon would face Taffy Williams on 27 July or 3 August although no venue had been finalised. The announcement, however, drew more criticism from the media because it was considered that despite being Welsh champion, Williams would be no test for Boon.

There was also more talk of a fight with Ronnie James, but the general feeling among the critics was that Eric would never be able to make the lightweight limit again. Even his greatest admirers, particularly those in the press, expressed concern about the fight going ahead. They were well aware that his punch was his main asset which he had relied upon in the past against more skilful opponents.

James was a class boxer equipped with a more than respectable punch, and during the previous 12 months had been undefeated in nine contests with no apparent weight problems. In the same period Boon's only fight was the somewhat fortunate victory over Dave Crowley.

Some critics therefore argued that with his weight difficulties Eric would be significantly weakened and mentally agitated going into the ring with a man of Ronnie's class. Although there were a number of reports that he had moved up to the welters, no comment to this effect had been made by Boon, his handlers or the Board of Control, or that he had any intention of relinquishing the lightweight title.

Despite Hulls' considerable efforts no engagement could be arranged for Eric in South Wales so during early August he made moves to secure a fight for him with welterweight champion, Ernie Roderick. Although no approach was made to the Board of Control to sanction it as a title contest, Boon was quoted as saying that he would be willing to vacate his lightweight title in order to get it.

It was certainly a period of rumour and speculation, especially where Boon was concerned. Despite him being in the RAF, he was still a high profile fighter and the stories about his weight problems rumbled on. Writing in the Daily Mail on 19 August 1940, Geoffrey Simpson remarked:

> Boon may be titled the lightweight champion, but since he has been drawing RAF rations, boxing's pocket Hercules has put on so much substance that the only thing light about him is his step.

Despite Hulls initial plans to stage the fight in London, Johnny Best was keen to put it on in Liverpool. He had discussions with Roderick's trainer, Nel Tarleton, who agreed to the contest provided it was a non-title affair at two pounds over the welterweight limit. Since getting established in the RAF Boon had been negotiating for a fight with former welterweight challenger, Norman Snow, which tended to suggest he was considering moving up a weight. A fight with Roderick, however, was a far more attractive proposition and one he had been seeking for more than a year.

After initial discussions with Jack Solomons, Best travelled to London for a meeting on 27 August, but in doing so experienced a six-hour air raid and some heated negotiations. Boon insisted that the fight be over 10 rounds while Best, representing Roderick, wanted 12. There was a great deal of debate over this topic with neither party prepared to yield. When asked by the promoter why he wanted the shorter distance, Eric replied: "I can set a fast pace over 10 rounds so that anything can happen."

Eventually Boon got his way, but Best would not agree to his demand for more money, arguing that Roderick was the welterweight champion and the fight was at his weight. Again there was some heated debate, but with everyone wanting the fight, agreement was finally reached and Eric put his signature to the contract. The contest would be staged at Anfield football ground on 21 September, a Saturday. The programme would commence at 4 pm and the contestants for the main event would be in the ring by 5.15 pm so as to allow spectators to return home before the blackout.

With Boon agreeing to meet Roderick at 10st 9, press speculation that he would never box at lightweight again, intensified. He strongly denied this, insisting that despite having been out of the ring for nine months, he could still make the 9st 9 limit. Although he had wanted the fight to be in London where he was a firm favourite, he never wavered when Liverpool was finally agreed upon. He knew that if he could beat Roderick the Board of Control would order an immediate rematch with the welterweight title at stake.

Like Boon, Ernie had also joined the RAF and both men were granted special leave to prepare for the contest. Eric set up his training camp under Mike Milligan at Astley Institute, Newmarket. He asked that fans wishing to watch his preparations pay a small admission charge which he generously offered to donate to the Newmarket and Racing Industry Spitfire Fund.

It was reported that training went well and that he was punching as hard as ever. He rounded it off just two days before facing Roderick with a three rounds exhibition with Army Sergeant Gallagher on an afternoon promotion at Newmarket Town football ground in aid of the Spitfire Fund. It was the highlight of a massive event which included a number of contests between teams from the Army and RAF, the latter being seconded by former world welterweight champion, Ted 'Kid' Lewis, a sergeant in the service. The crowd exceeded 1,000. Over £70 was raised for the fund and Boon's wife Wendy drew lucky numbers for the raffle.

The following morning Boon and Mike Milligan travelled to London where they joined Jack Solomons before making their way to Liverpool. To a small group of reporters who met them, Eric said: "I am very, very confident I shall beat Roderick inside the distance. I am as well as I have ever been and will scale about nine stone twelve."

It was a brave statement to make because there was no doubt that he faced a massive task. Roderick was one of the classiest boxers in Britain who had never been on the floor in his long professional career which started in 1931. Henry Armstrong couldn't do it and nor could any of a number of middleweights he had faced. He had engaged in over 100 contests and won the British welterweight title in March 1939, knocking out Jake Kilrain in seven rounds. In his only defence he outpointed Norman Snow in July 1940. He possessed tremendous defensive skills modelled on the lines of his trainer, former featherweight champion, Net Tarleton.

Roderick looked tremendous in training working with Blackpool boxer Frank Lennox who told the *Liverpool Echo*: "Don't be surprised if a knockout comes from Roderick's gloves." Lennox claimed that Ernie hit harder than any other man he had faced, and that was when he was wearing 'pillows'.

*   *   *

At the weigh-in for the fight at 2 pm Boon went to the scales partly clothed and was comfortably inside the agreed limit of 10st 9. Roderick was a shade over, but made the weight after removing his socks. The contest had originally been expected to pull in a crowd of up to 50,000, but fans were put off because local people were receiving up to a dozen air-raid warnings each day leading up to the fight. Inside the stadium the crowd looked sparse despite newspaper reports claiming the official attendance was about 18,000. Due to further air-raid warnings many people left before Boon and Roderick were in the ring.

In many respects the fight was a disappointment because Eric was comprehensively out-boxed. Although he showed great courage and was always a threat with his right hand, it was a very one-sided affair. He never at any stage measured up to the skill of the Merseysider whose defence was superb. On the retreat his cool deliberation was a feature of a brilliant all-round display. Roderick won so clearly that it shattered Boon's hopes of a quick shot at the welterweight title. He more than met his match, finding Ernie a far different proposition to anyone he ever faced at lightweight.

Boon was on the floor five times during the contest, the first as early as the opening round. He had bustled forward throwing short arm punches to the body while Roderick replied with sharp lefts. Suddenly, Ernie stepped back then leapt in with a brilliant right to Eric's head. Had the punch not landed slightly high it could have resulted in a sensational first round defeat for the Chatteris man. Instead, smiling broadly, Boon was on his feet almost immediately and found Ernie's chin with a great left as the bell ended the round.

Roderick easily won round two by upright boxing despite having to ship some rough treatment to the body from Boon in close-quarter exchanges. The local favourite, quickly realised, however, that his superior boxing skill was the way to beat Eric and from that stage he adopted a confident jab and move strategy.

Boon's defence was poor and when he dropped his hands in round four it was inviting trouble. Roderick, however, was prepared to bide his time and use his skill to open Boon up. In the fifth he drove him to a neutral corner and rocked him with a big right. Continuing to chase the Chatteris man, he floored him in round six with a barrage of lefts followed by a heavy right cross. Always the sportsman, Eric stayed down on one knee and jokingly counted with the referee while resting his head on his gloves.

Boon took counts of 'four' and 'nine' in round seven, but each time rose gamely and tried to battle his way back into the fight. Roderick, however, would not be denied and won the next two rounds by sheer skill. As they left their corners for the start of the final session, Boon's left eye was closing rapidly from the effects of Roderick's accurate left jab. Although he took another count from a volley of sharp lefts followed by a right cross, he threw everything into attack in the final seconds in an attempt to score a dramatic knockout. It was not to be and at the final bell, Eric and everyone in the crowd knew the result. Referee, Eugene Henderson's decision in favour of Roderick was a formality.

As his opponent's arm was raised, Boon could still muster a broad grin. He had taken his punishment magnificently, but only in that respect did he match his conqueror. To be put down so often

219

during a fight and then suffer defeat was a new experience for him. His powerful punches had been ineffective against a bigger and more skilful opponent, and it was perhaps fortunate that Henry Armstrong had not been in the opposite corner.

Apart from taking a beating, Eric didn't fare well financially, taking only £168 for his pains because he chose to go on a percentage of the gate. Jack Solomons later claimed that his man had not prepared properly for the fight believing that German activity over Liverpool would prevent it from taking place. It sounded like sour grapes because local newspaper reports indicated the contrary when Boon was training at Newmarket. In his disappointment Jack was just looking for excuses.

There were also conflicting stories about Boon's future. One of the problems was that whilst the critics had differing views, the boxer never confirmed or denied them. General opinion at that stage was that to have any chance of remaining at top level, Eric had no option but to fight and beat Ronnie James.

*   *   *

Returning to full time service duties, Eric moved with his squadron to RAF Newmarket less than three weeks after losing to Roderick. Two days later, on 3 October 1940, he was promoted to Aircraftsman 1st Class. Postings were kind to him and in mid-December he was transferred to RAF Mildenhall and on 8 February 1941 to No 3 Headquarters at RAF Exning, both in Suffolk.

Despite the disappointing setback against Roderick, Boon continued to combine boxing with his military service. He trained daily and in early January 1941 boxed a brilliant exhibition with Harry Silver at Watford Town Hall on a show in aid of the Mayor's fund for sufferers of the war. The promoter was Eddie Mallet, a prominent manipulative surgeon who, through his shows, had raised more than £5,000 for local hospitals and charities.

The following month Eric was one of a number of top boxers, including Harry Mizler and Jack London, to appear on a big charity show at The Odeon, Leicester Square, (formerly The Alhambra). Such was public generosity that the Marquess of Queensberry later announced that more than £6,000 had been raised of which £4,000 would go to the Royal Air Force Benevolent Fund. A Canadian visitor was reported to have paid £1,000 for an autographed photograph of the Prime Minster and another £100 was raised by auctioning maps captured from German planes.

All contests on the show were over six rounds and although there were no surprises, Boon had to work hard to outpoint Corporal Dave Finn in the final bout of the afternoon. One report stated that he started so slowly that for almost three rounds an upset looked likely. In round four, however, he opened up and Finn had to defend desperately to survive. Throughout the final session, Boon tore into his opponent as if to remind the audience he was still a champion.

During March, American promoter, Mike Jacobs, and Nat Fleischer, Editor of *Ring Magazine,* proposed that a match be organised between American world champions and British champions. They suggested that one contest be between Boon and Lew Jenkins, who became world lightweight champion in May the previous year by stopping Lou Ambers in three rounds. If Eric couldn't make the weight the fight would be offered to Ronnie James. Although it was an intriguing proposal which would undoubtedly appeal to boxing fans, the British Government blocked it for security reasons before it got off the ground.

Determined to keep Boon in the spotlight, Sydney Hulls attempted to stage a fight between him and Jack 'Kid' Berg over 12 rounds at Peterborough football ground on Easter Monday, 14 April. Although those plans fell through he secured the fight for the London Coliseum at St Martins Lane seven days later. The venue, which could accommodate a crowd of over 3,000 had hosted many spectacular sporting events in the past, but no big fights had ever been staged there.

This was a natural in every sense of the word and made more attractive by the events of the previous year when Boon dramatically pulled out. With seat prices ranging from four shillings to one pound, and standing room available for 300 on the stage at twopence, a full house was expected.

Although *Boxing News* predicted it could be the fight of the year, most critics believed Boon would win inside the distance. That view was shared by the bookies who made him a strong odds-on favourite, but few could have predicted the eventual outcome.

The programme commenced at 4.30 pm and Boon and Berg, who was also in the RAF, entered the ring two hours later. The fight was such a big attraction that it was recorded by the Ministry of Information to be relayed to America as a propaganda exercise to demonstrate that Londoners were able to come up smiling from a blitz and enjoy themselves at a boxing match.

Weighing 10st 7, one pound lighter than his more experienced opponent, Boon made the pace from the start. He swept into Berg as though intent on an early finish, driving him around the ring under a barrage of vicious swings from both hands. Jack appeared completely devoid of defence as the Chatteris man scored repeatedly to the head. One hefty clout sent him to his knees for a short count.

Although Berg retreated around the ring in an attempt to stem the tide, he appeared flat-footed and arm weary. He was sent rocking to his heels as Boon continued to score with solid shots to the head from both hands. Jack's performance was a complete mystery. He seemed to be in a daze and didn't land a worthwhile blow in the opening round, yet Boon failed to finish him.

Amazingly, Berg sprang into life at the start of round two. Fast two-fisted attacks from all angles completely bemused Boon and when he tried to hit back he was tied up at close quarters. Suddenly, Eric didn't know how to handle the old campaigner whose experience included more than 60 contests in American rings.

In sheer frustration, Eric lashed out wildly with most of his punches going wide of their target. When he switched his attack to the body one shot went low. Berg tottered, held on desperately and complained that he had been fouled. His seconds all yelled 'foul', but referee, Mr C B Thomas, ignored their pleas and waved the boxers on. Almost immediately Boon went low again bringing loud boos from the crowd. Again Berg's seconds rushed up the ring steps and remonstrated with Mr Thomas who again ordered them back.

By keeping on the move Jack held Boon at bay until another heavy blow crashed low into his abdomen. Berg fell to the canvas where he rolled about in excruciating pain. Without a moment's hesitation Mr Thomas ordered Eric to his corner and awarded the fight to Berg whose seconds had to carry him to his stool. It was fully 10 minutes before he was able to leave the ring.

Berg never forgave Eric for his indiscretions and years later in his biography, '*The Whitechapel Whirlwind*', he remarked:

> ....I chased him all over the place in the first round and he knew he wasn't going to win so he fouled me....

Jack's version of events, however, didn't correspond with those of the sports writers, many of whom had expected Boon to win by a knockout. Yet Eric was never a dirty fighter and general opinion was that sheer frustration led to his downfall.

Although still not licensed by the Board of Control, Jack Solomons continued to handle Boon's affairs. In a press statement he insisted that despite scaling 10st 7 for the Berg fight, Eric could still make lightweight. He said that they wanted to make a title defence against Ronnie James, but it was claimed he was otherwise engaged. In order to keep busy the champion was set to return to the ring at

Granby Halls, Leicester, on 1 September against Irish welterweight champion, Paddy Roche.

First and foremost, however, Boon's activities were controlled by the Royal Air Force and in the meantime he was transferred from RAF Exning to an airbase at Stradishall just a few miles away. Two weeks later he moved to RAF Marham, Norfolk, where, on 1 July, he was promoted to Leading Aircraftsman. Later that month he became an Acting Corporal (unpaid).

By this time Eric and wife Wendy had moved into married quarters at 9 Stretton Avenue, Newmarket, a short distance from the bases to which he was attached. On 2 July 1941, the day after her husband's initial promotion, Wendy gave birth to a baby daughter, Wendy Diane, at Brunswick Nursing Home in Cambridgeshire. The little girl would later be known as Erica.

During the course of his training to meet Paddy Roche, Eric fixed up a fight at RAF Marham for his former Chatteris Boxing Club mate, Ray Buddle. He was a farmer's son and an old school friend of Boon's, having boxed with him on many occasions. He was also trained by Arthur Binder and when he turned professional many of his early fights were at the Devonshire Club. He was a popular, big punching light-heavyweight and many local fans hired coaches to travel and support him. In a letter Boon told him to get fit although his opponent "would probably only go one or two rounds." The prizes would be war savings certificates.

Eric was extremely fortunate that, apart from when he was doing his initial training, he was stationed at RAF bases in Norfolk and Suffolk, all of which were in easy reach of Chatteris. He used this to his advantage and when he had some spare time often went home to see his family. He also made frequent visits to The Manor at Doddington where he played the family piano. There were five evacuees staying there at one stage and they used to take turns to visit the Boon household at Chatteris for tea on Sunday afternoons.

One such trip that Eric made, however, resulted in disaster. During the afternoon of Sunday 17 August 1941, he took a motorcycle from his base, but left it late before returning. Being familiar with the narrow, winding Fenland lanes, he sped towards his camp at about 50 mph during the blackout. Suddenly, at about 9.30 pm, on the Newmarket to Fordham Road, he crashed into a stray cow which loomed up out of the darkness. The impact sent him hurtling from the motor bike and crashing into a wooden fence at the roadside. The cow was killed instantly.

Boon was seriously hurt and laid in a crumpled heap beside the wrecked motor cycle for some while until a bus taking passengers from Newmarket to Fordham stopped at the scene. Shortly afterwards a local farmer arrived in his car and took Eric to White Lodge Hospital, Newmarket, where examination revealed fractures to the skull, nose, left elbow and right thumb. He lapsed into a coma and when he eventually came round a doctor told him he must never box again.

Although he knew he was lucky to be alive, it never occurred to him that it could be the end of his ring career. The news was shattering. "Boxing is my business," he protested bitterly, "I must fight again."

The doctor shook his head and told him it was impossible. He had a blood clot on the brain and to go into the ring again would be like signing his own death warrant.

Boon was detained in hospital for four weeks, but despite the seriousness of his injuries he made a steady recovery. On 21 October 1941 he relived the events of the accident when, described as Corporal Eric Boon of the Royal Air Force, he attended Newmarket Police Court in roles of both witness and defendant. As a witness, he gave evidence in a case against Harry Smythe, a small-holder, of Glebe Farm, Fordham, who pleaded not guilty to a summons for allowing a heifer to stray on to the highway at Fordham on 17 August.

Eric described how he was riding the motorcycle and ran into the animal which was about two feet away from him when he first saw it. The next thing he remembered was waking up in hospital. Sydney Reed, a farmer from Carlton, told the court how he came across the dead heifer lying in the centre of the Newmarket to Fordham Road. An airman, who he identified as Boon, was lying beside a badly damaged motorcycle about 15-20 yards away. He appeared to be seriously injured so he helped him into his car and took him to hospital.

Police Constable Parmenter from Fordham said that he attended the scene of the accident. He saw the dead heifer lying in the road on what would have been Boon's nearside about 80 yards from the flax factory. The next morning, when it was light, he returned and examined the fence of a nearby field and could find only one possible point through which the animal could have strayed.

The defendant, Harry Smythe, stated on oath that all the cows were in the field at about 9.30 pm. He could not understand how one could have got out. He was found guilty of the offence, fined two shillings and sixpence, and ordered to pay 18 shillings and two pence costs.

Boon then stepped into the dock and pleaded guilty to using a motorcycle without insurance. Police Constable Hill from Woodditton told the court that when he interviewed the boxer he produced a certificate of insurance in his father's name for a car.

Although Eric was covered to drive the car it did not extend for him to ride a motorcycle.

In mitigation, Boon told the magistrates that he borrowed the motorcycle to travel home because it would not use as much petrol as his car. He would not have used it if he had known the insurance didn't cover him.

After hearing all of the evidence, Chairman of the bench, Mr Grafton Pryor, said they were satisfied that Boon was under the honest impression that he was covered by insurance. Under the circumstances the magistrates did not consider it necessary to impose a period of disqualification. He was fined one pound.

The following week, on 27 October, Boon again appeared before magistrates, this time at Grimston Police Court, Norfolk. He was one of four airmen arrested 12 days earlier at Westacre for poaching. They all pleaded guilty to being unlawfully in pursuit of game, having in their possession game unlawfully obtained and pursuing game without a shotgun licence.

In evidence, Police Constable Robinson from Castle Acre said that during the night of 15 October he was on duty at West Acre when he saw a car containing four airmen stop opposite some sacks lying on the edge of the road beside woodland. As he walked towards the vehicle he saw the barrel of a shotgun pointing out of the back window. He called out that he was a police officer in uniform and told the occupants to put the gun down.

On searching the vehicle he found a .22 rifle and four cock pheasants lying on the floor. More dead game birds were in the sacks at the roadside. When asked for an explanation, Boon, who was the driver, said: "We only did it for a bit of sport. We didn't realise we were doing any harm."

Imposing fines of £17 on each defendant, Chairman of the Magistrates, Mr F K North, said there was far too much poaching on the estates by people with cars. The only way to stop it was by the court imposing substantial fines.

Many years later, in recalling memories of the war years on a social website, a former member of the RAF remarked that Boon was a frequent visitor to RAF Feltwell, a distance of about 15 miles from Westacre. He enjoyed the company of many comrades in the Sergeant's mess, and the writer remarked: "I think he had a bit of a racket going between him and the cookhouse sergeant – strictly legal of course!"

*   *   *

Throughout Boon's period of incapacity questions were continually asked as to why he and Ronnie James had not been matched. Most critics remained convinced that the champion could no longer make the lightweight limit, but *Boxing News* was particularly critical of a lack of action by the Board of Control. The view of the publication was that Eric had received favours and as a result basked in adulation for almost two years without being called upon to defend his title.

James, meanwhile, had been kept waiting with just the occasional promise to indicate there was still a Board of Control. The publication strongly believed that the lightweight title should be declared vacant and fought for by James and Dick Corbett.

Other critics were scathing and even sarcastic about the Board's apparent lack of control and even suggested that the Stewards were afraid to ask Boon if he could still make 9st 9. Since he was disinclined to provide any information on the subject it was suggested that promoters should force the issue.

Being an exceptionally fit and strong individual, Eric made a remarkable recovery from his injuries. So much so that the urge to fight again became so great that he became irresponsible and, disregarding the medical advice, started training again. It was a far call from his initial feelings when told by a doctor that his boxing career was over.

In an article in a Sunday newspaper some years later he recalled the moment reality set in:

> *Sick with disappointment and half crazy with worry, I had to force myself to accept the situation. There was nothing else I could do about it. I had never been a quitter, but death was an opponent I couldn't fight. Quite frankly, the thought of dropping dead in the ring scared me cold and I made up my mind I would never go near a gymnasium again.*

Eric eased back into action at the beginning of November 1941 at Downham Market Town Hall which brought back happy memories because it was there that he had one of his earliest contests as a schoolboy. On a show staged by the Air Training Corps, he boxed a two-rounds exhibition with Private Lunn (Beds & Herts Regiment). He showed dazzling speed and looked in magnificent shape, and later in a training display, demonstrated that he had maintained a high level of fitness.

Determined to recover from his injuries, and infuriated by the constant remarks that he could no longer make the lightweight limit, meant that Boon had a point to prove. Being an extremely proud man he agreed to have a public weigh-in at Kings Lynn in early November and surprised many critics by scaling 9st 13 ½ .

Sydney Hulls had carefully monitored Eric's recovery and planned to get him back into the ring on 30 November in a contest at 9st 12. Although he had hoped to stage it at a London theatre nothing materialised. In a subsequent statement, however, he announced that Boon would have a series of fights against welterweights starting with Norman Snow at Seymour Hall on 2 February 1942.

Meanwhile, *Boxing News* kept up its campaign on behalf of Ronnie James prompting Jack Solomons to state publically that Boon would defend his title against the Welshman in Cardiff during April provided he beat Snow. Eric trained hard for that fight and on the day scaled 9st 12 to Snow's 10st 3 ½. Despite getting no sleep the previous night due to a bilious attack he gave a convincing display in knocking out Snow in the fourth round.

In what was described as one of the hardest punching fights seen for some while, Boon used his left jab effectively. He showed speed and strength of punch which were too much for his courageous opponent. When resisting a gallant attack by Snow, a bricklayer from Northampton, Eric landed a powerful left hook to the chin which sent his opponent to the floor for a count of 'seven' in round three.

Snow weakened from that point and was knocked out in the following round by a vicious body shot. There were some questions about the final blow with one national reporter writing: "The blow certainly appeared low to me and a number of my colleagues, but it was obviously an accident."

Another stated that referee, Teddy Waltham, admitted he was unsighted, but as he had no evidence of a foul he was not prepared to condemn Boon. In view of the controversial ending to the fight, attempts were made to stage a return at Seymour Hall on 2 March. For a variety of reasons, however, plans fell through as did further efforts to match Boon with Ronnie James.

Although he boxed an exhibition with Leading Aircraftsman Hamilton at Peterborough in early June, Eric found it difficult to get sufficient leave to prepare for bigger fights. Having been promoted to Temporary Corporal, then Corporal followed by Acting Sergeant (unpaid), he took on more responsibility. His military duties came first amongst which was an intense three week training course in the Scottish Highlands. Proposed contests at Ipswich on Whit Monday and against Freddie Simpson from Basingstoke set to take place at The Peoples Palace, Mile End, therefore fell through.

The military did, however, appear to be more accommodating when fights were on shows in aid of charity. Jack Solomons told L V

Manning of the *Daily Sketch* that starting in August, Boon hoped to fight once a week on dates and venues to be announced. All contests would be above the lightweight limit and wherever possible on charity promotions including those for 'In Aid of Russia'. Although no mention was made of plans to defend the titles Jack assured the reporter that Boon could still comfortably do 9st 9.

The fact that the Board of Control still put no pressure on the champion brought more condemnation from *Boxing News.* The paper argued that he was still being allowed to keep his title without showing any willingness to defend it, yet was able to secure other contests as and when he liked despite being in the RAF.

Boon's answer to this was that he would need at least two months solid training to prepare for a title defence. That would not be possible because service commitments would prevent him being granted such an amount of special leave. As for fighting on a regular basis he pointed out that plenty of servicemen played football and cricket at least once a week.

Some critics saw his remarks as hollow citing the fact that he was able to get leave to train for and take part in easy money, overweight matches. Yet this was unfair to Boon because in reality he was only getting away with it because the Board of Control allowed him to. It has always been the case that a boxer usually defends his title as and when called up to do so by the Board.

Between 26 August and 11 November, Boon engaged in bouts with Dick Wheeler, Frank Duffy and Jake Kilrain (twice). All were non-title affairs scheduled for 10 rounds yet during that period no requirement was made by the Board for the champion to defend his title. The harsh press criticism of the controlling body was therefore fully justified.

18

CAREER CROSSROADS

After Jack Solomons surrendered his Board of Control licences, Boon effectively became self-managed. Yet, apart from the period when the two were at loggerheads, Jack had maintained a friendly interest and helped him whenever he could. Eventually, however, he felt that the boxer should have a manager in his corner during contests, but not holding a licence in any capacity made it impossible for him to fill the role. After cordial discussions he eventually reached agreement with Dave Crowley's manager, Harry Levene, to take over the role. "Levene and I have a perfectly amiable understanding," Jack told L V Manning. "I shall continue to have the same advisory interest in Eric's corner, but I will be around the corner instead of in it so to speak."

The story appeared in the *Daily Sketch* on 12 August 1942, but became a matter of concern to the Board of Control who had not been notified of the new arrangement. Consequently, Boon and Levene were called to a meeting of the Stewards on 8 September. In the meantime boxer-manager contracts were filed with the Board and approved for a period of 12 months thereby clarifying the situation and preventing disciplinary action being taken.

Against Dick Wheeler at Watford Town Hall on 26 August, Boon scaled 10st 8, one pound inside the agreed limit. He was in good form and the man from Bournemouth took counts of 'four' in the opening round and 'eight' in the second before being knocked out in the third by a left and right to the head.

Within a few days west country promoter, Captain Prince-Cox, announced that Eric would face Frank Duffy (Bootle) over 10 rounds at 10st 10, at Colston Hall, Bristol on 12 September. Duffy was a capable, hard-hitting fighter and a contender for the Northern Area welterweight title. In announcing the contest, the promoter described Boon as "probably the most colourful fighter in the world." He told the *Bristol Evening World* that the fight was the most expensive he had ever staged surpassing amounts he paid to engage top men including Tommy Farr. Local people were thrilled that Eric had been persuaded to fight in Bristol and interest in the contest was enormous. With Boon being a sergeant in the RAF and Duffy holding a similar rank in an infantry regiment, there was bound to be an edge to it. Tickets priced from two shillings and sixpence to ten shillings sold rapidly.

After a public weigh-in at 2 pm which attracted several hundred people, Boon was taken to Eastville Stadium where he was introduced to the crowd before presenting a trophy to the owner of a greyhound, Irish Choice, which had won the Golden Crest race. Despite requests, Eric refused to make a speech and stepped aside to allow stage and radio personality, Sandy Powell, to entertain the audience.

A huge crowd attended Colston Hall that night, but they went away disappointed after Boon was disqualified for a blatantly low blow which put his opponent out of action. Up until that point it had been a good battle between two well-matched boxers. Duffy gave a good account of himself, moving cleverly and scoring well with his accurate left jab despite lacking Boon's power. He was marginally ahead on points when, shortly after the start of round six, he suddenly crashed to the floor writhing in pain from an extremely low blow. Referee, Mickey Fox, immediately disqualified Boon. The crowd booed and whistled loudly as Duffy was eventually lifted over the ropes and carried to his dressing room by ambulance men where he was attended by a doctor. It was fully half an hour before he recovered from the effects of the blow.

Boon hung his head as he left the ring to more boos from the crowd expressing their displeasure at the way the fight had ended. In his dressing room he insisted that the final blow which felled Duffy was a pure accident. The indiscretion resulted in Eric being called before the Board of Control to explain his action. The Stewards were also concerned about an article which appeared in the *Evening World* on 29 August which appeared to suggest that the promoter had submitted a list of six names to the Board as possible opponents for Boon and they had selected Duffy. This was incorrect. In accordance with standard practice, Duffy's record was reviewed by the General Secretary who took the view that he was a suitable opponent at that stage of Boon's career.

As regards his disqualification, Eric notified the Board that due to service duties he could not attend the meeting. After dealing with reports from the referee and inspector, a letter was sent to the boxer asking him to provide details of his expenses for that contest. No reply was received and despite three requests being made, Eric still failed to attend. He was therefore notified that the Stewards took a serious view of his disqualification and subsequent conduct. As a result he was severely reprimanded and cautioned as to his future conduct whilst a licensed boxer. It was unanimously agreed that he would receive only £25 of his purse of £100 for the fight with Duffy, the outstanding £75 being passed to the Board Benevolent Fund.

Meanwhile, the debate over Boon and Ronnie James continued. Former Welsh flyweight champion, Billy 'Kid' Hughes from Maestag, who had taken over as Ronnie's manager, deposited a cheque for £100 with Bill Phillips, Secretary of the Welsh Area of the Board of Control, in an attempt to bind a contest between the two. Writing in *Boxing News* on 10 September, Andy Newton, junior, said that Boon and his supporters knew he couldn't make 9st 9 and even found it difficult to make the welter limit. He too asked the question why the Board of Control continued to allow him to hold on to his title. Newton suggested the Board stripped Boon and allowed James and another contender to fight for what could be called 'The Wartime Championship.' The winner could meet Boon once the war was over provided he could make 9st 9.

Eric and his handlers made no public response to the latest round of criticism. On 21 October he faced Jake Kilrain at the Queensberry Club, (formerly the London Casino), at Old Compton Street, Soho. Kilrain, real name Harry Owens, was a Scotsman fighting out of Bellshill in Lancashire, who held the British welterweight title from June 1936 until March 1939 when he was knocked out in seven rounds by Ernie Roderick.

As soon as the match was made Boon planned to train down to under 10 stone for the contest made at 10st 9. In doing so he hoped to answer the critics who constantly claimed he could no longer make the lightweight limit. Although he had service commitments he trained for this contest as though it was for a championship. Despite intensive effort and good intentions he scaled 10st 3 ¾ confirming to some extent what his critics had been saying for some while.

Boon against Kilrain was an attractive matchup, but yet again there was an unsatisfactory ending. It started slowly and both men received warnings in the opening round for continuous holding. The ending came suddenly in the first minute of round two when a vicious left hook sent Jake crashing to the canvas. As he went down his seconds screamed "foul", but referee Moss Deyong ignored them and counted Kilrain out.

Writing in the *Daily Sketch,* L V Manning was of the opinion that the blow was low. Other critics disagreed saying the punch was perfectly legal because Kilrain jumped up as it was delivered which made it look low. In a subsequent interview Boon confirmed that view whilst his opponent maintained it was a foul.

The crowd were unhappy, booing Boon loudly as he left the ring. After speaking with both boxers promoter, John Harding, took the microphone and announced that a return contest would take place at the same venue on 11 November for £50-a-side.

Just a few hours before the return contest, representatives of the two boxers met at the Queensberry Club to decide who should referee it. Both sides would have welcomed Barrington Dalby, but he was unavailable. Since the outbreak of war it had been the custom of the Board of Control to try and use local referees in an attempt to keep promotional costs down and also avoid upsets through travel difficulties. In May, a newly introduced entertainment tax at 60% was hitting big time boxing hard.

Although Kilrain lasted the distance in a hard contest where punches were thrown freely, Boon won by a wide margin. He floored his game opponent for a count of 'nine' in the opening round, but Jake got up and fought back well. He was the better man at close quarters, but Boon's heavy punches soon began to tell. During the course of the fight Kilrain was floored on eight occasions all by combinations to the head and he did well to last the distance. Eric was extremely careful about going to the body and although there were three occasions when the Scot made minor appeals for low blows it was clear to ringsiders that all were legal.

After the fight Kilrain again made excuses for defeat stating that as he was working in the pits he was unable to train properly. Before the weigh-in he had to take a fair amount of weight off at a Turkish bath at Russell Square.

A few days later Harry Levene stated that Boon would not defend his lightweight title until the war was over. He was not ducking Ronnie James and would willingly fight him at 10 stone for a side stake of £500 in war bonds. Despite this announcement another report predicted a fight between them for the title would definitely take place in Wales early in 1943.

*   *   *

Although Boon had not been involved in any top level contests since losing to Ernie Roderick in September 1940, almost everything he did seemed to be reported. He wasn't very active during the early part of 1943, but local newspapers still regarded him as front page news.

In early January that year he caused a stir when he withdrew from a 10- rounds contest against Dick Shields at Oxford Town Hall. Eric told the promoter, Benny Huntman, that he needed more time for training than the RAF were prepared to give him. He was replaced by Harry Lazar, but as the show was in aid of prisoner of war funds, the promoter persuaded him to box an exhibition. This, however, was no consolation to the audience who had bought tickets hoping to see him in a real fight. When he was introduced he was greeted by boos and jeers. It was not an experience he was used to so he promptly withdrew from the exhibition, stormed back to his dressing room and hurriedly left the building.

Boon did take part in a number of other exhibitions for charity, one being at Luton on 26 March. Another was at the Rainbow Club on what was described as the first all-American boxing show staged in London during the war. British and Empire light-heavyweight champion, Freddie Mills, also boxed an exhibition on the bill which featured both amateur and professional boxers.

In December 1942, Eric was posted to RAF Downham Market and although he maintained his involvement in boxing, he occasionally suffered from severe headaches and blackouts which stemmed generally from his accident in 1941. After stringent examinations by the services medical board he was declared physically unfit for any form of air service duty under Kings Regulations and Air Council instructions. He was therefore medically discharged from the Royal Air Force on 17 May 1943.

He had been due to fight Laurie Buxton at Watford Town Hall on 25 May, but pulled out claiming to have injured his left elbow in training. A few days later he took a safer option playing as pitcher in a baseball match at West Ham Greyhound Stadium between teams representing Canadian Military HQ and First Canadian General Hospital.

With Boon out of the services, *Boxing News* resumed their campaign on behalf of Ronnie James who the paper claimed was being described as the uncrowned lightweight champion. In one editorial it was said that as Eric had always used being in the RAF as an excuse for not meeting James, he should now get the fight on.

In another article on 10 June, Andy Newton, junior, took another view. He raised the issue of Boon's claim that at times when in the RAF "things went black on him." Having been discharged on medical grounds it was unlikely that any promoter would risk using him. The writer believed that the Board of Control should prevent him from boxing again and declare the lightweight title vacant.

Amazingly, Boon was examined on behalf of the Board by Dr D Minton who issued a certificate dated 9 July 1943 stating that he "had examined the boxer and found him to be in perfect health and fit to take part in a serious boxing contest." This was placed before the Stewards who agreed that his licence could continue. On reflection it was an extremely dangerous decision and demonstrated just how lax medical requirements were in boxing during that period. Boon had apparently sustained a fractured skull, had a blood clot on the brain, yet had been permitted to resume his ring career less than six months later. Although he was subsequently declared unfit for duty in the services on medical grounds, a Board of Control appointed doctor gave him a clean bill of health. It was abundantly clear therefore that the Royal Air Force took individual medical conditions far more seriously than the boxing authorities.

The previous day, Andrew Newton, junior, wrote another article in *Boxing News* criticising the situation of Boon being allowed to remain champion without facing Ronnie James:

> Billy Hughes has done all in his power to get Boon to meet James in a title bout, but the "clique" behind Boon would not hear of such a match. Justice is one of those things that thousands of our lads have sacrificed their lives for, but where is just and fair play when it comes to a lad seeking what he is entitled to in the fistic ring?"

Newton again stressed the point that Boon clearly couldn't make the lightweight limit, and had also been medically discharged from the RAF:

> He has been allowed to hold on to his title, pick up good money in catchweight matches and exhibitions, yet James, a fit man still serving with His Majesty's Services, is overlooked.

In the same edition, the Editor of *Boxing News* expressed his displeasure at the continuing situation:

> When you say that Boon should not be granted another licence, I have also read Boon's own story concerning the motor accident. Also the reason for his discharge from the RAF. Any person of intelligence would know that in these circumstances Boon could not do himself justice. It would also not be fair if his opponent won and that the accident would surely be brought up as a reason for his defeat. I am forced to criticise the Board of Control for reluctance to insist on Boon defending his title.

The day after he was examined by Dr Minton, Boon travelled by plane from Liverpool to Belfast for a fight with Northern Ireland welterweight champion, Tommy Armour. The contest, made at 10st 6, aroused tremendous interest throughout the country and during the week leading up to it promoter, Bob Gardner, reported heavy bookings. He believed it would be one of the greatest contests staged in the region for years. Some critics, however, were sceptical because the local favourite had lost three of his last five contests, one of which was to Norman Snow who, 18 months earlier, had been knocked out by Boon in four rounds. They therefore saw it as just another payday for the British champion.

The promotion, an open air event starting at 3.30 pm, was part of Belfast's Holidays-at-Home programme and on the day a crowd of about 10,000 packed into Cliftonville Gardens. Although Armour started quickly and generally outscored Boon at long range for the first three rounds, the fight as a whole was best described as dull. Eric did have some success with heavy rights in round four, but it was not until the fifth that there were any real thrills.

Knowing that he hadn't won a round, Boon pressed forward trying to get into the fight, but in doing so became careless and let his guard drop. Seizing his chance Armour crashed a left hook to the chin which sent the Chatteris man to the floor for a count of 'nine'. It was the beginning of the end for Boon who was sent down heavily three more times. Although he bravely got up and tried to mix it, Armour finished the fight with a vicious left hook to the chin, but in his excitement followed up with several more blows while Eric was still on the floor. Despite loud protests from Jack Solomons, Boon was counted out for the first time in his career.

Yet again there was a controversial ending in a fight involving Boon. Solomons was furious and afterwards gave a press statement in which he said he was disgusted at what happened in the ring. "Armour got in a punch in the fifth and Boon went down," he remarked, "and whilst on the floor he was struck three times. Boon looked at the referee thinking Armour had been disqualified, but the timekeeper went on counting so I waited for Boon to get up. Immediately Armour rushed at him and put him down and while down he did the same thing."

Jack insisted that he had nothing whatsoever against the Irishman and considered him a clean fighter, but believed he lost his head in his eagerness to finish it. Immediately after the fight Solomons protested to a representative of the Northern Ireland Area of the Board of Control and demanded a return contest. He was told to put his complaint in writing which he did, asking that the decision be reversed and Armour disqualified. On his return to Liverpool the following day, Jack telephoned the Board in London reiterating his complaint.

Despite his disappointment Eric displayed warmth and a great sense of humour. After the fight, when approached by a fan who wanted his programme signed, he only endorsed it "Eric Boon - was I lousy?"

On returning to London, Solomons continued to make a big issue over Boon's defeat. Although the Board took no action over the complaint, Eric was still very much in demand. Within a few weeks he was matched with Lefty Flynn of Jamaica over eight rounds at the Royal Albert Hall. It was the perfect way for him to redeem some of his lost pride because in the past three months Flynn had twice outpointed Ronnie James, the most recent being at Swansea on 31 July. Unfortunately, just a few days before the contest, Flynn had to withdraw because of injuries he had sustained during a West End street brawl.

Harry Mizler was brought in as a substitute and this too was an extremely interesting contest. He was six years older than Boon and a former British lightweight champion having won it in January 1934 by outpointing Johnny Cuthbert. After successfully defending it against Billy Quinlan at Swansea he lost it to Jack 'Kid' Berg who stopped him in 10 rounds in October the same year. The old champion, however, was almost at the end of his career and had lost two of three fights that year. Arthur Danahar stopped him in eight rounds and Harry Lazar outpointed him over eight. With this in mind Solomons believed Harry was the perfect opponent for Boon at this stage of his career, but things didn't go according to plan. Mizler took an overwhelming points decision leading the critics to believe if that was the best Eric could do he would be taken apart by James if they ever met.

Boon only won the opening round and after that was kept on the end of a persistent and deadly accurate left jab. He did shake Mizler with a good left hook to the head in round two, but didn't land a single shot of note thereafter.

The veteran had no trouble containing him. After the fight Boon claimed that the eight rounds distance was too short for him, but it was a weak excuse because he had done nothing to indicate he could have turned things around. In reality he appeared to have lost, not only his capacity for measuring distance, but also his power. At the end he had a badly cut right eye and looked tired whereas Mizler was unruffled and unmarked.

Eric did beat Billy Jones of Cwmparc on points over eight rounds in a dull fight at Blackburn the following month, but again looked a shell of the man who beat Crowley and Danahar.

The day before the Jones fight the Board of Control rejected an application from manager, Tony Vairo, to recognise a proposed contest between Boon and Harry Hurst of Canada as for the vacant British Empire lightweight title. The Stewards decided that no consideration would be given until Boon had defended his British title against Ronnie James. On reflection it was a strange statement to make because whilst appearing to acknowledge that the fight with James should happen, the Stewards displayed their continued weakness by failing to make a direct order to the champion.

Eric was supposed to have faced Scottish lightweight champion, Joe Kerr, at St Andrews Hall, Glasgow, on 28 October, but withdrew due to a shoulder injury. Having done very little apart from boxing since he was a young teenager, it was at this stage he found himself at the crossroads in his life. With a wife and young daughter and no regular employment, he had too much spare time on his hands.

Having always been a great supporter of local charities Eric spent some of his spare time attending boxing shows throughout East Anglia to help raise money for worthy causes. In December he was at Ely Corn Exchange for a promotion organised by the 2nd Battalion, Isle of Ely Army Cadet Force, in aid of welfare funds. On 18 January 1944 he was at Wisbech Corn Exchange at a show in aid of North Cambridgeshire Hospital at which there were bouts between boxers from Wisbech Amateur Boxing Club, Army and Royal Air Force. He met up with several former service colleagues and received great applause when the Master of Ceremonies announced that he was ready to defend his title against Ronnie James.

Earlier that month Eric had spent a week at Denham film studios. He had been given the part of a gangster in an underworld epic entitled "Champagne Charlie" which starred Tommy Trinder. His presence attracted members of the press most days and during intervals the subject of Ronnie James was always high on the agenda. Boon said he was prepared to face him at an early date and that it could be staged at the Royal Albert Hall.

James had been a logical contender since 1940 and this was confirmed at a meeting of the Board of Control Stewards on 9 March. He was nominated along with Hal Cartwright, Jackie Rankin, Jack Carrick, Joe Kerr and Dave Crowley, but after due consideration the Stewards unanimously agreed that James was the leading contender. In accordance with the relevant regulation Boon was given up to and including 30 June 1944 to defend his title. It had taken the Board four years to make what was a relatively straight forward decision and it was now up to the promoters, managers and boxers to get it on.

Boon took a warm-up fight against Jimmy Malloy, a Liverpool seaman, at the Royal Albert Hall on 26 April. Looking trim and much fitter than for some while, he climbed through the ropes to great cheers. With Malloy having the reputation of being a big puncher the crowd expected fireworks. Regulars at the venue remembered how, in December the previous year, he forced Harry Mizler to retire after four rounds. Four months earlier Mizler had outclassed Boon.

Sadly, things didn't turn out as expected and the contest developed into a maul largely because of Malloy's tactics. Although Eric tried his best the crowd jeered and stamped their feet. At times they broke into singing "dear old pals" accompanied by the slow hand clapping and the stamping of feet all of which were unfair on Boon.

The champion scored with ease during the opening round mainly because Malloy's left jab was ineffective. His pace was good and by the end of round two the Liverpool man looked to be on the verge of a knockout following a good right to the jaw. For the remainder of the fight, however, Malloy frustrated Eric by mauling, smothering his attacks and holding at every opportunity. The champion had to be content with a wide points victory. Weighing 9st 12¼, Boon was almost a stone lighter than when he fought Billy Jones at Blackburn eight months earlier. Although he got plenty of stick from the press the following day, he boxed with real skill, won practically every round and showed he was getting back to form. The critics, however, believed he had a long way to go if he was to overcome James.

Boon (seated) is taught Yiddish by his close friend, Harry 'Kid' Silver.

Boon pounds the heavy
bag at The George
Hotel, Chatteris as he
prepares for the Reynard
fight.

Boon and wife, Wendy, at home during happy
times of their first marriage.

Boon trains for his fight with Norman Snow in 1942 watched by Jack Solomons (right) and trainer Harry Stokes.

Boon (right) and Ronnie James sign contracts for their fight at Cardiff in August 1944. Jack Solomons and Bert James look on.

Boon works at his father's forge following his
medical discharge from the RAF in 1943.

Boon (right) attacks Billy
Stevens at the Royal
Albert Hall on 19th March
1946.

Boon (left) lands a solid left
hook to the jaw of European
champion, Robert Villemain at
Harringay in April 1948.

A rare attack by Boon (right) against Gwyn Williams on 31st May 1948 at the Royal Albert Hall.

Boon returns to London Airport in early 1949 after his unsuccessful trip to America.

Boon with girlfriend, Dee Glavey, an ex-nurse, in August
1958 when he attempted to launch her into a modelling career.

Boon (left) shakes hands with Ernie Roderick
at the weigh-in for their welterweight
championship fight on 9th December 1947.
Benny Huntman and Nel Tarleton look on.

Boon training in South
Africa in 1947.

Alf James (left) with
Boon in South Africa in
early 1947.

19

RONNIE JAMES AND OTHER DISASTERS

Boon's fight with Ronnie James was originally set to take place at Tottenham Hotspur Football Ground on 8 July 1944, but was postponed until 29 July. Promoter, Jack Chappell, planned to stage it on the same bill as a British heavyweight title contest between Jack London and Freddie Mills. Although the Board of Control had ordered the fight, Jack Solomons had concerns because he believed Eric had not recovered sufficiently from his motor cycle accident in 1941. The champion, however, insisted that the fight went ahead and, knowing the task he faced, had remained in training since his fight with Jimmy Malloy. He even went back to his father's forge and put in hours of hard graft on the anvil to toughen himself up. Apart from being confident of beating James, he knew that the fight would give him his biggest pay-day since he faced Dave Crowley back in December 1939.

Eric was happy with his fitness so when the postponement was announced he broke from training and spent a week at Whitley Bay with his wife and three-year-old daughter, Erica. He returned to Chatteris on 8 July and boxed an exhibition with Jimmy Cain in what would be his last public appearance before facing James. It took place at Cromwell School at an event organised by the Chatteris Branch of the National Farmers Union where more than £300 was raised for the Red Cross Agricultural Fund. A boxing tournament proved to be a popular conclusion to the event and Boon's presence was an added bonus for the fans.

The previous week Eric featured in a radio programme, 'Shipmates Ashore', which was broadcast from the Merchant Navy Club in London during which he was interviewed along with other celebrities from sport and show business. He spoke frankly about his boxing career and recent film making experiences, and after much persuasion revealed details of his part in "Champagne Charlie" which until then had remained a secret. He also referred to his fight with Jimmy Malloy saying what a game fighter Jimmy was. Fittingly, as the broadcast was for merchant navy personnel, he sent Jimmy his best wishes and hoped he was listening. Boon told listeners that he had promised his daughter that if he won a second Lonsdale belt, he would give it to her. It was a tall order because first he had to beat Ronnie James and then two other contenders.

Meanwhile, the James fight was postponed again, this time at the express wish of the British Government who saw it as a major risk.

Bookings had been heavy and with so many people present it would make the open air venue a massive target for German bombers. Following discussions with government officials the Board of Control instructed that all championship contests be moved to the provinces prompting an immediate interest from promoters to stage the contest at either Leicester or Wolverhampton which would have been convenient for the masses of Boon fans. The most attractive offer, however, came from Nossie Sherman, a member of the pools and bookmaking family. As a licensed promoter, he acted on behalf of the Glamorgan Territorial Associations Welfare Fund and local Jewish Board of Guardians who wanted to stage the contest on a big charity event at Cardiff.

Sherman travelled to London and had a meeting with Jack Chappell and Jack Solomons who, apart from being Boon's manager, was also Chappell's matchmaker. They thrashed out a deal for the fight to take place at Cardiff Arms Park on 12 August for which Boon as champion would receive £3,000 which at the time was the largest purse ever paid to a lightweight. Chappell agreed to hand over his contract to the new organising committee after which the requisite articles were completed on 12 July.

The new agreements were accepted by the Board of Control who also approved an application for the fight to be broadcast on BBC radio on the usual terms. The Welsh Area Council of the Board granted permission for a film of the fight to be made provided both boxers and their managers agreed terms regarding fees received. Each boxer should receive 25 per cent of the fee with the balance going to the promoter. An application by the BBC to televise the contest was refused.

The Stewards also considered a further application on behalf of Harry Hurst to fight the winner of Boon and James for the vacant British Empire lightweight title. This was rejected on the grounds that Hurst must first prove he could make the 9st 9 limit. If successful he would then have to box an eliminator to establish his right to a title fight.

The news that James had finally got a crack at Boon created tremendous interest because it was a fight which had probably provoked more debate and argument than any other for years. There were demands for tickets from all parts of the United Kingdom, and all seats except the most expensive ones were sold out within a week of going on sale. An entire block of ringside seats were taken by top manager, Ted Broadribb, who steered Tommy Farr to his world title fight with Joe Louis in 1937. With plenty of standing accommodation available in both the old and new stands of the Arms Park, a crowd of at least 30,000 was expected.

James had been chasing Boon for over four years and to finally get him on home ground created great excitement throughout the Principality. Wales was a real hot-bed for boxing and this was one of the most attractive contests to be staged there for years.

Once the fight was finally agreed Boon set up his training camp at the Crown Hotel at Slough which had been selected by Solomons because he considered it to be safe and out of the range of doodlebugs. Eric was trained by Snowy Buckingham and his sparring partners included Harry Davis of Bethnal Green and undefeated Eastleigh middleweight, Vince Hawkins, who two years later would win the British title by outpointing Ernie Roderick. Jimmy Malloy also joined the camp during the later stages.

Boon settled in well at Slough and loved the area so much that in his spare time he looked around for a business. Within a week he found a roadhouse which he wanted to take over and run after the fight with James. Although Solomons loved the idea, and agreed to waive his manager's commission to help him get started, it was just another of Eric's pipe dreams that never reached fruition.

At the start of his preparations, Boon scaled 10st 13, but with intense workouts the weight fell off him. He then reached a point where the final few pounds proved difficult to shift and it became evident to those close to him that he would have difficulty getting down to the 9st 9 limit. He was therefore check-weighed at regular intervals each day and his diet monitored more stringently.

Five days before the fight Eric went to bed weighing 9st 11 ½ , and after drying out was expected to be 9st 10 the following morning. To the amazement of Buckingham and Solomons, however, he had put on one pound. They couldn't understand it, but all became clear later in the morning when Eric mislaid something and they went to his room to help him search for it. There, under the bed, Solomons found several empty fruit juice containers. Boon confessed that he had been so thirsty at night he smuggled them in and hung them out of the window on lengths of string.

Despite putting in extra work in the gym he still scaled 9st 12 with just two days to go. Drastic steps had to be taken, so late that night Solomons got on a bicycle and set the pace alongside Boon as he pounded six miles through quiet streets heavily clothed. When they returned to their hotel Eric weighed exactly the same. There was no alternative but to get him to a Turkish bath.

Boon's weight problems were kept strictly in-house and when contacted by William E. Allen, Boxing Editor for the *South Wales Echo,* Solomons said he was in splendid condition, but fully aware of the task he faced. Eric told Allen he was confident of victory and gave nothing away regarding the difficulties he was experiencing. "I am down to 9st 9 and will give James something to think about," he remarked.

Although some reporters appeared to accept what they were told by the managers and trainers, others stated there were rumours that both men were having weight problems. William E. Allen, however, was of the view that they were completely without foundation. He had visited James' camp at his father's farm at Pondardawe in West Wales and knew he was comfortable on his weight. The reporter added that in regular communications with Solomons, he had always been assured that Boon was within a pound of the limit.

Despite all the bluff, experienced boxing correspondents for a number of national newspapers worked out exactly what was occurring with Boon. The fact that Solomons had taken the unusual step of refusing to allow them into the training camp was a clear indication that all was not well with the champion. This was virtually confirmed when word got out that Jack had given instructions that no soft drinks were to be delivered to his camp.

Boon left his training quarters at Slough during the afternoon before the fight and, accompanied by Solomons and Buckingham, travelled to Cardiff on the 5.55 pm train from Paddington. A huge number of London fans also made the journey over a 24-hour period taking plenty of money with them in order to back the champion. Eric was still exceedingly popular and a number of telegrams and messages of goodwill were sent to him via the *South Wales Echo* all of which were handed to him when he reached Cardiff.

James arrived at the weigh-in at 2 pm on the afternoon of the fight in the uniform of an army sergeant which gained him a lot of patriotic support. He was first to the scales and was one pound inside the limit. Boon followed and was announced as being one ounce over, but after skipping for about 10 minutes he returned and scaled exactly 9st 9. The true extent of Boon's problems were not known until much later when it was admitted that he hadn't

CHARITY BOXING TOURNAMENT
in aid of
GLAMORGAN COUNTY WELFARE AND COMFORTS' ASSOCIATION
and CARDIFF JEWISH BOARD OF GUARDIANS.

Lightweight Championship of Great Britain
15 (3 min) ROUND CONTEST
ERIC   RONNIE
BOON   v.   JAMES
(England) Champion   (Wales) Challenger

8 (3 Min) ROUND CONTEST
CYRIL   HARRY
GALE   v.   LAZAR
(Cardiff)   (London)
Amateur Champion Gt. Britain   Contender Lt.Wt. Championship

CARDIFF ARMS PARK, SATURDAY, Aug. 12th, 1944.
Gates open 4.30 o'clock.   First Bout 6 o'clock.

BLOCK   Row E   Price
B   Seat No. 16   £3 3 0
TO BE RETAINED.

RINGSIDE—County Club Entrance

242

eaten for two days. In a newspaper article some years later he claimed that he fainted three times in the hours leading up to the weigh-in.

James was made a firm odds-on betting favourite despite having lost his last three contests on points to Lefty Flynn and Arthur Danahar (twice). Before that, however, he had suffered just one defeat in 26 contests between April 1939 and March 1943. During the same period Boon engaged in just 15 bouts, losing five, and appeared to be on the decline.

After turning professional in 1933, James developed into a top class lightweight, but the nearest he got to a championship contest was in April 1939 when he was disqualified in six rounds against Dave Crowley in an eliminator at Swansea. Now he was a man on a mission. He had plenty of grievances, particularly against the Board of Control for not forcing Boon to face him much sooner.

*   *   *

The scenes in Cardiff were reminiscent of the old days when Jack Petersen and other great Welsh fighters were in their prime. Fans descended on the city early in the afternoon, many wearing rosettes – red for James and white for Boon. They formed long queues for tickets costing five shillings and upwards, and were content to wait in the ground for up to four hours soaking up the atmosphere until the show commenced at 7.30 pm. Many others climbed on to roofs of nearby buildings to watch the fight through binoculars.

Boon looked finely drawn as he climbed into the ring and it soon became obvious that making the weight had been a mammoth task. In the opposite corner James looked fitter than he had for some years.

The fight started slowly as both men were cautious and respectful of each others reputations. There was so little action that midway through the opening round referee, Eugene Henderson, told them he expected more action. "This is a championship contest," he snapped firmly, "start making it look like one."

James was the first to open up and Boon's weakness became apparent as early as round two when a short hard right to the jaw made his knees sag and he dropped to the canvas for a count of 'two'. As if embarrassed the champion shook his head, smiled and got to his feet, but the smile was unconvincing. His body language seemed to indicate that he knew what to expect. He looked listless and weak, and gone was the early fire and punch of the man who had won the title at the age of eighteen.

Boon tried to get going with two-fisted attacks, but James countered with solid left jabs several of which seemed to shake the champion who, even at this early stage, looked to be fighting a losing battle. In the third round, he was sent to the floor for a count of 'nine' by a left hook to the body followed by a right to the jaw. There were loud protests from his corner that the body shot was low, and the champion also appealed to the referee. Mr Henderson, who was perfectly positioned, rightly ignored the protests because it had been a well executed punch to the solar plexus.

Although Boon landed the heavier single shots, James was much busier. Boxing cleverly, he mixed his attacks from head to body and put plenty of power into his punches. He floored Eric twice in the fifth for counts of 'nine' and 'two' from head shots, and things got worse for the champion in round six. Looking really weary, he took counts of 'nine', 'three' and 'nine' as James piled on the pressure. Well placed body shots were really taking their toll, sapping Boon's strength, and his legs wobbled every time James connected downstairs.

The seventh was a see-saw round in which the challenger also began to look tired. Although he dropped Boon for a count of 'three' he was also sent to the floor. Showing great courage as he bravely tried to stage a comeback, Eric crashed a right to the jaw giving the huge contingent of Welsh supporters their first moments of anxiety since the opening bell. James, however, was up at 'two' and nullified Boon's attempts to follow up his advantage.

The champion looked out of it in round eight and it was a tribute to his courage that he managed to keep going in an attempt to hang on to his precious title. He was down for counts of 'nine' and 'eight' in the ninth, and looked extremely tired as they came out for round 10.

James remained patient, knowing it was only a matter of time before Boon folded. When Eric dropped his guard he crashed a hard right to the bridge of the nose followed by a perfectly placed hook to the stomach. The champion crashed to the floor for the final time with not the slightest chance of beating the count. Mr Henderson called 'out' at two minutes 10 seconds of the round.

Victory made James the first Welshman to win the British lightweight title since Freddie Welsh in 1912. He was the perfect tactician and although honours came to him rather belatedly, there appeared to be no other lightweight of his class in Great Britain. He gave a masterful exhibition of copybook boxing and hitting bringing the record Arms Park crowd of 35,000 to its feet time and time again. His victory was totally justified.

Ever the true sportsman, Boon accepted his defeat with true grace. No more sporting tribute could have come from a beaten boxer than the one he spontaneously issued to William E. Allen in his dressing room shortly after the fight. "I could not have lost to a better man," said Eric. "Ronnie surprised me with his punching power and I have no excuses to offer. He is a great champion."

Jack Solomons agreed, but gave a more honest account than the one he related to Allen a few days earlier. "Eric lost the fight on the scales," he remarked. "It had been an effort to get down to the weight and now he will try his luck as a welterweight. James is a great boxer and champion without question."

Most critics believed that Boon was finished as a top class fighter, but his lack of height would be his greatest handicap should he continue in the higher division. Recalling the knockout by James in an article entitled "Eric Boon Confesses" published in *The People* newspaper some years later, the former champion said:

> *I remember thinking in the split second the body blow exploded in a blinding flash of coloured stars, that he had killed me. I must have blacked out for a few seconds. I fuzzily came to my senses and dimly, as though the sound was coming from the end of a long dark tunnel, I could hear the sound of the count and the faint roar of the crowd. I couldn't move. The last ounce of strength and resistance had been hammered from my body, but all I felt was immense relief. But the experience had scared me so much that I vowed I would never fight again.*

*   *   *

On 26 October 1944, a case was listed before Mr Justice Hilbery in the Kings Division of the High Court in London as Boon v Masters & Another. Boon, whose address was given as 17 Grand Parade, Raynes Park, South London, had issued libel proceedings against W R Masters and George Reynolds Limited, respectively, proprietor and printer of *Boxing News,* in respect of articles published in that periodical on 13 May and 10 June 1943.

Mr Valentine Holmes of Counsel represented Eric and Mr Colin Duncan of Counsel appeared on behalf of both respondents. Announcing that a settlement had been reached between the parties Mr Holmes said that the two articles in question concerned boxing generally and the plaintiff in particular The articles were long, and for people who did not know much about boxing, not easy to follow. There was criticism of Boon for not fighting Ronnie James, but the general gist was to belittle him and suggest that he was more of a talker than a boxer. The action had been settled to the plaintiff of a substantial sum as damages and an indemnity as to his costs. Mr Duncan told the court that the respondents regretted having published the articles and wished to apologise publicly. Mr Justice Hilbery agreed to the settlement, the details of which were not made public.

*   *   *

During 1945, Jack Solomons was granted a Boxing Board of Control promoter's licence and joined forces with Sam Burns. Having got started they came up with the idea of staging a big double championship bill at a London football ground. Freddie Mills, who had lost on points to Jack London for the British heavyweight title in September 1944, would get a return, and Boon would be matched with Ronnie James in an attempt to regain the lightweight title. Although the initial plans looked fine, the V2 bombing raids caused them to abandon what would have been a massive attraction.

The ambitious Solomons, however, never gave up and once peacetime returned he staged a big open air show at White Hart Lane, the home of Tottenham Hotspur football club on the 17 July 1945. Top of the bill was Jack London defending his British heavyweight title against up-and-coming prospect, Bruce Woodcock. The chief supporting contest would be a 10 rounds welterweight contest between Boon and Henry Hall from Sheffield.

This was another ambitious, and somewhat irresponsible move by Solomons because, apart from being retired, Boon was also badly out of condition. Having kept away from the fight game and everyone connected with it since losing to Ronnie James, he had also drifted into the champagne and cigar nightlife of London's west end. The bright lights and female society had always intrigued him and he enjoyed both thanks to his fistic fame. For several years he had the ambition to run his own business and recoup some of the money he had spent as a playboy. So, with the help of certain connections he opened a nightclub in Soho. The Top Hat Club was a plush little place with a cosy dimly lit bar, small dance floor and a three-piece band.

On the opening night, wearing a new dinner jacket with a red carnation buttonhole, Eric stood proudly at the entrance welcoming his guests. Inside, the bar and dance floor were packed with celebrities from the world of stage, film and sport who had gone along to wish him luck in his new venture as a night club owner. It was dawn before the celebrations ended and Eric sat down quietly in the bar with a glass of wine to think things over. "This is the life for me," he thought quietly. "No need to worry about finishing up walking around on my heels like the other punch-drunks I have seen so often and pitied."

Eric loved the glamour of the West End and the lifestyle first introduced to him by Ollie Franks when he was a teenager. If the first night at the club was anything to go by, business was going to be good. Exuberant dreams began to flash into his head and he became convinced that he could eventually open other clubs in Paris, Cannes and even New York. Fate, however, was waiting just around the corner, and three weeks later the Top Hat, into which he had sunk most of his capital, was raided by Police and closed down. It was a devastating setback, but Boon was never a quitter. With some money still in the bank he was convinced there was still a fortune to be made in the club business in a period when people seemed to have money to burn.

At the time London was full of American servicemen scattering dollar bills like confetti at a wedding. They all wanted a good time so, determined to cash in on the spending boom, the former champion acquired new premises at Denman Street just off Piccadilly Circus. Within a few months he opened the Inverness Club which had a bar that ran continuously from 3 pm to 11 pm seven days a week. With the overheads being considerably less than the Top Hat with its band and large staff, the new club had the potential to become a goldmine. By the end of the first week they were taking £100 a day and turning people away.

Unfortunately, Eric was very naïve to the goings-on in clubland and failed to recognise the plain clothes police officers who posed as customers several days running. After a period of observation the Inverness Club was raided and closed down having lasted just a week longer than the Top Hat. It left Boon a great deal poorer and brought to an end his dreams of becoming a nightclub king.

Knowing his assets didn't amount to much, Eric desperately needed to get his hands on some ready cash. He was in a dilemma because although several doctors and specialists had warned him about continuing his ring career, fighting was the only trade he knew. He thought long and hard and came to the conclusion that he had little choice but to get back in the gym. After a few workouts and sparring sessions he felt comfortable so he went to Solomons and said he wanted to resume boxing. Without asking any questions, the promoter agreed to put him on his big Tottenham bill.

For a couple of weeks his preparations went well, but suddenly while sparring with his old friend, Jock McAvoy, who was also training for a comeback, Eric blacked out. Recalling the incident a few years later he said: "When I came to my senses and realised what had happened, all my old fears returned. I tried to fight against them, but it was hopeless. I was scared and in the end I went to Solomons and asked him to release me from my contract."

Boon didn't tell Jack why he wanted out. He just made the excuse that he couldn't get himself fit in time. The promoter, however, pleaded with him to fight saying: "I've already got one substitute on the bill, I can't ask the customers to accept two."

It was clear that Solomons' priority was the quality of his show. He was not prepared to make allowances for the well-being of the man who had been largely responsible for his rapid rise up the boxing ladder. On the verge of becoming London's top promoter, his manipulation worked and for old time's sake and all that Jack had done for him in the past, Boon foolishly agreed to go through with the fight. It was another example of his naivety.

Although he was taking part in only his sixth professional contest, Henry Hall, a stablemate of Bruce Woodcock, was ABA welterweight champion in 1944. It was claimed that he had won about 290 of 300 amateur contests between 1937 and when he turned professional five months earlier.   Despite a lack of experience in the paid ranks he showed that he was a smart boxer and possessed a terrific punch as Boon soon found out.

Looking confident Eric scored freely from the opening bell and there were some heavy exchanges. Although Hall edged the first round he was floored by a left hook in the second. Boon fought viciously in the third, but Hall was the more accurate and harder puncher. In the fourth he scored repeatedly with fast stiff punches to Eric's head and, almost on the bell, drove a vicious punch to the solar plexus which sent him to the canvas in agony. Boon's seconds struggled to lift him to his stool, but he slipped to the floor moaning, "Leave me alone."

Although he made an effort to respond to the bell for round five, Eric was in such a helpless state that the referee wisely intervened. His performance did not go down well with the 38,000 crowd who booed him as he left the ring. On reflection it should have been Solomons they booed for allowing him into the ring knowing he was unfit.

Eric got £200 for his troubles, a huge drop from his purse against Ronnie James less than 12 months earlier. It was clear that he had seen better days and despite moving up to welterweight he was well past his best. He recognised this and after the fight told a small group of journalists it was time to hang up his gloves. "I think I shall have to have a shot at journalism," he said with a smile.

Much of Eric's condition was due to the good life he had been living. He had been surrounded by hangers-on, a not unfamiliar happening in the fight game in those days. It dug deep into his already dwindling bank balance and for weeks he didn't go to bed before dawn. Describing some of his worst times he said: "I was tortured with insomnia, blinding headaches and frightening moods."

20

COMEBACK

Despite having announced his retirement, it wasn't long before Boon had the urge to get back into the ring. Already convinced that he still had something to offer, his mind was finally made up when he went to London's Seymour Hall on 11 December 1945 to look after his pal Harry Silver who was fighting Bob Ramsey. The top of the bill contest featured British welter and middleweight champion, Ernie Roderick, who was outpointed by Bert Hyland in a scrappy eight-rounder. Eric was unimpressed and by the end of 1945, he was working out daily at a gym behind Piccadilly Circus. It wasn't long before rumours circulated that he was to make a comeback.

Boon was still a man who captured public imagination and the newspapers fed off the story. Reporters began drifting to the gym and one day at least a dozen gathered to watch him train. They were impressed with what they saw and their visits became more regular, but on New Year's Day they got a story they could never have hoped for.

Wearing a heavy sweatsuit and 16 ounce gloves, Eric worked out with a well known professional. During a session of sheer ferocity he floored his 'opponent' several times with vicious body punches before knocking him out with a perfect left hook to the chin. It was accomplished with the speed and ferocity of his best championship days and the following morning the story appeared on the sports pages of most national newspapers.

Writing in the *Daily Mail,* Geoffrey Simpson said the job was done so expertly that everyone gathered there began to wonder what Eric had been doing to lose so often and so badly as he had over the past few years. His performance in the gym that day ridiculed stories of him being a worn out shell of an ex-champion. Simpson was discrete enough not to name the unfortunate sparring partner who he knew well and had seen win many good contests.

Jack Solomons, whose admiration for Boon was unshakeable, remarked: "There is no mystery to what has occurred, it is just a matter of his conditioning."

He revealed that Boon's outlook on boxing had changed dramatically because his wife and child had rejoined him after several years of evacuation. "There is no doubt that he is now very fit," continued Solomons, "and I can understand why he is telling people that if he does not win his comeback fight he will quit the ring for good."

Eric had been due to meet Welsh welterweight champion, Gwyn Williams, at Seymour Hall on 8 January 1946, but he was replaced by late substitute Cyril Wills from Shrewsbury. In what was a must win fight he gave an exhibition of hard accurate punching and in less than two minutes dropped Wills with the perfect combination of a right to the head and a left to the jaw. The Shrewsbury man fell flat on his face, his right cheekbone badly cut. He rose at 'nine', but was glassy-eyed and defenceless against a vicious left swing which crashed against his chin flooring him for another count of 'nine'.

Wills bravely rose again, but leaned helplessly against the ropes as Boon rushed forward. Another accurate left swing put him down for a third time. Although he crawled along the canvas and attempted to find his feet, it was a futile effort and he was counted out after two minutes 45 seconds.

Not for some years had Eric looked so fit and he proved to his critics that he had lost none of his old power. Apart from flooring his opponent three times he also inflicted cuts above both his eyes. There was, however, the reservation that Wills was a comparative novice who had no means with which to combat the old champion's attack once his guard had been broken down. His original opponent, Gwyn Williams, would not have been expected to fall so quickly. One headline, "Boon is back" was surely rather premature.

At the same time as Eric was preparing for his comeback, a Johannesburg businessman, Mr J F Coetzee, was in London to purchase British machinery. He also had a mission to recruit some established British boxers willing to face South African champion, Laurie Stevens. Boon, by this time was managed by Benny Huntman whose stable included quality fighters Jack London, Jimmy Davis, Dickie O'Sullivan, Billy Thompson, Jimmy Webster and Gwyn Williams. He invited Coetzee to the Boon – Wills fight and the businessman was impressed by the Chatteris man's performance. After talks with Huntman he agreed to recommend him to the South African promoters he represented.

The following week John Harding, who was busy winding up the Queensberry Club after its tremendous war effort, told Bob Crisp of the *Daily Express* that he was willing to back Arthur Danahar in the amount of £200 to £100 in a fight against Boon. A couple of days later the challenge was taken up by Huntman who said he was willing to back Eric in any amount up to £500 provided the fight was made at 10st 7. Such a demand meant that if a contest between them was staged, Danahar's Southern Area welterweight title would be at stake.

With Solomons concentrating on promoting the plan was to keep Boon busy and hopefully build him back towards championship contention. He and Huntman knew that a winning Boon would be a tremendous draw at the box office. The fight with Wills was therefore the first of a series of six contests alternating between Seymour Hall and the Royal Albert Hall at fortnightly intervals.

The campaign continued on 22 January at the Albert Hall on a show topped by Arthur Danahar against Omar Kouidri. Boon's opponent, Paddy Burgin, was described as the light and welterweight champion of Eire, but he was no match for the Chatteris man who floored him for counts of 'nine' and 'two' in the opening round and cut him over the right eye. Early in round two Burgin was sent sprawling again for 'nine' from a vicious right hook. When he rose, referee George Garrard stopped the fight.

The crowd rose to Eric as he left the ring, and in his report in the *Daily Mail* the following day, Geoffrey Simpson wrote:

> The best punching of the show came from the reconditioned ex-champion Eric Boon who treated Burgin like a sparring partner.

Next up was useful French welterweight, Jean Wanes, who gave Boon plenty to think about by flooring him with a left hook to the body in the opening round. Eric protested that the blow was low, but referee Mickey Fox ordered him to box on. Boon responded in the only way he knew sending Wanes to the floor in the same round and again the third with powerful body shots.

At the end of round three the Frenchman returned to his corner wincing and gripping his left side. He carried on gamely through the fourth and even floored Boon for a count of 'six' from a body shot. Again Eric protested that it was low, but was again ignored by Mr Fox. On rising he tore into Wanes and a sharp left raised a huge lump over his left eye which was almost closed when the bell sounded.

The Frenchman looked to be in agony during the interval as he clutched the left side of his rib cage. Boon showed no mercy and threw a hard right to the damaged area in the opening seconds of round five. Wanes gasped and sunk to his knees for 'seven'. When he rose Boon drove another right to the same area and as the Frenchman fell, his manager, Pierre Gandon, a former cruiserweight who had fought many times in England, threw in the towel. It was quickly thrown out by Mr Fox who later explained that this method of surrender was not accepted under British rules. After more excited gesticulation from the French corner, the referee accepted Wane's retirement. It was later revealed that he had a fractured left rib.

After the fight Dave Crowley went to Boon's dressing room and wished him luck in his comeback. During their conversation he explained that due to an injury to his left eye he would never fight again.

The following day there were reports that arrangements had been made for Eric to travel to Johannesburg in March. Possible opponents were South African welterweight champion, Laurie Stevens, Alf James, the lightweight champion, and Charlie Catterall, the featherweight champion who planned to move up to lightweight. On 7 February, however, it was revealed that Boon would not be making the trip.

Writing in the *Daily Mail,* Geoffrey Simpson said that the South African promoters hesitated when the proposals were first discussed. They could have got Boon for a comparatively low fee, but that was before he became the rejuvenated and much talked about fighter he was after three quick victories within a matter of weeks. As the reporter pointed out:

> It is a case of a missed opportunity. Why should he go now he is back in the money? A little patience will bring him a fight with Arthur Danahar that will command a bigger purse than any he might earn overseas. Their fight in 1939 is still being talked about and a return at the higher weight would fill any hall.

Boon continued his comeback with a one-sided victory over Mick Magee, a southpaw from Belfast, who Jack Solomons described as the undefeated lightweight champion of Northern Ireland. His best performance had been a draw with Johnny Watters who had beaten 'Kid' Silver and put up a good losing battle against Henry Hall. On a visit to Northern Ireland, Joe Louis described Magee, as a future world champion.

Boon was again in destructive form and ended the fight at the Royal Albert Hall with a short left hook to the body midway through the second round. As Magee sank to his knees the referee dismissed appeals from his corner that the blow was low. The moment the count was completed a doctor climbed into the ring and attended to the stricken Irishman who was having his first fight at welterweight.

Magee had been outclassed from the start being cut over the right eye and floored for a short count in the opening round. He rallied briefly at the start of the second, but Eric's short blows to the body carried tremendous power and it was clear the regular contests were helping him get back to something like his former self.

There were some boos as Magee was counted out and the following day the press criticised the quality of Boon's recent opponents. Those behind him, however, knew that he had to be brought back carefully because in recent years the sparkle had gone from his performances. Despite this everyone knew he could still punch. He was an exciting, flamboyant performer guaranteed to draw large crowds. As the plan was to build him steadily towards another championship contest it was important that he kept winning.

Three weeks later, on 5 March, Boon survived the sternest of tests in his comeback campaign when he faced Maurice Ouezmann, a French North African, at Seymour Hall. Throughout the first six sessions of the eight-rounder he was a mere shadow of the old Boon as the experienced Frenchman neatly and accurately caught him with good shots every time he charged forward.

Only in the fourth and fifth rounds did Boon land solid blows to the jaw, but Ouezmann took them without flinching. Even when trapped on the ropes or in corners, he fought his way out with rapid two-fisted volleys frequently sending the Chatteris man back on his heels.

By the start of the seventh Boon was well behind on points and his left eye was almost closed. He looked a beaten man, but knowing that defeat was not an option he turned the fight around in sensational style. In some respects it was like the old Boon when, seven years earlier he snatched losing championship fights out of the fire against Dave Crowley and Arthur Danahar.

Attacking with renewed fire and ferocity he threw big punches at the confident Frenchman and the effect was instant. A vicious left hook crashed against Ouezmann's chin sending him to the floor in an untidy heap. Blood from his injured mouth dripped onto his chest as he rested on one knee before rising on shaky legs at the count of 'nine'. He was badly dazed and referee, Mickey Fox, took a careful look at him before allowing the bout to continue.

Sensing a dramatic victory, Boon moved menacingly forward again and slammed another fusillade of heavy blows to the Frenchman's face. Blood streamed from his nose, and a deep gash opened beneath his left eye. A left hook to the body followed by a right to the jaw sent him down again for 'nine'. Although he bravely climbed to his feet he was immediately pounded on the ropes as Boon went for the 'kill'. "Enough, enough," shouted Mr Fox as he stepped in and pulled the Chatteris man away with just two seconds of the round remaining.

Meanwhile, a number of fights had broken out at the ringside among a section of the betting fraternity who had shown uncalled for hostility towards Boon from the moment he entered the ring. The sudden turnabout of the contest had apparently been too much for them and Eric was disgusted at their lack of sportsmanship.

254

The drama and excitement generated by Eric's sensational finish to the fight was sadly dampened by what was becoming unacceptable behaviour by those individuals with absolutely no sporting interest in boxing. Writing in the *Daily Express* the following day, Frank Butler gave a frank and accurate account about the conduct of members of the betting fraternity at boxing promotions:

> Professional boxing will be ruined unless quick steps are taken by promoters to prevent ringside outbursts like those which marred the Boon-Ouzemann fight. Ringsiders who went to watch boxing by sportsmen were so disgusted by the brawls by betting hooligans and the unwarranted abuse directed against Boon in the sensational seventh round when he turned almost certain defeat into victory, that I can safely say many will not return until a clean-up is staged. It is up to the promoters to stamp out this evil.

> I sympathise with Boon. His loud-mouthed critics were those who had taken odds of 4-1 against him and they were angered when "a good thing" was snatched from them by one punch. Full credit must be given to him for his great comeback, but in many other respects he was a shadow of the old Boon. Too often he showed he was hurt by a body blow from the light punching Frenchman. Too often he was caught by right swings and too often did he miss his opponent by feet.

Boon made only one excuse for his poor display in the earlier rounds, claiming he had double vision in his left eye. "As the Frenchman was flicking about in front of me it was like watching an old-time silent movie," he told reporters who crowded into his dressing room after the fight.

The important thing was that Eric still retained his great hitting power. In the dressing room next door Ouezmann stated that he had never been hit so hard during his 10 years of fighting.

Boon was still a huge draw and with five quick victories behind him within the space of two months he received offers for fights all over Britain. Others came from America where he was offered large sums of money for 10-round contests. The London fight fans, however, wanted to see him against a more worthwhile opponent. When it was announced that he would face Irishman, Johnny Watters, at the Royal Albert Hall on 19 March, he was considered to be the sternest test for the former champion in his comeback so far. Unfortunately, as so often occurs in the fight game, Watters sustained a training injury and had to withdraw. He was replaced by Billy Stevens of Glasgow and their eight-rounds contest became the chief support to a fight for the vacant European bantamweight championship between Jackie Patterson and Theo Medina of France.

Boon was given an unexpectedly hard struggle by Stevens who was elusive, cunning and awkward. He baffled and teased Eric throughout the first six rounds by continually changing his style and stance. He jabbed well and the Chatteris man had no answer to his tactics. In his frustration he was unable to steady himself to land his big punches.

Eric was clearly well behind on points, but in almost identical fashion to when he faced Maurice Ouezmann two weeks earlier, he came out for round seven looking like a killer. A left hook followed by two right swings to the chin sent Stevens heavily to the floor. Although he rose at the count of 'nine' the fight was effectively over because Boon rarely let an opponent off the hook.

The Scot showed tremendous courage and absorbed some awful punishment as Eric went all out for the finish. Vicious left hooks sent Stevens crashing for three further counts of 'nine'. Even when he was floored for a fifth time he made a valiant effort to rise and only just failed to beat the count. He received massive applause from the appreciative audience as he left the ring and afterwards even challenged Boon to a return.

Boon proved yet again that he was still one of the hardest punchers in the country and a few days later issued a £1,000 challenge to British welterweight champion, Eric Roderick. It was immediately accepted and within an hour Jack Solomons stated that he was willing to promote the contest.

Roderick's rapid acceptance was easy to understand because he gave Boon one of the worst beatings of his career whey they met at Liverpool in 1940. Speaking from Newport, the champion said: "When I met Boon six years ago he took a count in every round. I can repeat that and to show that I mean it I am willing to stake the British welterweight championship as well as taking Boon's side-bet."

Writing in the *Daily Mail,* Geoffrey Simpson said:

> Few of us are fond of return matches, but this is one I should like to see if only to get the true measure of Boon's recent form. Of all the recent six opponents who have lost to him inside the distance, none were of top class.

*　　　*　　　*

By this stage Boon was a natural welterweight. Since embarking on his comeback in January1946 his weight had been constant with 10 st 7 ¾ against Paddy Burgin being the heaviest and 10st 5 ½ for his fight with Mick Magee the lightest.

Despite having no immediate intention of retirement, Eric still had ambitions to set up his own business. With that in mind, he asked a close friend, journalist Terry Leigh-Lye, to look for premises in the West End which were suitable to be turned into a gymnasium which he wanted to run.

After a lengthy search, an estate agent told Leigh-Lye about a disuscd billiard hall at 41 Great Windmill Street on the edge of Soho which had rooms above it which he considered would be suitable for the purpose. Eric took Jack Solomons along to view it, but quickly acknowledged that he could not afford the rent.

Already an astute and established businessman, but always looking for new horizons, Solomons recognised the potential for a high quality gymnasium in the heart of the West End. The premises at Great Windmill Street were ideal for what he had in mind so he quickly negotiated a deal to take over the tenancy.

After considerable internal work the gym opened in March 1946 and was run by Nat Seller. On Sunday mornings entry was strictly limited to invitation only and Nat, having staged novice competitions each weekend at his Whitechapel gym, offered Solomons a similar programme.

During the same month concerted efforts began to match Boon with Arthur Danahar to settle the long and outstanding arguments as to who was the better of the two. London promoters knew that a return between them would fill any arena in the capital, especially as Boon appeared to have recaptured some of his old flair and punching power.

Since their memorable meeting in 1939, Danahar had been far busier than Eric having had 53 contests of which he lost just six, one of which was on points to Ernie Roderick in September 1941 for the British welterweight title. He had also been more successful than Boon by scoring victories over Roderick (points) in 1938, Norman Snow, whom he stopped in six rounds to take the Southern Area title, Harry Mizler, who was outpointed in 1942 and stopped the following year, and Ronnie James who he outpointed in 1944 (twice) and 1945. During the same period of time, Boon had taken just 23 fights and lost seven.

As two of the best supported London based boxers for years a return between them was a natural. Jack Solomons eventually succeeded in matching the pair and made the contest the chief support to the world light-heavyweight championship fight between Gus Lesnevich and Freddie Mills at Harringay on 14 May. Articles were signed for the bout to be over 12 rounds at 10st 7 and the Board of Control approved an application from the promoter for it to be an eliminator for Ernie Roderick's British welterweight title.

As soon as the fight was announced *Weekly Sporting Review* ran a front page story headlined "He's Front Page News Again" which was illustrated by a handsome pose of Boon. The Editor, Isidore Green, was confident that despite the passing of the years and restrictions imposed by war, both men were still capable of putting up a great fight. Although Boon still relied on his murderous punching power to decisively settle most battles, the writer was of the opinion that he wouldn't get away with it this time because Danahar would not have forgotten the lesson he learned back in 1939. His boxing skill was far superior to Boon's who was not as alert as in his earlier career.

Harringay Arena was packed for what was the first important London promotion in peacetime. Mills against Lesnevich was a huge attraction as was the contest between Boon and Danahar. On paper it had all the elements of thrill and spectacle and despite the passing of time, fans and critics alike expected another terrific battle. The outcome, however, could not have been more different because it opened tamely and ended amid bewilderment and uncertainty.

Both men were ultra cautious during the opening rounds with little or no action from either. Boon appeared to have no intention of wading in and being continuously caught by Danahar's immaculate left jab. Arthur himself was reluctant to set the pace for fear of being nailed by the Chatteris man's vicious counter punches. The outcome was that for the best part of four rounds they served up what is known in the fight game as a real stinker.

As the fight progressed it became clear that Boon was biding his time waiting to land his big punch. Using the ring well he avoided most of Arthur's attempts to jab, and then midway through the fourth he exploded into action. Clearly frustrated at getting nowhere he suddenly opened up with all his natural ferocity.

A left hook to the head followed by a terrific right to the chin sent Danahar crashing to the canvas. He looked badly shaken as he looked up at the referee's counting fingers before instinctively rising to his feet at the count of 'nine'. With great courage he stayed upright on wobbly legs desperately trying to hold off the thoroughly wound-up Boon who tore into him in an attempt to end hostilities. Doing what he always did best, Danahar landed a few jabs to the head and opened a cut beneath Eric's right eye, but the bell saved him from certain defeat.

During the one minute interval the Bethnal Green man got a new lease of life and came out for the fifth with a renewed air of confidence about him. Standing beautifully erect in contrast to the determined, low-crouching Boon, he carefully pumped left jabs to the face with deadly accuracy as the former champion waded in. It was during one of these wild rushes that sensation suddenly occurred.

With Boon wide open, Arthur sunk a terrific right deep into the body. Eric half turned, sank to his knees and rolled over on his haunches, his face contorted in agony. With tears streaming down his face, he clutched his protector with his left hand while thumping on the canvas with his right. Outside the ring his seconds angrily screamed that he had been fouled.

Danahar looked on in amazement and even the referee, Mr C B Thomas, seemed puzzled. Although he had started to count, he abandoned it at 'six' as Boon attempted to rise angrily shaking his fist at Arthur indicating that he had been hit low. Almost immediately Eric sank back to the canvas, his gloves covering his face because of the excruciating pain. He bent almost double in the centre of the ring when he rose again, but it was obvious he was unable to continue and Mr Thomas helped him to his corner.

There was utter confusion all around the ringside with some fans and critics believing that Danahar had been disqualified. Others thought Boon had failed to beat the count. The situation only became clear when the Master of Ceremonies announced that the referee had stopped the contest because Boon was in no condition to defend himself. Some critics believed that Mr Thomas had been unsighted and therefore unable to determine what caused Eric to drop.

Boon was still in agony as a doctor examined him back in his corner. He insisted he had been hit low and indicated the point where the blow landed. Benny Huntman examined his protector and on finding it was dented immediately crossed the ring and protested to the Board of Control Stewards sitting opposite. He was politely told that the referee's decision must be final.

There was a mixed reception as Eric was helped from the ring with many in the crowd believing he had been fouled. Supporters of Danahar, however, cheered the decision loudly. Boon was very disappointed because had he been victorious plans were in place for him to travel to America for a fight on the Joe Jouis – Billy Conn bill in New York on 19 June. If he remained undefeated it was hoped that he would challenge Marty Servo for the world welterweight title.

There were differing opinions about the legitimacy of the blow which ended the fight. Some critics were adamant that it was low while others claimed it was border-line. Writing in the *Daily Express*, Frank Butler said that he could not comment because

Danahar had obscured his view, but contrary to other opinions he believed that the referee was in a perfect position to decide. Butler believed that Boon boxed intelligently, weaving and using the ring to avoid most of Danahar's work.

Following medical treatment in his dressing room, Eric recovered quickly and within a short time sat fully dressed a few rows from ringside watching the Mills – Lesnevich fight which many critics saw as the most exciting fight in Britain since Boon met Danahar in 1939.

By his victory Danahar gained a revenge of sorts, but general opinion was that both men were mere shadows of those in 1939. Had it not been for the war both would probably have gone on to bigger and better things.

The day after the fight, Boon and Benny Huntman went to the Board of Control offices at Dean Street and asked for the decision to be reversed. They took the dented body protector along as evidence that Eric had been hit low and hard. The doctor who examined Boon was also of the opinion that he had been hit low, but under the rules of the controlling body, the referee's decision is final.

Although the decision would stand, Huntman was told to put his complaint in writing and it would be put before the Stewards at their next meeting. This took place on 31 May and after hearing all the evidence placed before them they were satisfied that a low blow had been struck by Danahar, but the referee had been unsighted. There was no criticism of his action and it was decided that there should be a re-match on a date to be agreed.

Despite his dip in fortune, Boon lost none of his public appeal and together with Jack Solomons he was guest of honour at a big boxing show at RAF Henlow on 21 May. Media coverage of his attendance was no different from the days when he was at his peak. The following week films of his fight with Danahar and that between Mills and Lesnevich were the star features of a programme at the Cameo Theatre, Charing Cross Road. At the time they were rated amongst the best big fight films ever produced with the photography greatly enhanced by the crystal clear quality of the Cameo screen. Although time limits prevented the whole fight from being shown, all shots were captured with the maximum of thrill and suspense. In particular there was an excellent close-up of Benny Huntman's vigorous protest after Boon had been declared the loser.

The controversial defeat to Danahar certainly did Eric no harm because within a few days he received a firm offer for a series of fights in South Africa. If successful there was also the chance of big money contests in America. Things were certainly looking bright again for the former British champion, especially when the Board of Control announced that Ernie Roderick would not be permitted to defend his British title until a return between Boon and Danahar had taken place.

21

SOUTH AFRICA

On 13 June 1946, Boon and Benny Huntman flew from Croydon Airport to South Africa on a plane specially chartered by the White City Sporting Club of Johannesburg. Sport, especially boxing, was booming in South Africa, and over the preceding few months several promotional representatives had travelled to England to try and lure British boxers to those shores. Former British heavyweight champion, Jack London, also managed by Huntman, had been expected to travel with Eric, but decided to join them on a later date because he needed to lose weight and get into condition.

The initial plans were for Boon to fight Laurie Stevens and Alf James. Although nothing definite had been agreed, Huntman told *Weekly Sporting Review* that provided he was successful and remained unscathed he would probably return to London to face Arthur Danahar again in the autumn. Boon was the first British boxer to travel to South Africa by air and as a means of keeping fit played squash at RAF stations on route before arriving there on 20 June. Some years later he gave his version of the flight in a Sunday newspaper claiming it took 36 days not seven:

The pilot was permanently drunk. We were supposed to touch down in France for a few hours, but unfortunately he went out on the binge. We were there for ten days. We spent all our money the first night thinking it would be the last, and for the next nine days we just stayed in our hotel

To make matters worse we had no documents – you needed a visa to go to France in those days. After ten days we had a visit from the Police wanting to know what was going on. It was touch and go, but eventually the Police took us to the airport so we could see if the plane was airworthy. We had told them the only thing we could say which was that there was something wrong with it and we'd been waiting for repairs to be done.

We got to the airport and there was the pilot dead drunk crawling about on his hands and knees. Anyway, we got into the plane to check things over, so he said, and the pilot promptly opened up the throttle and we were away. But it was a long, long time before we finally made it to South Africa. There were times when we wondered if we would ever make it.

The story was clearly fabricated to a large extent. Perhaps the old champion's memory was failing badly, or more likely sections of his account were all part of his wonderful sense of humour. Whatever the truth, it made light reading at the time it was published.

There was some misunderstanding about Boon's time of arrival at Johannesburg and as a result he and Huntman were kept waiting at the airport for two hours before being collected.

The initial plans were for Eric to meet Laurie Stevens in Johannesburg at the end of June and then face South African lightweight champion, Alf James, in a contest at 10 stone. On arrival in South Africa, however, Boon stated that he needed at least three weeks to prepare for Stevens and in view of the fact that he was also required to have yellow fever injections, the contest was put back until 27 July. That against James was cancelled.

Reg Haswell, Secretary of the White City Sporting Club, at whose house Boon was staying, told the press that it would be unreasonable to expect the former British champion to fight within a few days of his arrival after a long flight.

Eric commenced light training at the Rand Physical Culture Institute gym on 21 June and was introduced to the Johannesburg public the following day at a professional promotion at the Olympic Ice Rink. A few days later Benny Huntman was taken seriously ill with a throat infection and confined to hospital for several days. In the meantime Boon took on forty-one-years-old, Harry Best, a former RAF instructor, as his trainer.

Stevens, meanwhile, decided to take a warm-up fight against American southpaw, Jimmy Ainscough. In the days preceding that contest bad feeling developed between Huntman and the American's manager, Joe Basco, who brashly boasted that his man was likely to prove a bigger menace to Stevens than Boon.

Huntman, who had recovered from his illness, responded by saying that he was prepared for Boon to meet Ainscough for £500-a-side. "Put your money where your mouth is," he told the American manager when they came face to face.

Tiny Dean, Secretary of the Transvaal National Sporting Club, also got in on the act by stating that having watched Ainscough in his final try-out before facing Stevens he believed he was a bigger threat than Boon. "I'm not knocking Boon," he told the *Rand Daily Mail,* "I think he is a great fighter, but on paper I think Stevens has a greater chance against Boon because there isn't the difference in age there is between him and the American."

Dean's remarks also infuriated Huntman who, on a visit to the *Rand Daily Mail* offices on 3 July, said: "I don't want to be too hasty on this, but I certainly don't know how Tiny Dean can compare Ainscough with Boon who was a contender for the world lightweight title after he won the British title at the age of eighteen. He is now a contender for the British welterweight title." He went on to say that Eric was a much bigger name in America than Ainscough.

"Before we came out here I received an offer for Boon to go to America to fight the man who is welterweight champion of the world," continued Huntman. "It was only because we had given our word to Reg Haswell to come to Johannesburg that I did not take up the offer. I don't say Ainscough isn't any good, but he should have proved himself in this country to justify Tiny Dean making any such statement as he has."

Huntman's remarks proved to be justified because Stevens comfortably outpointed the American over 10 rounds. After he and Boon had watched the fight Benny said that he was willing to put up £500 against half that amount staked by Tiny Dean that Boon would stop Ainscough inside six rounds. The challenge, however, was quietly dismissed because the South African Boxing Board of Control had always frowned upon side-stakes on fights.

As Eric settled into his training routine it was revealed that if he beat Stevens he intended to take up residence on The Rand. Reg Haswell told the press that he had arranged employment for the British boxer and added: "There is no doubt that he will be a very welcome addition to our active boxers. He is only twenty-six-years-old, a fighter of the type crowds want to see and still has a good many ring battles in him."

Haswell said that Boon was committed to a return with Arthur Danahar so whatever happened against Stevens he would have to make a quick trip back to Britain at the expiry of his contract with the White City Sporting Club. Benny Huntman revealed that Jack Solomons had already telephoned him from London stating that he was anxious to stage the fight at Harringay during the first week in September. Solomons also offered Boon an overweight contest with Ernie Roderick, but in the event of him losing to Stevens, the South African would be given the chance to fight Roderick for the British Empire title.

Although Jack was carefully hedging his bets, Huntman insisted that the only time Eric would fight Roderick would be for the British title. "Boon is not fighting Roderick at any catchweights," he told the *Rand Daily Mail*. "When I told Solomons that he authorised me to offer Stevens a fight in London should he beat Boon."

Former British heavyweight champion, Jack London, arrived in South Africa on 13 July to prepare for a fight with Nick Wolmarans on 24 August. He stayed with Boon on a 52-acre estate about five miles outside Johannesburg where they did all their outdoor training which included six-mile runs each morning. Eric had been preparing steadily since arriving in the country and found that he was not at all troubled by the altitude.

He commenced public workouts on 15 July at the El Alamein Club at Commissioner Street which had been officially opened by the Mayor of Johannesburg two weeks earlier. Huntman engaged local boxers Jimmy McKay, Jackie Solomons, Teddy Brown and Tony Lombard as sparring partners and also extended invitations to any other local boxers to work with him.

During one intensive session, Eric did bag punching, exercises and shadow boxing before taking on Harry Best for two rounds of sparring. In a terrific workout watched by a large crowd Boon spared no quarter and asked for none in return. It developed into a real fight and the action was far more rigorous than anything seen in a training session on The Rand for many a long time. Best was left groggy from a terrific left hook and left the ring with a badly swollen right eye, a bleeding nose and bleeding teeth. "My whole jaw is numb," he remarked adding that Boon's left hook was the hardest punch he had ever taken in his 23-year ring career as a amateur in which he was only knocked out once. He was confident Boon would be too powerful for Stevens.

It soon became clear that the El Alamein and other local gymnasiums were too small to accommodate the crowds who wanted to watch the former British champion in action. Huntman therefore arranged for his training camp to be moved to the Whippet Ring at Maine Street which could hold at least 2,000 spectators. It was a shrewd move because nearly 1,000 fans, the biggest crowd ever to watch a boxer train in South Africa, paid a small entry fee to see Boon in his first public tryout. The money more or less covered the cost of a new car which Huntman purchased and intended shipping back to England.

First to face him was Bill Geogheagan, a former South African amateur welterweight champion, who took a terrific battering. It was like watching the old Boon as he let go a terrific battery of short left hooks to the body and right crosses to the jaw. There was no letting up and his sparring partner was glad to hear the bell.

Next into the ring was Jackie Solomons who kept back pedalling out of reach, but countered with several smart jabs to the face. It was clear, however, that Boon was holding back his punches and using his opponent's speed and skill to build towards his peak. It was then back to all out aggression as he battered Jimmy McKay relentlessly for the final two rounds of the tryout.

Boon created a great impression, not only with the public, but also the South African sports writers for the energy and vigour he displayed in the workouts, and also by his articulate manner during interviews. He had time for everyone and the newspapers, particularly the *Rand Daily Mail,* gave him coverage most days. There was an air of excitement about everything he did, particularly in his gym preparations. The press were united in their opinion that he was the hardest hitting man of his weight to have gone to South Africa for years.

The interest intensified as the fight with Stevens drew closer. He was mobbed when he attended East Rand Engineers Amateur Boxing Club's tournament at Germiston Town Hall in aid of the Dan Pienaar Memorial Bursary Fund. When he did his final try out at the Whippet Ring on 23 July, more than 1,500 fans turned up and hundreds more were refused entry as the stadium became packed. At the box office there were long queues most days as sports crazy South Africans clamoured for tickets. Reg Haswell told the press that takings had exceeded £6,000 and he anticipated a record attendance.

Benny Huntman kept the interest alive by saying that the final tryout would give an indication of Boon's capabilities. "Tonight folks will get a picture of the real Boon," he told the *Rand Daily Mail.* "They will be able to form their own ideas as to how good he really is. He will take some beating on Saturday even if his opponent is your favourite, Laurie Stevens."

Despite Huntman's promise, Eric had other ideas and revealed nothing of his true form. Whilst he was in amazing physical condition with masculinity written all over his toned and muscular body, he took things easy during four rounds of sparring with local boxers. He knew Stevens was a formidable opponent so the spectators expecting fireworks were left none the wiser as to what danger he posed on the night of the fight.

Boon was, nevertheless, extremely confident of success as were the promoters, so much so that exactly one week before meeting Stevens he signed a contract to fight Alf James at Durban on 15 August. At a special ceremony at the offices of *The Transvaal Sunday Times* in Johannesburg James said he felt confident he would do better against Boon than Stevens would because he was a boxer as opposed to a fighter.

Meanwhile, the Transvaal Board of Control for Professional Boxing had become alarmed about the extremely high level of illegal betting transactions being openly conducted at professional shows. The Boon-Stevens contest had aroused considerable interest and throughout the week preceding it many thousands of pounds had been wagered on the outcome. The Board therefore issued an instruction to promoters that all press advertisements must include a warning to the public that betting on fights was forbidden by law.

*　　　*　　　*

Laurie Stevens was one of the most popular boxers South Africa had ever produced. He was lightweight champion of his country from 1933 to 1937, held the British Empire title from 1936 until 1939 having beaten Jack 'Kid' Berg on points over 12 rounds at Johannesburg. Going into the fight with Boon, he was the leading welterweight in the national rankings.

Stevens, who owned a sports shop, took five weeks off work to concentrate on his training for the fight. "I know that Boon is a very good boy," he remarked," and it is out of respect to him as much as my own reputation that I am taking no chances about entering the ring as fit as it is possible to be."

The day before the fight press reports claimed that Boon was proving to be the biggest draw South African boxing had ever seen. In a telecommunication Benny Huntman told Frank Butler of the *London Daily Express* that the gate would fetch at least £10,000 exceeding the previous best by more than £3,000. Boon's share was 25% of the gate so with all expenses paid they expected to clear at least £2,000. On a visit to Durban, Reg Haswell was asked by a reporter from the *Natal Mercury* how he envisaged the fight going. "Boon is undoubtedly a top liner and is anxious to get his fights in South Africa over as he is due for a return with Danahar in England," he remarked. "Therefore you are likely to see the best of him out here. Stevens is a great fighter and knows all the tricks of the trade, but Boon is very fast, very fit and possesses a terrific punch. He will be extremely hard to beat."

Although Stevens was the idol of thousands of South African fight fans, those who sat among the crowd of about 20,000 in temperatures of minus three degrees at the Wembley Arena on 27 July, saw Boon hammer him with one devastating blow after another. It soon became clear that he was not going to last very long. Both men went to work from the opening bell with Stevens attempting to get to close quarters whilst Boon spoiled cleverly. He prevented the South African from using his renowned in-fighting skills and within half a minute shook him with a hard right to the jaw.

Midway through the round Eric pushed Stevens away from a close-quarter melee and threw a perfect right-left combination which landed with terrific impact. The South African's head jerked back and he toppled for a count of 'seven'. As the round drew to a close another powerful right staggered him badly, and a left and right combination had him rocking as the bell ended the round.

Stevens appeared to have recovered well as the second began and, showing no fear, set about Boon with several good lefts and held his own for most of the round. Suddenly, however, Boon opened up and staggered the South African with a series of great hooks. A right to the chin bounced him against the ropes, but Stevens rallied and the excitement reached fever pitch as they slugged it out toe-to-toe. The noise was so intense that neither boxer nor the referee heard the bell.

Stevens again started brightly in round three and had the crowd roaring and shrieking as he forced Boon to the ropes with an inspired two-fisted attack as if remembering the greatness of his past. There was a brief spell when many of his supporters believed the tide had turned and that against all expectations he could still beat the confident former British champion.

Boon, however, withstood the attack and, recognising that the South African looked too sure of himself, soon became the aggressor again. He launched a storming attack, switching punches to both head and body, and when Stevens momentarily dropped his guard, crashed a terrific left hook to his unprotected chin. The sheer power of the shot lifted the South African almost off his feet before he crashed to the floor. Although he gamely rose with the count at 'nine' he was badly dazed and a sitting target for the pumped-up Boon who was hovering impatiently.

Never a fighter to let an opponent off the hook, Eric flew at Stevens and smashed him back to the canvas with a lightening right cross. The crowd were dumb-struck as, eyes glazed, their idol tried desperately to rise. In a magnificently display of willpower he hauled himself up onto unsteady feet at 'nine' only to fall backwards and be counted out.

A few minutes later Laurie's limp body was being supported along the aisles to the dressing room. Thus ended what was the last fight of one of the most skilled and popular boxers in the South African ring. Boon was simply too powerful for him.

Although there was great disappointment among the huge crowd to see their idol dismantled so viciously, it spoke volumes for Boon's popularity that despite being several years past his best, he still left the ring to a great ovation for a thoroughly professional job.

Surrounded by friends back in his dressing room, Eric told reporters that Stevens was a very, very game fighter. "I did not think he would be able to retaliate quite so much after those punches of mine in the first round," he added. "Stevens was as tough as we thought he would be. He is a good fellow and a wonderful sportsman."

Benny Huntman added his tribute by saying: "No credit must be taken away from Stevens. He was one of the gamest boys I've ever seen in the ring."

The sheer scale of the fight as a sporting attraction was highlighted by the fact that about 2,000 fans scaled the perimeter fences of the venue to gain free admission. Back in London, however, there was a more negative reaction with newspapers relying on cabled reports. The *Daily Express* commented that Boon's victory meant that South African boxing had stood still during the war years. This was unfair on Boon.

The sequel to the Chatteris fighter's victory was a cable from Huntman to American promoter, Mike Jacobs, challenging world champion, Marty Servo, to a fight at £5,000-a-side. Reports claimed that if the champion agreed Johannesburg would be the venue for the biggest boxing promotion ever staged in South Africa.

Reg Haswell also cabled Servo's manager, Al Weill, in New York offering a purse of £5,000 free of income tax plus two return tickets for Servo to defend against Boon in Johannesburg on a convenient date.

Servo, who won the title by knocking out Freddie Cochrane in four rounds in February, was seen as a good thing for Boon because in March he had foolishly been drawn into a non-title fight with Rocky Graziano in which he took a terrible beating. Weill responded saying that they would be willing to face Boon provided Marty beat Sugar Ray Robinson in a fight set to take place in September.

A couple of days later, however, reports from London revealed that even if Servo agreed to the fight the British Boxing Board of Control would not recognise it as being for the world title. Despite Boon's success against Stevens, he still had leeway to make up against domestic fighters back home, the Board making particular reference to his defeats against Henry Hall and Arthur Danahar.

Anxious to identify a loophole, Huntman and Haswell discussed the alternatives. According to the Immigration Department in Pretoria, anyone born in Britain could become a South African National after living there for two years. The constitution of the Board of Control for Boxing in the Union of South Africa was less stringent in that it made no mention of nationality for registration as a professional boxer.

Much really depended therefore, on whether Boon would be permitted to challenge for the South African welterweight championship, and if he won it whether he could fight for the world title without obtaining authority from the British Boxing Board of Control. The period of residence was clearly the stumbling block to the current position so, on realising this, Haswell and the White City Sporting Club decided that the safer option would be to try and get Eric a fight for the British Empire title. At that point in time, however, his future became uncertain because despite having initially agreed for two contests in South Africa he was also receiving huge money offers for fights in America. The string of quick victories in London followed by that against Stevens had made him a much sort after fighter again.

Confusion set in because apart from the new offers, there was still the return with Danahar to consider although some critics were starting to believe it would never take place. Eric was also seriously considering settling in South Africa where he wanted to open a gym. If that occurred, the White City Sporting Club had reached agreement to buy his contract from Benny Huntman. They then hoped to induce Ernie Roderick and Arthur Danahar to travel to South Africa and fight him where the purses were much higher than in England.

Meanwhile, arrangements were well advanced for Boon to face South African lightweight champion, Alf James, at Durban in what would be the first big fight to be staged there. The promoters, Natal National Boxing Club, hoped to accommodate at least 5,000 fans, and made lavish plans for it to take place in the open air at Kingsmead, the region's main cricket ground. The ring would be situated between the stands and the actual cricket pitch square with 19 rows of seats around each side. A heavy Police presence would be in place to prevent 'jibbers' getting in through the many entrances on all sides of the ground.

The fight was set to cost the promoters purse money of about £2,000 with the winner taking sixty per cent. Boon was guaranteed a minimum of £1,000, but in the event of him weighing in at more than the stipulated weight of 145 pounds he would forfeit £250 to James. This was big money for Durban, but there was such tremendous interest in Boon as a boxing personality that the promoters were convinced that he alone would be a sufficiently attractive drawing card to generate a record gate. To ensure the fans got the best programme possible, it was planned to introduce many big name South African boxers.

A few days after the Boon-Stevens contest, James spoke to a reporter from the *Johannesburg Star*. "All the boxing men I've met greeted me with a pitiful smile," he remarked. "They did not say so in as many words, but they knew I was going to fight Boon next and they greeted me with a sort of smile given to a condemned man."

"Well, I smiled too," he continued, "because I am not going to fight Boon as Boon wants me to fight. I'm going to fight him my way. I'm going to use my feet and when I make him miss he won't look so good."

Boon arrived in Durban on 3 August and James the following day. As both required sparring partners a request was made in the *Natal Mercury* for willing feather, light and welterweight boxers to contact the promoters.

After a sight-seeing trip along the Victoria Embankment, Eric loosened up at the Fred Crooks gymnasium at the National Technical College during the afternoon. Photographs of him appeared in most local newspapers and he quickly became the centre of attention just as he had in Johannesburg. To pass away spare time between training he tested his angling skills trying to catch the elusive Durban bayfish.

It was not long before Boon again publically declared his desire to live in South Africa, and Durban in particular. In an interview with Jack Sacs of the *Rand Daily Mail* he said he found that the prestige of boxers, and professional sportsmen generally, was much higher in South Africa than in England. "In the Union the fact that a man can earn his living by fighting is accepted in the same way as a lawyer earns his money through the law and a doctor through medicine," he remarked. "My very short stay in this country has already convinced me that a boxer could not wish to be among more congenial and genuine friends than can be found in South Africa."

Benny Huntman supported his boxer's decision and added that they were sorry Eric had been the cause of Laurie Stevens retirement from the ring. "He has had a very gallant career and given the public their moneys' worth," he remarked. "However, I am sure that in Eric Boon the public will find a worthy successor and one who will guarantee to keep fighting. After last Saturday he is the only man in the welterweight division who can draw the crowds and there is no reason why opponents should not be brought here to meet him."

The day after the fight with Stevens a number of people called the *Rand Daily Mail* offices. One was Joe Basco, junior, the manager of American fighter, Proctor Heinhold. He complained bitterly of plans for Boon to face Alf James, stating that he should meet Heinhold instead. Huntman insisted that Eric was under contract to the White City Sporting Club for two contests and the terms would be fulfilled. He did not rule out a fight with the American saying: "Now that Boon intends to make his headquarters in this country there is no reason why he should not take on all-comers and I'm sure Heinhold would be one of the first he would like to tackle."

"In the meantime Heinhold should fight Stevens," said Benny. "If he beats him we can talk about a fight against Boon because then it will be more of a contest."

Boon had a public tryout for the James fight at the Royal Institute, an amateur boxing club in the centre of Durban, on 8 August. Several hundred fans packed in and were impressed by his tremendous speed and punching power. The South African press saw him as a hard man to beat.

Meanwhile, James told the media that he didn't fear Boon in the least. "While I was in England I sparred with him several times over a period of six months and know his style fairly well," he said. "I am confident I can outbox Boon over the first four or five rounds and from then on I'll get stuck into him."

In an interview some years later James claimed that in 1936 when he was boxing as a junior he used to buy two magazines, '*The Triumph*' and '*The Champion*', the centre spreads of which were devoted to boxing. "There I used to read about a seventeen-years-old British boxer named Eric 'Boy' Boon," he remarked. "I used to think to myself that if he could do it so could I."

Consequently, Alf went to Durban where he got a job as a deckhand on a freighter called 'The Ross' which was bound for Britain. Although he landed at Edinburgh he eventually settled in the east end of London and began training at Nat Sellers' La Boheme Gym in Mile End Road where he met Boon.

James spent just over a year in London and between January 1938 and February 1939 won 18 of 20 contests mostly at small arenas in the East End. He worked out regularly with Boon and was one of his main sparring partners for the return fight with Johnny Softley at the Royal Albert Hall on 3 March 1938. Now he looked forward to meeting him for real and was more than confident of the outcome.

Suddenly, however, there was huge disappointment because behind the scenes Boon had been secretly taken from his hotel to hospital on 9 August with a fever as a result of blood poisoning. After examination it was concluded that the problem arose through a cut he originally sustained over his left eye in the fight with Arthur Danahar which never properly healed. It reopened during the contest with Stevens and was further irritated during his public tryout at the Royal Institute.

As Eric's condition gave no immediate cause for alarm, Huntman kept it to himself in the hope that he would be able to leave hospital over the weekend and still be fit to fight. On learning that he was not responding to treatment, however, he had no alternative but to contact the promoter. A specialist was emphatic that Boon needed several days to recondition himself after which he would undergo further examination. Only then would a statement be issued regarding when he would be able to fight again.

Although he was discharged from hospital on 12 August the glands in his neck were very swollen and tender. He also had difficulty lifting his arms as a result of a series of 12 injections he had been given, and was advised that it was too dangerous to take a blow on his left eye for at least three weeks. The Natal Sporting Club therefore announced that the fight with James had been cancelled.

Resting at his hotel Eric looked pale and weak, but full of disappointment he said he was willing to meet James as soon as it could be arranged. Once he was well enough he travelled back to Johannesburg with Huntman and was present at Wembley Stadium on 24 August when Jack London outpointed Nick Wolmarans. It was announced from the ring that Boon would meet Alf James at that arena on 14 September, but within a few days the fight was postponed until 5 October. In the meantime having fully recovered from his illness, he would fight South African middleweight champion, Tiger Burns, at Wembley on 7 September.

The announcement provoked another outburst from Joe Basco, junior, who was angry about uncomplimentary remarks Benny Huntman allegedly made about his fighter, Procter Heinhold. "Huntman says Boon has everything to lose and nothing to gain by fighting Heinhold, "remarked Bosco. "His argument was that whereas Boon was in line for a shot at the world title, Heinhold hasn't got that far yet and therefore he has too much to lose. If he thinks Boon can beat Heinhold all I ask Benny Huntman is, why does he allow him to fight Alf James who is only a lightweight?"

"The only reason he has agreed to let Boon fight James rather than Heinhold is because James has got no punch and Heinhold has," continued Bosco. He added that should Eric lose to James the blow to his prestige would be a bygone.

"What I don't like," added Bosco, "is the way Mr Huntman wants to pick opponents for Boon. Tiger Burns, the middleweight champion, is a nice boy and a game one, but what does Mr Huntman want to pick on such an old man for?"

Huntman dismissed Bosco's ranting as publicity seeking because all Heinhold had really achieved was to get a draw with Alf James. "I brought Boon out here to fight James then Stevens," he remarked. "Had he got beaten by either at least it would have been by a national champion. If Boon fights Heinhold and beats him it wouldn't mean anything anywhere in the world."

*　　　*　　　*

Although he was tough and resolute, Burns, real name Dan 'Ginger' Levene, could by no stretch of the imagination be described as an outstanding champion. Known as 'The Fighting Postman' from his amateur days, he was also a well-known marathon runner. For some months he had been trained by Harry Best who prepared Boon for the Stevens' fight. In his opinion Burns would not be easy to beat and predicted that he would put on a great performance against the former British champion. "Tiger is tough and hardy," he told the press. "He has never been knocked out and is a much better boxer than he has been given credit for."

It was a great build-up by the experienced and respected trainer, but looking lean, hollow-cheeked and with a dull skin Burns, for all his 12 lbs weight advantage never looked to have a chance once he got into the ring.

Looking trim and muscular at 10st 8, Boon took things easily during the early stages of the opening round in which he even apologised to his opponent for hitting him as they emerged from a clinch. As the round wore on he gradually increased the pressure and floored the forty-years-old South African for a count of 'nine'. Even at this early stage it was obvious that the contest wouldn't last long.

Burns certainly didn't lack courage and made a couple of futile rushes which forced Eric to the ropes at the start of round two. At this point the Chatteris man upped his work-rate and after two solid left hooks to the head staggered Burns he dropped him with a terrific left hook to the jaw. The South African champion bravely struggled to his feet at 'nine', but Boon was waiting for him and immediately launched another two-fisted attack. Two left hooks paved the way and a solid right to the jaw sent Burns to the canvas for the full count.   Afterwards he said that he had never been hit so hard and explained that the only other time he was knocked out was when he was a sergeant in the Military Police some years earlier. He had been on riot duty outside Johannesburg City Hall when he was hit on the head by a brick thrown from the top of a nearby building.

Only as he sat in his corner did Boon permit himself a quiet smile leaving the more obvious pleasures to Benny Huntman who talked volubly. After visiting Burns' corner he rushed to the ropes where he called out excitedly to reporters sitting below. "Did you hear what he just said? Did you make a note of that?

"What did he say?" asked one journalist.

"He says he's never been hit so hard," replied Huntman.

"It hurts more as one gets older," was the cynical response of one newsman.

A few days later, whilst returning to his hotel after watching a film of his fight with Burns, Boon was involved in a motor accident. He sustained injuries to his right eye and a chipped bone in his left elbow which required hospital treatment. It meant that his fight with Alf James, scheduled to take place on 5 October, would have to be called off again.

By this time Eric had decided to take up residence in South Africa. Together with his business partner, Jack Miranda, a forty-one-years-old musician and band leader, he planned to concentrate on running a country club and gymnasium business nine miles outside Johannesburg.

Miranda had played clarinet in the Bert Ambrose Band during the late 1920's and later became a member of the Al Collins Orchestra. In the late 1930's he formed his own band, Jack Miranda and his Meanderers. He was a highly respected musician who had played at most of the luxurious West End nightspots including the Mayfair, Berkeley and Savoy hotels. He and Boon became good friends after being introduced in the days when Eric was a regular figure around the London music and entertainment circles.

Once Boon had made his decision to live in South Africa his managerial contract with Benny Huntman was taken over by the Treasurer of the White City Sporting Club, Gilbert Brown, a South African businessman, for £2,500.

In view of his injuries Brown advised Eric to return to England and wind up his financial affairs. He and Miranda planned to arrive in London on 17 September in time to get to Harringay to watch the fight between British heavyweight champion, Bruce Woodcock and Gus Lesnevich, but their flight was delayed. "The crew of the aircraft knew of our anxiety to get there," Boon told *Weekly Sporting Review* "so the pilot suggested we listened to it on his RT set. So instead of watching it in ringside seats we heard a crackled commentary as we flew eight thousand feet above the Libyan Desert."

His left arm in plaster, Eric said that after settling his private affairs he intended returning to South Africa within about five weeks when he and Miranda intended taking over the running of the Willowdene Country Club.

Alf James was bitterly disappointed and highly indignant at the latest cancellation of his fight with Boon especially as the former British champion had left South Africa before he was told. It was the fourth time in as many months that it had been postponed. "A fellow can't keep on training for a fight that doesn't take place," he told the *Rand Daily Mail*. He said that he had been offered fights in

Transvaal and had to turn them down due to his contract to meet Boon for the White City Sporting Club.

"Now the report is that Boon has gone to England to fix up his affairs and I am to await the pleasure of his return, not only to this country but also to ring activities," he continued angrily.

22

MORE SOUTH AFRICAN EXPERIENCES

A few weeks before Boon arrived back in England there was talk of a possible world lightweight title fight between him and Ike Williams. The American had successfully defended his title against Ronnie James whom he knocked out in nine rounds at Cardiff on 4 September and as the champion boarded his plane at London Airport four days later for his return to the United States, he waved cheerfully and called out: "Be seeing you soon." Both his manager and promoter Jack Solomons told Isidore Green of *Weekly Sporting Review* that Ike would most probably be appearing in a British ring again in November. The likelihood was that his opponent would be Boon.

At the time Benny Huntman was still Eric's British manager and expressed his willingness for the fight. Solomons knew it would fill any arena in London, yet any attempt made to stage it would be the biggest indication yet that Boon was being exploited. Only two years earlier he had been badly beaten by James. He had struggled for months to make the 9st 9 limit and since then had boxed only at or above the welterweight limit. Common sense said that he could never make lightweight again. Furthermore, the British Boxing Board of Control, having refused to recognise a proposed fight between Boon and Marty Servo for the welterweight title, would surely never have sanctioned it.

Shortly after returning to England Eric was offered a fight against Jean Wanes in Paris on 20 October. Although it was an attractive offer financially, it was turned down because he had important private matters to attend to. There was also talk of a fight in London with Welsh champion, Gwyn Williams, but this too was resisted because Eric had made up his mind to return to South Africa.

The Board of Control, meanwhile, were anxious to keep the welterweight division active and during January 1947 announced that Arthur Danahar would meet Williams in an eliminator. The winner would meet Ginger Stewart for the right to face Ernie Roderick for the title. As Boon had already made his intentions clear he was not considered for the eliminators.

Solomons pleaded with Eric not to return to South Africa because he wanted to match him with the winner of a European welterweight championship contest between the champion, Ernie Roderick, and Robert Villemain of France set to take place in Paris on 1 February. Jack knew that Boon against whoever won would guarantee another sell-out at Harringay a few months later.

Despite a substantial financial incentive, Eric resisted the offer and arrived back in Johannesburg during the third week of January. As soon as he arrived the White City Sporting Club announced that the long delayed but keenly awaited contest with Alf James would take place at Wembley on 3 March which was a Monday. This was because a ban had been imposed on Saturday night boxing as the stadium had been given over to football thereby making it impossible for boxing promotions to be staged there the same day.

Boon got straight back into action by boxing a lively three rounds exhibition with former South African lightweight champion, George 'Panther' Purchase, at the Rosebank showground. Top of the bill was a contest between Alf James and Bobby Ramsey from Stepney who was disqualified for a low blow in the fourth round of what was described as a free-for-all.

James had used the fight as a warm-up for his long awaited meeting with Boon although this suddenly looked to be in jeopardy because it did not meet with the approval of the British Boxing Board of Control who claimed Eric had not sought their authority.

A story appeared in the *Transvaal Sunday Times* on 23 February stating that the sale of Boon's contract to the White City Sporting Club the previous year, was being queried. Despite repeated demands by the promoters, the Transvaal Board of Control refused to issue him a boxer's licence which was seriously jeopardising the promotion of 3 March. It was claimed that this was entirely due to an attempt by the British Board of Control to interfere with the management of boxing in South Africa by questioning the validity of the contract sale.

Meanwhile, in London, Board of Control Secretary, Charles Donmall, disputed a Reuter's report that they had cabled their Transvaal counterparts asking that Boon's contest with James be cancelled. "We did not ask for a cancellation," he said. "We drew attention of the Transvaal Board to the fact that Boon did not apply for permission to fight in South Africa on his second visit."

Donmall stated that authority granted for the first trip automatically expired when Boon returned to the United Kingdom the previous year. A further application should have been made to the Board if he intended taking part in further contests when he returned to South Africa.   "There have been reports that Boon is taking out Union citizenship papers," continued Donmall, "and if he does so it would automatically cancel out the necessity to make application to the Board for permission to fight there."

Donmall maintained, however, that the Board was entitled to exercise control over Boon's boxing career for the entire two years preceding his qualification for nationalisation as a South African citizen.

According to the *Transvaal Sunday Times* it was further suggested that the rights sold to White City in respect of Boon's contract were of a restricted nature. Reg Haswell, Secretary of the Sporting Club, disputed this maintaining that White City purchased a complete interest in Boon as a boxer. The deeds of sales were available and had been produced for scrutiny by the Transvaal Board of Control. Haswell added that the money in respect of the transaction was transmitted to Benny Huntman's wife through a local shipping company. Ample evidence and sworn statements as to the transaction were available.

Boon himself made it clear that he was prepared to appear before any court of law to make a sworn statement as to the sale of his contract. He added that he was settling down in South Africa and intended to make the country his permanent home.

The granting of a licence to Boon was further delayed due to a serious illness to the Chairman of the Transvaal Board which prevented the promoters making direct representation to him. On 24 February, however, Reg Haswell approached Vice Chairman, Steven Pitts, and presented a demand for the immediate issue of a provisional licence to Boon.

Following discussion, the Transvaal Board eventually decided they were not prepared to allow the situation to develop further and thereby cause yet another delay to the Boon – James contest. They accepted that Eric was genuine in his desire to take up residence in South Africa and therefore granted him a licence. As his managerial contract had been purchased by the White City Sporting Club he would only be permitted to box under their auspices or with their specific permission. A cablegram confirming the decision was sent to the British Boxing Board of Control, but no response was ever received.

The attitude of the British Board caused a great deal of bad feeling in South Africa because it dragged on too long and threatened to damage the prestige and respect which existed between the two controlling bodies. The general feeling was well documented in an article in the *Transvaal Sunday Times* part of which read:

> While the British Board no doubt have jurisdiction over his boxing activities if Boon ever fights in Britain, it is obvious that they have neither the right nor the power to interfere with his professional boxing career in South Africa. It is the duty of the Transvaal Board of Control to protect all connected with the sport in the Province. With the ample and substantial evidence before them regarding the purchase of Boon's contract it is surprising that

there has been all this delay in protecting a legitimate right of a local promoting body which has fully conformed with all of the Board's regulations for some years and has also contributed handsomely to the Board's revenue.

Once he realised that the fight could finally go ahead a relieved Alf James said: "A win over Boon will put me right back on top of the list as a draw card. It's a golden opportunity and I'm going to make the most of it. I don't think there is anything I don't know about his methods. It is possible he may bust me with a knock-out punch within five rounds, but that is his only hope. If he doesn't win in five rounds the fight is mine."

Meanwhile, Dolph du Plessie, a well known South African boxing trainer visited the *Rand Daily Mail* offices and issued a challenge to Boon on behalf of his boxer, Gillie van de Westhuizen, who he claimed was the most outstanding welterweight in South Africa. Only by fighting Boon would he be able to prove there was nobody else there to beat him.

Boon continued to be a massive attraction in South Africa and his forthcoming fight with James had the fans buzzing. It was another massive sporting occasion and during the build-up both men gave a number of press interviews. Having waited for eight months James was relieved that it was at last going to happen. "Boon is the one man standing in my path so far as the welterweight championship of South Africa is concerned," he remarked. "It wasn't my fault it hasn't taken place already."

James believed that as Boon had been out of the ring for so long he needed a contest or two. "That will all worry him on the night," he told the *Rand Daily Mail.* "Boon is two types of fighter and so far in South Africa we have seen only one kind, the man who is a killer over the short distance. He is at his most dangerous for the first four or five rounds of a contest."

Boon was irritated by some of Alf's remarks to the press and said: "One would think I am going into the ring just to be made to look a mug. It's hardly worth my trouble to carry on with the fight because James has already won it!"

"According to the way he has the fight all mapped out, all he would have to do is dance in and out for five rounds and completely frustrate all my efforts to land a knock-out punch," continued Eric. "After those five rounds I would be so exhausted I will hardly be able to hold my hands up. That's a very pretty picture, but I've got news for him. That is not the way fights are won."

Boon insisted that he had done plenty of training at a city gym and road running during the evenings out of town. He was as fit as he possibly could be and just as anxious as James to get the fight over and done with. "One would think that just because I have taken an interest in a nightclub and am helping to run it that I am all washed up and out of condition," he remarked angrily. "I have been in this game too long to take any chances. Running a nightclub is easy compared to fighting a contest."

Boon may not have been the fighter he was in the late 1930's, but he was still proud and determined. He knew there was good money to be made in South Africa and there was never any question of him cutting corners during his preparations for James. The South African, however, had trained equally well and during the first six rounds of the fight outboxed Boon with footwork that would have made a ballet dancer jealous.

From the opening bell it was clear that James intended fighting to a defensive plan based on the knowledge that he didn't possess the power to deter the Englishman. Boon, for his part, predictably tried to bomb his opponent out, although generally his punches were wild. Many missed the target as the South African moved and held.

The fight suddenly took a dramatic turn in round seven when James cornered Boon and caught him with three stiff lefts to the stomach. Eric winced as the third landed and sank to the floor where he rested on one knee before rising as the count reached 'nine'. Believing his opponent was in trouble James moved in to finish it only to be caught by a spectacular left hook which crashed against his temple and sent him heavily to the floor. With a huge swelling at the side of his head the South African gamely rose at 'eight', but tottered badly. The Boon of old was hovering and another powerful left hook smashed him to the floor for the full count which was completed at one minute 50 seconds of the round.

A few seconds after it was officially over, James struggled to his feet and moved towards Boon as if to continue the encounter. After a couple of steps he collapsed in the centre of the ring and had to be helped back to his corner. Boon's left hook was the decisive factor and although he was clearly outboxed for long periods there was a feeling the fight was only going to last for as long as it took him to connect properly.

In some respects the British boxer was fortunate not to have been disqualified at the end of round three. As the bell sounded James dropped his guard and turned towards his corner. In a split second Boon crashed a terrific left hook to the head which opened a gash under the South African's right eye. He momentarily sank to his knees and was clearly in some distress as he sat on his stool during the interval.

281

Instead of disqualifying Boon, the referee went to James' corner and asked if he was prepared to continue. He acknowledged that he was. It was, nevertheless, poor judgement by the official to put the onus on the boxer who was clearly dazed. Although the illegal blow by Boon was unintentional he was given an unfair advantage by the weakness of the referee by not enforcing the rules. Most critics were of the view that Boon became more aggressive from that point whereas James, despite still stealing the points, was more cautious.

A crowd of over 8,000 watched the fight and Boon's purse was reported to have been in excess of £1,000. Interviewed in his dressing room afterwards while quietly sipping a brandy, he looked none the worse for wear except for a slightly swollen left eye. He said that he fooled James into believing he was hurt in the seventh round. "That was the only way I could get him to come to me," he said with a smile. "I really did think I could have licked him earlier, but didn't want to take any chances. I wanted him to come to me."

"He never hurt me and I wanted to teach him a lesson," continued Eric. "He is quite a clever boxer, but I took exception to the fact that he said he would make me look like a monkey."

Boon was adamant that the blow he landed after the bell at the end of round three was an accident, but considered James very sporting for not claiming a foul. "I just didn't hear the bell, "he remarked. "After that I gave him two chances when he slipped, but at the start of the seventh I told my trainer, Harry Best, I was going to do him."

At an after-fight party at the Willowdene Country Club where Boon was based, James admitted that he had been 'foxed' by the Chatteris man and demanded a return. Although Eric agreed, rumours circulated that the fight had been fixed, but in the heat of the moment Boon had forgotten the script. General feeling was that the allegations were without foundation, although in subsequent press reports comment was made that if they were true, Boon and James deserved praise for the best acting performances seen in Johannesburg for many a year. The reality was that there was nothing fake about Boon's pay-off punch. The Transvaal Board of Control, however, took the whispers seriously and refused to sanction a return contest. A statement issued to the press stipulated that it was not in the public interest.

In the same statement, Gilbert Brown, Boon's South African manager, stated that the former British champion would be kept busy. His next engagement would be at Wembley Stadium on 31 March against Transvaal middleweight champion, Freddie Vorster. That contest, however, was subsequently cancelled because Eric had to undergo an operation to have his tonsils removed.

Depending on his fitness he would face former opponent, Maurice Ouezmann, at Wembley on 28 April.

Although there were conflicting reports from London regarding his future, and in particular that he was expected to return and battle his way towards a challenge for Ernie Roderick's title, Boon dismissed them. In a letter to Isidore Green he said: "I'm happier here in South Africa than I've ever been in England. The conditions here make it easy for a boxer to get fit and keep fit."

Shortly after his victory over Alf James, another London journalist, Maurice Woolf, believed Eric would be better off back home. Writing in *Sporting World* he said:

> If Boon would come home to this country he could still earn thousands of pounds, and with Jack Solomons bringing over champions Eric may yet win a world title. One thing I must say about him is that when he hits somebody you may as well get ready to go home. I'd back Boon to knockout a heavyweight if he caught him correctly.

*　　　*　　　*

During early April, Eric met up with British light-heavyweight champion, Freddie Mills, who had arrived in Johannesburg to fight Johnny Ralph on 14 April. Mills, who was accompanied by his manager, Ted Broadribb, and South African heavyweight champion, Don McCorkindale, was staying at the Langham Hotel. Anxious to hear news from back home, Eric was taken to see him and they became good companions. Mills trained at Eric's gym, and on 11 April nearly 3,000 people watched his public try-out at the White City Stadium during which Boon and Alf James each sparred a round with him.

Mills' contest with Johnny Ralph was subsequently cancelled when the South African broke his hand. He was then matched with Nick Wolmarans on the bill featuring Boon against Ouezmann scheduled for 28 April, but put back a day because of heavy rain. Freddie had a relatively easy task, knocking out his South African opponent in five rounds, but the fight between Boon and Ouezmann was sensational in that Eric actually won it twice.

With an advantage of just half a pound, he floored the Frenchman with a left hook to the jaw in the opening round. Ouezmann only rose to his feet after referee, Willie Smith, had counted him out, but when he realised what had happened he protested bitterly. As he couldn't speak a word of English, an interpreter was called into the ring. The last thing Boon wanted was to win that early under controversial circumstances so at his request, and with the authority of the Transvaal Boxing Board, the fight was allowed to continue.

Drawing on his experiences from their previous encounter, Boon dictated the course of the fight throughout. Although skilful, the Frenchman lacked power in his punches which allowed the former British champion to get close and whip in heavy hooks to head and body from both hands. In rounds four and five Ouezmann took several long counts and in the sixth the referee issued a warning to him through an interpreter for going down too easily. When he went down again from a left hook which badly damaged his nose, Mr Smith called it off. Boon had again shown much of his old power and only instinct and courage kept the Frenchman in the fight for six rounds.

Eleven days after beating Ouezmann, Boon knocked out Alf James in five one-sided rounds at N'Khara in Northern Rhodesia. Due to accommodation difficulties both boxers remained in their respective regions until the day of the fight.

Meanwhile, the Johannesburg promoters, keen to cash in on Boon's incredible popularity, were finding it difficult to get him a meaningful contest. Attempts to match him with Ernie Roderick for the vacant British Empire title fell through as did a proposed fight with Giel de Roode of Holland, regarded as one of the top welterweights in Europe. Although a series of contests were staged involving de Roode, James and Ouezmann, none emerged as a fighter likely to fill an arena against Boon. De Roode won and lost against James whilst Ouezmann, having already been stopped twice by the Chatteris man, would not be accepted again by the local sporting public.

Everyone in Johannesburg understood the situation and it prompted Dolph du Plessis to visit the *Rand Daily Mail* offices on 18 August and issue a further challenge to Boon on behalf of Gillie van der Westhuizen. "So far Boon has not met a puncher with Gillie's power," said du Plessis who was anxious for his man to get a shot at the Englishman.

Having been out of action for more than three months, Eric agreed to a third meeting with Maurice Ouezmann, this time at Capital in Pretoria on 22 August. It would be the first international contest to be staged in Pretoria and the joint promoters, Pretoria Sporting Club and White City Sporting Club, made it a big open-air event at the Caledonian Sports ground with a number of local boxers also appearing on the bill.

Boon arrived in Pretoria two weeks ahead of the fight and became an instant hit with the public. On 14 August he boxed a two-rounds exhibition on a show staged at the City Hall by the Garrison Boxing Club in aid of the Air Crash Victims Fund. There were 14 contests between Army and Air Force personnel, and Eric entered the ring wearing his cherished Lonsdale belt.

On the morning of the fight rumours circulated to the effect that the contest had been postponed owing to the indisposition of Boon. This was flatly denied in a statement issued by Sonny Rolt and Reg Haswell on behalf of the promoters who described it as mischief making by a fraction opposed to boxing. Haswell confirmed that he had been in touch with Eric and there was absolutely no truth in the rumour. Unfortunately, the damage had been done and the crowd of about 1,500 was far less than expected.

Having been attracted by Boon's reputation for winning his fights in spectacular fashion the fans witnessed a drab affair with little or no action until the later rounds. From the first bell it was obvious that Ouezmann was not going to take chances. He back-pedalled throughout the round with Boon stalking him ready to strike. The Frenchman's tactics, however, left little or no chance for Eric to land the big punches everyone was expecting. Although the occasional one got through his follow-ups were smothered by the skilful yet somewhat negative Frenchman.

Following a fierce exchange in round four, Ouezmann emerged with a badly swollen right eye which Boon played on until it was almost completely closed. It was not until the eighth, however, that he made his big punches count. A left hook sent the Frenchman to the canvas for a count of 'six' and a similar punch floored him for 'eight' in round nine.

Ouezmann started the final round as though he was going to stand and trade, but a few wild swings from Boon made him think again. He wisely reverted to his defend-and-survive tactics to reach the final bell on his feet and lose widely on points. It was doubtful if he won a round.

Meanwhile, Giel de Roode was nominated as the official contender for the European welterweight title. Seeing this as an incentive for Boon, the White City Sporting Club reached agreement with both men for them to meet on an open-air show at Wembley Stadium on 8 September. The twenty-six-years-old Dutch welterweight champion had impressed British fans the previous year with a clear-cut victory over Ginger Stewart. He turned professional in 1942 and had never been knocked out although most South African boxing critics predicted Boon would shatter that proud record.

During the build-up to the fight Eric and his White City advisors claimed he had never been in better shape due largely to him acquiring extra vitamins through regular meals of juicy South

African steaks. Although de Roode was seen as a credible opponent the promoters didn't anticipate him giving Boon too many problems and were somewhat naively looking beyond the impending contest.

They wanted world junior welterweight champion, Tippy Larkin from New Jersey, to defend his title against the Chatteris man in Johannesburg before the end of the year. The promoters saw it as a great opportunity because it was 12 months since the American put his title on the line. Furthermore, he had been knocked out by Charlie Fusari and Ike Williams in non-title fights earlier in the year. All Boon had to do was beat de Roode, but that looked to be no easy task. In his final workout at Benoni, the Dutchman impressed observers as he did 10 rounds flat out with his team of sparring partners. At the end he wasn't even breathing hard. "He gave the impression he could last forever and has the lungs of a horse," his trainer Walter Liebenberg told Paul Irwin of the *Transvaal Sunday Times.*

Boon, meanwhile, was trained by Fred Davidson who handled Maurice Ouezmann who was matched with George Angelo on the same bill. Although by this time Eric's interest was divided between boxing and the theatre he was reported to have trained harder than for any of his previous contests in South Africa. With the prospect of a fight with Tippy Larkin he knew he had to be more convincing and decisive than against Ouezmann in Pretoria.

Despite there being only five contests on the programme, including three of just four rounds duration, a crowd of 7,000 turned up at Wembley expecting fireworks from Boon. They went home bitterly disappointed because he was much slower than usual and appeared casual to the point of laziness. During the early rounds, particularly in the second, he didn't land a single punch of note. His performance was by far the worst since he first arrived in South Africa 15 months earlier. From the third round onwards there was only one man in it as de Roode skilfully plotted his opponent's downfall.

The first hint of trouble came during round five when a sharp right rattled against Boon's chin sending him to one knee for a count of 'eight'. As referee, Willie Smith, counted over him, Eric spat out blood and a tooth. Another right to the jaw sent him down again in the ninth, but he rose quickly with a wry grin and shaking his head as if to say he wasn't hurt.

Boon's only successes were a vicious right under the heart in the opening round and a combination in the fourth which opened a cut over the Dutchman's right eye. Presumably, reflecting on previous occasions when he had pulled off dramatic victories, he spent too much time waiting to land the one important shot. This time he faced an extremely fit and confident opponent who simply wore him down.

Despite having a two pounds weight advantage, much of Boon's strength seemed to have left him and he had no counter to de Roode's attacks during the final round. Bleeding heavily from the nose, he was forced to the ropes several times and under pressure on shaky legs when the bell ended the fight. He had been outclassed throughout and de Roode's wide points victory was one of the biggest upsets in South African boxing for some time.

A couple of days later, Alf James told the *Rand Daily Mail* that he wanted to fight Boon again. "Now that he has been beaten by de Roode, there is no reason why the Board of Control should not agree," he remarked. "I beat de Roode in Durban recently and if he can beat Boon I will certainly have a chance. It must be remembered that I was leading on points until the seventh when I fell into his trap."

James also claimed that when Eric beat him in five rounds in Rhodesia he was suffering from malaria and had a temperature. He only boxed because no substitute could be found and he didn't want to disappoint the crowd.

Boon, meanwhile, was far from satisfied with his performance against de Roode and had no interest in another fight against James. Although the promoters still hoped to secure a contest with Tippy Larkin, Eric told reporters he wanted a couple more contests before agreeing to face the American. He gave no indication that his career might take a different course.

*　　*　　*

Many of the critics in South Africa were convinced that Boon's poor performance against de Roode stemmed from the fact that boxing appeared to have taken second place to his business and social life, but he told another story.

Some years later he wrote several pages of notes intended as the basis for a biography. He made particular reference to the period in South Africa before and after the fight with de Roode which, if accurate, would explain his sudden dip in form. The biography never materialised, but the notes remained in Eric's possession until his eventual passing. The relevant section read:

> *I telephoned my wife and asked her if she would come out to live in South Africa if I could buy a business there. She was delighted and I booked a passage for her and my daughter on a boat which left in about a week. In the next few days I bought the business, a lovely country Club standing in 42*

acres of beautiful grounds, with tennis courts, riding stables and a swimming pool. I arranged for the opening night to be on my wife's second day in South Africa. At the same time I was rehearsing for the lead part in the boxing play Golden Boy. I was busy, fit and happy.

The day came when my wife arrived in South Africa. I drove down to Durban in my new Buick convertible and wouldn't have changed places with the king when I saw them both waving to me from the deck of the ship. Perhaps you can imagine how I felt when my wife greeted me with the words: "I have fallen in love with another man."

She told me she wanted to go to join him in Tanganyika as soon as possible. I was too stunned to speak. I think if I opened my mouth I would have cried. And so we drove back towards Jo'burg with only the chattering of my five-year-old kid to break the silence. With an effort I started to talk to her, telling her that I had bought her a pony, and that she would be able to swim in the pool every day, and that she would have a coloured maid all to herself, and a million other things. Before we completed the 400 mile journey she was asleep and my wife turned to me and said: "You shouldn't have told her all that Eric, she'll want to stay with you."

I couldn't believe my ears. I flatly refused to let my kid go. I said that I knew my wife had had a tough time since I left the Air Force and I did not even blame her for falling in love with someone else, but I was certainly not going to allow her to take Erica to Tanganyika with her. And there we reached deadlock. I would not let her take Erica, and she would not go without her.

I played the lead in Golden Boy and received good notices and offers for further plays, but somehow it didn't matter any more. Then to keep faith with the promoter who bought my contract I agreed to fight again. The club had opened and was doing good business. I lost the fight on points and the betting crowd accused me of deliberately throwing the contest. The papers said I had not tried – none of them knew the real reason for my bad display.

*　　　*　　　*

The play Golden Boy, originally created by Clifford Odets, was a Broadway hit before the war which made William Holden a Hollywood star and also featured Barbara Stanwyke and Adolphe Menjou. It was a story about Joe Bonaparte, an ambitious bright-eyed young man who sacrificed his career as a violinist because he could not resist the attractions of prize-fighting and the big money it held out for him. Golden Boy became one of the most enthusiastically received plays ever sent to Britain and in September 1938 sold out to houses at the Hippodrome, Golders Green, and the St James Theatre in London.

During his second trip to South Africa, Boon made contact with Henry Gilbert, a British actor he first met in London several years earlier. Henry was a keen amateur boxer at the time and a friendship between them started in the dressing room of an arena. Gilbert later went to South Africa where he rapidly worked his way to the position of one of the countries leading character actors. When Eric returned to Johannesburg in January 1947, the threads of their friendship were taken up again.

At the time Gilbert was the producer and casting manager for a reproduction of Golden Boy which was due to open at the Standard Theatre in Johannesburg on 10 September. He was also to play the part of Joe Bonaparte's father. Eric told him that he still had a hankering to swap boxing for the theatre and explained about his vaudeville performances back in England and how he loved acting. Gilbert was impressed and offered him an audition. The former British champion gave such a glittering performance that he was offered the leading role of Joe Bonaparte.

Asked by a reporter from the *Transvaal Sunday Times* what prompted him to exchange floodlights for footlights, Eric said: "I always loved the theatre. If I am good in this show I am saying goodbye to the boxing game."

Boon fitted the role of Bonaparte perfectly because he was very handsome, rugged and had a sharp brain. Most importantly, he was a real life boxer. After six weeks of rehearsal, the play opened just two days after Boon's defeat by Giel de Roode. When the curtain went up for the first performance the audience saw a boxing ring on stage in which Boon and Maurice Ouezmann sparred in a special scene written by Gilbert. Ouezmann had agreed to it because he had so much respect for Boon who, for the first time in South Africa, wore golden trunks as if to celebrate his new role.

There was tremendous interest in the play, and Boon in particular. After the final curtain on the opening night, he admitted that he had faced many crowds in Johannesburg and been nervous, "but last night I was scared stiff," he remarked.

In general, the critics liked Eric's performance although comments did vary from paper to paper. *The Star* was supportive saying:

> Scared or not, he gave a neat performance as Joe Bonaparte which came across because of his sincerity. Most of the parts in this quick-fire Clifford Odets play were cleverly cast. That kind of authenticity

can cover up a lot of histrionic short-comings. I don't doubt that the theatre will be packed for several weeks.

Elsewhere in the same paper another critic remarked:

> Henry Gilbert's experiment in theatre – the choice of the boxer Eric Boon for the principal role was, in this respect, more akin to artifice than art, and the piquant mixture of the ring and the stage attracted a wildly different audience from the usual first-nighters.
>
> Boon was, in fact, to use the analogy of surrealism, the real apple on the painted canvas, and his audience metaphorically ate him up. It is far too early to say whether the boxer may be turned into an actor and absorbed into the complex background of the theatre, but interest centred around him on this stage and this part of Joe Bonaparte. Henry Gilbert, as his father, the old unworldly fruit-seller, was superb.

A *Transvaal Sunday Times* arts critic was more explicit saying:

> Stronger producing would have made Eric Boon give more to the part of 'Golden Boy'. His occasional burst of dramatic fervour suggested an understanding of the role, but this understanding was not given scope to express itself. Boon's range of motions was restricted. The fact is that he is too theatrical. His power parlance wasn't natural for the part and this goes with the knowledge that his acting was curved making it difficult to assess his potentiality as an actor. On the whole he played easily, but if he sticks to the stage he will have to learn to speak out to his audience.

The only seriously negative comment about Eric's performance appeared in the *Sunday Express* where it was described as "his second Waterloo in a week."

The play was originally given a three-week booking, but was forced to close after only 10 days because Johannesburg City Council condemned the Standard Theatre as a fire hazard. After the final performance on 20 September the closure of the building marked the end of an era in theatre life in Johannesburg.

Golden Boy had been a huge success playing to sell-out audiences each night. Henry Gilbert therefore decided to take it to Pretoria, but despite having originally agreed to continue, glamorous twenty-one-years-old British actress, Gay Gibson, who played the part of prostitute, Lorna Moon, asked to be released in order to return to London. She booked a third class passage aboard the Dutch vessel, Orangefontein, but a few days later cancelled and booked first class accommodation aboard the liner Durban Castle. She was never seen alive again.

Boon was also keen to return home mainly for personal reasons. Despite the conclusive defeat by de Roode he was still ranked as the leading welterweight in South Africa, but knew he would no longer be able to command the big pay days of the past 14 months. He had been considering his options since July following cables from Jack Solomons who insisted that if he returned to London he would get him some big money fights. Jack pressed home the point that Eric was still a great attraction wherever he fought.

The cables from Solomons reached Boon at a time when he had become very unsettled. His business had run into debt largely because he was too easy with his customers, and his marriage was also in difficulty. Although he and Wendy had been happy for a while, she told him that if he fought again she would not be there when he came home. To make him realise she was serious she packed her bags and booked a passage on a ship bound for England. She told Eric that if he still wanted her and Erica he would have to go with them. He agreed, sold his business at a considerable loss and made arrangements to leave South Africa.

In his biography notes Boon made no reference to what occurred with Golden Boy. He merely wrote:

> *Then my wife asked me to go back to England with her and Erica to start again. She said that if we were back in England things would be different, so would I try? I sold the club and we sailed home. We had only been back a few days when she said she wanted a divorce. At that moment I gave up. I gave her all the money I had for Erica's sake and went to see Solomons to ask him to arrange another fight.*

Throughout his second trip to South Africa, Boon kept in touch with a number of people in England, particularly Isidore Green. There were no great surprises to hear that he lost to de Roode because he had given the journalist the impression that he was not so enthusiastic about the fight game as he was two years earlier. He made it clear that he was in it for what he could get out of it while he still remained a box-office attraction.

Green knew for some while about the interesting enterprises Eric was involved in, but made the point that it was difficult to predict with certainty what he would do. He had become a restless, roaming character and even his closest friends were unable to say what his immediate plans were.

Meanwhile, Boon's pal, Freddie Mills, had also suffered a shock defeat in June at the hands of American, Lloyd Marshall. His trainer, Nat Seller, believed that preparations for that fight had been wrong and when Mills was matched with Pol Goffaux for the European light-heavyweight title he suggested they set up a training camp at Chatteris. "Remember what Eric Boon said in South Africa," said Nat, "and he's right, you know. I trained him there and it's a wonderful place."

Seller was a hero to the Chatteris folk because they always remembered what he did for Boon, so when Mills and his party took up residence at The George Hotel for three weeks they were made extremely welcome. Freddie's visit made him the only fighter of championship status, apart from Boon, to set up camp there. When asked why then had chosen Chatteris he said they had been impressed by everything Eric had told them about the facilities.

Freddie caused a real stir amongst the local people. He trained daily at The George, helped make hay on a local farm and did billposting for a local cinema in the neighbouring villages as he did his daily running.

Recalling his time at Chatteris in his autobiography, *Twenty Years,* published in 1950, Mills said:

> Several times we found our way to Mrs Boon's place for a cup of tea before the evening meal. Eric's father was still the local blacksmith and I even tried my hand at shaping a shoe, but found it was not as easy as it looked.

Not since Boon rose to fame almost a decade earlier had the Chatteris folk taken such an interest in a boxing champion. On 8 September while Eric was losing to Gil de Roode in South Africa, they turned on their wireless sets and tuned into the light programme to hear Mills become European champion by knocking out Pol Goffaux in four rounds.

*   *   *

Boon returned to England aboard the Orangefontein during mid-October to learn that Gay Gibson had been reported missing from the Durban Castle. He told a reporter from the *London Evening Star* of her ambitions and how they appeared together in Golden Boy. "When I last saw her on about 24 September she was full of joy and living," he remarked.

When the Durban Castle docked off the Isle of Wight on 24 October, detectives from Hampshire Constabulary went aboard and commenced a full-scale investigation into Gay Gibson's disappearance. During the course of the enquiry Boon was interviewed and provided an affidavit as did most members of the Golden Boy production. He was subsequently called as witness number 33 at the trial of James Camb, a deck steward, who was charged with murdering the actress and casting her body to sea. At his trial at Winchester Assizes in March 1948 Camb was found guilty and sentenced to death, but following a change in the law that was commuted to life imprisonment.

Boon, meanwhile, was having his own difficulties. On arriving back home he had very little money and, convinced that there was nothing left for him but boxing, he went and saw Jack Solomons. True to form the promoter said all the right things and assured him he was still good enough to win a British championship. Eric knew full well that he was on dangerous ground with Wendy, but these were desperate times.

23

BACK HOME

Boon's arrival back in England certainly added interest to the fistic scene. He was in fact an extremely lucky young man because within just two weeks Jack Solomons announced that he would face Ernie Roderick for the British welterweight title at Harringay on 17 November. Although the contest was subsequently postponed until 9 December because Ernie sustained a cut eye in training, it was a controversial situation which brought about plenty of complaints.

Not only had the Board of Control withdrawn Eric from eliminators, he had also been in South Africa for almost 18 months where he insisted he would take up residence. Questions were therefore asked as to why he had been given an immediate title shot. Not surprisingly newspaper sports desks received telephone calls from indignant managers claiming, rightly or wrongly, that their particular fighters should face Roderick ahead of the Chatteris man.

General opinion among the boxing correspondents was that Benny Huntman, who Eric had re-engaged as his manager, was very instrumental in securing the contest. He also managed Billy Thompson, Gwyn Williams, Jimmy Davis, Jimmy Webster, Danny and Dickie O'Sullivan and Jack London, and was the British agent for Gus Lesnevich and Marcel Cerdan. He had a close working relationship with Solomons who, by this time, was the leading promoter in the country. Jack's association with Boon went back more than 12 years and the Chatteris boxer had been largely responsible for his rise to the top. It was fitting therefore that his former protégé should headline one of his major promotions.

The fact remained that Boon was always good value for money. He was a colourful, dynamic fighter who had always been a box-office favourite, and was still regarded as probably the hardest puncher, pound-for-pound, in Britain.

Some years later, however, Boon put another slant on how the fight with Roderick actually came about. In his biography notes he claimed:

> *Solomons phoned the secretary of the Board of Control and after telling him he would send him a case of whisky and see him alright, he told him he wanted to put me in with Roderick for the title. He then gave me two contracts to sign, one with Roderick and the other to fight his latest protégé,*

Eddie Thomas, if I won the title. I couldn't have cared less so I signed both.

Although Eric's recollection of his early life and career was basically accurate there were sections which gave cause for concern. By the time he compiled the notes he had fallen out with the Board of Control and for that reason some doubt must exist regarding his version of how the fight with Roderick was arranged. He may, of course, have been telling the truth because a grey area did exist in that it was never satisfactorily explained why the Board approved the contest with such speed and overlooked more worthy challengers.

Some reports at the time claimed that Eric actually jumped for joy when he heard the news that the Board of Control, at a special emergency meeting, had agreed that the fight would be for the British title. There was one stipulation that in the event of him winning he would have to forgo the usual six months grace before defending the title. Boon claimed that a few days earlier Solomons bet him five shillings to half a crown that the fight would be for the championship. "A title fight for half a crown is well worth it," he told L N Bailey, boxing correspondent of the *London Evening Star*. "I'll put up the fight of my life."

Shortly after contracts were signed it was claimed that Boon had been using the services of a mesmerist. He was a Canadian doctor who insisted on remaining anonymous and during consultations put Eric to sleep and then instilled confidence into his self-conscious mind. It was planned that he would sit next to his corner during the fight and exert his influence.

There were plenty of sceptics when the story broke especially when it was claimed that Boon walked around repeating to himself: "I will win, I will win, I must win." Eric never denied the stories and insisted that the therapy only worked on people who believed in it. He did, and was convinced that Roderick, at the age of thirty-four, had seen better days and was ready to be taken.

The fight quickly became a sell-out partly because Solomons realised the days of the 20 guinea seats were over. For this show almost two-thirds of Harringay seats would be available for between 10 shillings and one guinea. Not since the Bruce Woodcock – Joe Baski fight 18 months earlier had there been such a clamour for tickets

Boon again engaged Honey Francis who had trained him for his comeback fights during the early part of 1946. He was an experienced man who had assisted Henry Armstrong in his final preparations for the fight against Roderick in London during May 1939. He and Eric were a good team and years later in a newspaper

295

article the Chatteris fighter praised him saying: "He proved himself as my friend by giving me fresh heart when I thought I was finished as a boxer."

For the Roderick fight they set up camp at Solomons' gym where Eric sparred good men including middleweights Jimmy Davis (Bethnal Green) and Alby Hollister (Islington). Lightweight prospect, Harry McMurdie and former British Empire and European featherweight champion, Al Phillips, were used for speed while Eric was permitted to practice punch power on young heavyweight prospect, George Dawson.

There was a wonderful atmosphere at the gym affectionately referred to as the 'Palace of Sock.' Situated in the heart of the West End, just a couple of hundred yards from Piccadilly Circus, it was frequented by most of the London boxing 'faces'. Benny Huntman, Nat Seller, who ran the place for Solomons, and Sam Burns all took their boys there for training at half a crown a session. The gym, which opened at twelve noon, was situated on the second floor and the ring was the one which Jack had used at the Devonshire Club. He had his office in the corner, the walls of which plastered with photographs mostly of himself with his famous friends.

The perpetual sounds of punch bags being pounded, bells ringing, grunts and groans could be heard coming from the building every afternoon. It was a place of blood, sweat, a few tears and a touch of adventure. There was always something happening which made newsworthy snippets.

One afternoon in mid-November, Maurice Woolf was surprised to find a group of about 20 schoolboys watching Boon sparring with Cliff Anderson. They were members of Quintin College at nearby Regent Street, but to an over-zealous official they shouldn't have been there. As he was about to hustle them out, Solomons shouted: "Leave them alone, they are my customers for five years time."

Later the same afternoon there was an air of concern in the dressing room area at the rear of the building. As an anxious looking Boon watched over them, Mike Milligan, Honey Francis, journalists Maurice Woolf and Tim Riley, crawled about on their hands and knees searching for something with the aid of lighted matches. They peered through floorboards, turned up carpets, looked in trouser turn-ups and were all in a panic except Boon who remained calm. Just as they were about to give up, Riley found what they had been looking for under a table – Eric's solid gold ring.

A few days before the fight Boon told a group of newsmen who visited the gym that he had never felt so fit in his life. It was a remark he had made several times previously before important contests, but the fact that he scaled only 10st 3 ¼ at the official weigh-in was an indication of how hard he had trained. Roderick was 10st 6.

It was a cold December evening when Boon faced Roderick at Harringay. The public saw it as a fight which could go either way and consequently the great arena was packed. Apart from the main event Solomons had put together an attractive programme of supporting contests featuring British lightweight champion, Billy Thompson, European flyweight champion, Maurice Sandeyron of France, Dickie O'Sullivan from Finsbury Park and young Welsh welterweight prospect, Eddie Thomas, who had backing of up to £1,000 for a contest with Boon, Roderick or Gwyn Williams.

It was less than a week short of nine years since Boon sensationally smashed Dave Crowley to defeat at the same arena to become British lightweight champion. In some respects this was a similar contest because Roderick, the older man, was champion and a crafty ring veteran.

Born in Liverpool in 1914, Ernie had his first professional fight at the Lyric Theatre in 1931. He won the British welterweight title by beating Jake Kilrain in seven rounds in 1939. By the time he faced Boon he had made successful defences against Norman Snow, Arthur Danahar and Gwyn Williams, all on points. In 1945 he outscored Vince Hawkins to take the vacant middleweight title, but lost it to him the following year. Between those contests he added the European welterweight title to his trophies by outpointing Omar Koudri, but lost it to Robert Villemann in Paris on 1 February 1947 when he was forced to retire with a badly cut eye.

Since meeting Boon in 1940, Ernie had engaged in a further 39 contests, winning 25. Although he had won only three of the last eight, his successful title defence against Gwyn Williams took place at Harringay the night Eric was beaten in South Africa by Giel de Roode.

Boon looked in tremendous shape as he climbed into the ring to huge applause from the several bus loads of fans who had travelled from Chatteris and other parts of the Isle of Ely. Most wireless sets in that region were tuned in to the BBC light programme. As he awaited the introductions Eric looked around the arena and nodded confidently to friends seated at ringside. He had predicted he would win inside the distance.

Across the ring Roderick looked pensive as he stood in his corner. Victory over Boon would give him a second notch on a second Lonsdale belt which he wanted to win to emulate his manager, Nel Tarleton, whose sister he had married. He also hoped to be able to give a belt to each of his two children.

At the opening bell, Boon moved forward half crouching and ready to pounce. Roderick knew exactly what to expect and countered any aggressive move with an accurate left jab to the challenger's face. It was a ploy he rarely deviated from and had the challenger guessing during the early rounds by showing masterful ringcraft. Every time Boon rushed forward he jabbed, side-stepped or moved backwards making the punches hit thin air.

The fight quickly settled into a pattern with Roderick generally in control. Although Boon threatened, he was rarely allowed to get close enough to land the big shots. Consequently, there were times when it was monotonous to watch and there were only brief moments of excitement during the early rounds.

Roderick was shaken briefly by a powerful left hook in the second and Boon was cut under the left eye in the fifth. The champion was again hurt by a powerful right to the stomach in round seven, but recovered quickly and boxed his way clear of trouble.

As the rounds slipped by Eric became more desperate because the fight wasn't going to plan. Although he was throwing plenty of big punches, they weren't slowing his older opponent down. By the end of the 10th concern was written all over the faces of Boon's cornermen, Benny Huntman, Jack Gutteridge, Honey Francis, and Mike Milligan, who had been granted special permission by the Board of Control to work with Eric for this fight. The champion was well ahead on points and their man's face was sore and reddened from the stream of accurate left jabs. Eric was in a familiar situation of knowing he had to do something dramatic in the closing rounds.

As the bell signalled the start of round 11, Roderick carried on where he had left off. A sharp left to Boon's head was followed by a right cross and a vicious right uppercut narrowly missed the chin. Eric was being made to look like a novice as left after left pumped into his face. Then with only 30 seconds of the round remaining the tide unexpectedly seemed to turn as the ever patient Boon landed a thumping right to the jaw. Roderick wobbled briefly, but despite bleeding heavily from a cut beneath his left eye, kept his composure and boxed cautiously until the bell.

There was a buzz of excitement around Harringay as Boon, sensing his chance, was quick off his stool and into the attack at the start of round 12. Well behind on points and with his left eye cut and swollen, he had only one thing on his mind. At first, Roderick kept his jab working, but then Boon, eyes blazing and biting hard on his gum shield, hurled himself at the champion and crashed lefts and rights into his face. Two left hooks smashed into the damaged eye which was looking the worse for wear as he reeled against the ropes.

Suddenly, as he ducked and weaved, a dynamic right smashed against Roderick's chin sending him to the floor for the first time in his career, amateur or professional. A huge roar went up as blood streamed down Ernie's face. The betting boys were yelling that the fight was over, but the proud champion got to one knee and listened carefully to the count. Wiping the blood from his eye he looked towards his corner where Nel Tarleton signalled to him to keep his chin down and his left hand out.

Only instinct and pride forced Roderick to his feet with the count at 'eight'. "Boon, Boon, Boon," chanted the crowd as he wobbled like a drunken man on a Saturday night. Many vividly recalled how Eric downed Crowley and Danahar in the later rounds when he was a long way behind. Was it about to happen all over again?

Although Boon waded into the attack and pasted Roderick in an attempt to close proceedings, the tough, skilful champion turned his back, swayed his shoulders and held desperately in his attempts to survive. He was a different proposition to Crowley and Danahar, a wiley ring veteran who knew the art of survival. He demonstrated it admirably by instinctively prodding out jabs as Boon hurled leather from all angles.

One perfect punch smack in the mouth halted the challenger and broke up his attack. The champion then beat a tattoo of punches to Eric's head and body shattering any hopes he had of scoring another knock-down. Before he could regroup the bell ended the round.

In the corners the seconds worked overtime. George Tarleton tended swiftly to Roderick's damaged eye whilst Nel whispered advice in his ear. Across the ring Benny Huntman implored Boon to control his punches because he sensed victory was still within their grasp.

Although flat-footed, Roderick looked to have recovered as they came out for round 13. Knowing he couldn't win on points Boon threw everything he could at the champion. A few shots got home, but plenty of others hit thin air as the skilful champion fiddled his way through the round. Although one big shot did shake Roderick, there was a feeling at ringside that Boon had a problem with his hands. On a number of occasions during the fight Isidore Green noted that he did not deliver solid punches with the knuckle part of the glove, tending to throw them sideways instead of straight.

Boon shook the champion briefly early in round 14, but in what was a quieter round Roderick was not in any trouble. It was a classic boxer against fighter encounter in which, despite some hairy moments, the boxer just kept control. Remaining calm, he fiddled, ducked and swayed away from danger in what was a wonderful exhibition of survival.

The crowd roared as they came out for the final round of what had been an absorbing championship contest. Boon was the first to land and a good left hook shook Roderick. Unruffled, the champion stuck to the tactics which had served him well. Although Eric swarmed all over him, rasping in great shots from either hand, Ernie took them and despite being very tired continued pumping out the left jab to nullify most of the challenger's aggression.

Boon's fitness was incredible and at the final bell he was still pressing forward hoping that one more huge shot would bring him victory. It wasn't to be because the night belonged to Roderick, a truly wonderful champion who rightly took the referee's decision. Yet he had come within an ace of losing his title when Eric went for broke.

Fans stood all around the arena to salute two tremendous warriors. At the end they fell into an embrace before acknowledging each others seconds. It had been hard fought, but in a fine spirit. There was a moment during round nine when the crowd applauded Boon for his sportsmanship in stepping back to allow Roderick to recover after accidentally slipping to the canvas.

Boon was a great loser. Although subdued for long periods, he had chased the champion, hunted him down, yet couldn't snatch the title from his grasp. His desperate efforts during the closing rounds were reminiscent of the Boon of old as he set up the same two-fisted tearaway attacks. Against Roderick, however, he was facing a man who seemed to understand him and was therefore fully equipped to deal with his tactics. Consequently, it was the first time in his career that Eric had been forced to travel the full championship course of 15 rounds. At the end he accepted that he had been beaten by a better man.

Although Roderick had retained his title by scientific brilliance he looked a sorry state at the end. His arms were badly bruised and there were gashes down both sides of his face and across his left eyebrow. He looked terribly fatigued, so old and worn. Being younger and relatively fresher, Boon issued a challenge for an immediate return and said he would agree for it to be on a winner-take-all basis. Huntman agreed, adding that he was confident his man would do better because both his hands had been damaged as early as the fourth round. The following day x-rays confirmed serious bruising, but revealed no fracture.

Afterwards in the dressing room Boon did not look nearly as bad as Roderick, but because of the injuries to his hands he couldn't even hold a cup of tea. Although he was naturally upset at losing when he thought he had victory 'in the bag', his only comment was: "It was a good fight and I tried, but my hands went. Still, that's how it goes – that's the fight game."

The unhappiest man in Boon's dressing room was Mike Milligan who had only ever missed one of his fights since he first went to the Devonshire Club. "He should have done it," said Mike with tears in his eyes. "He left it a little too late, but he's still got the old Boon punch."

Writing in *Sporting World* the following week, Maurice Woolf said he still believed Eric would be the next welterweight champion. He added:

> I am sorry for Boon who came so near to winning the title only for his hands to go back on him. He can take some consolation from the fact that he made boxing history by being the first man to knock Roderick down. Even the phenomenal Henry Armstrong failed to do that and in doing so Eric proved once again that he is the most destructive puncher Britain has produced for years.
>
> I thought he had never boxed so well, but he left his effort too late. If he had gone all out in about the fifth and caught Ernie, that eye would not have stood up and Ernie may not have been able to box his way out of trouble for 10 rounds.

*   *   *

Within a short while of losing to Roderick, Boon stated that he was anxious to keep busy and willing to face any welterweight in the country. Early in 1948 he received a challenge from Jim Wellard of Northampton for a fight at £500-a-side. This was ignored, but on 28 February a 'wanted' poster appeared in *Sporting World* offering a reward of £100 to anyone who could entice Eric into the ring with Wellard on any conditions. It was asked that all communications be sent to his manager, Jack Spencer, at 58 Brighton Road, Stoke Newington.

This latest challenge was also ignored mainly on the grounds that Wellard was a relative novice who had lost three of his nine contests the previous year. Huntman explained that victory over him would do nothing to enhance Boon's chances of another championship fight.

*   *   *

A few days after Boon's defeat by Roderick, the Board of Control ordered a further series of eliminating contests in the welterweight division. One was to be between Gwyn Williams and Eddie Thomas with the winner to face Boon. These proposals didn't go down well

301

with the press and were certainly of no interest to Eric and Benny Huntman. All they wanted was another shot at Roderick.

As a warm-up for his eliminator, Thomas outpointed Henry Hall over eight rounds at the Royal Albert Hall on 26 January 1948. Boon was at ringside and the following day he telephoned Maurice Woolf, editor of *Sporting World,* saying that although Eddie put on a great performance he wouldn't pose him any problems. "Let them all come," he remarked. "Roderick, Hall, Thomas, I'll beat the lot. I mean to win the British and world welterweight titles and I can do it too."

Never a man to mince his words, Woolf was always proud to admit that he and Boon had been close friends since Eric's Devonshire Club days. He became editor of *Sporting World* in 1939 and at the age of just nineteen was probably the youngest editor in Fleet Street. He joined the RAF during the war and saw service in North Africa, Italy and Greece during which time he ran several newspapers. He was demobbed in 1946, redeveloped *Sporting World* and concentrated on boxing.

He referred to Boon's telephone call in *Sporting World* the following week and issued a response in which he said:

> I couldn't agree more Eric, but it means a training period of 24 hours a day for weeks. If you agree to settle down to that I'll back you against anyone in the world. It's up to you – I'm behind you, but at the moment you are about the only British boxer, with the exception of Freddie Mills, who could capture a world title. Train please Eric, like you did for your Danahar fight.

Boon made no public response, but continued to demand a return with Roderick. Their fight had been described as one of the greatest seen at Harringay and Eric knew that by fighting with all his old flair and fury he had come within an ace of winning the title. When he had Ernie on the floor for the first time in his long career it was touch and go if he would beat the count.

To mark time, Boon was matched with Omar Koudri over 10 rounds at the Royal Albert Hall on 1 March. Koudri, a French Algerian, was regarded as a top class fighter having contested the European welterweight title on three occasions. In 1941 injury forced him to retire after eight rounds against Marcel Cerdan, whilst Ernie Roderick and Robert Villemain outpointed him in 1946 and 1947 respectively. In England he had put up credible performances against Arthur Danahar and Henry Hall before losing both on points. It was claimed that he had never been stopped or knocked down in over 100 contests.

A packed house at the Albert Hall expected an evening of excitement, but ended up disappointed because five of the seven scheduled contests ended inside three rounds. By 9 pm the two main events were over, including that between Boon and Koudri. Controversy was to follow because subsequent revelations left a nasty taste as to what may or may not have occurred.

Looking in perfect physical condition at 10st 8, Boon was less finely drawn than against Roderick, while Koudri, at just half a pound heavier, was squat, swarthy and muscular. Both looked ready for action and the crowd anticipated fireworks.

Boon wasted no time and let loose powerful shots from both hands. A hard right which crashed against the side of Koudri's head shook him badly, but he retaliated in a flash. Appearing to be at his aggressive best Eric seemed to relish the exchanges because there was no Roderick type left jab to bother him.

Fighting in spurts, Boon looked to be the more powerful of the two and during one thrilling exchange he dropped the Algerian for a short count with a good right to the chin. It was absorbing stuff and the big crowd looked like being compensated for the early finishes which preceded this one.

The pair set about each other with bad intentions at the start of round two. Boon threw vicious punches many of which went wide or were avoided by Koudri cleverly slipping away from them. One short right to the chin did send him to the floor for another short count, but on rising he immediately went on the attack.

For a while Boon appeared to ease up although it was thought that the Algerian's awkward style was proving effective. Eventually Eric switched to the body before throwing an uppercut which opened a horrible gash on Koudri's mouth. As blood gushed heavily from the wound he fought back fiercely, but at the bell looked in a bad way.

Within seconds of the boxers reaching their respective corners, ringsiders could see that the contest was not going to continue. On one side of the ring Boon was rubbing his left shoulder and screwing up his face as though in considerable pain. Koudri, meanwhile, was having a heated argument with his manager and chief second who had called referee, Sam Russell, to the corner because of the boxer's badly injured mouth. The official needed only the merest glance to know that he could not allow the Algerian to continue. As Russell crossed the ring to award the fight to Boon, Koudri stamped around the ring protesting at not being allowed to continue. The official result was that he had been retired by his corner.

A doctor who later examined Koudri in his dressing room told reporters that the laceration to his mouth was one of the worst he had seen in a boxing ring. One newsman stated that it looked as though he had been sliced with a knife.

In the other dressing room three curious reporters asked Boon about his apparent problems. Tim Riley, boxing correspondent for *Sporting World,* had noted an ostentatious display of pain by the Chatteris man as he walked to his corner at the end of the second round. He was puzzled by a look of disappointment on Eric's face when he returned to the dressing room. "It was not only the fight," muttered Boon as the reporter gently probed him, "but something someone said as I came out of the ring."

Yet Boon appeared edgy and was not the normal chirpy character reporters were used to interviewing after a fight. He was strangely sullen and not even Honey Francis seemed able to console him as he dabbed blood away from his chest and body.

"Leave it," muttered Boon, "it's only French blood."

Something was clearly bothering the Chatteris man prompting Riley to ask further questions. Boon's handlers, Benny Huntman, Mike Milligan and Francis all stated that the boxer had complained of pain in his left shoulder whilst training at Chatteris. To make matters worse he ricked it during his warm-up in the dressing room before the fight. Eric said he thought he was suffering from arthritis in his left shoulder and had another attack during the second round. He and Huntman repudiated any suggestion that he intended retiring as soon as he reached his corner.

"Not on your life," snapped Boon. "It was the easiest fight I ever had." He insisted he was boxing well and punching much harder than Koudri.

"Retire?" asked Huntman. "What, against Koudri? Eric is as strong as a lion. Listen, if he is after a return fight he can have it whenever he likes."

Even before everyone left the Albert Hall there was talk that a return could take place at the same venue on 5 April. Boon said he was eager for the match if only to scotch some of the wild rumours that were flying around. "I heard the rumours even before I left the ring," he remarked.

It was the second time in consecutive fights that he had floored a man who had never previously taken a count, the other being Roderick. Talk of a quick return with Koudri, however, was utter nonsense because of the seriousness of the Algerian's injury.

*　　　*　　　*

Immediately after the Boon-Koudri fight had ended trouble erupted around the ringside amongst individuals involved in gambling. The scenes were reminiscent of those at the same venue two years earlier when Boon dramatically stopped Maurice Ouzemann when he looked destined for defeat.

For some years ringside gambling had been a problem at promotions, particularly in London. Those concerned had become a thorough nuisance because boxing didn't mean a thing to them. Their screaming and yelling nauseated the true sportsmen, and remarks hurled at referees and contestants were insulting to say the least. In most cases they were directed to influence or intimidate officials and on other occasions affect the performance of a particular fighter.

Following the trouble at the Albert Hall, Jack Solomons, backed by Harry Greenberg who promoted at Seymour Hall and small venues in the East End, decided to take action against the ringside pests. Jack went as far as sending well-worded letters to those he knew were involved at his shows. He made it clear that they were no longer welcome and if they attended future promotions admittance would be refused. If the warnings were ignored he would apply to the courts for injunctions against the particular individuals.

The letters caused a real stir amongst those who had got away with their actions for so long. Solomons received numerous telephone calls pleading for another chance with the promise of good behaviour in the future. It made no difference because he was adamant the bans would remain in force.

A week after the Boon – Koudri fight, *Weekly Sporting Review* ran a story about Jack's action under the headline "Boxing Betting Boys Warned Off." General opinion amongst the boxing correspondents was that it was long overdue. Whilst the press and boxing public were aware that gambling on fights was rife, the full extent of the problem was not general knowledge.

In an article in *Sporting World* Maurice Woolf said that he had been told that if the betting boys were kept away from the arenas, shows would be a flop. "I thought the smaller halls would suffer," he remarked, "but I was agreeably surprised when I attended Caledonian Road Baths and found the ringside full."

Other reporters attending promotions at West Ham Baths and Leyton found a similar situation, and reports from around the country indicated likewise. The crowd problem had also alerted Police and a few weeks later officers carried out a raid at a promotion at Kentish Town Baths in relation to illegal betting.

*   *   *

Despite all the doubt and suspicion surrounding the Koudri fight, Maurice Woolf still had tremendous faith in Boon. So much so that he wrote an open letter to him on the front page of *Sporting World* on 6 March. It read:

> We of the British boxing public have a great chance to add the world welterweight championship to our collection. At the moment the only boxer who can give us that honour is you, Eric Boon. In 1939 I thought you would give us the world lightweight championship, but unfortunately war intervened and you were prevented from boxing for that crown.
>
> There were many ugly rumours flying around about your contest with Omar Koudri. I was never one to pull my punches so I may as well tell you what the stories were about. The punters say you were going to turn it in at the end of the second round. You assured me that come what may you were going to continue with the fight even though you were suffering from arthritis in the shoulder. I myself, on the form you displayed in the two rounds, would back you against any welterweight in the world. You have to meet the winner of the Eddie Thomas – Gwyn Williams contest and I don't think you will be very much troubled by either of those two boxers.
>
> Many people said that when you went over to South Africa your fighting days were over. On your return to this country the British Boxing Board of Control nominated you as the leading challenger for Roderick's crown. You proved that step was the correct one, putting Roderick on the canvas for the first time in his career.
>
> Eric, you can win a world title if you decide to train seriously and treat every fight as a step towards the championship. I never want to see you box any better than you did in those two rounds against Koudri. Not even Nel Tarleton could have done better.
>
> On this form I would back you against Ray Robinson, but you have to settle down to the game and train 24 hours a day and never forget that we in Britain depend on you to give your best. The whole of the boxing public are behind you. You can win the world title, but you must settle down to the game.
>
> Maurice Woolf.

*   *   *

Almost two years later Boon gave a dramatic insight into what he claimed occurred before and after the Koudri fight. Writing in *The People* under the heading 'Eric Boon Confesses', he said:

It was about a fortnight before my fight with the fuzzy-haired Omar Koudri that I was tackled by the betting boys. "Fancy doing business Eric?" The offer was for £3,000 to take a dive. A wad of easy money just to lie down and quit. Well I was tempted. Times had changed. I knew my fighting days were numbered and that there was little chance of ever earning big dough again.

I was worried sick about my future. Most of my money had gone and I had no idea how I was going to earn a living. So I was tempted. I asked 'the boys' to give me time to think it over, although I had almost made up my mind to turn crooked. "Good boy Eric," they said. "Now you're being smart."

On the day of the fight Boon got a shock when Jack Solomons called him into his office. Huntman was also there and from the look on their faces Eric knew instantly that there was a problem. Solomons didn't waste any time or words. "Listen Eric," he snapped, "Benny and I know what's up. We've heard a rumour that you're going crooked tonight."

Boon was stunned and tried to stall. "I don't know what you're talking about," he stuttered.

"Don't be a young fool," yelled Jack. "We've heard all about it. You've been offered three thousand nicker to lose, but we won't let you get away with it."

Things got really heated as Solomons read Eric the riot act. He reminded him of everything he had done for him over the years and how he built him into a champion. He tried threats and friendly persuasion and when he ran out of words Huntman adopted a similar theme.

After listening in stubborn silence Boon decided he had no alternative but to come clean. "Okay Jack," he said sheepishly, "you can set your mind at rest. I guess I must have been crazy to think of throwing the fight. Just watch me tonight, I'll knock him out inside three rounds."

They all shook hands and as far as Solomons and Huntman were concerned the matter was over. Boon, however, had other ideas.

I came out of my corner with no fixed plan in my head. They told me that Koudri was a tough customer and could take plenty of punishment so I thought I could wade in and make it look really good for a few rounds, but the first time I hit him on the chin he went down. I stood back against the ropes wondering whether he would beat the count.

When he got to his feet I went straight into a clinch and held him up. For the rest of the round I treated him like porcelain. Koudri on his feet meant three thousand quid to me. On the canvas he meant trouble – trouble in a big way from 'the boys.'

When I went back to my corner Benny Huntman, whose shrewd eyes hadn't missed a trick, was hopping mad. "What's the game Eric? Have you forgotten your promise?" he whispered as he leaned over massaging my shoulders. "You could have knocked him out in the first minute."

I didn't pay much attention to Benny. I had my own problems and was busy trying to figure out what to do. Then suddenly I realised what a fool I had been. I made up my mind to win, and win quickly.

Early in the round I dropped Koudri again. He was still groggy when he got up so I just messed him around looking for an opening until the last few seconds. Koudri walked into the very last punch I tossed. I caught him awkwardly on the corner of his mouth and ripped it open. As the bell rang he staggered away with blood gushing from the cut like water from an open tap.

As I walked back to my corner I knew it was all over. I had a close-up of the terrible gash and knew Koudri could not possibly fight on with such an injury. As I turned to sit down I could see that his seconds and the referee were already examining his ripped mouth. I knew that I was watching three thousand quid slip down the drain, but I had come out clean.

When the MC announced me as the winner there was pandemonium around the ring. The crooked betting boys, who thought they were "in the know," had dropped thousands of pounds and it seemed that any moment private fights might break out in the hall.

I went back to my dressing room with my head in a whirl. I figured that 'the boys,' having promised me £3,000, must have bet at least £6,000 on the fight. Now they would think I had double-crossed them and although I had never received a penny or agreed to square the fight, they would be out to get me. I don't mind admitting I was scared.

Although the boxing finished early, Eric didn't leave the Albert Hall until after midnight when he slipped out of a side door and made a dash for a taxi. There was nobody about and as far as he knew he wasn't followed. Nevertheless, he spent a week in hiding fearful that if he was cornered he could be beaten up, slashed and most probably maimed for life.

For weeks Boon didn't set foot outside his home after dark. He kept the door locked and windows barred. Even in broad daylight he was constantly on the alert for a sudden attack. As the days and weeks passed and nothing happened he began to think he had over-reacted and nothing would happen, but he was wrong.

Late one night as he was walking home he suddenly became aware that he was being followed. He looked back and saw three tough looking characters under a street lamp about 100 yards behind him. He had a bad feeling so after turning the next corner he quickened his step. When he looked behind him again they were still there only a little closer. He crossed the road, turned another corner and sprinted for about 50 yards, but couldn't shake them off.

Eric knew he was in trouble. It was past midnight and there was nobody else about. The streets were deserted. He stopped running to gather his breath and walked until he reached a wall where he turned and faced his would be assailants. The three men walked towards him and when they were about five yards away they stopped and spread out. Simultaneously their hands went into their pockets and he saw a glint of steel as they slowly and quietly moved towards him. "Okay you cowards," yelled Boon more out of bravado than anything else. "Come and get me. Maybe I won't win, but I'll tear the throat out of the first one I get my hands on."

He was in a blind rage, half crazy with fear, but he faced up to them. "Come on you yellow rats, let's see who's got the guts to start."

The three thugs hesitated and glanced uncertainly at one another. Rapidly regaining his confidence, Eric took a step away from the wall and moved towards the thug on his left. His tactics worked because the man took a step back, turned and ran. "One gone, two to go," yelled Boon as he faced the others. As he yelled blood thirsty threats they too backed away and ran for it. Remaining where he was for a few minutes to compose himself, Eric realised he'd had a lucky escape.

Four years later Boon's revelations about his intentions were confirmed in part by Sam Russell who refereed the fight with Koudri. Writing in the *Sunday People* he said:

I have to disclose that on one occasion Jack Solomons and the public were taken for a ride by Eric Boon. As referee the night Boon met Omar Koudri I can say without a second's hesitation that Boon tried to sell that fight. He won it, but he wanted to lose and the scene in the ring when it happened must have been one of the most amazing in the whole history of boxing.

Boon started really well and was soon forging ahead. Then I heard strange sounds coming from the ringside. The betting boys were laying odds of 2-1 on Koudri to win. This was so against the position of things in the ring that I began to have my suspicions.

Then during the second round Koudri stopped a terrific one on the mouth and when the bell went his manager called me to his corner to show me that his boxer's mouth had been split right through. Koudri urged me to allow him to continue, but I refused and went across to Boon's corner to declare him the winner. To my amazement there was Boon in his dressing gown. He stated he was retiring because he had hurt his shoulder. "Don't be silly, you have won," I replied. "No I haven't," said Boon, "I retired first."

I insisted on declaring him the winner much to his annoyance. He was still protesting when he left the ring.

Russell believed that Boon tried to sell the fight without Jack Solomons' knowledge, and it was perhaps the only time in the history of boxing that a fighter was forced to win a fight he wanted to lose.

In the years to come, Eric remembered the Koudri fight for all the wrong reasons, not least because he lost his wife Wendy. When he was discharged from hospital after his motor cycle accident in 1941, doctors told her that if he boxed again one punch in the wrong place could be fatal. She had been living in fear ever since.

Only a handful of people knew the extent of his injuries because instead of getting out of boxing with his health intact, he made her swear she wouldn't tell a soul. Although she threatened many times to leave him if he ever boxed again, she was always there when he arrived home.

She begged him again the day before the fought Koudri, but like a fool Boon was convinced they couldn't get by without the money Solomons was paying him. He didn't consider his well-being or that of his family. He also remained certain that his wife would never leave him.

"But she meant it that time," he recalled. "That night she walked out of my life. When I got home she and Erica had gone."

24

ONE LAST STAND

One of the things which made Jack Solomons a great promoter was his incredible judgement where boxers were concerned. He was present at ringside at the Palais des Sports in Paris in 1947 when Robert Villemain took the European welterweight title from Ernie Roderick and liked what he saw in the Frenchman. He promptly engaged him to fight Gwyn Williams at the Royal Albert Hall in his next contest. Villemain won a great contest so Solomons was determined to use him again in the future.

Jack also saw the Frenchman successfully defend his European and French welterweight titles against Omar Koudri in Paris on 17 December the same year. He recognised both men as good opponents for Boon especially in view of Eric's recent showing against Roderick. After Boon beat Koudri, Solomons saw Villemain as the natural opponent for his next fight. He moved quickly and agreed terms with the Frenchman to meet Eric at Harringay on 20 April 1948 in the chief supporting contest to a British heavyweight title eliminator between Freddie Mills and Ken Shaw. He also got an assurance from the European Boxing Union that Boon would get an immediate return for the title if he won.

Another incentive for Eric was that following weeks of correspondence, negotiation and transatlantic telephone calls, Solomons and Benny Huntman had plans to take him to America. Win, lose or draw against Villemain they hoped to leave on the Queen Mary on 2 June. Huntman told *Weekly Sporting Review* that Eric would fight in New York rings and it was hoped that his first opponent would be Rocco Bassano, a hard-hitting welterweight from the Bronx. If he was successful he could meet Sugar Ray Robinson two or three fights down the line.

Boon trained hard for the fight with Villemain who was a massive test for him. Eric had clearly gone back somewhat since his glory days of the late 1930's, but in an attempt to be at his best he set up a training camp at the King William IV public house at Chatteris, and even revived the partnership with his old trainer, Arthur Binder.

Villemain was a brilliant champion and at the peak of his career. He turned professional in 1944 following a successful amateur career in which he lost only three of 110 contests. He became French amateur featherweight champion after just 16 months. As a professional he won the French welterweight title in October 1946 and the European title by beating Ernie Roderick early the following year. Going into the fight with Boon he was unbeaten in 30 contests.

The big Harringay crowd gave both men rousing receptions as they made their way to the ring and the arena buzzed with excitement. When the dressing gowns were removed both looked in great condition, Boon very muscular and Villemain tanned and toned. Both had scaled inside the stipulated weight of 10st 10 which had been agreed in order to protect the Frenchman's European title. Boon was the lighter by five pounds.

At the opening bell Villemain started confidently. He adopted a typical continental crouching style, his swarthy face cushioned behind his gloves as he sought an opening. He soon found it with a good left jab and although Boon hit back most of his punches missed their target.

Eric had difficulty avoiding the jabs throughout the first three rounds and in some respects the fight developed into a similar pattern to that with Roderick. Although the Chatteris man showed the aggression of old he was seriously lacking in accuracy. At times he appeared confused by Villemain's skill although the crowd roared whenever he lashed out. From the back of the arena his attacks made it look as though he was getting on top, although ringsiders could see the Frenchman swayed out of danger most times.

Boon continued to attack in round four throwing heavy shots from all angles. Villemain willingly joined in the action and their toe-to-toe exchanges brought the crowd to its feet. Midway through the round Eric landed one terrific right which the Frenchman took well and countered with a shot of equal power sending the Chatteris man to the floor for a count of 'four'. It stung Boon into action and on rising there was a lively exchange just before the bell.

During the fifth Eric landed his best punch of the fight, a powerful left hook which crashed against its target. Although it had floored Crowley and Danahar amongst others, Villemain was a much tougher man. Despite being shaken, he stood his ground and fought back fiercely. The crowd expected Boon to pounce again, but he didn't get the chance as the Frenchman bobbed and weaved his way out of trouble. By the end of the round his left jab was again pumping into Eric's face.

Things were going much the same in the sixth until a right to the jaw sent Boon reeling into the ropes. Eyes blazing he retaliated immediately and hammered home fast two-fisted barrages to head and body. His fans re-lived the glory days as Villemain's guard dropped and Eric smashed a powerful left hook to the face. The Frenchman rocked under the onslaught, and the excitement reached fever pitch as Boon gave it all he had. Fighting mad he slammed home hooks, swings and uppercuts forcing Villemain across the ring and, for the first time, unable to respond.

All around the arena fans screamed encouragement as the former British champion sought to bring his rival down. Villemain, however, was an extremely tough man and in wonderful condition and it must have broken Eric's heart to see him still on his feet at the bell.

Many of the fervent fans expected Boon to finish it in round seven, but they had taken so much out of each other that it was something of an anti-climax. Villemain, having recovered well, boxed cleverly on the retreat. Poking out his left jab he picked up points consistently although for the second time in the fight referee, Tommy Little, warned him for hitting with the open glove. Boon, meanwhile, became strangely subdued and flat-footed and it appeared that his reserves of stamina were drying up. Time and again in this round the Frenchman made him miss with simple shots.

His confidence fully restored Villemain again took command with his jab in the eighth. Advancing on Boon he brushed aside a flurry of punches and smashed a massive right hook to the jaw. Although badly shaken Eric hit back gamely and once again they fought furiously in the centre of the ring. Two huge shots to the head rocked the Frenchman back on his heels.

Villemain was the first to land in round nine when a good right to the head staggered Boon. Yet again he came back exploding savage blows from both hands. As they fought another bitter toe-to-toe struggle, the crowd were again on their feet. It was anybody's fight and there were a few anxious moments when Eric briefly went to the floor more from a push than a punch. On rising he let rip more great punches and hard as they yelled their man on, the fans had to admire the way Villemain stood up to his task. He seemed impervious to anything Boon threw at him.

Eric punched himself into a state of exhaustion and his final effort, a huge overarm right, missed completely and propelled him off balance. He fell to the floor as the bell sounded and a quick glance from him towards his opponent seemed to indicate he had played his trump card and lost. As he flopped on to his stool Benny Huntman knelt on the canvas in front of him. "Eric," he pleaded, "there's £20,000 out there for you. Go out and get it."

With those words echoing in his ears, Boon sucked in the air and flexed his muscles for one big final drive. He tried all he knew in that final round, but all he had left was a tremendous heart. Sensing his opponent's weakness, Villemain, looking fresh and ready, tore into the attack. His fists pumped like pistons, but Boon stayed with him and traded punch for punch.

The crowd roared their admiration for two great warriors, but the shrewd Frenchman was alive to the situation and biding his time. Suddenly, as Boon rushed forward he was sent spinning to the floor by a left hook which crashed against his chin with sickening force. Slowly gathering his senses he got to his feet as the count reached 'nine'. Yet again he drove himself forward, but his power had gone and he was a sitting target.

Villemain calmly despatched another right flush on the chin and Boon crumbled to his knees finally devoid of any strength. Although he valiantly struggled to get to his feet, Mr Little counted him out with just five seconds of the fight remaining.

Eric was more exhausted than hurt at the end as he knelt on the canvas with blood streaming from a cut above his left eye. The Frenchman was clearly ahead on points, but it was an absolute tragedy for Boon to have lost in that way having given such an amazing display of courage. Although he was beaten by the better man it was no consolation to have been greater in defeat than he had many times in victory. In fact it was a sad reward for such a glorious effort.

There could have been fewer braver performances in a fight described by many critics as one of the greatest ever seen at Harringay. In some ways it even surpassed that between Boon and Danahar with some experienced correspondents believing it was the finest contest of Eric's career. At the end of the year readers of the trade paper, *Boxing News,* voted in their thousands to select it as the best contest of 1948 resulting in both fighters receiving a silver trophy. In an article published on 9 February the paper commented: "It will live in boxing fans' memories for many years."

Applause thundered around the arena as the two men left the ring and continued for fully five minutes. Some years later Jack Solomons remarked: "Of all the fights I put on at Harringay the memory of this one remains etched in my mind blow-for-blow." The remark was a fitting tribute because neither man had been prepared to take a backward step. It was a contest long remembered by those lucky enough to witness it.

Although Eric claimed he had damaged his hands during round five, he still accepted defeat gracefully. "I don't want to make the slightest excuse," he told reporters in his dressing room afterwards. "I was fighting fit, never felt better and went all out to win."

It turned out to be Boon's last stand because what occurred in his career during the months and years to come bore no resemblance to the truly great fighter he was. There has long been a saying that a boxer is the last to know when it is time to quit the ring. Sadly Eric was one of those men.

*   *   *

A few days after the Villemain fight Solomons told the press he wanted to stage a European title fight between Boon and the Frenchman on his big promotion at the White City on 26 July. It would be the chief support to a world light-heavyweight championship contest between Freddie Mills and Gus Lesnivich.

Jack said that he had made Villemain a very attractive offer and before returning to Paris the Frenchman promised to consider it. "At ten stone seven I believe Boon could beat Villemain," added Solomons who claimed the purse he would put up would be a record for a European welterweight title fight. Despite his efforts, the EBU refused to sanction the fight and in any event Villemain moved up to middleweight and did not defend his title again.

By his performances against Roderick and Villemain, Boon was clearly still a great attraction. Solomons therefore matched him with Welsh champion, Gwyn Williams, over 10 rounds at Harringay on 31 May in what was labelled as an official welterweight championship eliminator. Williams had already beaten Eddie Thomas in another eliminator at the same venue in March. Boon was at ringside that night where he met up with Ernie Roderick and fans enjoyed seeing them having a warm conversation. After the fight he told Maurice Woolf of *Sporting World* that he was definitely going to win the welterweight title as he was confident he could beat both Williams and Thomas.

Despite his defeat by Villemain, Eric was a regular figure at the big promotions. He and Williams were present at the Royal Albert Hall on 26 April and introduced from the ring prior to the main event between Henry Hall and Yrgoe Piitulainen. During the evening Eric was heard telling anyone who would listen that after Williams he was looking forward to returns with Roderick and Villemain.

Eric trained for the Williams fight at Chatteris under Arthur Binder with Chris Adcock from Rochdale as his sparring partner. At the weigh-in he looked in good condition at 10st 6 which gave him an advantage of just over a pound.

Boon and Williams, both managed by Benny Huntman, had sparred together on many occasions. Out of loyalty to both men, Huntman refused to work a corner, but visited their dressing rooms before the fight to wish them luck. He later disclosed that he couldn't bear to watch the fight and waited elsewhere in the arena for the result.

A professional for 10 years, Williams had mixed in good company. Although he had lost nine of 49 contests, they came at the hands of good men such as Lefty Flynn, Arthur Danahar (three times), Ronnie James, Henry Hall (twice), Robert Villemain, and Ernie Roderick who outpointed him in a British title fight at Harringay in September 1947. A classic boxer against fighter encounter was therefore expected, but it turned out to be a disgrace. It was in fact such a poor spectacle that it threatened to disrupt the whole show. Fortunately the next contest between Robert Villemain and Mark Hart of Croydon at middleweight was a cracker.

There was a huge clash in styles and at no time did it look like coming to life. After issuing warnings for more action in the third and fifth rounds, referee Ben Green from Leeds finally lost patience and sent both men to their corners early in the sixth. He declared the result 'no contest.' It had been such a dull and uninteresting affair that there were bouts of slow hand-clapping and whistling. During round three one wag in the audience blew a whistle. The following day one sports writer described the bout as "one of the sorriest exhibitions by two championship contenders ever seen in a British ring."

Despite the poor quality of the fight both men were unhappy at the referee's decision and were anxious to meet again as soon as possible. In his dressing room afterwards, Boon was dejected as he sat sipping a cup of tea while the bandages were cut from his hands. Several sympathisers stood around saying how unlucky he was.

"It was just one of those things," he remarked. "He would not come into me and you know I don't fight like that. I said before we left the ring, 'you tried Gwyn and I tried. What else could we do?' Had it been the other way round I suppose everyone would have been patting us on the back."

When Eric was informed by a Board of Control official that his purse money would be withheld pending an enquiry somebody remarked: "I don't think that's fair. When Eric put up a smashing fight against Villemain and Arthur Danahar the Board didn't come along and say 'here Eric, here's another £50!' but they are quick to come along and take money from a fighter."

When asked by a reporter about his performance, Boon claimed he couldn't understand what went wrong. "I was fighting fit," he remarked, "and simply waiting for Williams to carry the fight to me."

Williams was of a similar frame of mind saying he knew Eric wanted to mix it so he kept out of range and tried to score with long lefts. "Surely they did not expect me to go in and fight against a man like Boon," he remarked. "My plan was to box. It's the first time I've been in a 'no contest' issue and I've never been disqualified."

Benny Huntman, who managed both fighters, was also annoyed at the outcome. "Both men have always given their best," he told Maurice Woolf. "They ought to be given the opportunity to wipe out this smudge on their careers as soon as possible."

In view of the referee's decision, Boon and Williams were called to a meeting at the Board of Control offices on 15 June. Although Williams attended, Benny Huntman wrote a late letter apologising for the fact that neither he nor Boon were able to attend. He asked that consideration be given to the past records of both boxers.

The Stewards decided to hear the case in the absence of Boon. In answer to questions by the Chairman, Williams gave his version of events. After hearing other evidence, including the referee's report, the Stewards agreed unanimously that the names of Boon and Williams be withdrawn from further eliminating contests. Their purse money was also considered and it was decided that Boon would receive only £82 of his £1,000 purse. An amount of £500 would be paid into the Boxers Benevolent Fund and the remainder given back to the promoter in respect of tickets and tax. Williams received £190 of his £1,000 purse and the Stewards further decided that both boxers be strongly warned as to their future performances in the ring.

*   *   *

One of the saddest parts of boxing is seeing a household figure being exploited by others during the twilight of his career. Whatever the reasons it has always happened and Boon allowed himself to fall into that very trap. The hard battles, late nights and good times on the society scene and the effects of the accident had all combined to take their toll of a once great fighter. To make things worse his life was in turmoil because his marriage had folded and he was broke. His great effort against Robert Villemain was his last roll of the dice.

Boon was as brave as they came and still possessed a tremendous punch and those factors alone would still draw the crowds. Unfortunately they now became obstacles because the people behind him, particularly Solomons and Huntman, were shrewd operators in the hardest game. They knew it wasn't possible to turn back the clock, but instead of persuading him to hang up his gloves, they continued to market him. In reality they were using him to line their own pockets.

25

EXPLOITED IN THE U.S.A

Early in June 1948 Boon sailed for America together with Solomons, Huntman, Sam Burns, Moss Deyong and British lightweight champion, Billy Thompson. Solomons main objective was to sign Gus Lesnevich to defend his world light-heavyweight title against Freddie Mills at the White City on 26 July. Although nothing materialised he had also hoped to arrange fights for Boon and Thompson on the Joe Louis – Jersey Joe Walcott bill in New York on 25 June.

From previous communications Solomons and Huntman knew that there was plenty of work available for Boon in the American rings because the fans there knew his style. Before returning to England on 24 June they reached agreement for him to meet Canadian champion, Johnny Greco, at The Forum, Montreal, on 5 August.

The fight had first been mooted in May when Huntman telephoned Maurice Woolf from Solomons' gym a few days after Boon's contest with Gwyn Williams. In officially announcing it Huntman optimistically remarked: "Boon likes to fight anyone and Greco is a man after his own heart." They knew it was a gamble because although past his best the Canadian still had a murderous punch. Huntman reasoned that if Boon won he would be an overnight success both in Canada and the United States.

With Huntman and Solomons having returned to England, Boon joined forces with American trainer, Johnny Sullo and spent several weeks working out at Stillman's Gym in New York. Matchmakers in the city tried to make a fight between him and Kid Gavilan, but his contract with Montreal promoter, Raul Godbout, forbade him to take another contest before meeting Greco.

Boon and Sullo arrived in Montreal on 29 July. The following morning Eric was up early and did some roadwork on the Mount Royal Mountain. During the afternoon he trained and sparred at the Palestre Nationale gym.

Greco, born of Italian parents in a suburb of Montreal, was a highly respected fighter who had done well in American rings. Although the fight with Boon was a 10-round non-title affair, press reports claimed the winner would move up the rankings and be on a short list for a shot against world welterweight champion, Sugar Ray Robinson.

Eric had never seen Greco, but knew all about him especially his fights with Beau Jack who he beat and drew with in 1946. "His record is impressive", he told Canadian journalists, "but mind you not too impressive. I've met some good men myself."

The sports reporters were fascinated by Boon because he had the reputation of being an American style fighter. He was described as being unlike most English boxers because he could box as well as punch. Promoter Godbout was excited about the pairing saying: "This fight is a natural. I feel better about it than the Greco-Beau Jack battle."

In a public workout on 31 July Boon went through five fast rounds with local fighters George Gervin, Ruby Margolin and Nick Primiani and impressed a crowd of 200 at the Palestre Nationale. He hurt all three, but refused to finish them off. A short distance away at Shamrocks Gym, Greco completed nearly 60 rounds of sparring against various opponents. He was in perfect condition and said he was confident he would take "the powerful Englishman."

A comparatively small crowd watched the fight, gross receipts being $13,282, much less than anticipated. Boon, who at 10st 2 was three quarters of a pound lighter than Greco, opened quickly. He had the Canadian bobbing and weaving to avoid a good left jab in the first minute and then crashed a hard right to the chin. Greco wobbled, but recovered quickly and chased Boon around the ring forcing him to the ropes where he scored with heavy punches to head and body.

Boon was more cautious in round two and tried to stay close to avoid the Canadian's powerful punches. He did have the occasional success with single shots, but most of the work was done by Greco who carried the fight to the Englishman.

Greco went straight on the attack in round three. Although Eric held him off for a while with his jab and landed a couple of hefty wallops, these seemed to fire the Canadian into a rage. A barrage of punches forced Boon to the ropes, but as he got set to smash back he carelessly dropped his guard. Seeing the opening Greco threw a short left hook which exploded against Eric's chin knocking him flat on his back. Although he struggled to get up at the count of 'four' his eyes were glazed. He didn't know where he was and the count was completed after 52 seconds of the round. The referee helped him to his feet, but he reeled helplessly on rubbery legs as he pulled himself free.

Boon returned to New York where a contract had been drawn up by the 20th Century Sporting Club for him to meet Kid Gavilan over 10 rounds at St Nicks Arena on 11 October. He would receive 20% of the gate.

Gavilan was a great prospect who at that time had lost only five of 53 contests and was being tipped for world honours. He had never been stopped and this had to be the best example yet of how Boon was being exploited. It was perhaps fortunate for his well-being that when Gavilan lost on points to Sugar Ray Robinson on 23 September the fight was cancelled.

A few weeks later it was reported that Eric would face Terry Young at St Nicks Arena on 15 October. Young was another rough, hard-hitting fighter who earlier in the year had two vicious contests with Paddy De Marco. He lost both on points, but in between beat Beau Jack on a split decision at Madison Square Garden.

At about this time Boon took on Ray Arcel as his trainer and when the fight with Young fell through he was contracted to meet Tony Janiro at Parkway Sporting Club, Brooklyn on 18 October. His purse was to be 25% of the gate. That contest also fell through whereupon he was matched with Beau Jack over 10 rounds at the Uline Arena, Washington on 28 October.

Between 1943 and '44, Jack held the New York version of the world lightweight title and his record included three championship battles with Bob Montgomery. In 1944 he was voted *Ring Magazine* fighter of the year. Realistically, Boon was not in this class, but the Americans saw him as a stepping stone for Jack to regain recognition after being knocked out in six rounds by Ike Williams for the world lightweight title in his last fight. Prior to that he had beaten Greco and Janiro.

A few days before the fight Arcel got to work at a press conference and really built Boon up. He had worked with plenty of good men in the past including Tony Zale, Joe Louis and Jack 'Kid' Berg, but claimed Eric could be his best. He said he was someone who could really fight and was ready for Jack. "Eric is one of the few European fighters who can punch," said Arcel. "He is fast and we will find out on Thursday night if he is going to be the fighter I think he is."

Ray's praise for Boon was a far cry from the first reports he had received about him. Early in 1948 he was in London on a European tour looking over fighters, but hadn't found anyone who to him looked especially good. Then Jack Berg called him one night and asked him to go to the Albert Hall. "Having nothing better to do I tagged along," said Arcel. "I didn't even know who was fighting, but everyone was talking about some Frenchman called Koudri who would murder a guy called Boon who was all washed up after a pretty good career."

Arcel told his audience that Boon came out, sparred a little and then "wham" he tagged Koudri. Although staggered the Frenchman survived the round.

320

"I began to ask myself 'what is this? Here is a guy, a two and a half to one underdog, smacking the favourite all around the ring'." Arcel described how Boon cut Koudri's mouth and won the fight.

"Right there and then I decided that was my fighter," he continued. "The guy can punch, and here we are."

Referring to the fight with Greco at Montreal, Arcel blamed the food Boon had been getting along on. "He has eaten good ever since," he claimed, "so there's no excuses this time. Come this fight, it's up to him."

Three days before the fight Boon did a public workout at the Liberty Athletic Club gym in Washington. The following day he attended a luncheon at which he was called upon to make a speech. Glancing over at Beau Jack who was also present he said: "I think the better man is going to win."

Although Jack was a 7-5 on favourite, Arcel disputed the odds. He had once trained the American and claimed Boon was a stronger, tougher and harder hitting fighter than even Tony Janiro who was the last man to stop Jack before Ike Williams did.

Despite Arcel's praise of Boon he was not in Jack's class and it came as no surprise to critics back in England to hear that he had suffered a crushing defeat. It was another example of him being over-matched for the sake of the big purses.

Before a crowd of less than 2,000 Jack won with ease and although not the fighter of a few years earlier he was still too much for Eric. Despite displaying all his usual gameness the Chatteris man was a mere toy at the hands of the tough American. Throughout the bout he pounded Boon unmercifully, holding him at arms length with his left and bringing up one sizzling right after another.

With Boon bleeding badly from the nose and mouth in round two Jack swarmed in to finish it and landed almost at will, yet it wasn't until the third that Eric weakened. He doubled up from a bolo punch early in the round, but then shook his head and retaliated with both fists flying. Yet it was to no avail because Jack stood his ground, threw a stinging right to the head which sent Eric reeling across the ring into the ropes. He was an open target as referee, Eddie La Fonde, quickly stepped in and called a halt at one minute 21 seconds of the round.

At the end Boon was showing real signs of wear. The gruelling battles had taken their toll and critics were unanimous that if he carried on he would be foolish to face the likes of Greco and Jack. There was no doubt that he should have called it a day at that point, but the lure of big purses was too great to resist. He was living the high life, visiting fashionable places, and completely by chance even met up with his boyhood sweetheart, Ollie Franks, again.

As he walked back to his hotel late one evening having just left a lady friend, he bought a newspaper. He casually turned to the entertainment page where he saw Ollie's photograph. Although the caption said the lady was "Kay Kenton, star of radio and television," Boon knew instantly that it was Ollie. His heart missed a couple of beats and in less than 24 hours he traced her. A week later they were on their way to Hollywood.

They saw a lot of each other and the next few weeks were idyllic, but the lifestyle to which Boon became accustomed cost money. In mid-November, when he was offered a substantial purse to fight Robert Takeshita at the Civic Auditorium in Honolulu on 14 December, he jumped at it, but promised Ollie it would be his last fight. "I didn't need much coaxing," he admitted later, "because I had come to dislike boxing as much as she did."

Boon's social life meant that he became less enthusiastic about training, but as soon as the fight was signed Ray Arcel set about getting him into shape because it was going to be a major event in Honolulu. Takeshita had won 31 of 33 professional contests, many inside the distance, so it was built up as a 'puncher' against 'puncher' fight. On the advertising posters Boon was billed as being 'the greatest puncher to fight in Hawaii'. He was also said to be the first Englishman to fight in a local ring since the legislation of boxing on the island in 1929.

Boon and Arcel arrived in Honolulu on 7 December and were given a typical Hawaiian welcome. At the airport Sad Sam Ichinose, the manager of Takeshita, draped a lei around Arcel whilst top Hawaiian boxer, Dado Marino, who would later become world flyweight champion, did the same with Boon. Huge photographs of them appeared on the sports pages of the *Honolulu Star Bulletin* the following day. The press gave the fight massive coverage with local critics predicting it would be a hectic brawl which wouldn't go the distance. They believed the local man would win, but only after being floored.

Sports journalists in Honolulu loved Boon and he was in great form during a number of interviews. "Don't worry about me," he remarked one afternoon, "I don't have a glass jaw. Since I was fourteen I have fought in four hundred and twenty-eight amateur and professional bouts. I have been stopped ten times." Whilst he was spot on with the latter, he more than exaggerated the number of fights he'd had.

Arcel, described as Boon's American manager and trainer, told the press that Eric had trained in New York for a month before they set off for Honolulu. He was confident his man would beat Takeshita.

On his first full day in Hawaii Boon trained at the 49th State gym and impressed locals with a brisk seven-round workout. The following day he looked good in his first sparring session with Richard Miyashiro, a veteran who had recently returned to the island after eight years in the United States. Eric also worked with local boxers, Richard Cabral and Jimmy Perry, until two days before the fight. Locals who attended the gym were fascinated by Boon because he always had a cup of tea after his workouts.

Meanwhile, some difficulty arose getting the contracts signed because Sad Sam Ichinose was under the impression that the fight had been made at 140 pounds (10 stone). Arcel insisted that he agreed with the joint promoters, Angie Curtis and Leo Leavitt, for it to be at 147. A compromise of 143 was eventually agreed and that is what Boon scaled at the official weigh-in. Takeshita was one and a half pounds lighter.

The fight drew a crowd of over 4,100 and they gave Boon a greater reception than Takeshita when they were introduced from the ring. In the opening round Eric lived up to all the complimentary things written about him in the pre-fight reports. Big over arm rights sent the local man to the floor four times for long counts in that round and at the bell he looked a beaten man.

It was Takeshita's toughest ever fight, but the twenty-five-years-old gave an exhibition of raw courage rarely seen in Honolulu rings. From being a badly beaten fighter he rallied magnificently in round two and through sheer aggression turned it in his favour. Keeping a cool head he belted stiff hooks to Boon's chin, but Eric wasn't finished. Another overarm right exploded on Takeshita's jaw sending him to the floor for a count of 'eight'.

Displaying incredible courage and powers of recuperation he rose once more to carry the fight to Boon. A few seconds later a vicious left hook to the stomach had Eric doubled up and in obvious pain only to be saved by the bell.

Boon vomited in his corner during the interval and hadn't fully recovered when the bell sounded for the third. Never short of courage he was determined to go out fighting and sprang from his stool to attack his opponent. Takeshita knew he had the upper hand and was determined not to let the chance slip away. The round was only a few seconds old when he side-stepped Boon's rush and drove another powerful left hook to the stomach. Eric sagged to the floor where he was counted out by referee, Walter Cho, after just 28 seconds of the round.

"It was my fault for losing the fight," said Boon in his dressing room afterwards. "I couldn't believe anybody could take so much punishment as Bob did and still be as strong as ever. I got careless after I dropped him in the second round."

The fight was widely reported, particularly by the *Honolulu Star Bulletin* which ran a large illustrated story under the bold headline 'Takeshita ko's Boon in Year's Most Sensational Fight.' It had been a frenzy of fast and furious hitting which had the crowd roaring from start to finish. It was the most stunning victory of Takeshita's career and lasted just six minutes and 28 seconds.

"A great fighter, he'll go far," was Ray Arcel's tribute to the Hawaiian boxer before he and Boon left for America the following day. Both said they hoped to be back in Honolulu the following year for a return. Boon, however, was a shot fighter and could no longer expect the big purses he had been getting in the States. There was nowhere else to go so Arcel advised him to return to England.

*   *   *

Within 12 months Boon gave a very different account of the Takeshita fight to those in the Honolulu newspapers. At the time he made his extraordinary revelation in *The People* about being asked to throw the Koudri fight, he also went into great detail about how he was told to take a dive against Takeshita. He claimed that he had also been approached in a similar vein prior of meeting Arthur Danahar in London in 1946. After describing his encounter with the thugs following the Koudri fight he said:

> *I never had any more trouble with gangsters in this country, but the incident was brought vividly back to me nine months later in Honolulu. I had flown there with my boyhood sweetheart, Ollie Franks, to fight Robert Takeshita. I didn't even bother to train for this bout. It meant nothing to me except an opportunity to pick up a little extra money.*
>
> *I had promised Ollie that this would definitely be my last fight, and we spent long, lazy hours together on the sun-drenched beach with the palms whispering over our heads as we talked over my plans for a stage career. I was living in a romantic dream world and couldn't have cared less about Mr Takeshita or the result of the fight. So on the night of the contest when I got a surprise from the "fancy doing business?" boys I let them talk.*
>
> *Wearing wide-brimmed Stetson hats and rainbow ties my visitors looked like a couple of characters from a George Raft or James Cagney film. Laconically they informed me that they had come from the 'Boss' – I never discovered who he was – and that the 'Boss' fancied doing business.*

I had to smile because it seemed that boxing racketeers spoke the same language all over the world. The approach was almost identical to the first time I was invited to throw a fight. That was when I fought Arthur Danahar for the second time at Harringay in 1946. The 'boys' on that occasion wanted Danahar to win, and since they never like taking unnecessary risks, they propositioned me.

I was guaranteed £3,000 in pound notes if I agreed to lie down or arrange by any other means that it was Danahar's hand that was raised as the winner. I didn't mince my words with their emissary that first time. I didn't like his looks anyway. I told him that unless he was out of my sight in two minutes I'd break off his arms and tie them in a bow around his skinny neck – or words to that effect! And that was that.

But, as I have explained, things were very different in Honolulu. It was to be my last fight and, remembering how, after all, I had lost to Danahar, although I had done my level best to lick him, I thought I might as well find out what was cooking.

"It's this way kid," said the leader. "The boss wants the local boy to win. See? You take a dive in the third and you collect two grand. See?"

"Maybe," I said, "but I don't know you. How do I know I'll get the dough?"

"Don't worry," he said. "You play ball and you'll get your cut."

"And if I don't?" I asked.

"That'll be just too bad kid – for you," he grinned. "Honolulu can be very unhealthy this time of year. Remember, you dive in the third, and no monkey business. The boss don't like monkey business."

There was a big crowd at the fight and as soon as I ducked under the ropes I spotted the two in ringside seats near my corner. They both gave me a broad wink and the thumbs up sign as I sat waiting for the bell. Frankly, I hadn't made up my mind what to do. It wasn't the two thousand dollars that was worrying me so much as what would happen to me if I didn't play ball.

In the first few seconds I went after the Hawaiian boy tossing half-hearted lefts and rights, and down he went like a ninepin. He only just managed to beat the count so I quickly grabbed him and walked him around the ring in a clinch.

325

Then I gave him a couple of digs in the ribs just to make it look good and down he went again.

As I backed away to a neutral corner I caught sight of the two pay-off boys. They were both making frantic signs to me to keep away and ease up. But that South Sea Islander was harder to miss than a barn door. Every time I hit him he keeled over. Altogether he took five counts in the first round and when I dropped onto my corner stool the two gangsters were bobbing up and down in their seats with temper. One of them caught my eye and drew his finger across his throat with a villainous leer.

Meanwhile, my trainer, Ray Arcel, was leaning over me with a happy smile. "Nice going Eric," he whispered. "You're going to give the crowd their monies worth before you take this mug to the cleaners, eh?"

"That's it Ray," I said unhappily. I was wondering what it would like to be taken for a one-way boat ride to be fed to the sharks!

The second round was almost as bad. Short of propping him up with a couple of steel bars there seemed to be no way of keeping the Hawaiian champ off the canvas. After he had taken three more counts I clinched and he held on until the end of the round.

So we came out for the third round and I still hadn't made up my mind what to do. Can you blame me? The two boys sitting near my corner were giving me very dirty looks and I didn't need a crystal gazing ball to read what my future would be if I didn't box to orders.

The trouble was that the Hawaiian had been so busy getting up and down off the floor that he hadn't landed a punch hard enough to burst a cream puff. Nor did he look as though he was about to. So I backed away and dropped my guard. I figured it was better to be knocked out than murdered.

The Hawaiian champ took the hint and let fly with a peach of a hook that caught me smack on the whiskers. Once down I stayed down. Indeed I couldn't have beaten that punch if I wanted to, but I wasn't worrying. To hell with the two thousand I thought as they carried me back to the corner after the ref had counted me out. At least I shall leave Honolulu alive.

Boon's account of events in Honolulu made gripping reading, but as with that involving the Koudri affair there were grey areas, not least his version of the actual fight. The Honolulu press reports the following day described the fight in great detail and presumably accuracy. They described Takeshita taking five counts during the fight, not eight as claimed by Boon. Furthermore, the ending came from a destructive body punch not one to the jaw. Eric's memory of course may have become blurred. On the other hand there may have been other motives for his dramatic story. Whatever the truth there was always the suspicion that fight fixing went on especially during that period of time.

26

END OF THE ROAD

Boon returned to England in early 1949 a washed-up fighter whose career looked over. The American trip had been a disaster, but his main problem was that he was virtually penniless. Instead of announcing his retirement he was at ringside at Harringay on 7 February and watched welterweight champion, Henry Hall, and contender, Eddie Thomas, score points victories over American opponents Tony Janiro and Billy Graham. He was not impressed with their performances and afterwards issued challenges in the belief that he still had enough to beat them both.

A few days later he went back to Jack Solomons and pleaded for one more chance. The promoter didn't need much persuading and after discussions with Benny Huntman, who was still Eric's British manager, they matched him with Hall over 10 rounds at the Royal Albert Hall on 22 March.

Hall had won the British title by outpointing Ernie Roderick in November the previous year and Solomons used this fact to try and market the fight to the press. He insisted that it would give Boon the chance to avenge the defeat Hall inflicted on him in 1945. He also claimed Eric was still a force to be reckoned with and just the man to bring the best out of Hall who had been described as stereotyped in recent contests. The promoter omitted mentioning the three crushing defeats Boon suffered in America the previous year or even consider what effect they may have had on him.

After the fight had been announced Maurice Woolf still maintained his admiration for Boon. Writing in *Sporting World* on 12 March he said:

> Boon still has a fortune in those golden fists of his and if he will settle down to training as he did in his Devonshire Club days he could still fight his way to the top. He has been given more opportunities to make good than any other British fighter with the exception of Jack Doyle. This must be his final chance.

There could be no more ardent and loyal supporter of Boon among the sporting press, but Woolf had either overlooked or failed to recognise that the good life had destroyed Eric as a top class fighter just as it did to Doyle a decade or so earlier. Although his charisma would ensure attraction at the box-office, recent contests had shown his form had spiralled rapidly downwards. Many people failed to understand how, after his showing against Gwyn Williams and three bad defeats in America, Solomons could justify using Boon in a top-of-the-bill contest. The answer was simple – he remained a box-office attraction who the public would still go to see because he could always bring over a big punch that would turn a fight around.

Continuing the support for his friend, Maurice Woolf wrote:

> A victory or a great contest for Boon and he is back at the top. It's up to Boon. He can get back to the top, but it all depends on himself. He is as unpredictable as a woman's moods, but if he boxes as well as he did against Robert Villemain then he will certainly topple Hall. Anything below that form and it's curtains for him.

Writing in *Sporting Life,* Joe Bromley made the point that opportunity rarely knocked twice on the door of any fighter, so Boon could consider himself one of the luckiest boxers in the country. When he returned from South Africa he got an immediate title shot at Roderick and now, after three bad defeats in America, found himself matched against the current British champion. Bromley figured that were he to win his flare would probably guarantee him another title shot ahead of more worthy contenders.

Always the optimist, Boon trained for the fight at Solomons' gym at Great Windmill Street. He couldn't be blamed for the situation he was in because it was Solomons and Huntman who continued to use him and the Board of Control who approved the contest. As usual there were plenty of reporters at the gym and although most were interested in triple Australian champion, Dave Sands, who was preparing for a contest with American, Tommy Yarosz, at Harringay on 4 April, there was still great intrigue about the Chatteris man. He drew them like a magnet and as usual he got them writing. "A belt within two years or I quit," he told a group at the end of one training session."

Eric knew he had been his own worst enemy by allowing his activities outside the ring to control his life and affect his performances. He was an intelligent man and appeared sincere when he told his audience: "I have no further ambitions in that direction. I am really going to get fit and win a title. Every post in the ring must be a winning post."

Boon's only problem was that he was unable to accept the real picture, that his best days were long gone. Questions continued to be asked in the press regarding justification over him topping the Albert Hall bill against Hall. In the end it didn't matter because about a week before the fight Hall sustained a cut eye in training and had to withdraw. This left Solomons in a quandary because he was unable to find a suitable British opponent at such short notice.

He therefore contacted the Board of Control and sought permission to engage Italian welterweight champion, Fernando Jannilli as a substitute. After discussions between the Board and the Ministry of Labour, the Italian was granted a work permit and a match was made over 10 rounds at 10st 10.

Little was known about Jannilli in Britain other than in his only contest there he drew with Stan Hawthorne over eight rounds at Paisley the previous year. He was undefeated in his last nine contests and a number of critics felt he would be too good for Boon.

After preliminary training in London, Eric moved to the Star & Garter at Windsor. His main concern was a lack of sparring partners which caused Benny Huntman to put an appeal in the newspapers. The situation only added to Boon's problems because during the build-up to the fight the press were not as warm to him as he had been accustomed. Whilst some reporters wrote the contest up as an intriguing one others had not forgotten how he was on the verge of pulling out against Koudri at the same venue 12 months earlier. Neither had they forgiven him for his dismal showing against Gwyn Williams at Harringay three months later.

Despite those shortfalls, Boon's flair and power of punch still pulled in the fans. The press tables were also full with the scribes keenly interested to see if one of his special punches would make the headlines again or whether they would be watching him in action in a British ring for the very last time. Sadly it was the latter.

Against Jannilli, Eric was just a shell of the man who was probably the most popular fighter in the country when he won the lightweight title 10 years earlier. His speed, aggression, timing and power of punch had all gone and he didn't seem to have the energy or will to make a fight of it. In a most disappointing display in which he didn't land a significant blow in the opening round, it became clear that he could no longer be regarded as a top class performer.

With considerable handicaps in height and reach, Boon found it difficult to get close to an opponent who used a straight left jab to good effect and displayed good footwork and defensive skills. He was so ineffective that by the end of round two the crowd stamped and booed their displeasure.

Midway through the fourth referee, Teddy Waltham, lectured both men for insufficient action. In the next round the crowd again became restless as the Italian's left jab and fast feet dominated a very poor contest. Although he went through the motions Boon rarely got close enough to land a decent punch. He returned to his corner at the end of the round with boos ringing in his ears.

If anything, round six was even duller as Boon still failed to land a decent punch against a mediocre opponent whose only weapon was a jab. It was a sad spectacle of a once great fighter who, but for the war, may have become the best in the world.

Mr Waltham gave them another lecture before the start of round seven although it was difficult to understand why he directed any of his displeasure towards Jannilli who was at least scoring. The end came midway through the round when the referee deemed that Boon had made no effort to increase his work-rate. He was disqualified for not giving of his best.

The decision was cheered from all parts of the arena by fans who had been badly let down. They paid their money to see a 10-rounds international contest and were entitled to show resentment for what was a farce.

Boon had hit an all-time low and it was sad to see him humiliated in this way after all the excitement he had generated over the years. He looked a forlorn figure as he trudged away from a British ring for the last time. Although financial difficulties were the main reason for him continuing to fight, much of the blame had to lie with Solomons and Huntman for encouraging him to do so.

There was an icy silence in his dressing room after the fight. Nat Franks, who had trained Eric, packed the bags without uttering a word and Benny Huntman just stood rubbing his face with his hands. The silence was only broken by former opponent, Dave Crowley, who was really upset and criticised members of his team for a lack of preparation. He told Eric he should have laid off working the heavy bag.

"I told him that myself," snapped Huntman, "didn't I Eric?"

"It's no good," groaned Boon as he turned to Maurice Woolf. "I have to have a fighter who comes to me. I chased the Italian, but could not get in. Every time I went to position myself for a punch, he was away again."

Another sympathiser was South African welterweight, Tony Lombard, who earlier in the evening had outpointed Cliff Anderson. "I only wish I had your style Eric," he said telling the Chatteris man he thought he was very unlucky to be thrown out.

Having sat at ringside, Maurice Woolf finally conceded that his great friend had reached the end of the road. In his column in *Sporting World* the following week he wrote:

> It hurts me to say this, but if Eric can't do better then he may as well turn the game in. I was practically raised in the fight business with Boon, but when the crowd hooted him last year I felt bad. I know they expect miracles from the ex-champion, but even I couldn't find an excuse for his inglorious display.

The disqualification led to Boon being called before the South Eastern Area Council of the Board of Control eight days later to explain his performance. He was questioned by members of the council who also considered the report of referee, Teddy Waltham, and a letter from Benny Huntman. The outcome was that he was ordered to forfeit all but £58 of his £400 purse and severely warned as to his future conduct whilst boxing.

Although somewhat belatedly, Eric finally accepted that his career as a fighter was over. Still wanting to be involved in the sport he applied for, and was granted, a Board of Control manager's licence. Unfortunately, his problems with the boxing authorities were not yet over.

In June the Board received a letter from a Miss Marion Steller from New York alleging that Eric owed her the sum of $360. The matter was taken seriously and he was ordered to attend a meeting of the South Eastern Area Council on 13 June. Although he was granted an extension of time he failed to appear at two subsequent meetings and was notified that if there was a recurrence the case would be heard in his absence. When he failed to attend another meeting arranged for 20 July, and made no contact with the Board, his manager's licence was suspended until such time as he did attend.

The action had the desired effect and Eric appeared before the Council on 10 August 1949 when Miss Steller's letter was read. Called upon by the Chairman to give an explanation, he agreed that he did owe her money, but claimed it was $280, not $360 as she had alleged. He was told that being a licence holder the Board took a serious view of the situation. In the circumstances he was instructed to write to her, send some money and offer an apology. The Council required copies of all correspondence between him and Miss Steller. Boon promised to comply.

In order to monitor the situation the Board had further communication with Miss Steller and it soon became apparent that Boon had ignored the Board request for him to address the situation. Furthermore, he failed to respond to a number of letters sent to him including one by registered post. As nothing had been heard from him by late November it was decided to hold the matter in abeyance until he applied for the renewal of his manager's licence.

Boon eventually wrote to the Board in February 1950 stating that he wished to surrender his licence. This was not accepted because apart from the outstanding matter the Board were also concerned about certain passages written under his name in the series of articles in *The People*. He was therefore asked to attend a meeting on 23 February which he did.

The articles in question were published over an eight week period between December 1949 and February 1950. Not only had he made the allegations concerning the Koudri, Danahar and Takeshita fights, he also made highly critical remarks about other aspects of boxing in Britain:

You can have the fight game. I want no part of it. So far as I am concerned you can, to quote from a current song hit, 'put it in a box, tie it up with ribbon and throw it in the deep blue sea,' the deeper the better. Take it from me, it stinks, and that's not sour grapes, for personally I can't complain.

Boxing bought me fortune and fame. It took me to America, South Africa, Honolulu and other glamorous places that would never have been anything but names on a map if I hadn't been a professional fighter. But then I was a champion. I was on the inside looking out. I was 'Eric' to the big-shots. I didn't have to wait cap-in-hand outside the promoter's door. I could walk straight in.

That's how it is when you're on top of the heap, but it's different when you're just small fry or a punch-drunk has-been on the outside looking in. Then nobody knows your name. It's "Hey you" or "shut up now", and you're on about the same level as a young heifer in a cattle market.

Mind you if I had a son I would certainly teach him to fight, but if ever a boy of mine wanted to turn pro I'd tell him not to be a crazy young fool. I'd sit down and tell him the inside story of the business as I know it. I would tell about the game, clean-living youngsters I have seen ruined. I'd tell him about the fixed fights and the crooked managers, the weigh-in scales with two sets of weights and all the other pleasant little carve ups.

And then I'd take him around the gymnasiums and show him a few of the mumbling half-witted punchies shuffling around like zombies. I'd prove to him that the fight game is twice as dirty and crooked as it is in the States. And if after all that he still wanted to be a pro, I'd have him certified.

I'm not trying to tell you that every fight is framed. Nine out of ten are straight, but the money that is made out of the odd one that is fixed would surprise you. And so too would the names of some of the boxers who are in the pay of the big-shot gamblers.

In the last article of the series Eric admitted that he wouldn't have missed a minute of his years in and around the ring. "Boxing has given me a lot," he admitted. "It has taken me around the world, poured money into my lap and I've actually enjoyed the fighting too."

Boon received a substantial fee from the newspaper for agreeing to write the articles and this enabled him to set up a small greengrocer's business with two lorries. The Board of Control, however, were furious about his remarks and at the meeting he was questioned at length. Although he provided an explanation, it was not accepted and as a result his manager's licence was withdrawn. That in itself was no concern to Eric because he had already asked to surrender it and was not managing any boxers. With the passing of time, however, the attitude of the Board still wrankled with him and he wanted everything in the public domain.

As he prepared the notes for his intended book, which were totally separate from the newspaper articles, he drafted an account of his version of what was said in the meeting:

> *Then I wrote an article in the press stating boxing in England stinks, and gave up my manager's licence. I was asked to appear before the Council to, as I thought, answer for my accusation, but all I was asked was: "Are you prepared to deny what you wrote in the press?"*
>
> *I told them I was not and nothing more was said or done about it. I told the Secretary that what I had written about crooked managers and promoters had been the truth. If it hadn't they would have sued me for libel. I asked him why these people's licences were not withdrawn. He made no reply.*
>
> *I then wrote to the Council asking for an interview. I wanted to tell my whole story and see what would be done about it. I was refused a hearing. Then I spoke to several Council members and told them I wished to make an official complaint about the conditions of boxing in England. I quoted their own rules on the subject and was told to write in again. I did, but was again refused a hearing. I wrote twice after that, but still they would not see me.*
>
> *I then went to see a Member of Parliament and put my case before him. He said he quite agreed with what I had said about boxing, but what could he do. I got little help there. He did say that Winston Churchill had told him that he (Churchill), would never go to see a fight.*
>
> *Then I saw another Member of Parliament who told me: "We know boxing is crooked, but what can we do?" I put forward*

Ray Arcel (left) watches a lei being placed around Boon's neck on his arrival in Honolulu in December 1948.

Boon, Tommy Farr (next to him right) and Terry Downes at an ex-boxers association outing to Slough Dog Racing Arena.

Boon (right) talks to Henry Gilbert at Winchester
Assizes on 22nd March 1948 where both were
witnesses at the trial of James Camb accused of the
murder of actress Gay Gibson.

Boon (right) and Omar
Koudri shake hands at Jack
Solomon's gym on 1st March
1948 at the weigh-in for their
fight at the Royal Albert Hall.

Robert Villemain (left) and
Boon weigh-in for their fight at
Harringay on 20th April 1948.
Dave Edgar, Benny Huntman
and Nat Seller look on.

Referee, Moss Deyong (left), Boon, Jack Solomons,
Billy Thompson and Benny Huntman arriving in New
York in early June 1948.

Boon awaits the start of a
booth fight at Strood,
Kent in 1952.

Eric faces Laurie Davis at
Charlie Woods booth at Strood
in 1952.

Eric remarried ex-wife Wendy at March Registry office on 1st
October 1966.

Eric training youngsters at Chatteris Amateur Boxing Club in 1964. Arthur Binder (far right) watches.

Boon (far left) with Arthur Danahar, Jack Solomons, Bert Nutt, Hal Bagwell and Peter Kane at a charity dinner at Bristol in 1973.

Boon (left) with Duncan Presst, Dave 'Boy' Green and Andy Smith at Smith's St Ives gym during the late 1970s.

Boon (left) and Arthur Danahar meet at a charity boxing event in West Sussex during the 1970s.

Len Wickwar (right) and Boon at one of Eric's charity film shows in Leicester in 1974.

Boon congratulates Dave 'Boy' Green on beating Derek Simpson at Cambridge on 12th February 1975.

In later life Eric retained his good looks, smartness and a full head of hair.

several suggestions, but apparently none were acceptable. I was told to see the Secretary of the Professional Boxers Association to see if he would do anything. I went to see him and found that he was the Communist member of the Council – the one I had been in hospital with.

In many ways it was sad that Boon's parting from boxing was so bitter. He had been good for the sport and it had been good to him. He had been exceptionally close to the major figures, especially in London, and must have known much of what went on behind the scenes. An autobiography written at the time would have been riveting, provided it wasn't blocked for legal reasons. Unfortunately, like so many of Eric's good ideas, it never reached fruition.

*   *   *

After his poor showing against Jannilli, Eric knew his ring career was over. Hoping to get back into acting he got a lucky break when he was engaged to play his original part in the boxing drama, Golden Boy, set to run for a week at the Richmond Theatre

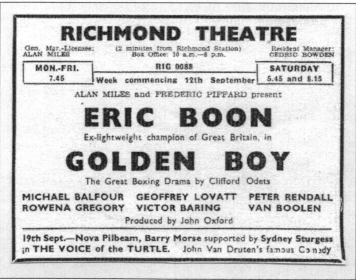

commencing on 12 September 1949.

In an interview with Bill Borne, who wrote a regular column 'My Friends the Stars', in the *London Evening News*, Eric said he was determined to pursue a career in acting. After completing his engagement at Richmond he hoped to go to a repertory company and learn how to master the techniques of the new art. Bad luck, however, struck again and he was unable to play his role due to the fact that he was suddenly taken ill with pleurisy and admitted to hospital the day before the show opened.

Boon never did join a repertory company, but on 21 October 1950, married his new girlfriend, Corrine Cooper, a twenty-four-years-old scenic designer, at West End Congregational Chapel, Lord Street, Southport. Although Corrine lived with her parents at 9 Lynton Road, Birkdale, much of her work was centred around theatreland in London's west end. She and Eric had met two years earlier at a party hosted by a close friend of his, Monty Levy, to celebrate the birth of his son. He became the former champion's best man.

In the months before the wedding Boon took lodgings at 31 Lynton Road to be near to Corrine, but after they were married they rented a flat at 132 King Henry's Road, Swiss Cottage, in north west London. They often visited Chatteris where, using his father's workshop and tools, Eric made wood carvings and stage scenery which Corrine painted and sold to help pay their bills.

With scarcely any money to his name Boon drifted from one job to another with little or no security. Nothing lasted for long and despite having married Corrine he became something of a lost soul. During the early 1950's he often turned up at Bill Klein's gym situated in a Fitzroy Street basement off Tottenham Court Road to wile away the hours. He was first taken there by Jack Solomons just before the war and in later years it became something of a bolthole for him. Down on his luck, Eric could be seen warming himself beside a fire and drinking a mug of tea as he watched young fighters being put through their paces. Shabbily dressed and with a cap pulled over his head he was living on memories as he savoured the gym atmosphere. "I had plenty of regrets," he once remarked, and often thought back to what might have been.

Evidence of Boon's plight was the fact that on a Friday night during the spring of 1952 he was paid £2 for lasting six rounds on Charlie Woods boxing booth staged at a fair at Strood near Rochester in Kent. He had been in the crowd when the Master of Ceremonies called for challengers to face booth fighter, twenty-one-years-old black boxer, Laurie Davis. Eric put up his hand and thrust his way forward making no attempt to conceal his identity. Men, women, and schoolchildren jostled around the wooden platform and watched intently as he battled hard and lasted the distance.

"We were very surprised to see Eric," remarked Woods afterwards, "but our pros are there to take on all-comers."

Boon's attitude was just as realistic when approached by an interested newspaper reporter. "I needed the money," he remarked bluntly. "I heard about this fairground booth and decided to cash in."

Nursing a bruised right hand he gratefully collected his money and before setting off for home signed dozens of autographs for delighted youngsters.

On another occasion the same year, he was seen taking on all-comers at a booth pitched on Woolwich Common in south London. Chatteris man, John Salisbury who, as a schoolboy, was often taken for rides in Eric's sports car, was posted to Woolwich Barracks prior to a period of military service overseas. The evening before embarking he and a group of mates went to the fair and John couldn't believe his eyes when he saw Boon in action.

One project which did earn Eric some much needed cash was a small illustrated instruction book entitled *'How to Box.'* Assisted in the writing of it by his good friend and author, Terry Leigh-Lye, it contained none of the bitterness he released in the Sunday newspaper articles a few years earlier. Some of his remarks had caused resentment among Chatteris people who, at times when he returned home, turned their backs on him. Although he told the stories for a price, their reaction annoyed him. "A few weeks ago all these people would have cleaned my boots for me," he told a friend.

A measure of Boon's continued popularity, however, was realised by the number of good-luck messages he received as his book neared publication. They came from all quarters, particularly the world of boxing and entertainment. Terry Sandford, joint author of the popular BBC serial 'Knockout' wrote:

> Eric Boon was one of the great personalities in the fight game. His name produces tremendous memories in the mind of every boxing fan – memories that are the real nostalgia of the greatest of all sport. To that compact exponent of the dynamite and the friendliness, which are the basic stuff from which championships stem, I send my humble and enthusiastic wishes for future success, both to the book and to The Golden Boy himself.

Other good wishes came from Ernie Roderick, Nel Tarleton, Nat Seller, Peter Kane, Jack Solomons, author Louis Golding, and actor Bruce Seton who wrote: "May I wish you every possible success for your book? It seems a long step from that dangerous bet I once made doesn't it?"

Although the book was generally instructional, Eric made a number of references to his career. In respect of his second fight with Boyo Rees he said:

> *Apparently feelings were running high over the contest and as I walked to the ring a section of the crowd pelted me with orange peel. I said to Jack: "Let's get out of this place as*

quickly as possible" - a sentiment with which he heartily agreed. However, because I knew Boyo was a great fighter I anticipated an evening of hard work.

Boon claimed that he frequently met boxers who kept up a running fire of chatter during the course of the contest with the obvious intention of either distracting him or making him lose his temper. He insisted that he seldom spoke to an opponent during the course of a contest unless it was to apologise for an accidental infringement. He did, however, add that he occasionally allowed himself the luxury of repartee:

In my first championship fight with Dave Crowley I caught him with a hard blow to the jaw which I thought had hurt him. I don't know whether Dave was trying to trick me, but he said: "I thought you could punch Boon." A moment later I did undoubtedly shake him and could not resist saying: "I hope that convinced you."

Eric also made references to his battles with Jimmy Walsh, Dave Crowley and Arthur Danahar, highlighting their respective skills and how he dealt with them. It was clear from the tone of his script that he had huge respect for all three of them:

Boxing men like these was an education in itself and I cannot help thinking that it is a great pity that such masters of yesteryear are not given lucrative positions teaching youngsters the fast fading act of boxing.

When talking about Crowley he often described him as "my old friend." In respect of Danahar he said:

I would like to say here and now, in tribute to Arthur, that I don't believe any of the former great champions could have boxed better than he did in the first eight rounds of our historic contest. As I said to him afterwards, it was a shame there had to be a loser.

The book was eventually published in 1953 by which time Eric and Corrine had emigrated to Australia. Although they were happy as a couple, he had become restless and was constantly thinking that a move abroad could be the start of a new life. Although it hadn't worked out for him in South Africa, he remained optimistic. It wasn't long before news of his plans reached the ears of boxing promoters in Australia. Boon was still a big name and before leaving England in June 1952 he had reached agreement to fight George

Barnes at Melbourne on 8 August with the possibility of other contests to follow.

Although his sole motive for fighting again was money, Eric knew he would have to work extremely hard to get himself into condition. He had not been in the ring since meeting Fernando Jannilli in March 1949 and openly admitted he did very little serious training for that fight. Shortly after arriving in Melbourne he therefore commenced preparations at Alexandre's gym.

One of the first people he met there was British comedian, Tommy Trinder, who he had known since they starred together in the film 'Champagne Charlie' in 1944. Tommy was getting himself in shape for a Command Performance in Melbourne on 2 August. "Show business is tough," he remarked as they posed together for photographs which would appear in the Australian papers.

George Barnes, who was eight years younger than Boon, was a bright prospect and described as being the hardest puncher of his weight in Australia. Since turning professional in 1948 he had won 19 of 24 contests, his most recent being a 12-rounds point's victory over Wallace 'Bud' Smith of America. His meeting with Boon was tipped as being one of the most intriguing in Australia that year.

Despite his long absence from the ring, Eric showed good form during public workouts. During the actual fight, however, it was a different story. Although there were brisk opening exchanges, there was a clear difference between the two men. Barnes looked fresh and sharp whilst Boon, although showing glimpses of his former greatness, appeared jaded, sluggish and generally ring-rusty. When he was floored for a count of 'nine' during the opening round it became apparent that he would be no match for the hard slugging young Sydney fighter.

Only in round three did Eric really shake Barnes when he landed a good right cross followed by two solid left hooks. Apart from that the Australian was in total command, mixing up his attacks with hooks and accurate jabs to keep the former British champion at bay. He won rounds four and five by wide margins.

Although Boon started the sixth well he was soon on the floor when Barnes cleverly fainted with his left and slammed a right cross to the side of the head. He climbed to his feet at 'nine' and dropped into a clinch, but the Aussie pushed him off and ripped a left hook deep into the stomach. Eric gasped as he fell backwards through the ropes. On hauling himself back into the ring he was immediately knocked down by a heavy right hook. It was a sorry sight to see him being humiliated in this way and a relief when referee, Terry Riley, quickly stepped in and called a halt.

Afterwards Boon claimed that he couldn't get going. Weighing only 9st 13, it was the lightest he had been since meeting Ronnie James back in 1944, but just didn't have the strength or fire of his youthful opponent. Eric Boon was a big name on Barnes' record and the victory clinched his claim for an Australian title fight with reigning champion, Frank Flannery.

Boon's poor showing against Barnes made no difference to the Australian promoters who were keen to put him in against young prospects. No sooner was the Barnes fight over than he was matched with novice, Pran Mikus, formerly from Lithuania, at Melbourne Stadium on 5 September. Although Eric was content to take the fights purely for money he was now in the trial-horse status. It was an identical situation to when he was exploited in America a few years earlier.

During the early rounds he bewildered Mikus with brilliant boxing, but eventually made the mistake of standing toe-to-toe with his tough young opponent. His first serious mistake came in round five when he landed a solid right to the jaw then rushed in with a two-fisted body attack. This suited Mikus who had been patiently waiting for an opening and soon had Boon hanging on grimly. At the bell he was bleeding heavily from a deep cut over his left eye.

Although Eric rallied in the sixth a hard right to the head sent him reeling across the ring. The Lithuanian punished him severely with good uppercuts and the leg-weary Englishman was unable to move away from danger. Typically, Boon showed great courage by throwing punches back and, try as he did, Mikus was unable to put him on the floor.

The end came at the end of the seventh when Boon, who had been fighting purely on instinct, staggered to his corner. His trainer promptly waved the towel at referee, Terry Riley, who after a brief conversation with Eric, accepted his retirement. Although he had been beaten by another young prospect he had given a spirited display and was cheered all the way to his dressing room by the crowd of over 8,000.

Another of Australia's bright young hopes was twenty-years-old Pat Ford from Orange, New South Wales, who had won nine of his 10 professional contests, eight by knockout. His handlers saw Boon as the perfect man to test his true potential and they were matched over 12 rounds at Brisbane Stadium on 31 October.

Boon once again impressed in training during the period leading up to the fight especially when sparring State featherweight champion, Carl Douglas. Sadly it was a false hope because when he faced Ford he suffered his third consecutive stoppage defeat since arriving down under.

Just as he did against Mikus he started well, but as soon as Ford upped the pace and put on the pressure Eric was a mere shadow of years gone by. The good life had caught up with him and the late nights, women and champagne had taken their toll.

Ford easily took the opening round by flicking out an accurate left jab to Boon's face. There were some fierce exchanges in the second during which Ford took a count of 'eight' from a hard right to the chin. On rising he attacked viciously, cutting loose with two-fisted barrages to the head which had Boon bewildered and defenceless.

Round three started sensationally when Boon let rip and sent Ford spinning across the ring from a well-timed right cross. A few seconds later the Aussie was on the floor, but jumped up without a count to knock Boon to his knees. He was still there as the bell ended the round with the count at 'five'.

Ford went straight into the attack at the start of the fourth and a savage two-fisted combination forced Eric back on his heels. The Australian followed up and a huge right uppercut lifted Boon off his feet and crashing into the ropes. As he slid slowly to the floor and in obvious trouble referee, Pat Hill, stepped in and called a halt.

The fight against Ford was Eric's last as a professional. The only man he had beaten in his last 12 contests was Omar Koudri. In reality he should never have returned to the ring. Unfortunately, it was a classic case of a desperate man taking desperate measures. He was broke and fighting was the only trade he knew.

At 9st 11 Boon had a weight advantage of three pounds over Pat Ford which was two pounds lighter than when he faced George Barnes almost three months earlier. Whilst the indications were that he had trained hard, his punch resistance had gone.

Barnes and Ford were great prospects who went on to build successful ring careers. George became British Empire welterweight champion in 1954 and held the title three times until losing it to Brian Curvis in 1960. Ford twice held the Empire lightweight title, the first time by beating Frank Johnson of Manchester within 12 months of stopping Boon.

Once he realised that his fighting days were finally over Boon got work in a steel factory and also did stints as a commentator for Australian radio. His main pastime was fishing and he often sent home photographs of his specimen catches. Eventually, however, he became homesick and in order to fund the return to England took a job working all hours distributing supplies to chemists' shops. He also sold items which Corrine had made.

Shortly after returning home, Eric and Corrine split up. He claimed it was because she was a domineering person who always wanted to be in charge. The remark, however, didn't ring true because it was well known that he was disorganised and liked doing his own thing. The likelihood was that she became as disillusioned as him.

Boon told a London newspaper reporter that he loathed Australia and got fed up with constantly being called a 'pom.' "The Aussies are so unpleasantly anti-British," he remarked.

His main problem was that he could never settle anywhere for long and be successful. It was the same in South Africa, and even when he lived in London he moved house several times, but usually ended up returning to his roots at Chatteris.

27

TWISTS AND TURNS

Since leaving school boxing had occupied most of Eric's life. Once it was finally over he had no other skills or trade to fall back on and as a consequence he was often broke. Over the next seven or eight years he drifted from one job to another, but with no real vision. Although he was full of good ideas nothing seemed to reach a conclusion due to the fact that his concentration level was low, a problem attributed to his accident back in 1941.

Despite his bitter fallout with the boxing authorities, he made one last ditch attempt to return to the ring in 1958 at the age of thirty-nine. Fighting was all he knew and announcing his decision in a Sunday newspaper he said: "I shall be champion again in two years."

Eric based his confidence on a course of treatment he underwent before leaving Australia. It involved monkey gland injections to rejuvenate his body. He continued the treatment on returning to England and, according to a prominent doctor at Paddington Nerve Clinic, it would "make him a young man again." The Board of Control, however, were unimpressed and refused his application to be re-licensed. Eric had too much history and before retiring had suffered a series of bad defeats. If he was allowed to fight again he was a disaster waiting to happen.

Boon, however, disagreed with the decision and in his biography notes wrote:

> *I started training again and in two months was as fit as I had ever been in my life. I applied for my licence to box again, but was turned down by the Board. I wrote asking for a chance to state my case personally at an interview, but again I was refused this opportunity. I wrote again and once more it was turned down.*

> *Finally, I went to the secretary of the Board and asked him why. He said it was because I had written that crooked fights had taken place in England and had made remarks injurious to those in control of boxing. I said that I had not written the story myself and that the whole thing had been a distortion, but even so both he and other members of the council had been known to be connected with fixed fights. He shrugged his shoulders and said: "But they don't advertise it."*

> *I went to see a Member of Parliament and put my case forward. The advice was that I should see the secretary of the*

343

Professional Boxers Association and ask them to fight my case. I saw the secretary, but I have so far received no practical help.

Part of what Boon wrote was a variation of remarks made earlier in a previous page of the notes. The contents, however, showed that he remained very bitter and at the time clearly wanted to expose what he saw as injustices within boxing.

Despite his attitude towards the controlling body, Eric was far from forgotten in the sport. He received a rousing reception when introduced from the ring at Harringay on 28 October 1958 at what was the final promotion there. It was appropriate that during the photo-call he stood next to Jack Solomons with Arthur Danahar immediately behind them. Other former opponents Dave Crowley, Ernie Roderick and Harry Mizler were also present.

The great arena was to be turned into a food warehouse and because of the many fine promotions staged there the *Daily Mirror* ran a competition inviting readers to nominate the best fight. Boon against Danahar in 1939 was the overwhelming favourite.

Aside from boxing the film industry was the only other thing that really excited Eric. He had always wanted to get involved in acting and before going to Australia played the part of a boxer in the film 'The Gambler and the Lady' which was filmed at Bray Studios. He got to know a number of directors and producers, and through them he was eventually invited to work as a stuntman. The challenges appealed to him and again he risked his health by jumping off bridges and falling backwards down stairs. "Sometimes I think a slate must have been loosened when I banged my head all those years ago," he once remarked. "It's a miracle that I've come through to good times."

People in the film industry loved Eric's warm inoffensive personality and nobody objected as he often spent hours just sitting at the side of sets during filming. Because it was common knowledge that he had fallen on hard times some people had a degree of sympathy for him, and having had experience of acting small parts eventually came his way.

In 1957 he appeared in 'Santa For Christmas' and three years later played 'Shorty' in 'Carry on Constable.' His good friend Freddie Mills featured as a jewel thief. In 1961 he was a young man in 'Carry on Regardless.' Both were filmed at Pinewood Studios at Iver Heath and featured a number of leading stars including Sid James, Kenneth Williams, Kenneth Connor and Charles Hawtry.

Between rehearsals and filming Eric had short periods of employment as a tube inspector, labourer, selling sports equipment, working for a public relations company and driving for a business distributing equipment to schools. Nothing was permanent, however, and the jobs were all intermingled with periods of unemployment. He also helped coach youngsters at an amateur boxing club in London, but nothing ever lasted for long.

Although he lived mainly in London throughout that period, he frequently returned to Chatteris to see his parents who still lived at Burnsfield Street. Whenever he was there he visited Fred Green and Arthur Binder and spent Saturday afternoons watching Chatteris Town football club matches.

After splitting from Corrine, Boon had a succession of girlfriends, one of whom was Dee Glavey, a former nurse he met at the Temperance Hospital in London when he had an appendix operation. Although he was working at the time he attempted to branch out into the world of modelling by promoting Dee who was an extremely attractive young lady. Like most things Eric did, the venture created great media interest, but again it was not a success.

Boon's relationship with Dee lasted for about two years during which time they spent a short holiday in Jersey. They stayed at Oaklands Lodge, Trinity Hill, on the northeast side of the island and were accompanied by their mothers. Whilst there Eric contacted officials of a local amateur boxing club and expressed interest in taking a team of youngsters from London to the island on a future date to raise money for charity.

In an interview with the *Jersey Evening Post,* he was very enthusiastic about a new type of punchball he had designed and a new air-filled glove he was experimenting with. He claimed that the punchball, which he hoped would be on the market by the end of the year, could be detached from its stand and screwed onto a wall. He hoped that the new glove would help eliminate injuries and even knockouts. "I feel this glove will help a lot in the improvement of skill in the sport and will be a good thing, particularly for the amateurs," Eric remarked enthusiastically.

Convinced there would be great interest in his invention, Boon formed a sports outfitting business in the hope of making big money. He also called at a number of Embassies in London to enquire about trading possibilities abroad. Having heard that there were good pickings to be made from careful use of international commercial information, he asked about other matters which he might be able to help them with. "Now it so happens that when I called at the Israeli Embassy in Kensington Palace Gardens about the boxing gloves, they mentioned they were on the lookout for general motor spares," he later revealed, "and by chance I had heard where that very commodity just might be obtained in large quantities."

Although nothing came of it, what did emerge from Eric's periodical visits was the chance to do business of a very different kind. Because of permanent hostility between Israel and neighbouring Arab countries, information about military secrets could be of great value to both sides. He was led to believe that handsome payments might be forthcoming for it so, being badly in need of money, he found himself drawn into a world far removed from boxing.

All was revealed one day at a lonely Sussex chicken farm where Boon was helping a friend. He was confronted by two reporters from a Sunday newspaper with facts they had discovered while investigating the activities of foreign powers in London. Eric subsequently admitted that what he became involved in began as a result of his unsuccessful efforts to find foreign markets for his new boxing glove idea. "During one of my trips to Kensington Palace Gardens, an Israeli official asked me if I could find out who in Britain was supplying arms to Arab countries," he remarked. "I think I had won their confidence because even though I am not Jewish myself, I can speak Yiddish."

Boon believed it would be possible for him to gather the kind of information the Israelis sought, the rewards for which would set him up for life. "I was promised ten per cent of the value of any arms which were seized by the Israelis as a result of information I supplied," he continued. "So, I knew that if I pulled it off it would not only save thousands of lives, but also help me with any future dealings with them."

Two weeks later Eric told the reporters he was able to provide his Israeli contact with details of large consignments of arms destined officially for Jordan. He even supplied names of the ships on which the weapons and ammunition were being carried together with dates and times of sailings.

Israeli intelligence agencies checked his information and in doing so discovered something that even Boon didn't know. Some guns and ammunition, supposedly bound for Jordan, were in fact to go to the Algerian rebels for use against the French. "It was arranged that my Israeli contact and I should meet Colonel Andrew Gille who was in the military attaché at the French Embassy in London," said Boon. "At a meeting in the Israeli Embassy I was told that my information had been proved absolutely correct. Colonel Gille thanked me and told me the discovery of the guns bound for Algeria would help shorten the war there and I'd be saving lives."

"He also spoke of a commission of ten percent of the value of any seized arms being paid for such information," continued Eric. "A week later I learned from my own sources that ships bound for Algeria had been boarded in French ports or French territorial waters and their cargos of arms amounting to four and a half million pounds confiscated, but when I went to my Israeli contact and asked about the commission, which should have been about half a million pounds, he said I would have to take the matter up with the French."

When he raised the matter at the French Embassy, Boon got another knock-back because he was told that the French had received their information from the Israelis. "As I had not informed them direct I had no claims to the reward," he revealed bitterly. "In the end I didn't get a penny out of it. All I learned was that the Algerian war ended a short time later."

It was an incredible story full of intrigue, but despite their probing the reporters failed to get any official confirmation from the Embassies concerned that Boon had supplied the relevant information. The cloak of official secrecy was too efficient.

Although Colonel Andrew Gille had since been transferred to Vienna they were able to establish beyond doubt that Eric was a well known and welcome caller at Israeli and Arab Embassies. At the Egyptian Embassy at Mount Street for instance when the reporters accompanied him there he was recognised immediately and ushered into the private offices of the naval attaché.

Despite Boon's hopes of substantial financial reward there was an air of inevitability about the eventual outcome. Not only did he have half a million pounds dangled in front of him and then snatched away, his punchball and boxing glove projects failed to succeed. He told the reporters that having settled back in the East Anglian countryside he wanted to take up farming. Sadly, with little or no funds it was another fanciful idea that never happened.

*   *   *

During the early 1960's rumours circulated around Chatteris that Boon had got himself involved with some London gangsters and there had been a falling out. It was also claimed that he had lent money to the son of a well-known politician. When he failed to pay it back, Eric administered his own form of justice which upset the wrong people.

Although he never publically disclosed what his problems were, this was at a time when organized gangsters in the capital often recruited former boxers to add muscle to their cause. Boon, however, was never a villain. Deep down he was still a naïve and gullible country boy who, whilst loving the buzz and glamour of the bright lights, was far from streetwise as regards dubious business dealings. In reality he was out of his territory.

His movements, however, tended to add weight to all the rumour and speculation. Over a lengthy period he was backwards and forwards between London and Chatteris in all probability to avoid those he had fallen foul of. His father, by this time, had another blacksmith's forge at West Street and Eric often hid there in a caravan for several days at a time. He always left his car several streets away and told relatives not to let anyone know where he was. Locals who saw him noticed that he was edgy and always on the move.

During this period Boon had a flat at Fairfax Road in the Hampstead district of north-west London. In 1963 he took occasional work as a debt collector for Commercial Purchase Limited, a company based at Hanover Square in London's west end. Although controversial, it was something he was comfortable about and with the passing of time much of the tension in his life seemed to evaporate. On occasions when he visited Chatteris he was seen to be more relaxed. There was a more carefree air about him and he often spent time shoeing horses and doing repair work at his father's forge.

Later that year he took a Ministry of Labour rehabilitation course in carpentry and the following year traded on his own account from his father's yard. Like most of his good ideas and intended projects, however, it lasted less than two years and he moved on to something else in what was the beginning of another difficult phase in his life.

Whilst he was still with Corrine one of his schemes was to make garden gnomes from plywood which she would paint. His intention was to sell them to Harrods and other major stores, but despite making a large quantity he gave up the idea and left them in his father's shed.

Another of his plans was to design and build caravans with foldaway tents, but it never got off the ground. Then one day he turned up at his father's yard with an old 45-seater bus which he planned to turn into living accommodation. After spending a few weeks stripping it out he got fed up and left it. The bus eventually disappeared.

Eric loved dogs and one day he arrived in Chatteris with a great dane. On another occasion he arrived with an Alsatian named 'Honey' which he left with his father before disappearing again.

After buying an old typewriter he started writing his autobiography. Like his attempts to write a play, it soon fizzled out.

*   *   *

Despite Boon's attraction for the bright lights of London and everything that went with them, his heart always remained in Chatteris. By the mid-1960's he had moved back there and, with time on his hands, he was persuaded by Arthur Binder, to help out at the local amateur boxing club.

His first job was to help Arthur and his assistant trainer, Hugh Daisley, get boys fit for the club's first open show at The Palace on 23 October 1964. His involvement generated tremendous interest and on training nights the gym was alive. There was a renewed enthusiasm at all levels and boys came from miles around to train at 'Eric Boon's Club' which already had established boxers in Matty Payne, Tony Brown and Bernie Wing.

The one thing that disappointed Boon was the shortage of equipment so he organised a fund-raising event. He even drew the winning ticket which he promptly auctioned and gave the proceeds to the club. It was a typical Boon gesture.

On the night of the club's first show of the season he was there in a dual role of cornerman and guest of honour. He got the boys ready, advised and encouraged them during their fights and later, smartly attired in evening dress, presented the prizes. His presence ensured that the venue was packed.

*   *   *

During the summer of 1966, Boon's life took another incredible twist, this time very much for the better. It arose when his ex-wife Wendy visited his mother at Chatteris one afternoon to invite her to their daughter Erica's wedding. She had been there about half an hour when the door suddenly burst open and in walked Eric. It was a complete shock to both of them because they hadn't seen one another since Wendy walked out in 1948 because Eric insisted on going through with his fight against Omar Koudri.

Wendy began to shake like a leaf, but as soon as his mother left the room to make a pot of tea Eric eased the tension. "Are you married?" he asked warmly.

"No, are you?" she responded.

When he said he wasn't they fell into a spontaneous hug and couldn't stop laughing. Despite having reached the age of forty-six, Boon had lost none of his romantic charm. That evening he took

Wendy to one of their old haunts, a plush restaurant by a river in the heart of the Cambridgeshire countryside. Without even offering her the menu, he ordered their favourite meal of duck with oranges and green peas. "I haven't forgotten," he remarked with a loving smile as he held her hand. "How could I?"

When the waiter said that duck wasn't on the menu, Eric explained that it was a very special occasion and asked if anything could be done to avoid disappointing a very special lady. His charm and politeness worked, but when the main course took a long time to arrive he convinced Wendy that the staff had gone to the river to catch a live duck.

They sat at their table chatting until well after the other diners had left and barely stopped for breath. It was a tremendous relief for them both as all the memories they shared, good and bad, came flooding back. They talked about Erica's childhood, the plans for her wedding and what they had been doing during the years they were apart. They quickly realised they were still in love with each other and acknowledged what fools they had been.

The previous year both had watched a television programme 'All Our Yesterdays' which featured their wedding in 1940. They knew then that they still loved each other. Because Eric was no longer boxing Wendy was certain that there was nothing to cloud their future happiness. So when he asked her to marry him again she readily accepted because it seemed the most natural thing to do. Once the news leaked out, the couple were hounded by the press. "The first time we were married we were too young, little more than teenagers," Boon told a *Sunday Express* reporter on 3 September, "but now we are older and a little wiser, we are both sure that this time it will be for keeps."

Eric and Wendy remarried at March Registry Office on the morning of Saturday, 1 October 1966. Word had got around, but when they arrived there was no parking space at the front of the office so they had to walk a short distance along Broad Street. Whispers of "Here he comes" soon had the weekend shoppers at a standstill.

At first only a dozen or so gathered at the small entrance to the registry office, but by the time the short ceremony was over the crowd had swelled to several hundred. The nearby War Memorial steps acted as a fine grandstand. Boon was still fondly remembered for his great fights and how he put the region on the sporting map. The crowd cheered him and his bride warmly and for a brief moment he was in the spotlight again.

The moving, and somewhat unique situation, appealed to writers from social, weekend and women's magazines because it was packed with romance and intrigue. The couple received hundreds of letters from well-wishers, some in the same position as themselves, advising them what to expect. When asked by one journalist the inevitable question about why their first marriage dissolved, Wendy replied: "It never really had a chance. We were apart so often what with Eric's boxing, my career and then him being in the RAF."

She explained how the subsequent worry and strain of the boxing eventually proved too much. "Also, he was very handsome and had a great attraction for women," she added, "so I finally divorced him."

After years of changing jobs Eric was unemployed and broke. He was back living with his parents at Chatteris, but said he intended starting a printing business at St Ives. "I hope to do well for Wendy's sake because I'm a lucky man to be given this second chance," he remarked. "There is so much lost time to be made up because I have never forgotten her."

Despite getting good media coverage Boon's fanciful business plans again failed to materialise. After living at St Ives for a short time he and Wendy moved into a council flat in Corby town centre and he got a job at a local steel mill. Yet his failures did nothing to deter reporters because he was a man about whom stories could always be written. He had been at the top of his chosen profession, travelled the world, mixed with society folk, particularly women, and appeared in films before crashing back to a working class existence.

There was an occasion in late 1966 whilst sitting on a packing case, dressed in an old sweater and rolling his own cigarette at their sparsely furnished flat that he poured his heart out to a female journalist. "You've got to swallow your pride – something I've only just learned to do," he remarked. "There are old hurts to forgive and forget as well as the odd pangs of bitterness and reproach."

"I suppose some of my old fans might think it's a bit of a comedown," he continued, "but believe me if Wendy and I had this sort of emotional security when we were first married I don't think we would have split up."

During their first marriage they had no permanent home for any length of time, but in Eric's mind everything was different this time around. He was totally relaxed as he spoke of his contentment. He said that since moving to Corby it was the first time in his life that he knew where he was going to be each day, how much money he was going to take home each week and who his real friends were.

"That would have been too tame for the old Boon," he admitted with a smile, "but I don't need the crowds any more. I just need

Wendy and enough in my pocket to pay the rent and eat reasonably well. We'll make it this time, Eric Boon, steelworker and Wendy Boon, Corby housewife."

*   *   *

Although it appeared that Boon had turned a corner in his private life, his financial problems came to the fore again when he appeared at Northampton Bankruptcy Court on 10 November 1967. Proceedings had been commenced against him by the creditor of a business with which he had been associated.

Through his London contacts, particularly those in the East End, he became involved with people operating what transpired to be dubious businesses. Whilst he liked the money he was paid he had no idea where it really came from. It was the age-old story of him falling under the influence of undesirable hangers-on.

As part of the court proceedings Boon submitted a statement of affairs showing his assets to be £3 against liabilities of £537. In his public examination he said that he had nothing left of the money he earned from boxing. It all went on managerial and other expenses. He had lent money to friends and acquaintances, and between £2,000 and £3,000 was still owing to him, but there was no chance of getting it back.

In answer to Mr Ronald Savage for the Official Receiver, Eric said his discharge from the RAF was due to loss of memory. He said that he was still solvent when he returned from Australia and later had an interest in three companies, but had since ceased to be associated with them.

During 1966 he took employment in the credit drapery trade with an understanding that he would eventually become a partner in the business. Without his knowledge or consent, headed notepaper was subsequently printed bearing his name as the sole proprietor. Consequently, a creditor of the business obtained a judgement against him and issued a bankruptcy notice.

Boon told the court that a Police investigation had been conducted into the business and he was expected to be called as a witness during a forthcoming trial. At that point the Registrar adjourned the hearing until 1 December. His public examination eventually continued on 10 May 1968 after having been adjourned three times pending his attendance at the Central Criminal Court as a witness in the trial of three men on charges arising from the credit drapery business with which Eric became involved.

Questioned by Mr Savage, Boon explained that he was only ever an employee of the business for a short period during 1966.

352

Although his name was used on the headed notepaper, he was never a partner. His former employers used him as a tool and made use of his name.

He explained that he gave evidence for the prosecution and during the trial a number of letters were produced on which his signature had been forged. These gave guarantees for payment for goods and as a result claims totalling £7,653 had been made against him. He insisted that they were all debts of the business.

Eric told the court that judgement had been made against him in proceedings which he had not defended. He agreed when Mr Savage remarked: "You were entirely the innocent party."

Continuing his examination, Boon admitted areas of failure on his behalf, in particular lack of business experience and entering into a business arrangement without seeking professional advice. "My main trouble has been loss of memory since I cracked my skull," he added referring to his accident whilst in the RAF.

Mr Savage suggested that his boxing career may have contributed to the loss of memory which impaired his ability to manage his affairs.

*　　　*　　　*

Although Eric and Wendy claimed to be happy at Corby, they didn't really settle. Boon gave up his job and within a year they moved into a small house at 36 Clare Street, Chatteris. It was in a poor state of repair, but with plenty of time on his hands Eric renovated it.

After a short while they moved again, this time to Wicken where they rented a 400-years-old cottage at 4 North Street which he also renovated. One of his neighbours was former sparring partner Walter Redit, who was the local blacksmith. Boon became more settled there and set up a carpentry shop so that he could use the tools he had acquired over the years. Woodwork, which he learned at school, had always been one of his few hobbies. His comforts at Wicken were two poodles and a rocking chair.

Eric's only connection with boxing was helping train youngsters and attending charity events. Once re-established in Cambridgeshire he was frequently invited to be guest of honour at amateur dinner shows. He was particularly popular at Peterborough where the Wirrina Amateur Boxing Club invited him to most of their events. Together with international cricketer, Colin Milburn, he was a judge at a local newspaper 'Top Girl' contest. He also opened a number of businesses in the area at a time when the 'do-it-yourself' craze was catching on fast.

In February 1969, Eric was a guest at the Jersey Dinner Club amateur boxing show at the Hotel de France. His visit attracted tremendous interest surpassing even that afforded to Brian Clough who was a guest speaker on the island two nights earlier. Photographers were at the airport to greet him and a picture of him parrying a punch from his wife Wendy as they stepped from the plane, appeared on the front page of the *Jersey Evening Post* the same day.

They spent four days on the island during which time Eric appeared on local television and met up with old friends at the local amateur boxing club. During sightseeing trips he was constantly asked for autographs. At the boxing dinner he received a rapturous welcome and speaking from the ring expressed his pleasure at being back in Jersey again. He wished the local club continued success and then sat ringside to watch a match in which Jersey ABA beat a Dorset select team by six bouts to two. He presented trophies to the contestants at the end of every contest and chatted to each one warmly.

Back on the mainland a BBC television programme, 'Great Moments in Sport' introduced by Harry Carpenter, featured the fight between Boon and Arthur Danahar. Anglia television also featured him in a programme 'Generations Apart.'

In 1971 Eric became an area sales representative for C.D. Monninger Limited, a large national company which marketed the largest range of wood cutting tools in Europe. It came about when he saw an advertisement in a local newspaper. In view of his interest in carpentry he went for an interview at the company offices in London. His initiative was rewarded and he was given the job the same day.

Initially, his area covered East Anglia, but his warm personality and communication skills with clients ensured that his first year in the job was a huge success. The company recognised this and duly rewarded him by giving him a much larger area to cover.

The local press loved a success story and with Eric being long overdue one he became headline news again. "I did the right thing for once when I got this job," he told a reporter from the Cambridgeshire Times. "It's like a whole new life."

28

CHARITY

Having finally settled into a job he really enjoyed Boon became a much more relaxed individual. The days of fast living were well behind him so to occupy his mind he put a lot of time and thought into working for good causes and helping others.

His kindness was never more apparent than in early 1973 when he heard that his former opponent, Dave Crowley, was going blind in one eye at the age of 63. It affected Eric so much that, without considering the possible implications, he publically offered to donate of his own eyes to his good friend. "When I was driving home from a meeting to arrange a charity boxing tournament for Dave, I couldn't help thinking about him," he told a *Daily Express* reporter. "So I closed one eye myself and tried to imagine what it was like and decided I must try and do something."

"Now I must see doctors to find out whether my offer can be taken up," he continued. "Dave and I were the best of friends before and after our fights and have been ever since."

Crowley was stunned when he heard the news. "I cannot believe it," he remarked. "It is a terrific sacrifice."

Eric discussed his proposal with his wife who gave him wholehearted support. Although it wasn't possible for him to go through with the transplant operation his offer came from the heart and he continued his involvement in organising a charity event at the Hilton Hotel in London on Dave's behalf. He was heartbroken when his former opponent passed away the following year.

"Dave was what boxing was all about," he tearfully told the press when he heard the news. "We had two great fights, remained good friends and he was genuinely pleased when I did well. He came to a lot of my fights and I'll really miss him."

With charity very much in his mind, Boon agreed to climb into the ring one more time. On 14 October 1974 he faced Harry Lazar from Aldgate over three rounds at Seymour Hall at an event organised by Tottenham Jewish Home and Hospital Aid Society. It was advertised as 'A Grand Night of Boxing and Entertainment' and featured a number of former Jewish boxers and others mainly from London's east end. The response was tremendous and on the night the venue was packed. Harry Mizler squared off against Bobby Ramsey and there were also contributions from Nat Franks, Lew Lazar, Dave Keller, and George Merritt who was sixty at the time.

They were men of differing ages, shapes and sizes, but had all been popular performers in their day.

The organisers offered Eric £100 to appear at the event, but he said that if they paid him he would donate it to the charity. He was billed as 'The Greatest Lightweight Champion of Our Time.' It got the press interested in the event and Boon in particular. "The only training I'll do for this comeback is to run some old fight films through a few more times," he told Sydney Hulls of the *Daily Express.*

Eric said that one of the reasons why he agreed to take part was because he had received touching letters from fans who had followed him to fights in wheelchairs. "They never moan," he remarked, "and as I have been blessed with good health it's the least I can do for them."

When Boon arrived at Seymour Hall a telegram awaited him. It came from Harry Lazar's grandchildren and read: "If you take it easy with our granddad we will send you some sweets."

After the bout Eric was concerned about his performance. "Did you think I made a fool of myself?" he asked Peter Batt of *The Sun*. The reporter did not and told him so although Boon wasn't sure if he was just being polite.

"That was the first time I've had the gloves on in over twenty years," he remarked. "I thought I wouldn't know where to put my feet and thought I'd probably fall over."

He did none of those things, his positioning, footwork and ringcraft, which carried him through a ring career spanning 20 years, proved to be as instinctive as riding a bicycle. Once learned, never forgotten! At only half a stone above his normal fighting weight the old champion looked more than capable of landing a knockout blow if pressed. There was even a chilling conviction in his voice when he remarked: "You can lose your speed and timing, but you never lose your punch."

Before leaving Seymour Hall, Boon insisted that he didn't go into the ring trying to relive past glories. "I've had enough kicks as a boxer, actor and playboy to last me the rest of my life," he said with sincerity. "I was up there because I felt I was needed. I know only too well what the bad times are like."

As he spoke to reporters, Eric knew he had just climbed out of the ring for the very last time. There was no party in his honour, no back-slappers or hangers-on to pester him, just the cold night air, a car parked in a nearby side-street and a lonely three hour drive home. Some years later as he recalled that night he said: "I loved doing it and if my involvement helped just one person it was worth it."

The only downside to the event was that the British Boxing Board of Control withheld support on the grounds that it was not in the interests of boxing. In effect it was unlicensed, but this annoyed Boon. "Surely charity is in the interests of everyone," he remarked to Peter Batt. "I'll stand on my head for charity and I'll striptease as well if they ask me.

*　　*　　*

In December the previous year Eric began what was his most concerted effort for charity. Despite his disputes with the boxing authorities he never lost his love for the sport or respect for its participants. He kept in touch by attending official functions and reunions of old-time fighters and therefore decided that showing old fight films would be a good way of raising large amounts of money.

Although he was working full-time travelling all over the country for Monninger's, Eric was able to arrange film shows in conjunction with his business trips. Still being a highly respected sporting figure helped him build good relationships with customers, many of whom were boxing fans. They supported his charity proposals and generously donated raffle prizes whilst others sold him cine equipment at greatly reduced prices.

Despite his initial outlay being high, Eric built up what he believed was the largest collection of big fight films in the country. Many had been imported from America and featured highlights of contests involving such great stars as Joe Louis, Max Baer, Primo Carnera, Henry Armstrong, Sugar Ray Robinson, Muhammed Ali, Joe Frazier and George Foreman. British fighters included Freddie Mills, Peter Kane, Benny Lynch and Henry Cooper.

Whilst the collection was mainly boxing it also featured highlights from most other sports especially golf, racing, football, cricket and motor racing. All were on 16mm film in black and white or colour. During the shows they were projected on to a large screen with amplified sound.

The Eric Boon film shows were a resounding success and rapidly gathered momentum. Crowds of 700-800 regularly gathered at Rotary and Round Table events, and in Working Men's Clubs around the country. He often put on three or four shows a week and whenever he had a business appointment he tried to organise a show in the vicinity the same evening. Distance was no object and he often had to drive home through the night and then be back on the road early the next morning. He once remarked: "There are four

357

thousand working men's clubs listed and I am going to do film shows in as many as possible."

Apart from the satisfaction of raising money for the charities there were some pleasant reunions for Eric at his shows. At an event at the Baker Perkins Sports Club at Peterborough in March 1974, he met up with former professional boxer, Arthur Wright, who lived locally. Arthur had sparred with Boon at Ely in 1938 when he was training for his first fight with Dave Crowley, but they hadn't seen each other since.

Later the same year when he staged a show at the Boot & Shoe Club at Leicester, Eric met up with his old friend and opponent, Len Wickwar. It was 35 years since their great fight in the town. Wickwar, an incredible man who retired from the ring with a record of 336 victories and 42 draws from 462 contests, was a founder member of Leicester Ex-Boxers Association. He loved meeting up with Boon and also attended further film shows at Spinney Hill and Belgrave Working Men's Clubs both of which had close connections with boxing.

By mid-1974, Eric's shows had gained international recognition and he received invitations to travel abroad particularly to Army and RAF camps in Germany. An agent even suggested a tour of South Africa where he was still fondly remembered.

The travelling Boon did was incredible, but apart from organising his own shows in conjunction with his work commitments, he never refused an invitation to attend a charity event. The size and quality of the venues differed vastly, between small Working Men's Clubs to posh five star hotels.

In late January 1975 he was the principal guest of Guernsey Dinner Boxing Club at the Duke of Richmond Hotel, St Peter Port, Guernsey at an event in aid of charity. Following a match between Channel Island boxers and an English Southern Counties select team during which he presented trophies, Boon showed a sample of his films to an enthusiastic audience. He promised to return to the island at a later date and present a full evening in aid of charity.

A few weeks later he presented a film show to an audience of 800 at the West Centre Hotel in London on a Metropolitan Police "B" Division amateur boxing show. Three months earlier he had shown films to another sell-out Metropolitan Police boxing event. It was fitting that his 100th film show was staged at Chatteris Working Men's Club.

Boon's fund-raising efforts were unique and frequently reported in local newspapers. "The films prove a point," he told a reporter from the *Peterborough Evening Telegraph*. "Standards are higher in almost every other sport these days. Athlete's performances are better, but boxing is the one sport that appears to have gone backwards in skill and everything."

"There are three hours of entertainment here to prove it," he continued. "Ali is an exception, but many people believe Louis would have pulverised him."

At most of Eric's film shows audiences asked to see the 1939 fight between him and Arthur Danahar. It was without doubt one of the most popular in his collection, but in an interview with Simon Euan-Smith of *Boxing News*, Eric said: "I get embarrassed about showing that one because I call the show 'The Great Champions' so it's a bit of a liberty to put one of my own fights in there."

Yet he acknowledged that audiences always cheered and shouted while the film was being shown. "You would think they were watching it live," he remarked. "I always get good audience reaction."

Boon always went to great lengths to explain that he had absolutely no intention of making anything from his charity ventures. Although he had about £4,000 worth of equipment this was never a case of self-indulgence. All the money he collected through entry fees, raffles and donations went to charity, particularly the then Spastics Society (now Scope). It was a cause close to his heart and he even got a Northampton caravan company to sponsor him. Once he got established he planned to raise about £3,000 a year. Within three years, however, it was stated in the press that his donations had exceeded £12,000.

Eric did plenty of other charity work, not least when, in November 1979 at St Ives, he launched an appeal fund for heart research. A few years earlier, despite having developed arthritis, he had taken up golf and had lessons at Newmarket Links Club. There he met Duncan Presst, an eighteen-years-old assistant club professional who took him under his wing. Despite the difference in their ages the two became close friends.

Duncan was a sports-mad young man who at one stage wanted to take up boxing. Still loving the sport Boon took him for training sessions at Andy Smith's gym at St Ives, the workplace of European champions, Dave 'Boy' Green and Joe Bugner. When Eric practised his golf swings and putts on Ely Golf course, Duncan was often at his side offering advice and encouragement.

In October 1976, Boon suffered a mild heart attack and was detained at Newmarket General Hospital for two days. On being discharged he knew he needed to take things easy so he gave up work, played more golf and devoted most of his time to raising money for charity. Although he continued with his film shows he didn't travel so far afield as in previous years. There were always requests for him to visit venues throughout East Anglia and more often than not Duncan Presst accompanied him, but would never accept payment for his work.

They formed an effective partnership, but in August 1979 disaster struck when Duncan, still only twenty-one-years-old, was involved in a fatal car crash. He was a passenger in a friend's Avenger estate car which crashed into a wall at Ely, and despite an emergency operation, he failed to survive.

With great courage and compassion his parents consented to his organs being donated to transplant surgery. A few days later, following removal at the RAF Hospital at Ely, Duncan's heart was donated to Keith Castle, a gravely ill patient from Battersea, South London. The operation, which was carried out at Papworth Hospital, was a great success.

Although devastated by Duncan's death, Boon was quick to pay tribute to him when contacted by the press. "Duncan had the heart of a lion," he said with great sincerity. "He was full of guts and determination, and was never the sort of guy who would give in without a fight."

Eric, who by this time was living at Soham, had so much respect and feeling for Duncan that three months after his death he launched an appeal in his name for heart research. At an event staged at St Ives Recreation Centre on 14 November, he said: "I think the kid's name deserves to live forever. He has given life to another man."

Praising Duncan as an athlete, Boon said: "He had great potential – he was so fit he could have made a success of anything he attempted in sport. He was full of life, ideas and suggestions for charity work."

Boon was joined at the launch by Keith Castle who for many years would be Britain's longest surviving heart transplant patient. He had made a special journey from his daughter's home near Northampton to be there. In a short speech he said he would give all the support he could to Eric's cause.

"Naturally, it must be the closest thing to me," he remarked. "Without Duncan I would not be here. He must have been a marvellous chap judging from what people have told me about him."

Addressing the audience Boon asked that contributions be sent to his address at 16 Cornmills Road, Soham, and made payable to the Duncan Presst Memorial Fund. He then presented a cheque for £500 to Major Ray Stokes, East Anglia Organiser for the British Heart Foundation Appeal.

29

CONFESSIONS

Having returned to the tranquillity of the Fens, Eric was thoroughly contented with his life. The only pressures were the amount of driving he did in connection with his job and the long hours required to carry out his charity work which in effect had become a hobby and gave him great satisfaction. All of his love was directed at Wendy and their two poodles, but this quiet lifestyle was light years away from the days when he lived in London.

For as long as boxing has existed the participants have had tales to tell and invariably Sunday newspapers have turned them into absorbing reading. Boon was no exception because, being an extremely handsome young man with a muscular physique, he quickly gained the reputation of being a ladies man. Even in his teenage days at Chatteris he was very much sought after and dozens of girls clamoured for tickets the night he fought Jimmy Walsh. After he made the headlines as British lightweight champion at the age of eighteen they were after him in droves. Wherever he went he was propositioned.

Some years later, when he was almost penniless, Eric referred to his experiences in *The People* newspaper articles. Although careful not to disclose names he was happy to reveal some of his experiences and the pressures he put himself under:

If there's one lesson the fight game taught me it is that peaches and punches don't mix. Those dizzy, hero-worshipping dames, who begin fluttering their big blue eyes as soon as they get within hooking distance of any up-and-coming scrapper, are bad medicine.

I should know. They began chasing me as soon as I was in the money and never stopped until I was out of it. Showgirls, society heiresses and plain glamour struck bobby-soxers – they were all in the hunt and they nearly drove me nutty.

I can see it all now, and as I'm through with boxing I might as well tell the truth and the whole truth. I shall never be able to go into the ring again because the doctors won't let me. It means I've come down to earth almost as rapidly as I went up, and believe me there aren't many kids from the country who've packed into a short life as much as I have done.

Yes, there's no doubt I tried the peaches and punches mixture right enough. From the moment I hit the headlines I was dealing with both in a big way for the reason that while I could hand out the punches I couldn't somehow keep the girls at distance. They just crowded me in.

Not all of them were simply after the £1,000 purses I was picking up. There was, for instance, one Mayfair debutante who offered me a fortune to marry her. There was another wealthy girl who tried to throw herself under a taxi just because I wouldn't answer her telephone calls. And in New York I had at least three proposals that would have put me bang on Easy Street.

It was those wild, wild women who first hung that 'Glamour Boy Boon' on me. It was the girls who gave me the appetite for the bright lights and a taste for champagne, night clubs, smart suits, monogrammed silk shirts and glossy motor cars.

I was just a country bumpkin when I first moved up to town from Chatteris – a wide-eyed, innocent kid of sixteen who didn't know what it was all about. Before I was seventeen I was head-over-heels in love.

Eric then described his relationship with Ollie Franks and how they planned to become engaged the following year. Jack Solomons, however, saw their closeness as a huge threat to his young champion's career and earning potential. When Ollie had to return to America he intercepted her letter to Boon who thought she had ditched him:

Maybe he was right. Maybe I was too young for romance, but things didn't work out the way he figured. Instead of settling down I began to kick over the traces. It was the birth of 'Boon the Glamour Boy.'

Until then I had been quite content to draw a modest weekly allowance and let Jack Solomons bank my wages. Now I insisted on drawing all my money. I moved into a West End hotel, bought myself smart suits and a flashy white sports car, and began stepping out around the town. I went to nightclubs and bottle parties, acquired the taste for champagne and the smart sophisticated kind of girls that went with it. And then my troubles began!

At one time I had three girlfriends living in the same hotel as myself. They moved in one after the other to keep an eye on me and I had to lock my room door and sit behind it wondering which one would knock next.

Then there was the night I called on the girlfriend of a very well known personality in the fight game. Just as we were

362

settling down with a drink apiece in a cosy atmosphere of soft lights and sweet music from the radio, the telephone rang. It was her boyfriend calling from the hall to say he was on his way up. "Eric," said the girl, "he mustn't find you here."

"You're dead right," I said, "but where can I hide?"

There was only one stairway and we were bound to meet on it. There was no room under the divan and there wasn't another place in the flat big enough to hide me. Just then there was a knock on the door. "It's me honey," said the boyfriend.

I didn't wait to hear any more. I opened the window and stepped out on to the ledge.

"I'll get rid of him as quickly as I can, Eric darling," the girl whispered as she closed the window. Then the curtains were drawn and I was left crouching on the ledge less than two feet wide and five floors above the street.

It was two o'clock in the morning, but it was in the heart of the West End and any moment I expected someone to look up and see me. It wasn't so bad for the first half an hour, but after that it got colder and colder. I crouched there frozen stiff listening to the murmur of conversation and the chink of glasses from the other side of the window.

After a while there wasn't a sound from the room, but I didn't dare risk opening the window until I got the 'all clear' from the girl. At last, however, when dawn began to streak the sky, I decided I must make a run for it. As I stepped over the sill the room was quiet and in darkness, but I didn't hang around to see who was there. I made straight for the door and went down five flights of stairs in as many seconds. I didn't breathe easily until I was out in the street. Then I walked slowly home vowing that I was finished with dames for good.

Although Boon married Wendy in April 1940, things didn't work out as he planned because even then he couldn't shake off his female admirers. The fact that he had just got married made no difference whatsoever. One of the most persistent was a beautiful young Mayfair debutante who regularly telephoned him at least a dozen times a day. When he pointed out that he was married with responsibilities she just laughed. Then one day she told him she would be inheriting £21,000 in a few months time. "I'll settle every penny on you Eric if you will get a divorce and marry me," she told him. He refused and luckily for him his movements were then controlled by the Royal Air Force.

In those days Boon loved to look upon life through the bubbles in a champagne glass and everything that went with that kind of life style:

> *It was fun to escort lovely women to expensive clubs and restaurants. It was fun to see their eyes light up when I was introduced as 'Eric Boon, the British lightweight champion.' In those days I enjoyed every moment of the flattery and adulation that came my way. I got a kick out of being recognised everywhere I went. I enjoyed the heady wine of fame, but I didn't realise how dangerous it could be. The trouble was that I couldn't resist the lure of any big city's night life. Nor, let's face it, have I ever wanted to decline the smiling, unspoken invitation of a pair of bright eyes. Looking back, it seems to me that the boxer who starts tangling with the fair sex can kiss goodbye to his dreams of fame and fortune.*

Boon went on to illustrate the kind of embarrassing situation a successful young boxer can find himself in by becoming involved with the dizzier type of female hanger-on:

> *This happened while I was staying in one of London's swankiest hotels and for once I wasn't to blame for what happened to me there. For weeks I had been pestered by a certain girl. She was only in her teens and was very lovely, but I wasn't interested. Unfortunately, she wasn't the type to take 'no' for an answer so I spent more time ducking and side-stepping to avoid her than I did in a dozen fights.*

> *Then, one night after I got back to my room after doing a round of the clubs, there she was sitting up in my bed. She was wearing a wisp of a nightdress that covered her about as adequately as a cobweb, but she didn't bat an eye when I walked in. "Hello Eric," she said, "I thought you were never coming home."*

> *I was in a spot. It was nearly 3 am and there wasn't a hope of smuggling her out past the night porter without being seen. There was only one thing to do – I went out again to a club for the rest of the night.*

> *When I went back after breakfast my room was empty. I was just congratulating myself that I probably wouldn't hear any more from her after such a pointed rebuff when the telephone rang. It was the girl's mother in a raging fury. "My daughter says she spent the night in your room," she screamed. "You should be ashamed of yourself."*

The woman continued to rant and rave so I couldn't get a word in edgeways. She finally hung up with a lurid threat about what would happen to me when the girl's husband came home.

About a fortnight later I had a phone call from a friend saying: "Remember that girl who gate-crashed your room? Well her husband is in town and he's on his way round to your hotel."

"Why should I worry?" I asked, "I've got a clear conscience and if he starts anything I guess I can look after myself."

"Maybe," said my friend, "but he's got a gun and he swears he's going to kill you."

Just then there was a furious banging on my bedroom door. I dropped the phone and made a dive for the wardrobe. I pulled the door behind me and crouched there hardly daring to breathe. Luckily, it was only my trainer, 'Honey' Francis.

The next week was full of similar alarms. Whenever there was a knock on the door I hopped into the wardrobe. In fact, I seemed to spend most of my time hiding there. I never moved out of the hotel without a bodyguard of three, 'Honey' Francis, my brother-in-law, John Elliott, and a Greek pal of mine named Thimedias.

Still the jealous husband didn't show, but then one day we left the hotel in our usual formation with John and 'Honey' on either side of me and Thimedias bringing up the rear. I felt rather like Al Capone taking an airing. Then just as we were stepping off the kerb to cross Coventry Street, 'bang, bang' came two deafening reports. "This is it," I thought as I clutched myself wildly to find out where I had been hit. I looked at my bodyguards and they were all as white as sheets. Suddenly, there was another sharp explosion and we all burst out laughing. It wasn't the pistol packing husband after all – just a passing car back-firing.

As a matter of fact he never did arrive, but that husband certainly threw a bigger scare into me than any fighter has ever done. So, once again, I solemnly swore that henceforth for me it would be strictly a man's world and that I wouldn't let another female within a mile of me. What a hope I had!

Six months later Boon was in New York training to fight Beau Jack and it wasn't long before he was right back on the romantic merry-go-round again:

Beau Jack wasn't my biggest worry in the States, it was the women, and once more there I was right bang in the middle of double-trouble. The publicity boys out there had done their normal good job and I hadn't even had time to unpack my bags before the phone rang in my hotel bedroom and a husky female voice said: "Hello Eric, you don't know me, but I think you're cute."

"You're crazy," I said and put the phone down. Five minutes later it buzzed again and it was the same girl. "Eric my pet," she said, "I still think you're cute. Where shall we meet?"

"Over my dead body," I snapped, "and in case it interests you, I still think you're crazy."

But she was only one of many. There was a blonde showgirl I met at a nightspot on 52nd Street. For a couple of weeks we did the rounds from Harlem to Greenwich Village. Then I got tired and tried to drop her, but she was only just getting her second wind. She chased me all over New York. I think there must have been a bloodhound in her family tree somewhere because no matter where I tried to hide she tracked me down.

Finally I ducked out to Gus Lesnevich's place in New Jersey. Only about three people in New York knew where I had gone and for one blissful week I was able to relax. Then one afternoon I was roused by the blaring of an automobile horn. I went out and there sat a famous American fighter in a shiny new convertible. "Hi Eric," he shouted, "I've brought a friend to see you," and there she was sitting next to him, the blonde from the 52nd Street club.

By that time there was another woman in my life. She was older, the wife of a millionaire businessman and a leader of what Americans call 'café society', part of the world of mink and diamonds. We danced and went to first nights together, and whenever I needed it I borrowed her big Cadillac coupe. Her husband never seemed to be around. Like most other big businessmen in the States he was too busy making money to bother about anything else.

That suited me fine for, although she had money to burn, I too had a fair share of dollars and together we had a wonderful time. But like so many of the others she wanted it to be forever. She even offered to get me a $10,000 a year job in her husband's business so we could always be together. I was nearly tempted because I didn't want to fight again, but then I saw the red light. Sparring for time I told the lady I would think it over. I never called her again.

Women? All I have to thank them for is the collapse of my boxing career. Those female wolves made the unholiest mess

366

of my life in the ring. Yes, it was fun while it lasted. I'm not denying that and I certainly don't intend glossing over my mistakes with any glib excuses.

30

THE FINAL YEARS

During the later years of his life Boon took great interest in young Chatteris prospect, Dave 'Boy' Green, who had also started his ring career at the local amateur club under the tuition of Arthur Binder. When Green stopped Jim Kelly of Peterborough in three rounds to win the Eastern Counties light-welterweight title on 1 March 1973, *Boxing News* described him as "the brilliant young Chatteris boxer who reminds one of his illustrious home town idol, Eric Boon."

Boon had always remained close to Binder and during one of their many social meetings Arthur told him he believed Green was a future champion. Having great respect for his old trainer's judgement, Eric followed Dave's career closely. When he was narrowly outpointed by experienced Terry Waller in the 1974 ABA light-welterweight semi-final he was convinced Arthur's assessment was spot on.

Green turned professional with Andy Smith later the same year and when he had his third paid contest at Cambridge Guildhall on 12 February the following year Boon was one of a number of celebrities in attendance. With two quick knockout victories already behind him, Dave faced Derek Simpson from Kilmarnock, a veteran of 50 fights, and forced him to retire after seven rounds. Eric was extremely impressed and after the fight went to the dressing room and congratulated the youngster on a fine performance.

"Marvellous, the boy has great potential," Boon told a local newspaper reporter anxious for his opinion. "I think a British title is a certainty and the world title is not beyond the bounds of possibility. He is improving so fast it is ridiculous. He is aggressive and knows what he is doing."

As Green continued to progress fans in Chatteris and beyond began to compare him with Boon because their aggressive styles were so similar. Dave was seen in the Fens as a reincarnation of their old hero who was regarded as a living legend.

Boon frequently attended Andy Smith's gym at St Ives to watch Dave train. He was often approached by local reporters and always gave a frank opinion as to the youngster's progress. "What I like so much is his will to win," he remarked one day as Green sparred. "He is the best young prospect I have ever seen."

After an unbeaten run of only 15 professional contests, Green was matched with Joey Singleton for the British light-welterweight title at the Royal Albert Hall on 1 June the same year. In the weeks approaching the fight it was like old times in Chatteris when Boon was preparing for his big fights. Newsmen from all over the country descended on the town seeking interviews and background stories from local people. Whilst there was massive interest and support for Dave, there were also plenty of stories about Eric as elderly folk turned back the clock.

The reporters loved it because they were getting two stories instead of one. The local boxing club had revived memories of Boon especially as he had got involved in training the youngsters. Although Mr and Mrs Cameron were no longer licencees of The George, there were plenty of pictures of the steamy fight days of years gone by hanging on the walls. Eric Boon was particularly prominent.

"The thing about Boon was he knew how to take a punch," one old-timer told a local reporter. "Greeny's the same – he's a good boy."

"Boon used to put 'em to sleep," said another old character playing darts in the public bar of The George. "Greeny does the same."

The older generation couldn't help recalling the great days of Boon and, with pens and tape-recorders to hand, the scribes noted every story.

John Peggs, a sprightly seventy-one-years-old, described how he once travelled all the way to Harringay to see Boon fight, but didn't see a punch because he and some mates got themselves ready with a couple of drinks in the bar. When they got back to their seats they saw two other boxers climbing into the ring and thought the order had been changed. "Turns out that Boon finished his bloke in half a round and was back in his dressing room," he said. "Chap called Ward from Ireland I think."

Bus driver, Dave Edgar, described how he saw Eric fight Johnny McGrory and others. "And I remember Lenny Wickwar saying he felt he'd been hit by a traction engine when Boonie knocked him out one wet night at Leicester football ground."

The excitement in the town was incredible, not just about Green's advance towards a title, but with the old folk enjoying recalling the great days of Boon. He put Chatteris on the map and they never forgot him. Now Dave had arrived they could compare him to their former idol and hopefully look forward to more great ring nights. There were so many similarities between the two, not least their powerful two-fisted style of fighting. Both had spent hours pounding away with heavy hammers at a local blacksmith's forge, and like Boon, Dave was an excellent body puncher and used the uppercut well.

On 1 June 1974, Boon was among an army of Fenland supporters who travelled to London by car, coach and rail to support Green in the biggest test of his career. "It brings it all back," said Eric before leaving his home at Wicken. "There is a tremendous feeling in the air. I think Dave will wear Singleton down and stop him."

Boon received an incredible reception when introduced from the ring at the Royal Albert Hall. Only that afforded to Green when he was pronounced champion following Joey Singleton's retirement after six rounds, was greater.

"You were great, simply great," Boon told Dave when he visited him in his dressing room later.

Green never forgot that moment and years later remarked: "It meant the world to me when Eric Boon came into my dressing room after the fight. He was my inspiration."

Boon had often said that he envisaged Dave Green as a British champion. "He is a dedicated boxer who has the will to win and that must be good for British sport," he told a reporter from the *Cambridgeshire Times*. "I think he has done Chatteris proud."

The one sad note connected with Dave's success was that Arthur Binder was not there to witness it. He had sadly passed away on 8 September the previous year. Paying tribute to him, Boon told journalists: "Arthur was a great, great man. A wonderful man with the patience of a saint."

"He was well liked by everyone," continued Eric. "Even now when I go all over the country with my film show you would be amazed at the number of people who ask about him. He took so many boxers all over the place."

Arthur had been at Boon's side for over 70 contests since the day he coaxed him into Chatteris Boxing Club. Whilst he was an exceptional trainer, Eric insisted that he was an even better masseur.

There was huge mutual respect between Boon and Green and they were often jointly invited to attend local functions. Together with Isle of Ely MP, Clement Freud, they took part in a darts match to help raise funds to enable Chatteris Boxing Club to purchase a new gym. On 23 April 1976, just four days before Green's fifteenth professional contest against Herbie McLean, he and Boon were guests on a BBC television documentary-style chat programme, 'Generations Apart' hosted by Harry Carpenter. Eric was relaxed and well-spoken as he recalled his early days at Chatteris Boxing Club. In response to a question from Carpenter he said he and other youngsters had very little to do in Chatteris because it was such a quiet town. "Mind you, we were always fighting," he said with a smile, "but not in the ring."

Boon described in detail the times in which he was brought up. He believed that although it was difficult, the people were much nicer, more content and willing to help each other. There were about 3,000 licensed boxers and there was much more of a will to win. "A purse of £2 was a lot of money," he remarked, "and I would have hated to miss the apprenticeship I had."

Eric smiled when Carpenter mentioned that he had a reputation for being a playboy who loved the bright lights, but was quick to say how he always returned to Chatteris at every opportunity. "I loved the place," he remarked, "and still do."

A few weeks after Dave Green became British champion he and Boon opened the summer fete at King Edward School where both had been pupils in their young days. Their presence attracted a crowd of over 1,000 and at the conclusion of speeches they and their wives were presented with buttonholes and bouquets of flowers by a group of pupils.

Similarities between the two continued to be identified and were not just confined to their fighting styles. The day after he had won the British title, Boon carried the prestigious Lonsdale belt triumphantly around Chatteris in a carrot bag. When Green returned to work at a Downham Market farm at 7.30 am two days after beating Joey Singleton, he had his belt in a sack in the boot of his car.

In December 1976, a few weeks after recovering from a mild heart attack, Eric was again in demand by reporters for his views on Green's forthcoming fight against Jean Baptiste Piedvache for the vacant European light-welterweight championship. Several called at his Wicken home the day before the contest and whilst Wendy made them tea and coffee, he happily made his prediction. "I don't think this Frenchman can do anything against Green," he remarked confidently. "Frenchmen are notoriously bad punchers. Green will lick anyone who cannot punch because of his aggression and stamina."

In deriding fighters from across the channel, Eric had obviously forgotten the hammering he took from Robert Villemann back in 1948. Yet, his prediction again proved accurate because Dave's power forced Piedvache to retire after nine rounds.

Although Boon never sought to interfere with Green's training he was a keen observer during his many visits to the St Ives gym. His views were always important to the reporters who were there most days. "He is very good, dedicated and a nice kid," he remarked one day as Dave went through his strenuous routines.

371

When asked for a comparison between himself and Green, Eric smiled and said: "I was never a very good fighter – I was a lover."

Boon was always a low-key modest man who saw no point in making comparisons. They boxed in different eras and he saw Dave exactly as he was – very professional and dedicated.

Green's continued success bought the old champion back into the news. The better the youngster got, the more reporters went after Eric for his comments. Their stories frequently referred back to his own successes and the atmosphere he created in his heyday. As Dave trained to meet John H Stracey in a world welterweight title eliminator in March 1977, it was Chatteris against Bethnal Green all over again as memories of the great Boon – Danahar fight came flooding back. "If Dave puts the pressure on as he can, I think it could end as early as four rounds," Eric told a *Cambridgeshire Evening News* reporter. "I think Stracey has lost his heart and guts. That beating from Palomino has taken everything out of him."

Boon's assessment was harsh on Stracey because the last thing a boxer loses is his pride. John always had plenty of that and although Green won by a stoppage after 10 rounds, Stracey was still on his feet at the end.

Eric always remained a great fan of boxing and had a high regard for Muhammad Ali, John Conteh and Ken Buchanan, but being local Dave Green was special to him. The Chatteris youngster also had great affection for Eric and in early 1978 when it became known that he was in poor health and in need of financial help, he and Andy Smith became members of The Eric Boon Testimonial Committee formed to stage an event in his honour. Others included Henry Cooper, OBE, (later to become Sir Henry), Dave Charnley, Harry Carpenter and Joe Coral.

Despite incessant bad weather throughout January and February, Green and Smith motored to London to attend meetings. With some roads blocked by snow their journeys often took as long as five hours. It was a classic example of the respect two great sportsmen had for the former champion.

The testimonial dinner took place on 22 March 1978 at the World Sporting Club in the Grosvenor House Hotel at Park Lane. During the evening many tributes were paid to Eric from people within sport, and also charities that had benefited from his tireless efforts. Harry Carpenter and Reg Gutteridge recalled his great days in the ring, both agreeing that he was the most exciting boxer in Britain for many years and undoubtedly the hardest puncher, pound for pound.

Jack Solomons openly admitted that Boon's success put him on the road to his own fabulous career as Britain's number one

372

promoter. "Eric Boon goes down in Boxing's Hall of Fame as one of the truly great ones," he remarked to a standing ovation.

Amongst the guests was Arthur Danahar, and a film of their epic fight in 1939 was shown during the evening. In a moving article in what has become an extremely collectable event brochure, Arthur described their fight in detail and paid tribute to his conqueror:

> At the end of the contest we both expressed to each other how glad we were that it was over and, for my part, I was proud to admit that I had lost to a great fighter, as game as a fighting cock, with the strength and ability to back it up in one of the best fights I ever had.
>
> Boxers are generally remembered for the contests they lose, as in my case with this particular contest, but Eric's game performance reversed that. He is unique – he is remembered for the fights he won!
>
> Over the years Eric and I have met several times in most pleasurable circumstances. I have always found him a gentle person with a pleasing character, one of the nicest fellows.
>
> It is unfortunate that ill health has stopped that endeavour, but I hope for him that tonight's testimonial will be fruitful enough to send him into a well earned and comfortable retirement. I will shake his hand and wish him 'good luck for the future and thanks for the memories.'

The evening was supported by a four-fight professional boxing bill headed by a 10-round contest between Peter Neal (Swindon) and Steve Angel (Hemel Hempstead) for the Southern Area welterweight championship. A splendid opening bout featured Steve Hopkin from Ely where Boon trained for some of his big fights. Hopkin took a points decision over Salvo Nuciford from Falmouth and at the end 'nobbins' were thrown into the ring by the appreciative audience. Hopkin immediately donated his share to the Eric Boon fund.

Like Boon, Arthur Danahar also suffered from ill health, and seven months later the London Ex-Boxers Association staged a benefit night for him at the Sobell Centre in Holloway. He was presented with a cheque for £750 made up of donations from individuals and a variety of organisations.

Although Boon was under the care of Cambridgeshire General Hospital and having problems with his sense of balance, he made the trip from his home at Soham to support his old opponent and friend. Despite his own problems he still made a donation.

For as long as he could get about Eric continued to attend boxing functions and keep in touch with the sport he loved. The following year he was one of 100 past and present champions to attend the British Boxing Board of Control 50th Anniversary Dinner at the Café Royal. He never forgot those close to him during his boxing career and in January 1980 was a guest at the World Sporting Club for a tribute dinner to Jack Solomons who had died a month earlier.

The passion for boxing never deserted Eric. He loved the people, the camaraderie and the memories. In the early 1970's he devoted a great deal of time to Lowestoft Amateur Boxing Club and regularly attended ex-Boxers Association meetings particularly at Ipswich and Chelmsford. He even tried his hand at training an army boxer who wanted to turn professional, but after a sparring session at Ely, Paddy McAleese, a gym partner of Dave Green, told Boon bluntly that the boy wasn't good enough.

31

REFLECTIONS

Eric spent his final years living quietly with Wendy in a small bungalow at 16 Cornmills Road, a cul-de-sac on the outskirts of Soham in Cambridgeshire. It was there, on the morning of Sunday 18 January 1981, that he suffered a heart attack and was rushed to Newmarket General Hospital. After a massive second heart attack in the early hours of the following morning, he died aged sixty-one.

News of his passing spread rapidly and reporters from newspapers across the Fens and beyond sped to Chatteris seeking tributes from people who knew him. They weren't disappointed because the locals spoke with passion about the man they loved and respected. Their vivid accounts summarised the old champion's life and career.

Harold 'Adge' Simpson, above whose paint shop Chatteris Amateur Boxing Club was originally set up almost 50 years earlier, knew Boon better than most. On hearing of his death he was so shocked that he sat staring into space for most of the day recalling memories of the Fenland folk hero. "I felt shattered," he told Mike Finnis from the *Cambridgeshire Evening News.* "There will never be another Eric. Nobody in the world was tougher – not a soul. He wasn't frightened of anyone and always gave all he had."

"A wonderful character," added Simpson. "What he did for charity no-one will ever know."

Fred Green, who by this time was aged seventy-four, had been one of the first people to recognise Boon's talent and potential. He was devastated and, with great sadness told a group of reporters: "Eric's death has stunned us all."

As a match-maker and small hall promoter, Fred got Boon his first schoolboy fight and helped arrange many of his subsequent ones. He recalled the time when he tried to get Australian heavyweight, George Cook, to take over his training, but was told Eric was too young and tender. "I smiled at this," he recalled.

Green, who like 'Adge' Simpson, was a founder member of the Chatteris Boxing Club added: "I've been in boxing for over fifty-five years and never saw a harder puncher, weight-for-weight, than Eric Boon. His efforts in the ring amazed us."

"He used to drive in much the same way as he boxed," continued Fred," fast and furious."

Ken Peters, Secretary of the Mid-Anglia Amateur Boxing Association, added his piece saying: "In the ring Boon just kept

375

coming with his arms flailing. He was more like Marciano than anyone else I have ever seen."

Years earlier Peters had been one of scores of village children who used to wait in Haddenham School playground to cheer Boon past on his daily runs. "He is the idol of the Fens," he remarked. "His death is the passing of an era." He added that Eric's reputation in the Fens was emphasised by his ability to fish with a rod in each hand and ice-skate without ever falling over.

Dave 'Boy' Green reiterated what he had said many times before about his feelings towards Eric. "He gave me my enthusiasm for the job when I first started boxing. He was the man I set out to try and emulate. He was my inspiration, but the difference is that I train much harder than he ever did."

As fighters, Boon and Green had many similarities not least with their aggression and power of punch. Their lives after boxing, however, took very contrasting routes and could not have been more different. While Eric sadly went downhill in some respects in that he could rarely settle into a solid career and was frequently broke, Dave became and still is, a successful businessman. Yet despite Eric's misfortunes Green never faltered in his love and respect for the old champion.

On hearing of Eric's death, old opponent, Arthur Danahar, said: "Our condolences go to Wendy and family. My wife Lynn and I met Eric and Wendy several times and I always found him a very nice and likeable man. We will always be remembered for that 1939 fight, but I used to remind Eric that we did have a return in 1946 and I stopped him. A great opponent and great sportsman and the most lethal puncher I ever met."

Not a bad word was uttered about Eric and over the next few days tributes to him appeared on the front pages of newspapers throughout East Anglia and surrounding areas. In obituaries most nationals also acknowledged his massive contribution to boxing. He deserved nothing less.

On the day after his death, Eric had been due to take a collection of old newspaper cuttings, given to him by a rotary club, to London to begin a new series of exhibitions in aid of 'the year of the disabled.' It was to be his latest charity venture.

"He was always willing to go anywhere for charity," his wife Wendy proudly told a local reporter. "He was always lugging the stuff around. It worried him that he couldn't get about like he used to, but he always kept his interest in boxing. Just about the last thing we watched on television was Muhammad Ali talking to Michael Parkinson."

*   *   *

Eric was survived by his mother and father, wife Wendy, daughter Erica and his two grandsons, Stephen and Michael who were born in 1967 and 1968 respectively. His funeral took place at Chatteris Parish Church, Market Hill, on 28 January 1981, and was conducted by the Rev. David Towers. Groups of people of all ages gathered in the street to see the hearse arrive and his coffin carried into the church. Mourners included members of his family, close friends, local people who grew up with him and many boxers past and present including Jimmy Walsh, Alex Buxton and Dave 'Boy' Green who, the previous evening, had fought at the Royal Albert Hall. He was accompanied by his manager and trainer, Andy Smith.

Burying a child has and always will be a parent's worst fear and Reg Boon found himself thrust into that very situation. Almost eighty-years-of-age by this time, he cried bitterly throughout the service. "It should be me in that coffin," he was heard to sob.

After the service mourners made the short journey to Chatteris Cemetery at New Road for the burial. It was not until November, however, that a gravestone was laid and this came about through the kindness and respect of members of Chatteris Boxing Club who never forgot Eric as a fighter. Following his death it was they who wanted to provide a memorial for his grave. Club representatives contacted Wendy and offered to make a collection among their members and supporters. On receiving her agreement the club instructed William Kent Memorials Limited of March to provide a stone to her specification.

By this time, however, the Jack Solomons Trust had been established. Its purpose was to help former boxers who had fallen on hard times or needed financial help due to poor health. In view of the important part Boon played in helping Jack climb to the top of the promotional ladder, members of the fund committee felt they should recognise it. Unaware of the boxing club offer just three days earlier they also contacted Wendy and offered to pay for a memorial.

Wendy was not in a position to refuse any offer of help, but felt it would be more practical for the fund to pay for the stone. She therefore contacted Tony Brown, a former heavyweight who had boxed for Chatteris and originally spoken to her about the club offer. After cordial discussions between the parties it was agreed that providing the stone would be a joint effort. The boxing club members would make all the arrangements and liaise with the stonemasons, and the Jack Solomons Trust would cover the cost.

Although it was provided by others, Wendy selected a simple stone and chose the words: 'Eric Boon 1919-1981, Lightweight

Boxing Champion of Great Britain 1938-1944. A Legend in his own Lifetime.'

A few days after the stone was laid Wendy made a pilgrimage from her home at Soham to see it and spend a few quiet moments beside her late husband's grave. Before leaving she placed a vase of white chrysanthemums by the head of the stone. "It was what I wanted it to be," she remarked, "simple and explicit."

Despite the passing of time Boon is still remembered with affection. Throughout the year small anonymous floral tributes ranging from chrysanthemums to a single rose can be seen on his grave.

*   *   *

At the time of his passing, Boon was hailed as the greatest lightweight Britain had ever produced. He was undoubtedly one of the most spectacular because whenever he climbed into the ring something dramatic always seemed to happen. Big punching, thrills and controversy – he gave audiences the lot and nobody who saw him fight would ever forget the excitement and atmosphere he generated.

A handsome, fun-loving lad, he was full of courage and one of the outstanding crowd-pleasers. He could give and take a punch, and throughout the history of boxing in Britain few lightweights ever punched harder than Eric Boon.

There were many occasions throughout his career and later life when he was asked how he developed his exceptional power. He always gave the same explanation. "I worked in my father's forge for a while which helped me build up my physique, but there was more to it than that," he remarked in one interview. "When I was swinging the big hammer my father always taught me to pull it back immediately on the point of impact. That gave me greater force and accuracy. When I started boxing I did the same thing. My nasty nature helped too!"

Boon was a magnet for members of the sporting media because they were always guaranteed a story. During the late 1940's several remarked that despite his fall from grace he was a man who got more chances than most. Eric knew his faults and took any criticism on the chin. He was frequently interviewed in the years following his retirement and made several television appearances. Sporting documentaries often included aspects of his life and career. One such programme screened by Anglia Television in 1973 featured David Jacobs interviewing Boon at his Wicken home and included footage of him coaching youngsters at Chatteris Boxing Club and working as a rep for a timber company.

During 1969, the epic contest between him and Arthur Danahar was featured on a BBC Television programme 'Great Moments in Sport.' Both men were interviewed by the late Harry Carpenter who asked Eric what he remembered about the fight. "Very little," he replied with a smile. "Looking back I think we must have been mad. We should have been certified."

Both agreed that had the contest taken place at the time of the programme, they would each have earned between £30,000 and £40,000.

Boon and Danahar had remained good friends ever since that fight and met quite often. One such occasion was at an amateur boxing show at Pagham on the West Sussex coast where Arthur lived in later life. As the guest of honour, Eric was introduced from the ring and asked by the Master of Ceremonies if he would like to meet Danahar again. When he noticed his old opponent climbing into the ring, Boon replied: "Yes, if he keeps his hands in his pockets."

Frank Butler, one of the most respected boxing correspondents of all time, considered the Boon – Danahar fight to be the greatest he had ever seen. Over the years he had watched and reported on many great world champions including Joe Louis, Henry Armstrong, Sugar Ray Robinson, Rocky Marciano, Tony Zale, Marcel Cerdan, Willie Pep and Muhammad Ali. "When it came to sheer excitement, Boon was right up there with the best of them," he once wrote.

Eric loved recalling the good times and never shunned a journalist. In another interview he said that he didn't rate the Danahar fight as his best performance. "I reckon my fight with Robert Villemain was the best," he remarked one day almost 30 years after the event. "It was a great fight and if I'd gone into the ring fully trained I'd have beaten him."

Giving his own version of events Eric said: "I took a bit of time to get going, but once I did I really let him have it. He was a heartbreaking fellow to fight because although I hit him with my best punches, he would not go down."

"He put his hands up to cover his face so I belted him on the gloves and broke his knuckles," continued Boon, "but he just wouldn't go down and I exhausted myself trying to put him away. In the end he knocked me out in the tenth, just five seconds before the end."

"It wasn't his punches that did me," claimed Eric, "it was my own fault. It really was sheer exhaustion. I was lying on the canvas looking up at him thinking what I'd like to do to him if only I could get up, but I just couldn't move."

Eric also got fed up with hearing about good losers in boxing and was quick to qualify his feelings. "There is no such thing as a good loser," he remarked. "You've got to go out there to win. In my day there was never all this rubbish about good losers. People fought because they had to, because they had a wife and kids to feed and this was the only way to earn a few shillings. So they fought, and they fought hard. No kid-glove stuff – anything went!"

When he wrote his series of articles in *The People* years earlier, Eric recalled what to him were vital stages in his development:

> *For fourteen years fighting was my trade. From the day I had my first lesson from Arthur Binder as he knelt on the floor in front of our kitchen fire teaching me to lead and counter-punch, I schooled myself to be tough.*
>
> *When I was only thirteen I tackled, for thirty bob, a rugged forty-years-old Negro welterweight named Sam Minto in a fairground booth. The first time Minto hit me I thought I had walked into the side of a house and every punch he landed afterwards hurt. But I still stayed three rounds with him and earned my money. That's how it must be in the fight game. If you want to reach the top you must learn to take it; to have what they call a 'fighting heart' – a heart that will pick you up off the floor when every nerve and bruised and aching muscle in your body urges you to stay down.*

In Boon's day there were more than 3,000 licensed professional boxers plying their trade in Britain mostly for a pittance. During the week in February 1939 when he fought Danahar, the trade paper *Boxing* reported on 48 separate promotions. The likelihood was that there were probably half as many again.

Despite having fallen out with the boxing authorities, Eric was always thankful for the sport. Apart from the money he earned it took him to parts of the world he would not otherwise have seen. His claim of having gone to 42 different countries, however, seemed a slight exaggeration.

A measure of Boon's personality and popularity was the fact that he always maintained a good relationship with all of the reporters who covered his fights. To Sydney Hulls of the *Daily Express* in the late 1970's he insisted that despite the low periods in his life he had no complaints. "We've got the most marvellous crowd of friends and I always found it a pleasure meeting my customers," he remarked. "I think an awful lot of it stems from my experiences in boxing. That's why I say 'thank god for the fight game'."

The financial hardships Eric suffered after retiring from boxing were very much self-inflicted, but sadly were an all too familiar story surrounding the sport. Despite those difficulties he never once made excuses or sought to blame anyone but himself. "Money just left my hands like red-hot lead," he was once quoted as saying.

One of Boon's main regrets was leaving school too early and in the later years of his life he frequently advised youngsters to stay on as long as they could to try and better themselves. He also encouraged them to play sport because being in a team was an important part of growing up.

He had been a good footballer and as a lad his favourite team was Arsenal. Once he settled in London he watched them many times at their Highbury ground. He was amazed at the skills of Alex James, but overall regarded Stanley Matthews as the finest player he ever saw.

During his visits to South Africa, Eric spent many Saturday afternoons watching football at Wembley Stadium. Years later when he had a flat in London, he occasionally went to watch Fulham's home games at Craven Cottage. Despite often being broke he managed to get complimentary tickets from his good friend Tommy Trinder who owned the club.

Nothing, however, equalled fishing whether it was with crude tackle on the Forty Foot drain at Chatteris or testing his skills for trout or salmon. He also enjoyed deep sea fishing when in South Africa and Australia, but admitted that he was a very poor sailor.

Boon was paid just three shillings and sixpence for his first professional fight. His purse money increased to 25 shillings when he first boxed at the Devonshire Club and as his popularity built they rose to 50 shillings a fight. When he fought Jamaican lightweight champion, Dodo Williams, on 18 February 1938, Jack Solomons paid him £7.10.0. The purses rose dramatically once he reached championship status.

"Some people say I made about half a million from boxing," he told a national newspaper reporter. "Maybe it was pretty close to that because I got good wages for my top fights. I also got £9,000 for three fights in South Africa and made £250 a week on the variety stage."

Reflecting back to his South African trips, Eric described how he ploughed his money into the 42-acre Willowdene Country Club project. The fights he took on his second trip were, according to him, to keep it going. "But like all other businesses I tried my hand at this one turned sour as well," he remarked with a hint of sadness. "I was too easy with the customers and the club soon ran into debt."

When he was broke Boon even pawned his Lonsdale belt and there were also claims that he eventually sold it. Unfortunately its whereabouts have never been traced, although it was once claimed in a newspaper report that he sold it back to the Board of Control for £500. Yet despite falling on hard times he always had a smile on his face and a cheery word for a friend or local admirer.

Boon was the first top class fighter to come from Chatteris and his remarkable achievements undoubtedly put the little Fenland market town on the map. Although he continued to box until 1953 he was never able to find the form that enabled him to beat the likes of Walsh, Crowley, Danahar and McGrory. Many critics believed that his motor cycle accident in 1941 was the start of his decline.

Ignoring medical advice never to box again Boon failed to reveal the extent of his injuries to the Board of Control. Boxing was all he knew, but despite suffering from headaches and the occasional blackouts he had just one aim – to earn much needed cash from the ring. The extent of his plight was revealed in the series of articles in the *People* during 1949 and '50 when he described how his defeat by Ronnie James had scared him so much that, once more, he vowed never to fight again. Money, however, was the deciding factor and he agreed to fight Henry Hall at Harringay in July 1945. Describing that and subsequent events Eric said:

> *The result was a fiasco. I simply couldn't muster the strength or courage to go in and mix it in my old tearaway style. I kept my chin tucked behind my gloves, scared of what might happen if I opened up and Hall caught me as McAvoy had done.*

> *Halfway through the fifth round he caught me with a sledgehammer slam to the body and as I knelt on the canvas fighting for breath with the crowd booing and cat-calling the referee stepped between us and stopped the contest.*

> *The same sort of thing happened, as the fans will remember, when I met Gwynn Williams in a British welterweight title eliminator at Harringay. The fight was stopped in the sixth round and declared a 'no contest'.*

> *Yet I still continued to flirt with death. I had no alternative. My fights were my meal ticket. I had to fight to eat and by this time I was beginning to suffer from complete blackouts. For instance, I went fifteen rounds with Ernie Roderick when he beat me on points for the welterweight title, but my mind was a complete blank from the second round.*

> *To this day I can't remember a thing that happened after I went back to my corner until I was in a taxi with Jack Solomons on my way home. "What was Jack Petersen saying to you in the dressing room Eric?" asked Solomons.*

> *"Who?" I said dully.*

"Petersen," said Solomons. "Jack Petersen. He was talking to you after the fight."

I looked at him blankly. "I don't know what you are talking about," I said. "I don't know anybody named Jack Petersen."

That's how it's been on and off for nearly seven nightmare years now, but thank heaven the fear of dropping dead in the ring is no longer with me. I have fought my last fight. What the future holds I cannot say, but at least I shall never again have to risk my life in the ring.

Despite his apparent sensible intentions Eric did fight again, three times in Australia during 1953. Again the lack of money forced the issue. The situations he described regarding his health, however, would never have arisen in modern times because of massive changes regarding the welfare of boxers. Following guidance from the British Medical Association, Board of Control rules are stringent and the problems Eric experienced following his accident would have been identified and his licence suspended.

Had it not been for the war there is little doubt that Sydney Hulls would have done everything in his power to secure a world title fight for Eric in London. Lou Ambers, who won the lightweight championship in August 1939, was six years his elder and had twice gone gruelling 15 rounds contests with Henry Armstrong. Such battles would undoubtedly have drained him and the fact that he was stopped in three rounds by Lew Jenkins in May 1940 was a good indicator that a young puncher like Boon could have done likewise.

Had Eric been matched with Armstrong, however, his career could have been cut short. This of course is pure speculation, but the fact remained that not getting the coveted world title shot was one of the greatest disappointments of his career.

Although he achieved success in the ring at a very young age, local people didn't regard Boon as a young man who had taken his place among the celebrities of the sporting world. They still called him 'son' and remembered him as a lad who ran around the streets of Chatteris in short trousers just a few years earlier.

As the years ticked by he didn't alter very much as a person. He was an articulate, well-spoken and courteous man who exuded personality and was a magnet for the ladies. He did acquire poise, sophistication and a taste for high-powered sports cars and expensive camel-hair coats, but remained as modest and unassuming as ever. He retained his good looks, a healthy head of hair and powerful physique, and despite all the wars he had in the ring, didn't have a mark on him in the later years of his life.

The memory of Eric's achievements kept the interest in boxing alive in Chatteris and it flared rapidly during the mid-1970's when Dave 'Boy' Green went from success to success. As thousands of fans from the Fens travelled to London for his big fights, it was like turning the clock back almost 40 years. Dave's rise to the top brought Boon back into the spotlight as journalists continually made comparisons between the two.

Much has been written about Eric since his death in 1981, not one shred of which was negative or critical. In a chapter in his book, 'The Big Punchers,' published in 1983, the late Reg Gutteridge aptly wrote:

> When Eric Boon hit, they stayed hit. Pound-for-pound, the 'boy' from Cambridgeshire matched the greatest. Many fighters at least two weight divisions above him could not produce such power.

Stories about Boon continued to roll off the press and in 2005 an absorbing article about him and Dave 'Boy' Green featured in the British Boxing Yearbook. Entitled 'Chatteris Champions' it was subsequently serialised in the *Cambridgeshire Times* over four weeks during October and November the same year.

The *Cambridgeshire Times* group had always been a strong supporter of Boon and reported his fights from the early days. Even in later life they told their readers everything about him that was newsworthy. One such article published on 24 December 1976, described how Urshella Berry, a twenty-five-years-old lady from Manea, spent hours at the newspaper offices searching for copies of Eric's fight reports. Her mission was to create a scrapbook about him for her father, Charles Short, who had been one of his many fans.

The idea came about when her father saw her compiling a scrapbook about Dave 'Boy' Green and said he wished he had kept one on Boon. In his younger days Mr Short often cycled from Manea to Chatteris in pouring rain to watch Eric fight and once went to London for one of his major bouts. The scrapbook made a special Christmas present.

Boon was one of the most remarkable young men ever to win a British championship. After he beat Dave Crowley boxing fans knew he was something special. His victory over Arthur Danahar made him a national hero and had it not been for injuries he would have won the Lonsdale belt outright in record time.

He was a fighter to the end and even struggled with paramedics as they attempted to put him into an ambulance for what would be the last time he left his home. Despite his downfalls and incredible bad luck he possessed immense pride right up until he drew his last breath. During his final hours he was in immense pain and was given doses of morphine to allow him to pass away with dignity.

Throughout his life, and in the years following his passing, Eric was a frequent topic of conversation. When the BBC radio programme, 'Down Your Way' visited Chatteris a number of locals made reference to him when interviewed. Although he was the biggest sporting name to come from the town, he did not take part, probably because he was too modest.

Moments of his career still exist. Local man, John Salisbury, a close friend of Boon's when he was a youngster, is the proud owner of the Troupadour harmonica the boxer often played in his dressing room before a fight. German made and bearing a hallmark, he gave it to John as a present together with a copy of the three-page sheet music of 'Boonie, Wonderful Boon.'

It was fitting that Eric should be laid to rest at Chatteris because it was there that his boxing career began almost 50 years earlier. He never forgot those early days and especially people like Arthur Binder and Fred Green who set him on his way to stardom. In effect he completed a full circle in life.

Apart from the early days at Chatteris Boxing Club, teaching never begot Eric Boon. Although many of his teenage contests were at the Devonshire Club, he was the product of no school or academy. He had natural aggression and learned by practical experience, making full use of his immense strength and never calculating the odds for or against him. He revelled in that strength, his abiding gospel being: "A fighter will always beat a boxer." His defeats of stylists Crowley and Danahar backed that belief.

Those magnificent championship contests at Harringay within the space of two months opened a new era for British boxing. In the Danahar fight, the amazing changes of fortune, the thrills, courage and sportsmanship displayed by both men gave boxing a tremendous lift.

Mentality has always played a big part in boxing, especially in major fights. Boon had the mentality for the big occasion because nothing worried or disturbed him. He was a bright young man with an active, impressionable and romantic mind. Possessed with such attributes he ironed himself nearer to greatness than any British lightweight since the world-beating Freddie Welsh almost three decades earlier.

Boon was a colourful character in and out of the ring. The memories of him are endless, not least the days when the railway companies put on special trains to convey thousands of fans from the Fenland towns and villages to London for his big fights. There

385

was excitement, anticipation and great atmosphere, but sadly those were days of a bygone era.

The likes of Eric Boon will never be seen again, but he will be remembered for as long as boxing survives. As his epitaph so accurately reflects, he was 'A Legend in his own Lifetime.'

Rest in peace old champ.

Books

Dalby, W Barrington	*Bedside Book of Boxing* Cassell 1961
Harding, John	*Whitechapel Windmill* Robson 1987
Herbstein, Denis	*The Porthole Murder Case* Hodder & Stoughton 1991
McInnes, Peter	*Clouting for Cash* P.R.M 1962
Odd, Gilbert	*Ring Battles of the Century* Nicholson & Watson 1948
Snelling, O.F	*Bedside Book of Boxing* Pelham 1972
Solomons, Jack	*Jack Solomons Tells All* Rich & Cowan 1951
Wilson, Peter	*Ringside Seat* Rich & Cowan 1979

Newspapers

Boxing/Boxing News
Brisbane Courier
Bristol Evening Post
Cambridgeshire Times & March Gazette
Daily Express
Daily Mail
Daily Mirror
Evening Standard
Guernsey Evening Press
Honolulu Star Bulletin
Jersey Evening Post
Leicester Evening Mail
Lincolnshire Free Press
Manchester Evening News
Montreal Gazette
Natal Mercury
Newmarket Weekly News
Peterborough Advertiser
Peterborough Evening Telegraph
Pretoria News
Rand Daily Mail
Southport Guardian
South Wales Echo
Sporting Life
Sporting World
Sunday People
The Age (Melbourne)
The Star   (London)
The Star (South Africa)
The Sun
The Times
Topical Times
Transvaal Sunday Times
Washington Post
Weekly Sporting Review

Eric Boon's Schoolboy Record 1932 - 1934

Date	Opponent	Result	Venue
1932			
Mar 17	Boy Marriott	L Pts 6	St Ives
Apr 1	Boy Rushton	W Pts 3	Huntingdon
June 24	Boy Cross	W Pts 3	Chatteris
Dec 17	Boy Kerr	W Pts 3	Chatteris
1933			
Jan 20	Boy Rushton	W Pts 3	Huntingdon
Feb 9	Boy Cole	W Pts 6	Whittlesey
Mar 9	Boy Maywood	W Pts 6	Whittlesey
Mar 24	Boy Wilson	W Pts 3	Chatteris
Apr 7	Boy Brittan	W Pts 3	Huntingdon
Apr 29	Boy Marriott	W Pts 3	St Ives
May 12	Boy Brittan	W Pts 3	Chatteris
Sept 29	Paddy Chilvers	W Pts 4	Chatteris
Dec 1	Paddy Chilvers	W KO 4	Whittlesey
Dec 7	Paddy Chilvers	W KO 3	Chatteris
1934			
Jan 24	Fred Kerr	L Pts 6	Manea
Feb 9	Boy Cole	W Pts 6	Whittlesey
Feb 14	Paddy Chilvers	W Pts 6	Manea
Mar 9	Boy Maywood	W Pts 6	Whittlesey
Mar 28	Boy Groves	W Pts 6	Manea
Mar 31	Bruce Scotney	W Pts 4	Chatteris
Apr 21	Bruce Scotney	W Pts 6	Downham Market
May 11	Abe Groves	Exh 4	Warboys
July 14	Young Hammond	WRSC 3	Long Sutton
Aug	Sam Minto	NC 3	Chatteris
Nov 2	Sid Badcock	WRSC 2	Warboys

Schoolboy Summary

Bouts Taken:	25
Won	21 (4 inside distance)
Lost	2
EXH	1
NC	1

Eric Boon's Professional Record 1934 - 1953

Date	Opponent	Result	Venue
1934			
Dec 13	Doug Claxton	W Pts 6	Peterborough
1935			
Jan 17	Young Snowball	W RSC 6	Peterborough
Feb 7	Teddy Royal	W Pts 6	St Ives
Feb 21	Darkie Brian	W RSC 1	Spalding
Feb 28	Jeff Smith	L RET 2	Peterborough
Mar 10	Young Higgins	DRAW 6	Hackney
Mar 24	Stan Yates	L Pts 6	Hackney
Apr 7	Teddy Softley	W Pts 6	Hackney
Apr 21	Yorkie Perkins	W KO 5	Hackney
Jun 2	Young Higgins	W Pts 6	Mile End Arena
Jun 23	Boy Bessell	W Pts 6	Hackney
Aug 1	Alf Eburne	W Pts 6	Grimsthorpe
Aug 28	Kid Savage	L Pts 6	Hackney
Oct 21	Charlie Smith	W Pts 6	Cambridge
Nov 25	Ginger Daniels	W RSC 2	Cambridge
Dec 4	Charlie Smith	W RSC 2	Watford
1936			
Jan 6	Young Burbage	W KO 4	Cambridge
Feb 3	Terry Ellis	W KO 1	Cambridge
Feb 15	Tommy Herbert	W Pts 6	Spalding
Feb 17	Smoker Smith	W Pts 6	Norwich
Feb 29	Fred Franklyn	W KO 4	Spalding
Mar 2	Young Hawes	W KO 1	Norwich
Mar 16	Young Griffo	W RSC 1	Norwich
Mar 21	Bill Boyd	DRAW 6	Spalding
Mar 30	Charlie Smith	W Pts 10	Cambridge
Apr 15	Jack Roberts	W KO 2	Hackney
Apr 18	Ginger Brant	L Pts 6	Spalding
Apr 27	Airman Sammy Baker	W KO 2	Cambridge
Apr 30	Bill Boyd	W Pts 6	Peterborough
Aug 2	Jock Nicholls	W Pts 4	Ely
Aug 21	Len Ash	W Pts 8	Hackney

Sept 4	Charlie Wise	W Pts 8	Hackney
Oct 1	Bert Whall	W RSC 2	Norwich
Oct 4	Teddy Larkham	W KO 1	Hackney
Oct 18	Len Ash	W Pts 8	Hackney
Oct 24	Jimmy Doyle	W Pts 8	Chelmsford
Nov 1	Jack Watkins	W Pts 8	Hackney
Nov 2	Ted Vincent	W KO 2	Bury St Edmunds
Nov 5	Fred Dyer	DRAW 8	Norwich
Nov 12	Bobby Lyons	W RSC 6	Norwich
Nov 16	Jack Kershaw	DRAW 6	Earls Court
Nov 22	Joe Page	W KO 1	Hackney
Nov 26	Jack Watkins	W Pts 8	Hackney
Nov 30	Nat Williams	W KO 5	Earls Court
Dec 9	George Cunningham	W Pts 4	Holborn
Dec 13	Nick Lucas	W RSC 6	Hackney

1937

Jan 3	Al Church	W RSC 6	Hackney
Jan 11	Bert Chambers	DRAW 6	Earls Court
Jan 14	Billy Bennett	W KO 2	Holborn
Jan 24	Billy Sheldon	W Pts 10	Hackney
Jan 27	Billy Griffiths	W KO 1	Hackney
Feb 1	Reg Jenkins	W Pts 4	Harringay
Feb 7	Mike Sullivan	W KO 4	Hackney
Feb 16	Dai James	W Pts 8	Reading
Feb 25	Chucky Robinson	W Pts 10	Norwich
Mar 1	Spin Anson	W KO 5	Bury St Edmunds
Mar 7	Tony Butcher	W RSC 5	Hackney
Mar 21	Harry Brooks	L RET 5	Hackney
Apr 6	George Bissett	W KO 2	Chatteris
Apr 12	Jocker Johnson	W RSC 5	Bury St Edmunds
Apr 15	Angus McGregor	DRAW 4	Harringay
Apr 29	Bob Barlow	W Pts 10	Norwich
May 7	George Kelly	W Pts 12	Hackney
May 10	Bobby Lyons	W KO 1	Bury St Edmunds
May 16	Ron Porter	W RSC 5	Hackney
May 28	Jack Lilley	W Pts 12	Hackney
July 2	Johnny Softley	L RET 7	Hackney
July 16	Bryn Morris	W Pts 10	Hackney
Aug 20	Albert Heasman	W KO 3	Hackney
Sept 3	Wilf Dexter	W RSC 7	Hackney
Sept 15	Charlie Wise	W RSC 3	Hackney
Oct 5	Benny Thackeray	W KO 4	Chatteris
Oct 17	Bryn Morris	W RET 10	Hackney

Oct 25	Fred Thackeray	W KO 2	Cambridge
Nov 5	Harry McKenzie	W KO 2	Hackney
Nov 11	Dave Wilding	W RSC 2	Chatteris
Nov 29	Bob Rowlands	W KO 2	Cambridge
Dec 10	Con Flynn	W DISQ 3	Hackney
Dec 13	Llew Thomas	W KO 3	Bury St Edmunds

1938

Jan 13	Alex Jackson	W Pts 8	Ipswich
Jan 21	George Reynolds	W KO 2	Hackney
Jan 28	Tommy Dowlais	W KO 1	Hackney
Feb 2	Jack Hardiman	W KO 3	Hackney
Feb 18	Dodo Williams	W KO 1	Hackney
Mar 3	Johnny Softley	W Pts 8	Royal Albert Hall
Apr 7	Johnny Ward	W RSC 1	Harringay
Apr 17	Matt Moran	W RSC 7	Hackney
May 2	Boyo Rees	W KO 1	Holborn
May 28	Jimmy Walsh	W Pts 10	Chatteris
June 21	Len Lemaux	W KO 1	Harringay
July 16	Raymond Renard	W RET 1	Chatteris
July 24	Billy Masters	W KO 2	Mile End Arena
Sept 2	Eric Dolby	W RSC 3	Manchester
Sept 27	Mitso Grispos	W Pts 8	Harringay
Oct 20	George Reynolds	W KO 2	Marylebone
Oct 31	Mac Perez	W DISQ 7	Earls Court
Dec 15	Dave Crowley	W KO 13	Harringay
	(British Lightweight Championship)		

1939

Jan 30	Boyo Rees	W RSC 2	Mountain Ash
Feb 23	Arthur Danahar	W RSC 14	Harringay
	(British Lightweight Championship)		
June 28	Johnny McGrory	W KO 9	Peterborough
July 17	Len Wickwar	W KO 9	Lcicester
Dec 9	Dave Crowley	W KO 7	Harringay
	(British Lightweight Championship)		

1940

| Sept 21 | Ernie Roderick | L Pts 10 | Liverpool |

1941

| Feb 20 | Dave Finn | W Pts 6 | Leicester Square |
| Apr 21 | Jack Kid Berg | L DISQ 2 | London Coliseum |

1942

Feb 2	Norman Snow	W KO 4	Marylebone
Aug 26	Dick Wheeler	W KO 4	Watford
Sept 12	Frank Duffy	L DISQ 6	Bristol
Oct 21	Jake Kilrain	W KO 2	Soho
Nov 11	Jake Kilrain	W Pts 10	Soho

1943

July 13	Tommy Armour	L KO 5	Belfast
Aug 23	Harry Mizler	L Pts 8	Royal Albert Hall
Sept 2	Billy Jones	W Pts 8	Blackburn

1944

Apr 26	Johnny Molloy	W Pts 8	Royal Albert Hall
Aug 12	Ronnie James	L KO 10	Cardiff

(British Lightweight Championship)

1945

July 17	Henry Hall	L RSC 5	Tottenham

1946

Jan 8	Cyril Wills	W KO 1	Marylebone
Jan 22	Paddy Burgin	W RSC 2	Royal Albert Hall
Feb 5	Jean Wanes	W RET 5	Marylebone
Feb 19	Mick Magee	W KO 2	Royal Albert Hall
Mar 5	Maurice Ouzemann	W RSC 7	Marylebone
Mar 19	Billy Stevens	W KO 7	Royal Albert Hall
May 14	Arthur Danahar	L RSC 5	Harringay

(British Welterweight Championship Eliminator)

July 27	Laurie Stevens	W KO 3	Johannesburg
Sept 7	Tiger Burns	W KO 2	Johannesburg

1947

Mar 3	Alf James	W KO 7	Johannesburg
Apr 29	Maurice Ouzemann	W RSC 6	Johannesburg
May 10	Alf James	W KO 5	N'Khana
Aug 22	Maurice Ouzemann	W Pts 10	Pretoria
Sept 8	Giel de Roode	L Pts 10	Johannesburg
Dec 9	Ernie Roderick	L Pts 15	Harringay

(British Welterweight Championship)

1948

Mar 1	Omar Koudri	W RSC 2	Royal Albert Hall
Apr 20	Robert Villemain	L KO 10	Harringay

May 31	Gwyn Williams	NC 6	Harringay
(British Welterweight Championship Eliminator)			
Aug 6	Johnny Greco	L KO 3	Montreal, Canada
Oct 28	Beau Jack	L RSC 3	Washington, USA
Dec 14	Robert Takeshita	L KO 3	Honolulu, USA

1949

Mar 22	Fernando Janilli	L DISQ 7	Royal Albert Hall

1953

Aug 8	George Barnes	L RSC 6	Melbourne
Sept 5	Pran Mikus	L RET 7	Melbourne
Oct 31	Pat Ford	L RSC 4	Brisbane

Career Summary

Bouts Taken:	141	
Won	110	(72 inside the distance)
Drawn	6	
Lost	24	
No Contest	1	

Eric Boon – Exhibition Bouts

Date	Opponent	Contest	Venue
1938			
Aug 20	Walter Redit	Exh 3	Chatteris
Aug 20	Eric Page	Exh 3	Chatteris
Sept	Harry Silver	Exh 3	Army Camp, South of England
1939			
Feb 6	Harry Silver	Exh 3	Earls Court
May 29	Wally Davis	Exh 2	Alexandra Palace
	Billy Cannon	Exh 2	Alexandra Palace
	Bobby Lyons	Exh 2	Alexandra Palace
May 31	Harry Silver	Exh 3	Ipswich
Aug	Harry Silver	Exh 3	Chatteris
Aug	Jack Martin	Exh 2	Chatteris
Aug 16	Harry Silver	Exh 3	Skegness
Oct 28	Harry Rashleigh	Exh 1	Southampton
Oct 28	Eric Thompson	Exh 1	Southampton
1940			
Jan 29	Harry Silver	Exh 3	Empress Hall
Sept 19	Army Sgt Gallagher	Exh 3	Newmarket
1941			
Jan 25	Harry Silver	Exh 3	Empress Hall
Jan	Harry Silver	Exh 3	Watford
Nov	Private Lunn	Exh 2	Downham Market
1942			
June 2	Leading Aircraftsman Hamilton	Exh 3	Peterborough
1944			
July 8	Jimmy Cain	Exh 3	Chatteris
1947			
Jan	George 'Panther' Purchase	Exh 3	Johannesburg